# U.S. ENERGY AND ENVIRONMENTAL INTEREST GROUPS

**Greenwood Reference Volumes on
American Public Policy Formation**

These reference books deal with the development of U.S. policy in various "single-issue" areas. Most policy areas are to be represented by three types of sourcebooks: (1) Institutional Profiles of Leading Organizations, (2) Collection of Documents and Policy Proposals, and (3) Bibliography.

Public Interest Law Groups: Institutional Profiles
*Karen O'Connor and Lee Epstein*

U.S. National Security Policy and Strategy: Documents and Policy Proposals
*Sam C. Sarkesian with Robert A. Vitas*

U.S. National Security Policy Groups: Institutional Profiles
*Cynthia Watson*

U.S. Agricultural Groups: Institutional Profiles
*William P. Browne and Allan J. Cigler, editors*

Military and Strategic Policy: An Annotated Bibliography
*Benjamin R. Beede, compiler*

# U.S. ENERGY AND ENVIRONMENTAL INTEREST GROUPS

*Institutional Profiles*

Lettie McSpadden Wenner

GREENWOOD PRESS
NEW YORK • WESTPORT, CONNECTICUT • LONDON

**Library of Congress Cataloging-in-Publication Data**

Wenner, Lettie McSpadden.
   U.S. energy and environmental interest groups : institutional
profiles / Lettie McSpadden Wenner.
       p.   cm.
   Includes bibliographical references.
   ISBN 0–313–25362–5 (lib. bdg. : alk. paper)
   1. Energy policy—Environmental aspects—United States.
2. Environmental policy—United States.   3. Pressure groups—United
States.   I. Title.
HD9502.U52W45      1990
363.7′07′0973—dc20         90–2705

British Library Cataloguing in Publication Data is available.

Library of Congress Catalog Card Number: 90–2705
ISBN: 0–313–25362–5

First published in 1990

Greenwood Press, 88 Post Road West, Westport, CT 06881
An imprint of Greenwood Publishing Group, Inc.

Printed in the United States of America

The paper used in this book complies with the
Permanent Paper Standard issued by the National
Information Standards Organization (Z39.48–1984).

10 9 8 7 6 5 4 3 2 1

# CONTENTS

—————————— / ——————————

# *PREFACE*

— / —

For twenty years I have read and written about various interest groups' use of the courts to press their legal claims concerning environmental and energy policies. It became evident to me through this experience that the variety and strength of organizations using the courts to advance their demands about energy and environmental policies have grown in the past two decades and continue to expand. Most such groups do not restrict their efforts to the courts any more than they do to the legislative or executive branches of government. They appeal to whatever policy makers they can find who will respond to their demands. As a result, I have expanded my own interest in these organizations to track their efforts in other parts of the policy process. This book is a direct outcome of that effort.

In the latter part of the 1980s, as political action committees have proliferated and the number of lobbyists in the nation's capital has increased, there has been a corresponding increase of interest among scholars in examining this phenomenon. Many have focused on pressure groups in general regardless of the kinds of issues they pursue, and have expanded on the theme that business groups predominate in this society (Wilson, 1981; Schlozman and Tierney, 1985). Others have focused on associations that make up the energy-policy network of groups (Knoke and Laumann, 1983; McFarland, 1984). Still others have performed the same analysis on environmental policy (Ingram and Mann, 1989).

What I have attempted to do in this volume is to define the universe of groups that lobby in the fields of environmental and energy policy regardless of which side of the many controversies in these areas they represent. I began this quest by reviewing the lists that have already been assembled by others, but I made my own judgment about which were important enough to include based on the frequency of appearance of such groups before Congress to testify about various environmental and energy issues, from fuel economy standards for cars to the disposal of toxic wastes. I had already assembled a list of over forty laws that constitute the base of policy regarding the environment in the United States through my work on the federal courts. These laws have been under constant scrutiny and review by Congress throughout the 1970s and 1980s. I began by searching the hearings about these laws in the relevant Senate and House committees that have responsibility for overseeing their implementation.

Using the master list developed from consulting others' research as well as the congressional hearings I have reviewed, I used the standard reference works to develop an up-to-date mailing address list *(Encyclopedia of Associations, 1990; National Professional and Trade Associations, 1989)*. In 1987 I mailed a questionnaire to 155 groups and a second wave a few weeks later to nonrespondents (see Appendix B). During the summer of 1987, through a grant from the Institute of Government and Public Affairs of the University of Illinois at Chicago I was able to spend two months in Washington tracking down other groups by phone and personal interviews. Eventually, of my original list of 155 some 13 organizations were eliminated because they had gone out of business, moved without leaving a forwarding address, or otherwise disappeared. Of the remainder, 65 were trade associations and of these 36 responded, yielding a response rate of 55 percent; 56 came from the public interest sector, and of these 35 responded, a rate of 63 percent; 21 professional groups were contacted and 12 responded, a rate of 57 percent.

Those unwilling to respond to the specific questions often furnished annual reports, journals, newsletters, and various other publications. From these sources and from various studies written by other scholars and journalistic reports I was able to expand my list of informants to the present number of 140. The responses to the questionnaire and/or the information contained in their own publications constitute the major source of information for the organizations profiled in this volume. In some instances this data could be supplemented by secondary sources because there has been considerable interest in the organizations by both scholars and the popular press. In other cases, nearly the only information available is contained in general reference works.

Some of these groups are large trade associations with many interests that go beyond the focus of this book on environmental and energy policies. They have been in business for many years and would not fade from view if they stopped all lobbying on these issues. They are, however, some of the most important actors in this area today, and to ignore them would be to turn a blind eye to the reality of the political process. Others are tiny associations that focus on one particular environmental issue. Their impact may be significant on one minor issue because of their ability to concentrate all their energies on it, or they may be of trivial importance in the larger picture. Many general organizations that have been created to lobby in the "public interest" are also included in this book. Although they do not specialize in environmental or energy issues, their influence is great because of their general reputation, longevity, and importance on the American political scene.

One general rule I observed in winnowing this list was to avoid all local and state organizations. Many of the included groups have state and regional affiliates, and these are mentioned in the individual profiles. However, a book of this length could probably be written for any one of a number of states whose political processes are also much influenced by organizations specific to their areas. A few associations in this volume have central headquarters in a city other than Washington and its surrounding suburbs, but most also have a presence in or near the capital as well. The major criterion for inclusion, therefore, is expression of a preference on one or more policy issues presently before the national policy-making establishment in the areas of environment and energy.

No claim of universal coverage of all such associations is made here. They come and go with great speed in Washington; I learned this as I struggled to keep my list current over the three years it has taken to assemble all this information and analyze it. Some are more reluctant than others to part with their publications, and although I attempted to find comparable data on all groups, this proved impossible in some cases. Hence, the reader will find that some entries are quite skimpy whereas others are both rich and complex. This is necessarily the case because some groups are engaged in a great many activities and interested in many issues, and others are smaller and more specialized.

All three categories of organization that lobby in the energy and environmental policy areas are included in this volume; trade associations, public interest groups, and professional/governmental organizations. All profiles are alphabetized together, although it should be clear from reading each entry which category the group represents. Many groups have changed their names over time, and I have cross-referenced these to their present titles. An asterisk (*) indicates that a group mentioned in passing has a complete profile in this volume. I have also included a list of groups whose description in the standard reference works appears to qualify them for inclusion in this work, but for which I have minimal information (Appendix A).

Many people deserve thanks for their support during the period it took to complete this book. Many of my former colleagues and students at the University of Illinois at Chicago were helpful in discussing the ideas behind this volume, including Barry Rundquist, Boyd Keenan, and Andrew McFarland. Students who assisted were Victoria Musselman, who helped devise a method for coding the data on the questionnaire; and Barbara Yarnold, who read many of the congressional hearings that helped form the initial list. Both of these women were more colleagues than students to me by the time the project had ended. My new colleagues at Northern Illinois University were also highly supportive and helpful in suggesting additions and improvements to the manuscript, especially Paul Culhane, Robert Albritton, J. Dixon Esseks, and my husband, Manfred Wenner. Mary Sive first suggested the project and Mim Vasan was especially patient in developing the manuscript. Alicia Merritt was the extremely efficient production editor.

# INTRODUCTION

## —— / ——

## INTRODUCTION: THREE TYPES OF GROUPS

Organizations that lobby in the energy and environmental policy areas generally fall into one of three types: (1) business corporations and their trade associations, organized around the profit principle and concerned with developing energy and other natural resources in the United States; (2) not-for-profit public interest groups, generally dependent on public subscriptions or foundation grants, motivated by a common philosophy regarding the environment; and (3) professional, research, and governmental organizations, some of which have come into being because of the existence of the issues. Generally, the third category is composed of professional people who have career interests in these public policies.

Trade associations and their affiliated corporations are the most fully funded of the three groups, held together by a common desire to make a profit. This is the least difficult type of organization to motivate, according to Mancur Olson (1965), because each member obtains a very specific benefit, profit, from their common effort. Pluralist theorists (Lindblom, 1977) and critics (E. E. Schattschneider, 1960) alike agree that business corporations have dominated the U.S. political system for decades. But their influence is due to the belief in free enterprise embraced by most Americans and not because of the specific benefits they offer members. For the most part, such organizations are in agreement on their goals: the development of all natural resources and especially energy and mineral wealth in the United States. They are exemplified by the American Petroleum Institute (API) and its corporate members, such as Mobil Oil and Exxon corporations, known for their uncompromising devotion to economic growth and development of oil and gas resources regardless of complaints from environmental groups, whom they characterize as hysterical.

However, in recent years a small number of environmentally oriented trade associations have been created that attempt to earn a profit from producing pollution control mechanisms or environmentally benign renewable energy resources, such as the American Wind Energy Association. These groups are, however, much smaller and less important than such typical trade associations as the American Petroleum Institute.

Public interest groups are more difficult to organize. They depend on a common belief system and work toward purposive goals that their members perceive as benefiting the public interest. However, since they provide few specific benefits to individual members, they are subject to the "free rider" problem that prevents many potential members from contributing because they assume others will do so. Mancur Olson (1965) has argued that organizations so motivated do not form easily, and their members soon lose interest if they do join initially. Nevertheless, many such associations exist in the environment and energy policy area. Some have existed for decades, and many new ones have been added in the 1960s, 1970s, and even 1980s despite a downturn in public and governmental attention to problems of environmental concern.

Of these public interest groups most adopt a conservation posture and argue for strict enforcement of environmental controls on business. However, there is a minority of development-oriented public interest groups that take the opposing point of view: that the best public policy includes only economic developmental goals without regard for conservation or environmental controls. They advocate increased use of all natural resources, including mineral resources found on public lands. These groups are especially prominent in the debate over nuclear power, represented by such organizations as the Coalition for Nuclear Power.

The professional, research, and government category of organizations has the smallest number of groups in it, but they are the most varied of the three types. Their membership is voluntary as is that of the public interest groups, but one of their reasons for joining is career oriented; hence, their motives are partly economic. Members work either for the public or private sector of the economy, and some move back and forth between the two, taking their professional values with them. Some may also join public interest groups because of the interests they develop in the course of their professional training and work experience. In a sense, these groups, though the smallest segment of the policy network, hold the balance of power between the other two because they represent a moderate, middle-of-the-road approach between the two extremes.

## HISTORY OF NATURAL RESOURCE POLICY

Natural resource management and energy development were for many decades characterized by the iron triangle or subgovernment method of formulating public policy in the United States (McConnell, 1966). Business interests determined what policy was most advantageous to themselves and, together with a congressional committee composed of representatives from the states where the interest dominated and an executive agency that shared the same interest, legislated and executed that policy with little or no opposition from other interests in the United States (Schattschneider, 1960; McConnell, 1966).

This process is best exemplified by the planning and construction of navigation and flood control projects through demands made by local chambers of commerce, boards of trade, manufacturers, flood control district officials, and engineering firms that reaped the benefits of constructing the public works. These local private interests made their needs known to their respective representatives and senators, who in turn urged the U.S. Corps of Engineers district office to investigate the need for the proposed project and report favorably. So successful was this symbiotic relationship among congressional pork barrel recipients, local interest groups, and the Corps of Engineers that the latter became famous for its favorable treatment in Congress and its ability to make many funding decisions on its own without waiting for allocations by the legislative branch (Maass, 1962, 45–46).

Other natural resources were managed in the same manner. When the U.S. Department of Interior's Bureau of Reclamation was created in 1903, it replicated the Corps' model with the irrigation interests of large western landholders and their respective representatives in Congress. U.S. public lands policy followed a similar pattern. The U.S. Treasury Department's Public Land Office gave away much of the public domain to states to finance the construction of public roads and canals to facilitate settlement in the western parts of the United States. After the Civil War the Department of Interior extended this public policy to private railroad companies which were awarded millions of acres of public lands for extending the transportation infrastructure of the nation (Foss, 1960, 15–16).

The lands left in the public domain were those least desirable for settlement: poor quality, desert, and high-country forested lands that had been passed over by homesteaders under various privatization laws in the late nineteenth century (Culhane, 1981, 43). The public lands were rapidly denuded by overgrazing by cattle and sheep owned by competitive stock growers, each trying to get the most out of the land before it was completely eroded by some other user, a typical example of the "Tragedy of the Commons" depicted graphically by Hardin (1968).

Although there was some public debate in the United States over the propriety of this giveaway of the public domain, public policy in the last half of the nineteenth century was dominated by major business organizations such as the railroad trusts and their allies in Congress and the executive branch of government. The dominant philosophy of the United States was that free enterprise could best serve the economic needs of the country and that government policy should be subservient to this important private interest (Lindblom, 1977). In fact, little distinction was made in the minds of many influential thinkers of that day between the public interest and the needs of the business community.

The business ethic has not dominated U.S. political thought completely throughout our nation's history. Many naturalists, such as David Thoreau, John

Muir, and Aldo Leopold, developed an alternative land or ecology ethic in the nineteenth century. As early as the post–Civil War period, some public and private citizens began to have second thoughts about the rapid depletion of American natural resources, and in some instances they succeeded in influencing public policy. In 1872, after much debate spearheaded by the naturalist John Muir, Congress established the first national park, Yellowstone, to preserve some of the most spectacular scenery in the United States. In 1876 Congress created in the U.S. Department of Agriculture an office of forestry, which became the Forest Service in 1905, designed to manage the national forests in such a manner as to maintain a constant supply of timber. By the turn of the twentieth century, many citizens, both in and out of government, had come to believe that the public lands were being so rapidly depleted by private exploitation that the carrying capacity of such lands would be permanently reduced if they were not protected.

This concern was exemplified by the debate that took place from the turn of the twentieth century until Congress passed the 1934 Taylor Grazing Act. Under the terms of this act, stock growers who owned lands contiguous to the public domain land could rent public lands for a minimal fee designed to raise revenues for the depleted public treasury and to provide some protection for the overused and abused public domain lands (Foss, 1960). Like most policy in this era, the law was formulated by an alliance of cattle growers with the U.S. Bureau of Land Management and important western members of Congress. Although some stock growers had urged passage of the law because they realized they could communally ruin the resource that was left, implementation of the Taylor Grazing Act followed the normal subgovernment political pattern. The Bureau of Land Management administers the law in a manner that allows local cattle growers to determine the number of permits given out, to whom, and for how many cattle (Culhane, 1981). A similar relationship now exists among the Forest Service in the Department of Agriculture, the timber industry, and the relevant committees in Congress.

Despite the continuing presence of the iron triangle and small subgovernments, there is another strain in American politics that does not conform to this pattern. Ever since the days of Theodore Roosevelt and John Muir, some public figures and private citizens have opposed the dominance of business in our society. They have argued the cause of conservation, and some heated debates have occurred over the development of certain areas of our country. The conservation community, though weaker and less well organized than the business community, has engaged in many political battles over the years. One of the most important was the effort in the late nineteenth century to establish a system of national parks to protect some of the most impressive scenery in the United States from commercial exploitation. In the 1930s the conservation community also prevented the Forest Service from being incorporated into the Interior Department's Bureau of Land Management, which was nicknamed at the time the "Bureau of Logging and Mining."

## TRADE ASSOCIATIONS

### Competing Goals

Trade associations dominated the energy and natural resource policy subsystem from their inception through most of the 1960s. Yet trade associations are not monolithic in their attitudes and demands on government. Although they all espouse a philosophy of free enterprise and an official belief in competition, most will use government policies whenever possible to gain an advantage over competitors. They agree about certain issues, such as reducing corporate and capital gains taxes, but they differ on other issues, such as protective tariffs, as some obtain more of their profits from overseas investments than do others. It is thus difficult for a peak association that represents many corporations, such as the National Association of Manufacturers, to obtain agreement within the business community in order to coordinate its policy demands on this important issue (Bauer, Pool, and Dexter, 1972).

This type of division over goals exists also within the energy and environmental field and is due partly to the competition that exists within the business community. Four types of trade associations dominate the environmental and energy field: electricity producers, oil and gas companies, chemical manufacturers, and automotive manufacturers. Divisions about goals exist among these four sectors of the economy as well as within each of them. The natural gas industry, for example, sells its product partly on the grounds that it is nonpolluting and hence more desirable than electricity generated from high-sulfur coal and oil. The gas industry finds Clean Air Act controls on the electrical industry helpful to its own position in the market. Competition within the energy industry thus causes some division within the broad industry coalition that defends itself against most government regulation of its activities.

In general, the oil and gas industry is united in urging the government to open all public trust lands for energy exploration. But it divides internally about other issues; for example, whether government should control prices of natural gas. Trade associations representing pipelines and distributors think wellhead prices should be controlled, but the suppliers do not. The latter believe "take-or-pay" contracts, which force distributors to buy a given quantity of gas regardless of demand, should be fully enforced.

In the automotive industry, Chrysler Corporation managed to meet corporate average fuel economy (CAFE) standards in 1986, and argued against Ford and General Motors' petition to the U.S. Environmental Protection Agency (EPA) to reduce those standards from 27.5 mpg to 26 mpg. Ford and GM were successful in getting the standards postponed until 1990 on the grounds that it would hurt the economy to force them to manufacture smaller, more fuel efficient cars. Nevertheless, this incident broke the normally united front that the automotive industry presents to Congress and the agencies.

The oil industry also differs with auto manufacturers from time to time. One example is a debate between the two giants about who should be responsible for reducing volatile gaseous emissions during refueling. The auto industry argues this can be efficiently done in gasoline stations by installing recovery devices on the pumps; this has in fact been done in some jurisdictions under stage two of the Clean Air Act. Oil refiners do not wish to reduce the volatility of their product and would prefer that the burden be put on auto manufacturers to provide canisters on cars to recover these emissions instead. Thus, competing technical solutions to the same problem cause different parts of the business community to divide along predictable lines over how it should be resolved. However, at another level, both the oil and auto industries are united in opposition to any controls on gaseous emissions. It is only when other actors in the political system force changes that such divisions over methods for achieving results occur.

In addition to normal competition between energy forms, some trade associations have grown up around particular environmental laws. For example, the Wind Energy Association exists partially because of energy conservation laws passed in the Carter administration that encouraged research and development of alternative sources of energy through the tax laws. Industrial cogenerators of electricity are organized around the Public Utility Regulatory Policy Act (PURPA), which orders electric utilities to purchase power from industries that generate their own electricity and produce a surplus. Certain manufacturers produce emission control equipment, and these businesses are clearly benefited by pollution control laws and regularly lobby for them.

A solid waste control industry has flourished in the 1980s as a result of the Resource Conservation and Recovery Act (RCRA) and Superfund, because these laws force other industries to use its disposal services instead of simply dumping liquid and solid wastes on their own land. Today that traditional method of disposal is illegal. New regulations have inspired a whole new industry of incineration and chemical fixation for hazardous wastes. It has had the secondary impact on the waste treatment industry of forcing out of business many small operators who cannot afford the high-technology equipment and investment in liability insurance that is necessary to run solid waste disposal facilities today. This has produced a consolidation of the industry into a few corporate giants such as Browning-Ferris and Waste Management, Inc. who are thereby able to resist more forcefully any public controls on their operations.

This policy is definitely a two-edged sword. The smaller, dirtier operations are easier to put out of business, but the industry then becomes dominated by sophisticated corporations capable of resisting any further environmental controls more effectively. This is illustrated by the hazardous waste incinerator ships, such as Waste Management's *Vulcanus*, which operate in international waters without emission controls because it is difficult for any national government to regulate activities there. It has also led to internationalization of the problem of hazardous waste dumping because large corporations now find it economic to transport wastes large distances and convince governments in developing nations that have not faced the problem of such wastes in the past and do not understand the dangers to public health they represent, to accept them.

### Differences in Tactics

Today most pluralists agree that business organizations occupy a preeminent position in the American pluralist system (Lindblom, 1977; Domhoff, 1967). Yet anyone who sets out to document how this result is achieved has been hard pressed to demonstrate how this has come about. A 1963 study revealed that Washington lobbyists rarely approach members of the opposition to influence them. Rather, each coalition of congressional representatives, staffers, their counterparts in agencies, and interest group representatives remain an unassailable coalition of individuals who know each other's needs and respond to them automatically (Milbrath, 1963). This finding contributed to the idea that policy is formulated within subgovernments that rarely confront each other, but it also pointed up the difficulty of clearly demonstrating the "influence" of any particular group of actors, since they rarely interact with opponents.

Nevertheless, some anomalous coalitions occur, as when environmental groups combined with the waste treatment industry to get RCRA loopholes closed, forcing small industrial waste generators to use the services of the waste management industry. Generally, however, trade associations prefer a developmental approach to the economy, and environmentalists prefer an ecologically sensitive orientation. Nevertheless, trade associations occasionally have difficulty in coordinating all their members' interests into one coherent, integrated policy position for a given issue. In those cases the trade association representatives may have to reach a compromise approach to the problem or avoid making any general statement for the entire industry.

This has led to more and more individual representation by executives of individual corporations as they come to rely less on umbrella organizations to make their demands known to Congress. As businesses have geared up to respond to challenges being made by environmental, consumer, and similarly oriented groups in American society in the 1970s, individual corporations have increased their presence in Washington considerably (Wilson, 1981). Given the fact that the income of many of these corporations far outweighs the resources available to any given trade association, their presentations are often as much, if not more, influential with Congress and the agencies than are those of the umbrella groups.

Major corporations that dominate polluting industries greatly outnumber any newer pollution control industries, such as the recyclers or the emission control manufacturers. In addition there is considerable overlap in membership between major energy trade associations representing polluting industries, such as the Chemical Manufacturers and the Chemical Specialty Manufacturers, and smaller groups such as the recyclers and emission controllers. Major gas and oil companies have also invested in solar and other renewable energy resources.

Hence one division of some of the most important polluting industries often belongs to such new trade associations as the Council on Alternate Fuels or the Manufacturers of Emission Controls.

Large corporations, such as Dow Chemical and Exxon, which have divisions that specialize in treating wastes and developing alternative fuels, cannot be expected to take any action that would hurt the interests of its major investment in oil and gas supplies. This was demonstrated in 1989 when Mobil Oil sold off its solar division in order to focus on development of its traditional sources of fuel. Major corporations may invest in competing technologies in order to eliminate them as happened when the automobile manufacturers bought up Los Angeles's transportation system in the 1930s.

Major conglomerates now own most of U.S. industry. Dow Chemical has invested in pollution-reducing companies, but this does not mean that it has abandoned its stance in opposition to almost any government-imposed regulation on toxic chemical emissions to the air or water resources of our country. The fact that the same giant corporations both own the polluting technologies and have the only capacity to develop technologies to clean them up does not predict any particular outcome. What it does mean is that the decision about which direction public policy will go in the future may be made primarily in boardrooms rather than in congressional hearing rooms or agency research labs.

There may be genuine disagreements within corporations just as there are within congressional committees about the appropriate balance to strike between economic development and environmental conservation. The fact that there exists such a monopoly on knowledge, however, may lead to a denial that any economically feasible solution to problems exists, as happened in the past, for example, with auto emission control technology. The fact that the preponderance of investment and resources lies with the polluting part of the industry has led many to predict that economic development arguments will far outweigh environmental conservation arguments in the boardrooms of America's industry. It may be that the American philosophical belief in the wisdom of free enterprise prevents any policy innovation from being undertaken unless some part of business can profit from the policy. If so, then the only possibility for change to occur is for segments of industry to discover profitability in recycling waste materials and finding alternative nonpolluting renewable energy resources. Given the traditional nature of business, it seems unlikely that such innovations will originate in industry, however. The initial impetus must come from individual entrepreneurs or groups not committed to the profit motive and the acceptance of the status quo that pervades most large economic organizations in this country.

## PUBLIC INTEREST GROUPS

### Differences in Goals

Environmental groups, as do trade associations, sometimes divide on the basis of policy goals, and at other times they separate along tactical lines. Since their beginning, conservation groups have been divided philosophically, and their rifts are much deeper than those found among industries, which are all motivated by the profit principle. Some conservationists, such as Gifford Pinchot, who was Theodore Roosevelt's Forest Service Director, are devoted to a sustained yield, multiple-use philosophy. They believe that natural resources should be utilized for the maximum benefit of humankind through a utilitarian philosophy. They wish to maintain ecological systems at their highest carrying capacity through tree farming, game management, and predator control. Hence they seek to influence public policy to keep natural resources producing commodities for the greatest good for the greatest number. Preservationists, represented by John Muir, the founder of the Sierra Club, on the other hand, emphasize the value of wilderness and natural resources for their own sake rather than the economic benefit of humans. They believe that unique natural places and phenomena should be preserved as they originally were for their own sake and kept that way for future generations to experience.

Another example of philosophical differences is represented by groups such as Ducks Unlimited and Trout Unlimited, which are composed of hunters and fishermen, or "sportsmen" as they prefer to call themselves. The largest wildlife organization, the National Wildlife Federation, was started by sportsmen, and its main membership today is made up of rod and gun clubs in communities. Their primary goal is to ensure a sufficient supply of game to kill, an entirely different philosophy from that adopted by the National Audubon Society or Defenders of Wildlife, which regard other species not as commodities but as common inhabitants of the planet from whom humans can learn. Both types of groups, however, seek to protect the breeding grounds for game and nongame wildlife alike. Sportsmen's clubs may have only recently added a concern for nongame species, but as wildlife habitat of all kinds has grown scarcer in the United States, they have come closer to the preservationists' concern about nature for its own sake. Both types of groups share a love of outdoor experiences and hope to preserve their respective methods of enjoying this depleting resource.

Environmental groups have been accused by some of being an elite movement with an interest only in preserving wilderness for their own enjoyment and indifferent to the economic needs of the poor. It is accurate to observe that the members of many environmental organizations do indeed belong to an affluent, educated class, as is true of most interest groups of whatever kind in the United States (Schattschneider, 1960). Scientists, lawyers, and other professionals indeed have sufficient resources to devote part of them to membership in social causes such as the Environmental Defense Fund (EDF) and the Natural Resources Defense Council (NRDC). When the philosophy of environmental groups is compared to that of their business-oriented opponents, however, this criticism pales. The latter's motives are wholly economic, and their concern for the poor dissipates when they face individuals as workers and consumers of goods.

Nevertheless, the backgrounds of members of environmental organizations are extremely diverse. Some members of the Sierra Club are indeed affluent professionals who enjoy the color photographs in *Sierra*; others, however, are working-class people who enjoy the wilderness on occasional backpacking trips which are less expensive than the motorized campers they compete with for space in national parks. Indeed many of the hunters' organizations probably consist of a majority of working people who do not need a college education to appreciate nature. Many of the newer, more militant organizations, such as Greenpeace and Earth First!, consist entirely of volunteers who live on restricted budgets while devoting most of their energies to "saving the earth." These groups are especially denigrated by critics of the movement who regard them as "crazies," outside the mainstream of American ideology. It is difficult, therefore, to justify the additional criticism that they are part of the privileged class.

## Differences in Tactics

Another difference of opinion among environmental groups concerns tactics. Establishment environmental groups seek funding and help from major corporations and foundations attached to and dependent on wealthy families and corporations. Some members of socially and economically prominent families in the United States, such as the Rockefellers and Mellons, have taken an interest in conservation causes. Hence they sit on the board of directors of many of the large, better-known conservation groups, such as The Wilderness Society, the Conservation Foundation, the National Wildlife Federation, and even the Sierra Club. Their mission on the board is usually to raise funds from their wealthy colleagues. Their tactics normally include establishment techniques, attempting to influence congressional representatives and administrative officials with whom they may have personal relationships.

Social movements are different. They are composed of people who are not well connected to the institutions of government and the economic establishment. Instead they emphasize grass roots support and action by individual people. The most extreme of these presently in the environmental movement is Earth First!, a militantly radical group, some of whose members believe that sabotaging industrial development is the only way to attract attention to their cause. Other groups with a slightly less militant approach are Greenpeace and Earth Island Institute, the latest brainchild of David Brower, a follower of John Muir's militant conservationism. These groups are devoted not to ecological sabotage as is Earth First!, but to direct action and symbolic acts of opposition to business tactics they consider destructive to the ecology. They eschew violence personally but often expose themselves to physical danger by putting themselves between industrialists and their objectives, whether trees or whales.

The main cleavage between established groups and mass movement groups is not clear-cut. It is possible for any one organization to move back and forth across this line, and the various organizations should be viewed as occupying a position along a continuum that may shift from time to time depending on the leadership and membership of the given organization. The Sierra Club, for example, began as a militantly preservationist group in the 1890s, and later matured into an elite establishment organization. Later, under the executive direction of David Brower in the 1960s and 70s, it reassumed a more militant tack in dealing with the government. It lost its tax-exempt status for lobbying and advertising for the cause of conservation. Later, however, its board of directors became more conservative once more; David Brower was forced out of the directorship, and the club has now adopted a moderate stance on many issues. It actively supports political candidates, although this varies around the country according to the preferences of local chapters. Individual Sierrans may become very active on behalf of individual candidates for public office at the state, local, or national levels. They generally eschew the more symbolic and militant tactics of Earth First! or Greenpeace.

The movement people are much poorer and their budgets and memberships are smaller than their establishment cohorts. They survive on a shoestring and avoid large infrastructures, buildings, professional staff in Washington, and administrative expenses. They are dedicated to grass-roots action and seek to keep their individual chapters independent and capable of setting their own action agendas, depending on the need for programs in local areas. They tend to regard their establishment colleagues as too concerned with professional advancement, salaries, positions, and playing the Washington game of being invited to the right parties, knowing powerful members of Congress and other Washington personalities, and being connected to the policy-making network.

On the other hand, the establishment groups, such as the National Audubon Society and the World Wildlife Fund, believe their own tactics are more effective than those of militant groups. They believe that environmentalists, if left out of the decision-making process, will make no impression on policy. Hence they cultivate politicians and business people more ecologically oriented than others and work on developing alliances with business and government. They prefer to negotiate and bargain, believing that they are more successful in preserving individual tracts of wilderness through the legislative and administrative processes than militants can be by objecting to all economic development. They seek and secure foundation grants that they believe will be most effective in advancing the cause of conservation in the long run. The Conservation Foundation and World Wildlife Federation are examples of this type of group and have proven their effectiveness by getting their president named by President Bush to be administrator of the Environmental Protection Agency in 1989.

Some environmental groups may specialize in particular areas, dividing up the work in order to maximize their impact. They combine forces and lobby together (Berry, 1984). On the other hand, some of the smallest groups and most-recent additions to the environmental lobbies may prefer to operate alone because they need to keep their membership and contributors believing that they afford a unique contribution to the cause (Godwin, 1988a).

Other organizations that occasionally combine with environmental groups, such as Common Cause and the League of Women Voters, are more generally oriented to multiple causes. These organizations were not formed around the environmental movement. Their origin was based on other issues: women's suffrage for the League and open government for Common Cause. However, over the years, they have developed positions on a variety of public issues in the United States. Generally they tend to support the liberal side of debates on such issues as pollution controls and natural resource conservation. They frequently join the conservation or environmental movement in supporting amendments to the clean air and water laws, wilderness bills, and toxic containment. Because of their size and establishment position, their efforts on behalf of such legislation may be more persuasive than that of some environmental groups because the latter are typed as representing a "special" interest. Hence the League and Common Cause are eagerly sought as allies by the Sierra Club and Audubon Society. Although their total effort is not directed toward environment or energy goals, their impact may be greater than that of the more specialized groups.

Some members of the legal profession have become involved in environmental causes in recent decades. Lawyers are divided by income level and in their philosophical orientation to public causes. Most lawyers who have joined environmental public interest groups, such as NRDC, EDF, or even TLJP (Trial Lawyers for Public Justice) are liberal to radical in their approach to the law. They tend to belong to the "plaintiff" bar (lawyers who represent individuals claiming to have been injured by faulty products or other business and governmental activity) rather than the "defense" bar, the establishment part of the bar that represents large corporations, especially insurance companies, and dominates the traditional bar associations.

EDF, NRDC, and other such groups draw their personnel from elite schools, but they tend to pay lower salaries than do major law firms. Their personnel and contributors, like American Civil Liberties Union (ACLU) lawyers, may have careers and clientele of their own from which they make their money. However, they donate much time and talent to environmental causes and attempt to recover some of their costs from attorneys' fees obtained from opponents in cases. Originally these groups were founded to litigate environmental causes in courts. More recently, they too have become involved in legislative and administrative lobbying in order to affect the process before it reaches the litigation stage. Crucial to such organizations are statutes that allow groups to become involved in litigation through such mechanisms as class action suits and private attorneys general, enabling citizens to sue in the public interest when agencies fail to enforce laws.

Another issue between the large and small groups is whether the leadership or the membership makes policy. In some large general groups, such as the League of Women Voters, there are elaborate meetings designed to poll the membership and set priorities for the state and national chapters from year to year. In smaller organizations maintained by mass mailings, the staff and leadership tend to set priorities and simply ask members for financial support. Movement people argue that the grass roots are the only people who can afford to maintain a radical posture, as lobbyists in Washington are too easily co-opted into the establishment and seduced by career advancement. On the other hand, some argue that the professional staff who deal in causes continually convince the membership, which tends to be more moderate in policy orientation, to follow their more radical lead. The Reagan administration, for example, accused leaders of the National Audubon Society of stirring up its members to write their members of Congress about causes, such as clear-cutting forests and acid rain, that they knew little about.

Just as trade associations have their anomalies, such as the Wind Energy Association, so too have public interest groups. There are a minority of these organizations that espouse not an environmentally conserving philosophy, but rather a business-oriented, developmental one. The reason they are categorized as public groups is that they are self-defined as organized around a purposive belief in particular values rather than economic self-interest.

Generally, the economically organized trade associations reflect developmental values, and the public interest groups support ecological ones. Yet there are also some anomalies in this data, as some public groups have been organized to represent economic concerns and directly oppose the ecological interests of such groups as the Sierra Club and the National Audubon Society. For example, the Americans for Energy Independence and the Americans for Nuclear Energy are both nonprofit membership organizations that solicit contributions from the public. Yet they both favor nuclear power and have been formed by industrial sponsors to advocate this policy. Presumably their sponsors could just as easily contribute more funds to the official trade associations, such as the Edison Electric Institute, which also advocate nuclear power. They have opted to form a not-for-profit group either for tax purposes or for public relations reasons. Yet presumably all other members in the policy network know their values and policy positions as well as their sponsorship.

Another manifestation of this desire by the private business sector to take on the aura of a public group is the National Legal Center for the Public Interest, dedicated to reducing, if not eliminating, government regulations and the ability of courts to award compensation to victims of product liability and other industry-caused grievances. Its regional organizations include the Pacific, Mountain States, Mid-America, Mid-Atlantic, Southeastern, Gulf, Great Plains, and Capitol Legal foundations. Its most famous member, James Watt, headed the Mountain States Legal Foundation before becoming President Reagan's first secretary of the interior. These conservative public-interest law firms work primarily to counter suits initiated by consumer and environmental groups such as the NRDC and the EDF. Their corporate sponsors can and do make similar legal arguments in their own suits. But by contributing to such public groups they gain standing to sue in a variety of cases their corporate status might not enable them to enter.

It may also serve a strategic public relations purpose, as they need not involve their public image in such cases.

Despite their recent growth in numbers, developmental public interest groups remain fewer in numbers than their environmental counterparts. The latter are often divided in terms of philosophy, tactics, levels of funding, and sections of the population to whom they appeal. Nevertheless on occasion they can all cooperate in a particular cause such as saving a particular wilderness area or attaching responsibility for toxic waste dumps to the dumpers.

## PROFESSIONAL, RESEARCH, AND GOVERNMENTAL GROUPS

The smallest category of organizations interested in energy development and environmental issues are professional, research, and government groups. Yet these are the most varied kinds of groups operating in this public policy arena. They range all the way from the American Medical Association and other health organizations that form around a concern for the public health to professional groups organized around an environmental mission. As epidemiological evidence has mounted connecting the incidence of disease with environmental factors, it has become impossible for such groups to ignore pollution issues, such as toxic wastes. However, like the League of Women Voters, these groups were not organized around such causes, and they remain only moderately concerned about them. Likewise, trade unions, such as the Oil and Chemical Workers Union and the AFL-CIO, are primarily concerned about other economic issues such as wages and hours of work. However, they too have become more concerned about epidemiological links between working conditions and their members' health. Although they are sometimes allied with management against such regulations as emission controls on cars because of the negative impact they perceive them having on employment in the industry, they often oppose management when decisions affect workers' health.

Health-oriented groups, such as the American Medical Association (AMA) and the American Public Health Association, are professional organizations and are primarily concerned about the well-being of their own members. Their professional training, however, leads these associations to become concerned about public health matters such as exposure of humans to toxic chemicals. The AMA, a politically conservative group, on occasion allies itself with such liberal groups as the EDF or NRDC to support government regulation of the environment. It is not so militant as the American Public Health Association, which is more concerned with preventive tactics and is more willing to give credence to evidence linking environmental pollutants with disease and mortality rates.

Government organizations, such as the League of Cities, the U.S. Conference of Mayors, the National Association of Counties, and Attorneys General, as well as the Council of State Governments and Governors Association, were organized for other purposes and generally were well established before they became interested in environmental policies. However, today, all levels and branches of government must be concerned about such issues as disposing of solid and hazardous wastes and finding their citizens a clean drinking water supply. Hence, each of these groups has developed a division or at least a committee whose primary purpose is defining the organization's official stance on energy and environmental policies. These groups are cross-pressured in the sense that they are often responsible for finding cost-effective means of disposing of wastes which marks them as targets of federal pollution control laws. At the same time they may benefit from the same laws by having their own authority and responsibilities increased, as state and local governments are often delegated primary responsibility for administering such laws. Hence members of these government agencies are ambivalent in their attitudes to these policies. The net impact of the laws has been to introduce into state, county, and local government bodies individual professionals, engineers, economists, and planners whose primary concern is for environmental impacts. Larger government organizations of which they now form a part have in this way been made aware of the importance of these issues in the United States.

In addition there are some professional organizations whose existence is dependent on this policy area. Some of these are government groups, such as the Association of State and Interstate Water Pollution Control Administrators. Others, however, draw on both public and private sector members, including the Water Pollution Control Federation, the National Association of Environmental Professionals, and the Society of American Foresters. In these groups professionals who work for industry, governmental agencies, and even public interest groups can meet and discuss mutual problems. In the early twentieth century conservationists considered the formation of the Forest Service a considerable advance for their cause. That is equally true today with the formation of such groups as the Water Pollution Control Federation, because professionals who meet in such a group are aware of the problems of water pollution control. They also have a professional stake in seeing the problem treated in a serious manner. The existence of the Clean Water Act and its predecessor laws has upgraded this portion of the engineering profession and caused schools of engineering to give serious attention to this subfield. Thus the existence of such groups adds a moderate voice to the debate between polluters and developers and those who would control them.

Simultaneously with the evolution of the environmental movement, professional groups have added to the variety of actors in the environmental issue network (Morrison, 1983). Men and women whose careers now depend on environmental legislation and regulation now form professional associations, such as the Association of Environmental Professionals. Although generally less militant than their voluntary counterparts, they form a permanent professional interest in the policy that represents a stable base of support for such policies.

The reason such private, public, and mixed professional organizations can be grouped into a single category is that their organizing principle is occupational/

economic. Nevertheless, individual members may share a philosophy that is close to the world view of several environmental voluntary associations, and in fact many of their members also belong to such groups. These people usually regard themselves not as advocates for a cause but as objective scientists and professionals who can help to find a common ground between the two contending sides, or even the one technically correct way to achieve the goals of the policy.

## CONCLUSIONS

Two decades ago the energy development/environmental policy field was dominated by an iron triangle of interests shared among businesses intent on exploiting all natural resources, members of Congress representing that private interest, and the executive agency designed to promulgate that interest, the Departments of Agriculture and Interior. Today there have been some modifications made in that scenario. Conservation groups that had long cautioned about the rapid depletion of our abundant resources, newly formed voluntary associations that were created around one or more concerns about the natural environment, and professional groups that represent men and women involved in the management not only of natural resources but human health have become more active in this policy domain.

This is not to argue that the scales have been balanced and there is equal representation of all sides in the policy debate. Groups organized for private profit still have a clear edge on all others in terms of resources they wield in the policy debate. Nevertheless, there are alternate voices now being heard. Much discord exists among these voices, as they disagree with one another about strategies and even goals. The appearance and techniques of the public interest group have been adopted by business leaders intent on increasing their influence. Today it is risky to predict the direction a group's policy preferences will take simply because it puts the word *environmental* in its title. There are as many, perhaps more, entrepreneurs on the right as on the left of this issue. Public interest groups aimed at economic development at any cost to the environment have a ready audience in the business community that may view their pleas for support as an easy way to take the onus of anti-environmentalism off their own corporate image.

At the same time that public groups proliferate on both sides of this issue, some private investors have turned to more environmentally benign ways of making a profit. For those who believe that the U.S. capitalist system will always provide more political opportunity for those who can provide economic incentives to their followers, this may be the last best hope for environmentalism. Logically it may be argued that it is easier to keep the loyalty of someone whose economic well-being is wrapped up in a cause than it is to depend entirely on ideology. Development of such small industries will not be the solution for all our environmental problems. The nascent alternative power industry and pollution control industry are often dominated by the giants that also have heavy investments in traditional methods of doing business. Innovation comes very slowly to such institutions as General Motors and Mobil Oil. It would be unwise to depend on such marketplace competition to rescue our environment.

It will always be necessary to have groups that are disconnected from the marketplace to make the counterarguments. One hopeful development is the increase in the numbers of government agencies at federal, state, and local levels that are now concerned about environmental problems. These groups also do not speak with one voice. They seem to stand somewhere between the two major opponents in their public policy preferences, representing a separate professional point of view, but one intimately associated with the members' careers. Such public bureaucracies are not immune to political pressure, as was well illustrated in the Reagan administration, when the U.S. Environmental Protection Agency was effectively prevented from tightening its controls on pollution. Truly autonomous agencies are dependent on being pressured from both sides, and in the 1980s the environmental point of view was nearly eliminated at least in the executive branch of the federal government.

What is striking about this research is the similarity of organization, tactics, and policy concerns of all sides of this issue area. Clearly there is an issue network at work and all participants know one another well. They are familiar with each other's methods and indeed respect them enough to have adopted some of them. This is not to say that we are any closer to agreement about the problems of the environment in the 1990s than we were in the 1960s. Indeed the problems have multiplied while we continue to argue not only about the means of achieving goals but indeed about what goals are appropriate in this policy domain.

# U.S. ENERGY AND ENVIRONMENTAL INTEREST GROUPS

# A

## /

**ADHESIVE AND SEALANT COUNCIL**
1627 K Street, N.W., Suite 1000
Washington, D.C. 20006

### ORGANIZATION AND RESOURCES

The Adhesive and Sealant Council, originally called the Rubber and Plastic Adhesive and Sealant Council, was founded in 1957 to represent the interests of manufacturers of adhesive products and their suppliers of raw materials. It is a relatively small trade association with 200 members and a limited budget of about $500,000 a year derived from the dues of its corporate membership who contribute according to their production and income. It has a professional staff of 10 in Washington, D.C.

### POLICY CONCERNS

The Council opposes any regulation of the industry for public health or environmental legislation. It was originally successful in obtaining an exemption from disposal regulation under the Resource Conservation and Recovery Act (RCRA) for small generators of hazardous waste. Their lobbyists testify consistently against any change in RCRA. The law, however, was amended in 1986 to include more small generators under RCRA control, partially because of the testimony of another trade association, the Hazardous Waste Treatment Council,* which sought to expand the market for its members' services.

### TACTICS

The Council publishes an annual membership directory and a monthly newsletter and holds semiannual conventions in March and October.

**AMERICAN CANCER SOCIETY (ACS)**
1599 Clifton Road N.E.
Atlanta, Georgia 30029

## ORGANIZATION AND RESOURCES

The American Society for the Control of Cancer was founded in 1913. Its name was changed to the American Cancer Society (ACS) in 1944. It is a nonprofit research and education organization dedicated to eradicating cancer. There is a staff of 300 at national headquarters in Atlanta. In addition, there are 58 divisional offices and 3,000 local groups distributed among the 50 states as well as Puerto Rico and the District of Columbia. The House of Delegates consists of over 200 doctors, health professionals, and researchers from around the United States. Of these, over 120 are members of the board of directors, and 25 serve as members of the executive committee.

The ACS has revenues of over $300 million a year, raised from public subscriptions and bequests (90 percent) and investments. Of this, 8.3 percent is used for general administrative services and 16.1 percent is spent on fund-raising. The remainder is devoted to programs funded by the Society: 28.3 percent is dedicated to financial support for research conducted by academic institutions and scientists on the causes, cures, and prevention of cancer; 18.4 percent is devoted to educating the public about ways of protecting itself through early detection and preventive behavior; 9.2 percent provides programs designed to improve the knowledge and skills of the medical profession about diagnosis and treatment of cancer; 13.2 percent is spent on programs assisting cancer patients and their families through home care, rehabilitation, and counseling; and 6.5 percent is devoted to community services provided in conjunction with local governments for community health facilities and clinics.

## POLICY CONCERNS

For several decades the American Cancer Society sponsored research about the link between tobacco smoking and cancer and considered it a major victory when the U.S. surgeon general issued his initial report against smoking in 1964. This was followed almost immediately by favorable rulings by the Federal Trade Commission (FTC) and the Federal Communications Commission (FCC) to restrict advertising of cigarettes. However, the Tobacco Institute countered with both lawsuits and appeals to Congress, which passed cigarette labeling and advertising legislation in 1965, which actually weakened and delayed the original FTC rulings. This was due, according to one student of the process (Fritschler, 1989), to the preponderance of resources the tobacco lobby was able to interject into the process. Since the original cigarette labeling battle, the ACS has been instrumental in recent years in publicizing dangers of passive (involuntary) smoking and advocates smoke-free areas in the workplace and public accommodations, including airplanes. A primary goal in the 1980s was to reduce the number of smokers in the United States, especially among young people, which was successful to a large degree.

The ACS has also taken positions regarding other carcinogens, advocating the passage of the Toxic Substances Control Act in 1976, and urging the Environmental Protection Agency (EPA) and Occupational Safety and Health Agency (OSHA) to adopt strict standards for known carcinogens in the air and workplace, including asbestos, vinyl chlorides, benzene, ethylene dibromide, and polychlorinated biphenyls. Officials of the Society have testified before Congress in support of funding the Comprehensive Environmental Response, Compensation, and Liability Act (CERCLA, or Superfund) to clean up toxic waste dumps and in favor of the employee's right to know about carcinogens in the workplace. It advocates that EPA place known carcinogens on the toxic substances list for control under the Clean Air Act, and argues for continuing research on the effects of other substances that have shown links to cancer through animal research.

The ACS is more cautious than consumer groups such as Ralph Nader's Public Citizen* regarding health risks from such substances as formaldehyde. It argues that more research should be done on the effects of such substances but does not support immediate controls as does Public Citizen. It issues guidelines about the use of radiation and advocates controls on the exposure of technicians. It advocates high standards in the nuclear industry and more research and attention to disposal of nuclear wastes, but refuses to argue for the reduction of U.S. dependence on nuclear power, although it has been urged to do so by the Nader organizations. The Society also advocates testing homes for radon exposure and continued research on radon's link to cancer.

## TACTICS

Although national headquarters is located in Atlanta, the Society maintains a public affairs office in Washington in order to present the views of the ACS to Congress and the federal executive agencies most important to its mission, i.e., Health and Human Services, the National Institutes of Health, National Academy of Sciences, EPA, OSHA, and the U.S. Department of Labor. It publishes an annual report and the *Cancer Journal for Clinicians* bimonthly, covering cancer treatment and prevention, and *World Smoking and Health* three times a year. It holds an annual convention in New York City.

## FURTHER INFORMATION

*Annual Report 1988* (1989). Washington, D.C.: ACS.

Fritschler, A. Lee (1989). *Smoking and Politics*. 4th ed. Englewood Cliffs, N.J.: Prentice-Hall.

Washington address: 1515 I Street N.W., Suite 1025, Washington, D.C. 20005

## AMERICAN CONSULTING ENGINEERS COUNCIL (ACEC)
1015 15th Street, N.W., Suite 802
Washington, D.C. 20005

## ORGANIZATION AND RESOURCES

The American Consulting Engineers Council (ACEC) was established in 1973 from a merger of the American Institute of Consulting Engineers, founded in 1910, and the Consulting Engineers Council of the U.S.A., founded in 1956. It is a trade association of 4,700 engineering firms that together employ more than 150,000 engineers and design public works projects for local, state, and federal agencies, as well as many private-industry projects. These include civil designers, mechanical and electrical engineers, and architectural specialists. Nearly a third of the firms are small, with only 1 to 3 employees, and 5 percent have more than 100 employees. It is organized regionally with 51 state organizations, including Washington, D.C., which select the board of directors. The latter selects a 9-person executive committee and oversees a professional staff of 48.

ACEC's budget is about $3.5 million a year, about half the size of the National Society of Professional Engineers,* the major professional association for engineers. Its membership dues, based on the individual firm's business volume, constitute 86 percent of the total budget. Over 35 percent of the annual budget goes for governmental and international relations, 45 percent is used for communications and membership services, and the remaining 19 percent for professional practices.

## POLICY CONCERNS

ACEC's primary public policy concern, like that of many other trade organizations, is to protect its members from liability suits. It raised $380,000 in addition to its regular budget in 1987 to try to change the U.S. civil justice system to lower court assessments for personal injury claims against professional engineers. All its state affiliates lobby regularly to get state legislators to reduce the strictness of the liability laws that the courts enforce. ACEC also lobbies on behalf of its members to obtain the most favorable tax rates possible.

ACEC's membership designs and builds the major infrastructure of the country. Hence it advocates greater public expenditures for roads, sewers, bridges, and other public works. Fully 45 percent of its member firms do some business in the environmental field; for example, designing publicly or privately owned sewage treatment plants. It supported the reauthorization of the Clean Water Act in 1987 over President Reagan's veto, and ACEC representatives testify regularly for more appropriation of federal funds for building sewage treatment plants.

ACEC also worked for passage of the Superfund Amendment and Reauthorization Act (SARA) of 1986 which established an expanded program to clean up toxic waste dumps around the United States. The new law includes a federal negligence standard that provides for indemnification for engineers working at Superfund sites, and ACEC has worked with the U.S. Environmental Protection Agency (EPA) to obtain insurance in the hazardous waste cleanup market.

In addition to working on environmental control projects, however, ACEC firms design many private and publicly funded projects considered environmentally damaging by many critics, such as highways, nuclear plants, and especially dams and other flood-control projects. Hence it advocates the increased expenditure of public funds on Corps of Engineer and Bureau of Reclamation projects that are requested by many local governments but are opposed vehemently by environmental groups.

Another public policy of great concern to ACEC are those laws dealing with energy, such as the Federal Power, Nuclear Waste Policy, Energy Supply and Environmental Coordination, Energy Policy and Conservation, and Public Utilities Regulatory Policy acts. It advocates both conservation and greater development of energy resources in order to permit the United States to move toward energy independence. It argues that governmental regulations stifle development of natural resources, and advocates removing regulatory constraints on the marketplace. It believes energy conservation may be achieved through developing new building construction standards by consensus in the profession.

ACEC wants the federal government to finance research into energy technologies and to pass laws that encourage cogeneration of power and small power production. It argues for tax laws and utility rate structures that will encourage energy conservation, cogeneration, and small-scale power production and development of all our energy resources. It advocates the elimination of all price controls, especially those on natural gas, because they distort the marketplace by encouraging inefficient use of natural resources. It advocates use of federally owned resources in order to develop the country economically, and opposes set-asides for wilderness and other noneconomic uses.

It advocates constructing nuclear waste storage facilities immediately and has launched a campaign to inform the public of the safety and efficiency of nuclear power. It advocates greater use of cost-effective nuclear power plants and more government research aimed at advanced nuclear technologies.

ACEC testified before Congress to remove the requirement that utility companies perform residential and commercial energy audits of buildings for their customers free of charge, because this reduces the market for such services by consulting engineering firms. ACEC provides services to its membership to help them in marketing their energy management services to potential clients on the grounds that energy audits and conservation advice will save them money in the long run.

*TACTICS*

ACEC has a political action committee that collects funds to donate to congressional campaigns. It coordinates most of its lobbying efforts with the National Society of Professional Engineers. Representatives of ACEC testify before congressional hearings as well as agency hearings. It educates its membership and encourages them to write their congressional representatives. In the late 1980s it helped to form the Rebuild America coalition of professional engineering associations dedicated to convincing the media and politicians of the need to invest more money in the infrastructure of the United States at the federal, state, and local levels. ACEC issues an annual membership directory, an annual report, and a weekly newsletter, *The Last Word*, to keep its members up on developments in government and ideas about marketing their services. It also holds semiannual conventions.

### FURTHER INFORMATION

*Annual Report* (1989). Washington, D.C.: ACEC.

## AMERICAN COTTON MANUFACTURERS ASSOCIATION
*See* American Textile Manufacturers Institute.

## AMERICAN COUNCIL FOR AN ENERGY EFFICIENT ECONOMY (ACEEE)
1001 Connecticut Avenue, N.W., Suite 535
Washington, D.C. 20036

### ORGANIZATION AND RESOURCES

The American Council for an Energy Efficient Economy (ACEEE) was founded in 1980 by a group of energy conservation researchers in academic institutions and the national laboratories. Its purpose is to conduct research and disseminate information to utilities, industry, consumers, and government officials at all levels about energy conservation policies and technologies. The ACEEE is not a membership organization; it is governed by a twelve-person board of directors selected by the previous board.

ACEEE's annual budget is $300,000, derived 30 percent from foundation grants, 44 percent from contract research, and 26 percent from publications sales. The MacArthur Foundation, World Bank, U.S. Department of Energy, Electric Power Research Institute,* California Energy Commission, Niagara Mohawk Power Corporation, and Owens-Corning Fiberglas Corporation are among its sources of grants and contracts. The ACEEE has a professional staff of three located in Washington.

### POLICY CONCERNS

ACEEE seeks to promote energy conservation through efficient use of heating and cooling plants, tighter building techniques, more insulation, and similar methods. It also promotes more-efficient household appliances; it has studied the cost-effectiveness of efficient appliances and the impact of federal standards, and has helped states such as Maine to develop state appliance standards. ACEEE staffers have also studied indoor air pollution and its link to energy conservation and ways of conserving electricity consumption in developing countries. It has studied the potential for reducing acid rain emissions through conservation of energy in the midwest.

## TACTICS

ACEEE seeks to provide a forum for government officials, industry, and researchers to interact on common concerns. It selects research fellows to write special papers and books on energy conservation. It publishes a semiannual booklet, *The Most Energy Efficient Appliances*, for consumers. It organizes conferences and publishes the proceedings every other summer on the efficient heating and cooling of buildings. ACEEE's professional staff testify at congressional hearings on energy legislation and supply individual representatives, senators, and staff with information. Its primary activities, however, are producing and disseminating information to the professional research community on energy efficiency through its list of publications.

## FURTHER INFORMATION

*Energy Efficiency: Perspectives on Individual Behavior* (1987). Washington, D.C.: ACEEE.

*Proceedings from the 1988 Summer Study on Energy Efficiency in Buildings* (1988). Washington, D.C.: ACEEE, 11 vols.

## AMERICAN FEDERATION OF LABOR-CONGRESS OF INDUSTRIAL ORGANIZATIONS (AFL-CIO)
815 16th St., N.W.
Washington, D.C. 20006

### HISTORY AND DEVELOPMENT

In 1881 Samuel Gompers founded the American Federation of Labor (AFL) and remained at its head until World War II. This first umbrella organization for trade unions recruited only skilled workers and, following its leader's philosophy, eschewed involvement in the political process to focus on improving the economic conditions of its members. During the depression of the 1930s, however, more-militant labor leaders, such as John L. Lewis of the United Mine Workers, pressed to organize unskilled workers. The Committee for (later Congress of) Industrial Organizations (CIO) was formed within the AFL, but was later forced out. Its leaders were willing to undertake direct political action and found several allies in Congress, such as Senator Robert Wagner, who succeeded in passing the Wagner Act which created the National Labor Relations Board (NLRB) and forced management to recognize the right of labor to bargain collectively. In 1946, however, organized labor suffered a setback when Congress passed the Taft-Hartley bill outlawing closed shops and greatly reducing the right to strike.

In 1955 the two organizations merged to form the American Federation of Labor-Congress of Industrial Organizations (AFL-CIO). Under the leadership of former lobbyist George Meany, who remained president until retirement in 1979, the AFL-CIO became more active politically. It had traditionally lobbied for such legislative innovations as child labor laws and compulsory public education for all children below age 16. During the second half of the twentieth century it associated with other liberal interest groups, such as the civil rights movement and militant farmers' groups. Throughout its history, however, its policy priorities have centered on increasing wages of working men and women and improving their job security and the safety of their work environment.

## ORGANIZATION AND RESOURCES

During the 1980s there has been a considerable decline in the number and percentage of workers organized into trade unions in the United States. In the late 1980s the AFL-CIO claimed over 13 million individual members who belonged to more than 45,000 local unions, which made up some 89 autonomous national and international unions affiliated with the AFL-CIO. Dues vary from union to union depending on their members' wages, and each member of an affiliated union pays $3.72 into the AFL-CIO's yearly budget. Total income for the AFL-CIO was approximately $50 million a year in the late 1980s.

Each of the eighty-nine unions that make up the AFL-CIO also have representatives in Washington to promote labor interests, ranging from the International Ladies Garment Workers to the American Federation of Teachers. Each has its own political action committee designed to influence public policy. The AFL-CIO collected almost $800,000 in the first three months of the 1988 election year as contrasted with over $2 million collected by the United Auto Workers of America's PAC, which ranked third among all labor PACs in 1988.

The AFL-CIO holds a national convention every two years to which all member unions send delegations. There the president and thirty-three vice-presidents are elected. Vice-presidents are frequently presidents of their respective unions, such as Albert Shanker of the American Federation of Teachers. President Lane Kirkland has served since Meany's retirement in 1979. All officers make up the executive council which governs the Federation between conventions.

## POLICY CONCERNS

The AFL-CIO's major policy efforts in the 1980s have concerned preserving jobs for American working men and women. It has advocated protection against foreign goods imported into the United States and argued in favor of a law that would require industry to give sixty days' notice to their employees before closing a plant. It also endorses policies to assist less-affluent citizens generally, such as affordable housing, national health insurance, and an increase in the minimum wage. The AFL-CIO also seeks to ensure workers a safe and healthful workplace; it was instrumental in the passage of the Occupational Safety and Health Act (OSHA) of 1970, which is presently administered in the Department of Labor.

Its concern about unemployment has led the AFL-CIO leadership to embrace many economic development policies, including major public works projects in the United States. Yet its concern for worker health also influences AFL-CIO leadership to support some environmental legislation, such as the Safe Drinking Water Act Amendments of 1986. In some instances its lobbyists have testified against environmental legislation, as in 1982 when they argued to relax standards, extend deadlines, and allow building and development in areas that did not meet Clean Air Act standards. The construction trades were especially adamant in their demands to keep employment up through development in the oldest cities. In some cases the environmental and job interests have coincided, as in 1986 when labor successfully argued to get Congress to extend funding for sewage treatment plants under the Clean Water Act.

However, the auto workers' union has stood with the auto industry consistently in resisting increased strictness concerning auto emissions in the hope of keeping prices down and sales up. At the same time the UAW Conservation Department has developed an "Adopt-A-Dump" program to assist communities where leaking hazardous waste sites are located. Working-class residential areas have typically been located near manufacturing plants where industrial wastes were for many years disposed of without regard for their impact on nearby water tables and homes.

### TACTICS

The Committee on Political Education (COPE) of the AFL-CIO regularly attempts to influence its membership to become more involved in the political process and to help to influence their congressional delegations. It seeks to convince more union members to become activists in their unions and voting citizens. COPE publishes *Legislative Alert*, a newsletter for subscribing members that comes out twice a month. Lobbyists for the AFL-CIO are recognized as some of the most knowledgeable professionals in Washington. Their soft-spoken tactics, however, do not appeal to all members of the labor movement, and some of the most militant unions, such as the United Mine Workers and United Auto Workers, do not belong to the AFL-CIO.

Although originally apolitical, the AFL-CIO later came to be closely associated with the Democratic party and endorsed candidates at the national, state, and local levels. In 1972, however, it refused to endorse George McGovern, the Democratic nominee for president because many of its members and leadership were offended by his anti–Vietnam War stance.

### FURTHER INFORMATION

*The Future of Work* (1983). Washington, D.C.: AFL-CIO.
*This Is the AFL-CIO* (1987). Washington, D.C.: AFL-CIO.
Wilson, Graham K. (1981). *Interest Groups in the United States*. New York: Oxford University Press.

## AMERICAN FORESTRY ASSOCIATION (AFA)
1516 P Street, N.W.
Washington, D.C. 20005

## ORGANIZATION AND RESOURCES

In 1875 a group of citizens, under the auspices of the American Association for the Advancement of Science and concerned about the rapid exploitation and destruction of America's forests, founded the American Forestry Association (AFA). Its primary purposes at the beginning were to control indiscriminate logging and forest fires through increasing public awareness of the threat to American forests.

In 1989, the AFA had 25,499 regular members and 34,750 associates and contributors. Its dues are $24 a year, although many contribute more than that, and corporate dues are $2,000. Its members are primarily professional foresters who work for federal and state conservation departments or for commercial timber companies and private individuals and companies who produce lumber for the commercial market. In 1988 AFA had a budget of $2,416,863. These funds came from: dues, 26 percent; programs, 17 percent; services, 13 percent; contributions, 19 percent; interest, 11 percent; and other, 14 percent. It was used for services to members, 64 percent; programs, 21 percent; administration, 11 percent; and fund-raising, 4 percent.

At the annual meeting to which all professional members are invited, the governing council elects a thirty-two-member board of directors. The board is made up of foresters from the U.S.D.A. Forest Service, various state departments of natural resources, private tree farmers, as well as academics from various schools of natural resources. AFA has a professional staff of seven in its Washington office.

## POLICY CONCERNS

Started by conservationists, the AFA has been in the middle of disputes over natural resources throughout the twentieth century. It was instrumental in the creation of the U.S.D.A. Forest Service, and it continues to prefer the Department of Agriculture's greater conservation orientation to that of the Department of Interior, which is more industry oriented. Its members tend to be on the conservation side of preservation/conservation arguments. They are careerists whose livelihoods depend upon a continuing supply of forest products. Hence, they favor multiple use of forests, including timber harvesting, but they tend to prefer that forests be cut at a rate that guarantees a sustained yield.

The AFA also promotes the acquisition of more national forests as well as state forests for recreation and other uses. It favors funding for the Forest Service and state departments of natural resources and promotes planting trees in urban areas in order to make the environment more attractive as well as to reduce air pollutants. In the late 1980s it began a campaign entitled "Global ReLeaf" in order to influence governments to plant trees throughout the nation and abroad in order to reduce global warming. AFA argues that the greenhouse effect caused by increased generation of carbon dioxide through fossil fuel use must be offset by revegetation of tropical forests that have been depleted in recent years through burning off areas in order to promote agriculture. It also seeks to ban imports of wood products from countries that refuse to implement forest conservation policies. This policy also promotes the use of U.S. wood products which is an economic interest of most of its membership.

AFA has joined with environmental groups in arguing for more-restrictive controls over the sulfur oxides and nitrogen oxides that create acid rain. In 1987 AFA produced a white paper on the effects of acid deposition on American forests, arguing that more research needs to be done on the causes of reduction in tree growth and general deterioration of the health of forests in various regions of the United States. The researchers took a measured approach to the problem but ultimately concluded that the costs of delay in imposing stricter controls over the causes of acid rain outweigh the risks of acting too precipitously and imposing unreasonable costs on the energy industry. They also concluded that other air pollutants such as toxic metals may be contributing to the deterioration of forests and should be investigated.

It differs with environmentalists over the use of pesticides as AFA sees the need for use of some chemical components to restrict the growth of pests such as gypsy moths. It generally supports the Department of Agriculture and EPA in allowing the use of herbicides and pesticides to control pests and promote growth in the privately and publicly owned forests of the United States.

## TACTICS

Seven professional staffers in Washington testify before congressional committees, monitor the voting record of Congress, inform their membership of crucial issues before the legislature, and encourage them to write their representatives. They also try to inform the public of the need to maintain and improve the value of trees and sponsor outings for their members.

AFA publishes a bimonthly, *American Forests,* a scientific journal with authoritative articles about the practice of forestry, which has wide distribution in the profession. It also publishes *Urban Forest Forum,* a bimonthly newsletter distributed free of charge to anyone who has an interest in planting and preserving trees in urban settings. It distributes to its membership a weekly newsletter, *Resource Hotline,* to keep them informed about pending legislation and litigation in the forestry field. The Association also publishes monographs on specific forestry issues, such as *The Battle for Natural Resources,* which describes the history of federal land management.

## FURTHER INFORMATION

*American Forests* (1989). Washington, D.C.: AFA, May-June.

*Background Information* 1989. Washington, D.C.: AFA

*Battle for Natural Resources, The* (1983). Washington, D.C.: Congressional Quarterly Incorporated.

Culhane, Paul J. (1981). *Public Lands Politics.* Baltimore, Md.: Johns Hopkins Press, Resources for the Future.

## AMERICAN GAME PROTECTIVE ASSOCIATION
*See* National Wildlife Federation.

## AMERICAN GAS ASSOCIATION (AGA)
1515 Wilson Boulevard
Arlington, Virginia 22209

### ORGANIZATION AND RESOURCES

Founded in 1918 by a merger of the Gas Institute with the Consumer Gas Association, the American Gas Association (AGA) is a trade association of nearly 300 gas pipeline and distribution companies representing over 80 percent of all natural gas delivered and sold in the United States. It also has 4,206 individual members. Included on the forty five member board of directors are chief executive officers of gas companies from the southwest to the northeast. AGA is one of the larger energy industry trade associations, with 420 staff in its Arlington, Virginia, office. Its long-time president is George H. Lawrence, who has been described by the *National Journal* as one of the most effective lobbyists on Capitol Hill, persuasive with influential members of Congress, and masterful at keeping divergent companies in line. AGA has an annual budget of over $20 million.

### POLICY CONCERNS

The most important public policies affecting the gas industry have to do with the price of natural gas and the tax on that industry. It agrees with the American Petroleum Institute *in advocating tax write-offs for exploration for new fossil fuel supplies. Hence it forms an alliance for tax policies with other parts of industry with which it is in competition on other matters.

On wellhead price controls and renegotiation of contracts for natural gas, AGA, which represents pipelines, is usually in disagreement with the Natural Gas Supply Association (NGSA).* Each seeks to influence the Federal Energy Regulatory Commission (FERC) to its way of viewing the problem of competition in the gas industry. The losing side in the regulatory arena is usually eager to take up the issue in the federal courts, and many court cases have been decided on these issues in various circuits with mixed results.

Natural gas prices have been controlled since 1938 under the Natural Gas Policy Act (NGPA) by the Federal Power Commission and its successor, the FERC. Gas pipelines and distributors take positions opposing gas drillers and suppliers on this issue. AGA tries to keep price ceilings on old gas because that regulation favors the distributors against the suppliers. However, AGA wants to bring down the regulated high prices of new gas. In 1987 it volunteered to exchange its use of the law to keep old gas prices down for free market competitive pricing for new gas and elimination of escalator clauses in contracts for new gas that tie its price to the price of petroleum.

AGA also opposes take-or-pay regulations that have been promoted by suppliers of natural gas. Under FERC regulations, gas pipelines and distributors are locked into contracts made with suppliers of natural gas that keep the price of natural gas artificially high while costs of alternative supplies such as oil may be dropping. It also opposes proposed legislation that would force pipelines to carry gas to all areas needing it on the grounds that voluntary transport has eliminated the need for regulation.

The gas industry is much more united and hence successful in its opposition to the Powerplant and Industrial Fuel Use Act of 1978 (PIFUA). This law was passed when natural gas and oil were in short supply and it was feared that there would not be enough to keep residences and businesses heated. It restricted the industrial uses to which natural gas could be put, especially for generating electricity. The gas industry had long argued that there was a limited supply of gas available in the early 1970s. In the 1980s, as gas prices increased and more gas came onto the market, gas suppliers and distributors urged Congress to repeal restrictions on the uses to which gas could be put, on the grounds that gas is a nonpolluting source of fuel that can be substituted for sulfurous coal and oil in many turbines and help relieve air pollution. In 1987 the gas industry was successful in getting the prohibition on use of gas for an industrial fuel withdrawn by the 100th Congress through a compromise with the National Coal Association* that stipulates that new electricity-generating equipment should be designed to someday use coal or a coal derivative as well as gas.

The gas industry, through the Gas Research Institute,* attempts to demonstrate how economical gas is as a fuel in competition with any other, especially electricity. It therefore investigates the costs of heat pumps and other electrical appliances and stresses the efficiency of new gas appliances. It supports in principle the establishment of federal appliance efficiency standards because this is preferable to a variety of state standards, but it argues that there is a bias in these standards against small gas furnaces designed for starter homes.

AGA also supports the Public Utilities Regulatory Policy Act's (PURPA) requirement that the electric industry provide backup power for cogenerated power because much of the latter is produced through burning gas. In this area of policy the gas industry supports environmental and solar power groups that advocate government support of cogeneration as an alternative to building more electricity-generating plants. Some individual members of the AGA, however, also distribute and sell electricity, such as Consolidated Edison of New York. Hence they oppose cogeneration, as does the chief spokesman for the electric industry, Edison Electric Institute.*

The gas industry also uses environmental arguments to advocate the substitution of gas-fired power plants for coal and oil burners as well as nuclear ones. It also advocated conversion of the idled Midland nuclear power plant in Michigan to a natural gas combined-cycle facility. AGA members who also generate and sell electricity from other sources do not necessarily agree with this policy either. AGA is one energy trade association that advocates greater control of sulfur oxides to control acid rain because gas is the cleanest burning of the fossil fuels.

In testimony before Congress, AGA focused on the availability of natural gas to supply the country's industrial base rather than encouraging Congress to adopt a strict scrubber rule for coal-and oil-fired boilers. But it was in the interest of the gas industry to see its major competitors faced with increased regulatory costs. AGA also advocates the use of trade-offs and bubbles to reduce all forms of air pollution, including nitrogen and sulfur oxides. Under such regulations, which have been approved by the EPA, a high pollutant source can be balanced off against a low one such as a gas-fired furnace, and thus eliminate the need for controlling the emissions from the high source.

In 1987 a representative from the Texas Gas Company testified to the Senate Committee on Energy and Natural Resources that free energy audits provided by local gas distributors should be eliminated. He argued that conservation of energy goes on without them, and only the middle class benefit from them since the poor are not knowledgeable enough to take advantage of them.

Pipeline companies argue that there is too much regulation of pipelines and that the gas industry is the safest form of energy despite its volatility. It approves the use of the power of eminent domain to condemn private lands to enable pipeline companies to gain rights-of-way. It applauded the petroleum industry's success in getting the Alaska pipeline built by congressional override of the Endangered Species Act objections.

AGA, along with other segments of the gas industry, regularly urges Congress and the Department of the Interior to expand their leasing program for oil and gas companies to explore for energy resources in offshore areas and other federally owned lands. It also argues the Department of Energy should increase funding for geoscience research to find new sources of gas.

### TACTICS

In addition to its own lobbyists in Washington, AGA calls upon the officials of various pipeline companies and local distributors to testify before Congress when issues important to the gas industry are before it. Some of these, such as the Peoples Gas System or the Texas Gas Transmission Corp, are important U.S. corporations with major lobbying offices of their own in Washington. It is connected to the Gas Employees Public Action Committee (GASPAC) that regularly contributes funds to political campaigns.

AGA provides public relations materials that it distributes free to schools, including 500,000 slide shows, films, booklets, teacher's guides, and kits to give the gas industry's view of safety and conservation issues. It maintains an energy resource analysis model to project future energy market conditions for its member companies to help them in their local efforts to influence government and educators. It has produced many monographs, such as *Regulation of the Gas Industry*, to put its point of view across to the public.

AGA produces two monthly journals, *AGA Monthly* and *Gas Energy Review*, for its members which discuss marketing problems as well as regulatory issues, employment opportunities, and the latest developments in technology. Its weekly,

*AGA Washington Letter*, discusses regulatory and judicial decisions affecting the gas industry. AGA also issues an annual report to its members and a biennial supply forecast which in the late 1980s estimated an ample supply of natural gas through 2010. It sponsors a nature series on public TV in order to bolster the image of natural gas as an environmentally benign form of energy, and it supports the weekly Izaak Walton League's* public affairs cable program, "Make Peace with Nature."

## FURTHER INFORMATION

*AGA Monthly* (1989). Arlington, Va.: AGA, June.
American Gas Association (1989). *1988 Report to its Members*. Arlington, Va.: AGA.
Davis, David Howard (1982). *Energy Politics*. 3d ed. New York: St. Martin's Press.
Rosenbaum, Walter A. (1987). *Energy, Politics, and Public Policy*. 2d ed. Washington, D.C.: Congressional Quarterly Press.
Soloman, Burt (1986). "Ganging Up." *National Journal*, July 19, pp. 1778–1781.
——— (1987). "Measuring Clout." *National Journal*, July 4, pp. 1706–1711.
Stanfield, Rochelle L. (1987). "Paying for Nothing." *National Journal*, April 4, pp. 812–814.

## AMERICAN HORSE PROTECTION ASSOCIATION (AHPA)
1000 29th Street, N.W., T100
Washington, D.C. 20007

### ORGANIZATION AND RESOURCES

The American Horse Protection Association (AHPA) is a nonprofit organization founded in 1966 to advocate the humane treatment of horses. It has an annual budget of about $350,000, derived almost entirely from dues of $15 each from its 15,000 members and other contributions from them. Its president is William L. Blue, and the chair of its board of directors is Joan R. Blue. Its 10-person board of directors included Lorne Greene until his death in 1987 and other celebrities, including Burt Reynolds, Ed McMahon, Imogene Coca, June Havoc, and Marsha Mason. The board meets annually to set policy, but it is governed by a 5-member executive committee that meets biweekly. It also has a 5-person professional staff in Washington, D.C.

### POLICY CONCERNS

The AHPA's most important legislative victory came in 1971 with the passage of the Wild and Free Roaming Horses and Burros Act. Since that time it has worked to oversee the administration of that law by the U.S. Departments of Agriculture and Interior, which together administer the public land holdings of the U.S. government. It opposes the reduction in numbers and removal of wild horses and burros from public lands, advocated by landowners in the west and by the Reagan administration. The Association advocates adoption of unwanted horses and burros by individuals who will provide homes for them rather than reselling them. Officers of the Association attempt to monitor wild horse round-ups by the government.

Another legislative victory of the Association was the passage of the federal Horse Protection Act written to ensure humane treatment of show horses, especially Tennessee Walking Horses. The AHPA argues that these animals are often trained to adopt their gait through the use of painful devices. Officers monitor the Department of Agriculture's implementation of the Horse Protection Act and argue before Congress to amend the law to outlaw presently legal devices.

### TACTICS

In 1985 AHPA purchased and maintains a farm north of Leesburg, Virginia, to provide a refuge for abused and unwanted horses. It issues a quarterly newsletter to its membership to keep them informed about developments in Washington that may affect the welfare of wild horses. It testifies before congressional committees and agency hearings in Washington as well as in states that are involved in animal protection legislation. It does not contribute to political campaigns and has no PAC, although it does monitor individual congressional voting records. It coordinates its activities with those of the Humane Society of the United States.

### FURTHER INFORMATION

*Annual Report* (1989). Washington, D.C.: AHPA.


## AMERICAN INSTITUTE OF CONSULTING ENGINEERS
*See* American Consulting Engineers Council.


## AMERICAN INSURANCE ASSOCIATION (AIA)
1130 Connecticut Avenue, N.W., Suite 415
Washington, D.C. 20036

### ORGANIZATION AND RESOURCES

The American Insurance Association (AIA) was created in 1964 by the merger of three other organizations: the National Board of Fire Underwriters, founded in 1866; the Association of Casualty and Surety Companies, established in 1926; and the American Insurance Association, founded in 1953. By the 1980s there were 195 companies involved in this major trade association with dues dependent on the premium values sold in a given year. AIA operated with a $20 million budget in the late 1980s, raised primarily from dues. There is an elected 25-member board of directors. The president directs a 150-person professional staff at the Washington headquarters.

### POLICY CONCERNS

The primary public policy of concern to insurance companies is state government regulation of the insurance industry and court settlements and awards to claimants. All the companies as well as AIA have argued that courts have been too generous to individual plaintiffs in insurance cases and have argued for state legislatures to put limits on "pain and suffering" compensation awarded by state courts. The crisis in insurance has led to steep increases in premiums in the 1980s and to denial of insurance to some customers, especially municipal government units such as park districts.

Product liability and environmental liability are two areas in which the insurance industry is attempting to keep down costs for their members. When the Comprehensive Environmental Response, Compensation, and Liability Act (CERCLA, or Superfund) was being drafted, AIA and its members were successful in preventing any victim compensation clause from being included. AIA argues that insurance costs are much too high now for hazardous wastes due to the way courts have interpreted CERCLA.

Whenever the federal government puts a toxic waste dump on the Superfund list it searches for responsible parties to share the costs of cleanup. Federal courts have generally agreed that strict and joint liability should be imposed on any contributors to the site, including past owners and users. This may mean that one or a few participants who created the dump may be held responsible for the entire costs of cleanup because other responsible parties have gone bankrupt or disappeared.

AIA representatives have testified consistently before congressional committees on energy and the environment that joint liability should not be imposed. Rather, the costs of cleaning up one dump should be distributed among the several contributors in proportion to the damage they caused. All are not equally guilty, and some distinction should be made between companies responsible enough to have insurance and those that had none. If insurance companies are held responsible not only for their clients' but also others' contributions to a dump, this will take away all incentive for industry to act responsibly in discarding their wastes. Therefore, AIA opposes any direct suits against insurers, and many companies have begun refusing to write policies for waste disposal damages.

## TACTICS

AIA has a public action committee that contributes funds to political campaigns. It publishes an annual report and sponsors an annual meeting. Its member corporations send representatives to Washington to testify whenever legislation that affects the insurance industry is under consideration.

## FURTHER INFORMATION

*Annual Report* (1989). New York: AIA.

## AMERICAN IRON AND STEEL INSTITUTE (AISI)
1133 15th Street, N.W.
Washington, D.C. 20005

## ORGANIZATION AND RESOURCES

The American Iron and Steel Institute (AISI) is the successor to the American Iron Association, which was founded by U.S. ironmasters in 1855. After the Civil War the name was changed to the American Iron and Steel Association in recognition of the growth of steel as society's most important industrial material. Because of the rapid expansion of the iron and steel industry at the turn of the twentieth century, another organization, the American Iron and Steel Institute, was incorporated in 1908, and in 1912 the Institute took over the functions of the Association as well.

AISI has some 51 corporate members, which together account for 80 percent of steel production in the United States; among them are such giants as Bethlehem and U.S. Steel. Dues to the trade association depend on the volume of business each corporate member does in a given year. It also has 1,300 individual members who pay dues of $35 a year. It has a budget of about $5 million a year and a staff of 45. Like most trade associations, AISI is divided into policy-making committees on which major executives from the important steel corporations serve. Two major policy committees are environment and energy.

## POLICY CONCERNS

American iron and steel manufacturers have been in an economic slump for many years, and their primary goals are convincing the federal government to erect trade barriers to foreign imports and to give tax incentives to the domestic industry to expand production.

One of the industry's major costs is for energy, and AISI favors any policy that would reduce the cost of energy to the industry. It therefore joins with the electric power industry in advocating fewer restrictions on fossil fuel–fired powerplants and development of more nuclear energy. Individual corporations such as Bethlehem also belong to such groups as the Electricity Consumers Resource Council,* whose primary purpose is to reduce energy costs to end users, and to the Cogeneration and Industrial Power Coalition of America* whose purpose is to force electric utilities to pay them for electricity generated in conjunction with industrial processes.

One of the primary problems that AISI and its members perceive is government regulation of such environmental problems as clean air and water. AISI pollution control experts regularly testify against the need for strict standards in the Clean Air Act (CAA) and for relaxing deadlines for the iron and steel industry because of economic pressure. They believe that the CAA was passed in a moment of environmental excess in the 1970s and that the U.S. Environmental Protection Agency has been much too zealous in setting new source performance standards for steel mills. AISI has instituted a number of federal court cases in which it has argued that lowest achievable emission rates (LAER) are unrealistic for steel mills in the dirtiest areas of the United States, and the best available control technology (BACT) standards should be substituted.

AISI testifies before House and Senate committees that the steel industry is in such bad economic shape that no increase in regulatory severity can be absorbed. One major issue regarding the CAA at the end of the 1980s was the designation of hazardous air pollutants, and AISI opposed all efforts to set standards for them. In 1986 it also opposed an acid rain bill to reduce sulfur oxides further as too costly for industry to absorb. Individual members of AISI such as LTV Steel belong to the Council of Industrial Boiler Owners,* which argues against any CAA controls on industrial sources of sulfur and that the electric utility industry is more responsible for acid rain than other stationary sources.

Although AISI supported reauthorization of the Comprehensive Environmental Response, Compensation, and Liability Act (CERCLA, or Superfund) in principle in 1986, it opposed any tax on waste generators to supplement the tax on the oil and chemical industries. If wastes are taxed, AISI favored doing so according to the toxicity of each waste. Like other industries, it opposed joint and strict liability and victim compensation being added to the law.

AISI representatives are also concerned about the Resource Conservation and Recovery Act (RCRA), which establishes stricter standards for disposing of hazardous wastes in landfills than for normal solid wastes. It argues that coke is not a hazardous waste, and it is not fair to include it in such definitions. AISI objected strenuously to RCRA regulations that make industrial on-site storage of wastes subject to commercial hazardous-waste landfill conditions. It argues that steel plants should be given interim permits and allowed to continue to use on-site disposal sites until states develop new guidelines. It also believes that the steel industry has led in the recycling effort and should not be forced by government regulations to do more.

*TACTICS*

As do other trade associations, AISI sometimes finds it difficult to get all corporate members to agree on a common policy stand. Often CEOs of individual steel and iron companies testify before Congress as to their own interests, and each has its own lobbying staff in Washington in addition to AISI whose people often meet with Environmental Protection Agency and Federal Energy Regulatory Commission staff in attempts to influence environmental and energy regulations. They tend to find public hearings less useful because these sometimes constitute forums for environmental groups to make their demands known. AISI staff usually make formal presentations to congressional hearings considering amendments to the major pollution-control laws, but they find informal contacts with congressional staffers helpful.

AISI publishes a regular newsletter to its membership to keep them informed about developments in the regulatory field as well as what is happening regarding corporate taxes and international trade. AISI also works to obtain favorable publicity for the entire industry in the mass media. It issues an annual statistical report about the industry and technical manuals and sponsors a yearly conference.

*FURTHER INFORMATION*

"Position Paper on Clean Air Act Amendment Amendments" (1987). Washington, D.C.:
   AISI.
"Testimony of David G. Boltz on S. 2773 Waste Minimization and Control Act of 1988"
   (1988). Washington, D.C.: AISI.

## AMERICAN IRON ASSOCIATION
*See* American Iron and Steel Institute.

## AMERICAN LEGISLATORS ASSOCIATION
*See* Council of State Governments.

## AMERICAN LUNG ASSOCIATION (ALA)
1740 Broadway
New York, New York 10019–4374

*ORGANIZATION AND RESOURCES*

The National Association for the Study and Prevention of Tuberculosis was
founded in 1904 originally to combat tuberculosis, a major threat to public health
in the United States at that time. In 1973 it assumed its present name, the
American Lung Association (ALA). It now has a membership of 1,500, mostly
in the health care profession, and over 120 affiliates representing all the states
as well as many major cities and counties. Its board of directors numbers over
100 individuals, and a professional staff of 167 are headquartered in New York
City. In 1983 the president established a council of selected business leaders to
enhance the ALA's image and fund-raising capacity among corporations.

ALA obtains much of its revenues through public subscription, primarily
through its annual Christmas seals campaign. It has an annual budget of over
$12 million, which it obtains from donations as well as grants from organizations
such as the Hospital Corporation of America, Smith Kline and French Labs,
MONY Financial Services, and The Upjohn Company. It spends about 22 percent
of its budget for support services, administration, and fund-raising. Its programs
are divided into research and information on lung disease, 51 percent; smoking
and health, 11 percent; community health program support, 8 percent; occupational health, 4 percent; and air conservation, 4 percent.

*POLICY CONCERNS*

Like the American Cancer Society,* ALA's primary concern is for the effect
of air pollutants on human health, not on the environment. It was involved in
the protracted campaign to get the surgeon general to warn against smoking in
1964 and to obtain restrictions on advertising by the Federal Trade Commission
and the Federal Communications Commission. It saw much of its efforts eroded
in Congress because of massive spending by the individual political action committees of such corporations as Philip Morris, R. J. Reynolds, Brown and Wil-

liamson, Lorillard, and American Brands, as well as rival expert testimony by the Tobacco Institute. These groups were successful in diluting and postponing health warnings against cigarette smoking and in keeping intact federal tobacco price supports because of their economic arguments.

ALA now makes its campaign against smoking on the grounds that medical costs for treating emphysema and lung cancer far outweigh the tobacco industry's economic claims. It fought for the sixteen-cents a pack federal excise tax on cigarette sales and advocates increasing it to thirty-two cents a pack and banning the advertisement and promotion of tobacco, especially that aimed at the youth of the nation. It has enlisted the aid of Patrick Reynolds, an heir to the R. J. Reynolds Tobacco Company fortune, who opposes smoking, in testifying before Congress.

ALA's representatives testified successfully for strengthening the Clean Air Act in 1977 and again in 1982. Its spokespersons also testify before U.S. Environmental Protection Agency hearings and generally advocate stricter standards for air pollutants, especially toxic pollutants. Its representatives testified in 1986 before Congress concerning the problem of acid deposition, arguing that national ambient air quality standards should not be relaxed and that sulfur dioxide emissions should be reduced further for public health reasons.

## TACTICS

ALA regularly issues press releases about the dangers of smoking and other health risks; it distributes information to schools and workplaces about indoor air pollutants. Its medical section, the American Thoracic Society, prepares research and position papers on respiratory diseases and provides fellowships to fund training of physicians and scientists. It holds an annual meeting for members.

## FURTHER INFORMATION

*Annual Report 1987–88* (1989). Washington, D.C.: ALA.
Fritschler, A. Lee (1989). *Smoking and Politics.* 4th ed. Englewood Cliffs, N.J.: Prentice-Hall.
Washington Office: 1101 Vermont Avenue, N.W., Suite 402, Washington, D.C. 20005

## AMERICAN MEDICAL ASSOCIATION (AMA)
535 N. Dearborn Street
Chicago, Illinois 60610–4377

## ORGANIZATION AND RESOURCES

The American Medical Association (AMA) was founded in 1847 in Philadelphia to represent the interests of the medical profession in the United States. It gained considerable fame for its successful prevention of socialized medicine in the United States despite major efforts by groups concerned about inequity in the distribution of medical services. It has maintained over the years that the profession is able to regulate itself and should be free from government interference. It is a membership association; anyone who holds a medical degree is eligible to join, although not all do so. In the late 1980s its membership nearly reached the 300,000 mark, including student and resident members.

The AMA is organized into a 400-member house of delegates, in which each state's medical association is represented, as well as over 50 medical speciality societies, including the American Academy of Neurology, Ophtalmology, and Pediatrics, among others. Sections represent particular groups inside the medical profession: hospital staff, medical students, resident physicians, medical schools, and young physicians. Federal services, including the air force, army, navy, U.S. Public Health Service, and Veterans Administration, are also represented. Each speciality and section has one representative in the House, and states are represented according to numbers of members; all are elected. The fourteen-member board of trustees is elected by the house of delegates annually, as are the speaker and vice-speaker of the house of delegates, the president, president-elect, and secretary-treasurer. The executive vice-president is selected by the trustees to administer the professional staff in Chicago and in Washington.

AMA's annual operating revenues reached more than $160 million at the end of the 1980s. About 40 percent comes from membership dues, 25 percent from advertising and subscriptions to its various publications, 12 percent from real estate and securities investment, and the rest from miscellaneous sources. Its expenditures include: 27 percent for representing the Association's interests, 27 percent for developing and distributing scientific information, 8 percent on educational standards, 6 percent on membership and federation expenses, and 3 percent on administration and management.

### POLICY CONCERNS

The primary policy concerns of the AMA in the 1980s involved the economic interests of its membership. It has attempted to prevent government control over the costs of medical care and advocates increased spending on Medicare and Medicaid. It argues that medical insurance is excessive and has tried to convince legislatures to put a ceiling on the kinds of awards that courts may give for medical malpractice suits. Since 1910 the AMA has had considerable influence on the quality of medical education in the United States by accrediting medical schools and approving residence programs, thereby controlling the numbers of doctors entering the profession in the United States. It argues that it does so in order to protect the quality of health care provided to the American public rather than to restrict the availability of medical care and thus influence the price of that care.

The AMA also has become involved in other types of public policy. It has argued consistently for continued use of animals in biomedical research in opposition to animal rights groups. Like the American Lung Association* and the American Cancer Society,* it argues that smoking is deleterious to human health and now advocates further controls on the tobacco industry and its advertising. During the 1960s fight over the initial warning on cigarette packages, however,

AMA leadership argued that control over tobacco should be exercised by the Congress rather than the regulatory agencies, which were more eager to regulate (Fritschler, 1989). In the 1980s it supported other health groups' initiative to ban smoking on domestic flights of under two hours. It also filed a petition with the Food and Drug Administration to regulate the new smokeless tobacco cigarette introduced by R. J. Reynolds Company as a drug.

Representatives of the AMA testified in 1977 and again in 1982 for reauthorization of the Clean Air Act. They argued to extend deadlines for areas not meeting standards and not to withhold money from states for sewage treatment plants when they did not meet standards. They also disagreed with the auto industry about relaxing auto emission standards. AMA representatives have taken a cautious stand regarding controls of toxic emissions. Generally they advocate more research on the effects of such substances, and have argued specifically that the dioxin danger has been exaggerated by other advocates of public health.

### TACTICS

The AMA and its state affiliates have numerous political action committees that contribute significant amounts of money to individual political candidates whom they perceive as favorable to their interests. AMA regularly claims a success rate of over 90 percent for congressional candidates it funds. AMA publishes the *American Medical News* weekly and the *Journal of the American Medical Association* and several speciality publications of professional interest such as the *Archives of Dermatology*. Its offices mail news releases to 3,000 journalists each week, broadcast a regular radio news feature, and distribute a weekly 90-second video news release. It hosts semiannual conventions.

### FURTHER INFORMATION

*Annual Report 1988* (1989). Washington, D.C.: AMA.
Fritschler, A. Lee (1989). *Smoking and Politics*. 4th ed. Englewood Cliffs, N.J.: Prentice-Hall.
*Health Legislative Issues* (1987). Washington, D.C. AMA, January.

Washington Office: 1101 Vermont Avenue, N.W., Washington, D.C. 20005

## AMERICAN MINING CONGRESS (AMC)
1920 N Street, N.W., Suite 300
Washington, D.C. 20036

### ORGANIZATION AND RESOURCES

The American Mining Congress (AMC) was founded in 1897 to represent the interests of the mining industry. Over the years its membership has depended on the state of the mining economy. At the end of the 1980s it had over 400 corporate members, including both mineral production firms, such as the Aluminum Company of America, AMAX, Inc., Exxon Coal, Inc., Genstar Corporation, and Peabody Holding Company, and engineering and manufacturing firms that produce equipment used in mining, such as Fiat-Allis, Bucyrus-Erie,

Caterpillar, General Motors, and TRW. In addition, some financial institutions that specialize in raising capital to finance mining operations belong to AMC, including the Chase Manhattan Bank and Touche Ross and Company. Dues depend on the production and sales level of the company.

The forty-four members of the board of directors are elected for either one or three year terms at the annual members' meeting in February. In addition, there are ten vice-chairs and a twelve-person executive committee selected from the board. A separate thirty-person board of governors is chosen by the manufacturing/engineering division of the Congress, with its own ten-person executive committee. President of the entire American Mining Congress is John A. Knebel, who directs a fifty-three-person office in Washington.

In the late 1980s AMC had an annual budget of about $5.5 million, 45 percent of which came from corporate dues. A similar amount was made from trade shows, and the remainder came from subscriptions to and sales of publications produced by AMC.

## POLICY CONCERNS

The American Mining Congress has numerous concerns about public policy issues. It has a resolutions committee of over sixty representatives who determine policy positions for AMC at the annual meeting. One of its primary concerns is the way in which the industry is taxed. AMC consistently argues that the federal tax system should encourage investment of capital in high-risk areas of the economy such as mining for the sake of national security, including depletion allowances for mined minerals. In the interest of keeping down costs of borrowing capital, the industry urges fiscal restraint in government and reduction of spending on domestic policies generally; it supports the Gramm-Rudman budget law. It also advocates maintaining a significant stockpile of strategic minerals for national defense purposes and opposes any reduction in purchasing for stockpiling purposes because of budgetary constraints.

AMC views as one of its primary problems the lack of competitiveness with foreign goods that have been driving out their U.S. counterparts. It argues that the U.S. government should work for free markets and international competition by protecting U.S. industry from unfair foreign competition including foreign government subsidies for its exports and dumping of mineral products on the international market. AMC advocates use of all existing trade remedies, including negotiating under the General Agreement on Tariffs and Trade, as well as revisions of current trade laws to permit more protection of the American mining industry. It also attempts to influence International Monetary Fund and World Bank policy to reduce loans to less-developed nations that encourage overproduction of minerals for export.

One reason the mining industry feels it is at a disadvantage competitively is the foreclosure of mining in some public lands. It advocates opening up more public lands to exploration for minerals and mining. Its officers have urged the Department of the Interior's Bureau of Land Management to revoke many withdrawals of lands and to avoid putting buffer zones around the areas withdrawn for wildlife refuges and wilderness areas. It also advocates amending the Wilderness Act to this effect. Local members of the AMC have been active in the roadless area review process in both the Department of Interior and Forest Service in designating which public lands should be open to mineral development. It also advocates amending the Federal Coastal Leasing Act to increase the number of coal reserves open to development on public lands.

One of its major lobbying efforts was devoted to passage of the Deep Seabed Hard Mineral Resources Act of 1980, which laid the groundwork for reaching agreement with other nations about dividing up the mineral resources of the ocean. It was instrumental in getting President Reagan to proclaim an exclusive economic zone (EEZ) for the United States within 200 nautical miles of its coast, including Pacific territories. It believes that the EEZ should not be restricted by the regulations of the Outer Continental Shelf Lands Act.

The AMC advocates modifying existing environmental statutes to increase coal leasing on federal lands and to facilitate mining on privately held lands by delegating to the states the enforcement of surface mining regulations. It advocates promoting competition of rail carriers to prevent price gouging in hauling coal and other minerals, but it does not promote reintroduction of regulation of the rail industry. It advocates the development of coal slurry pipelines and other alternatives to rail transportation. It argues for the continued development of nuclear power in order to promote uranium mining, and believes Congress should facilitate the licensing of new nuclear plants and devote public moneys to informational programs to schools and the public on the safety of nuclear power.

One of the federal laws with which the mining industry has long been concerned is the Clean Air Act. AMC representatives testified in 1986 against adding controls to sulfur oxide emissions to reduce acid rain. It argues, along with the electric power industry, that sulfur oxides have been reduced substantially by current regulations and there is no scientific evidence that more needs to be done. The metals industry is so sensitive to energy costs that it believes the whole economy will be injured by further controlling emissions from power plants. Such a new policy, according to the AMC, will have the secondary impact of substituting imported Canadian hydropower for domestic coal production and further damaging our balance of trade problems in the world economy.

Mining is a water-intensive industry, and AMC advocates allowing state governments to determine how water rights should be distributed rather than letting the federal government decide which water rights are reserved for Indian reservations, wildlife preservation, and other nonindustrial uses. It also argues that Indian mineral owners should have greater discretion in negotiating mineral agreements, as it perceives the Bureau of Indian Affairs as too conservative in assigning mineral rights to developers. AMC also advocates relaxing restrictions created by the Clean Water Act (CWA) to exempt certain new source discharges from permit requirements and to protect only sensitive and truly valuable wetlands from dredging and filling.

One of the major issues to be discussed by AMC in the 1990s is the matter of groundwater contamination. It is concerned about the impact increased regulation is likely to have on the industry. It argues that mineral extraction is an essential economic activity in the United States, and any attempt to establish the principle of nondegradation of groundwater should be avoided since any mining by definition changes the chemistry of an aquifer near it. AMC believes that state governments will be more realistic in determining how to protect their groundwater resources and at the same time permit necessary economic activities than will the federal government, and therefore argues that primary responsibility for protecting groundwater should remain with the state governments.

Regarding solid waste management, AMC contends that waste materials from extraction and processing of ores should not be designated as hazardous because of naturally occurring elements in the ores. It also believes state governments are the appropriate level of government to make specific decisions about which wastes should be regulated. It believes that Superfund has been funded at too high a level. It scored a victory by convincing Congress not to tax waste producers, but to continue to fund Superfund from a tax on feedstocks, which is aimed at the chemical and petrochemical industry.

## TACTICS

Members of AMC stay abreast of Washington news and developments in mining through the *American Mining Congress Journal*, published monthly, and the weekly *Washington Concentrates*, which focuses on the most current developments. AMC sponsors a coal convention each spring and a mining convention in the fall in addition to its annual meeting in Washington. Mining equipment expositions are also sponsored. Throughout the year AMC holds workshops and seminars on a variety of subjects such as mine safety, risk assessment, international trade, and taxes. The AMC prides itself on being the eyes and ears and the collective voice of the mining industry in Washington.

In 1987 its leadership advocated a new procedure in federal law that would supplement Executive Order 12293 issued by President Reagan in 1983 by which regulations must pass a cost/benefit examination before going into effect. In addition, before any new law or regulation could go into effect three additional questions would be asked: Will employment be adversely affected? Will U.S. trade be hurt? Will capital formation be impeded? If the answer to any of these questions was yes, the rulemaking could not go forward. This probably expresses the AMC's attitude toward government regulation for environmental or human health purposes most effectively.

The annual fall meeting in Washington is designed to facilitate individual members' meeting with their elected representatives as well as officials in the major administrative agencies that affect the industry, including the Bureau of Mines and Office of Surface Mining in the Department of Interior and the Environmental Protection Agency. The fact that the mining industry is concentrated in certain regions of the United States enables the AMC to develop major allies in Congress who represent mining states, such as Senator Robert C. Byrd of West Virginia. These members give AMC easy access to committees on subjects such as energy, important to the mining industry.

### FURTHER INFORMATION

*American Mining Congress Journal* (1989). Washington, D.C.: AMC, March.
Davis, David Howard (1982) *Energy Politics*. New York: St. Martin's Press.
*Declaration of Policy* (1987). Washington, D.C.: AMC.
McFarland, Andrew (1984). "Energy Lobbies." *Annual Review of Energy* 9:501–527.
U.S. Congress. Senate Committee on Energy and Natural Resources (1987). *Hearing on Groundwater Protection*. Washington , D.C.: Government Printing Office, June 1.

## AMERICAN ORINTHOLOGISTS' UNION

*See* National Audubon Society.

## AMERICAN PAPER AND PULP ASSOCIATION

*See* American Paper Institute.

## AMERICAN PAPER INSTITUTE (API)

260 Madison Avenue, 10th Floor
New York, New York. 10016

### ORGANIZATION AND RESOURCES

The American Paper Institute (API) was formed in 1964 by a merger of the American Paper and Pulp Association, founded in 1878, and the National Paperboard Association, founded in 1915. It is a trade association for 166 companies that produce paper from timber. It shares office space in Washington and many other resources with the National Forest Products Association (NFPA),* whose membership list includes most of the companies that belong also to the API. It has an annual budget of $10 million and a staff of 140. Dues depend on the volume of business done by member corporations. Its president is Red Covaney.

### POLICY CONCERNS

API's interests closely parallel those of the NFPA. It is especially concerned with the Clean Air Act (CAA), whose controls it hopes to relax. It seems logical that API's economic self-interest would influence it to advocate greater controls on sulfur emissions in order to reduce the impact of acid rain on forest growth in the United States. This is not the case, however, for most API members are located in the western or southeastern states where acid rain has had little impact. API representatives regularly testify before Congress that there is no consensus among forestry experts on the causes or effects of acid rain and that the issue should be carefully researched before any controls are imposed on industrial boilers. The pulp industry itself uses boilers that API argues are impossible to control economically.

Another API concern is the Clean Water and Safe Drinking Water acts (CWA, SDWA). Environmental groups in the late 1980s have put considerable pressure on EPA to control groundwater contamination by preventing runoff from industrial sites as well as farmlands. The API has defended the pulp and paper industry by arguing that wastes from wood are not harmful and should not be included under such legislation. It also opposes any change in Superfund that would tax waste producers to contribute to the fund. It also opposes any definition of hazardous wastes under the Resource Conservation and Recovery Act (RCRA) that would include chemicals used in the pulp industry.

Finally, API advocates opening up most wilderness areas to timber companies to cut old-growth lumber. Throughout the 1980s the U.S. Department of Agriculture Forest Service permitted large tracts of publicly owned forest lands to be cut and sold both in the United States and abroad. Environmental groups countered with lawsuits against these harvests and succeeded in getting some court injunctions in Washington State and Oregon. In response, API and other forest industries argued that jobs would be lost and the economy slowed by such decisions and launched a major public information campaign against preserving old-growth forests.

### TACTICS

The API coordinates its lobbying activities with the NFPA. It both testifies before congressional committees on such subjects as the clean air and water acts and contributes to public information campaigns, such as the American Forest Resource Alliance's advertisements against environmental "extremists" who wish to preserve wilderness for its own sake. API has a library of 500 volumes and issues a weekly report to members about developments in government and an annual statistical report. It holds a meeting in New York City in March each year.

### AMERICAN PETROLEUM INSTITUTE (API)
1220 L Street, N. W.
Washington, D.C. 20005

### HISTORY AND DEVELOPMENT

The American Petroleum Institute (API) was founded in 1919 to represent the interests of the petroleum-producing industry. During its first fifty years the API, along with its major corporate affiliates, enjoyed considerable success in structuring government policies in two major fields: restricting the supply of oil and controlling government taxation of the industry. First, states such as Texas and Oklahoma, and later the federal government, passed legislation to restrict the production of domestic oil in order to maintain the price and prevent competition. Later in the 1950s import quotas were introduced to prevent a flood of foreign oil from driving down the price of domestic oil. In the 1920s the oil depletion allowance was created allowing oil producers to deduct 27.5 percent of their gross income from taxable income to compensate for the fact that oil pumped from a field is nonrenewable, a tax write-off unprecedented in other industries. This high rate of success has been attributed to the strategic position in Congress held by oil-producing states, such as that of Senator Robert Kerr of Kerr-McGee Oil from Oklahoma (Oppenheimer, 1974).

In the early 1970s, however, interests opposed to the oil industry began to break into the closed circle of oil lobbyists, interested members of Congress and the U. S. Department of Interior, and state agencies in sympathy with the oil industry. The Nixon administration placed price controls on oil along with other commodities in order to cut inflation. When price controls were lifted in 1973, public cynicism regarding the oil industry's influence forced the government to keep controls on oil. Later, however, the Carter administration began and the Reagan administration completed withdrawal of these controls as well. Oil price surges in 1973–74 so alienated the population that Congress withdrew the oil depletion allowance in 1975 and passed a windfall profits tax in 1980 to recapture part of the deregulated price of domestically produced oil. The Reagan administration subsequently cut the tax and gave large reductions to Americans working abroad in the oil industry in the 1981 tax relief package (McFarland, 1984).

## ORGANIZATION AND RESOURCES

API now includes producers, refiners, marketers, and transporters of petroleum products. It represents over 200 domestic and 28 foreign oil companies, including all the major integrated petroleum corporations: AMOCO, ARCO, Atlantic Richfield, British Petroleum, Chevron, CONOCO, Ethyl, Exxon, Marathon, Mobil, Pennzoil, Phillips, Shell, Standard Oil, Sun Oil, Shell Oil, and Texaco, as well as many smaller independent oil producers. All of the large corporations also maintain substantial offices in Washington, and many have major political action committees (PACs), but the API integrates and coordinates the oil industry's efforts to influence policy.

During the late 1980s, a period of decline and belt-tightening for the oil industry, API had a budget of about $50 million, 96 percent of which came from corporate dues, which vary in terms of each company's production. About 5,000 individuals also belong to API and contribute $250 annual dues. The president of API, Charles J. DiBona, heads a staff of 400 at headquarters in Washington. Regional offices in Dallas and New York and 34 state division offices employ an additional 140 persons.

Policy is made by an elected board of directors of 121 members and a 30-member executive committee, which meets twice yearly. The management committee, which considers important policy matters as they develop, meets 10 times a year and consists of the board chair, President DiBona, and 6 members elected by the board. The committee on public issues, consisting of representatives of senior management of large, medium, and small member-companies makes recommendations to each meeting of the management committee. Seven vice-presidents have large departments in the national office dealing with finance, analysis and statistics, law, public affairs, field operations, health and environment, management and budget, federal government affairs, and industry affairs. The vice-president for industry affairs, for example, is responsible for exploration and public lands, fire and safety, marketing, measurement, production, refining, and transportation.

### POLICY CONCERNS

Traditionally the industry and API's first priority has been to press for significant tax deductions for the industry in the form of depletion allowances and intangible drilling cost deductions. Over the years these tax advantages have fluctuated, but the industry continues to enjoy considerable influence on the tax code due to its extensive lobbying efforts. However, API has lobbied unsuccessfully to repeal the 1980 windfall profits tax. API's primary argument is that government ought to tax the oil industry in such a manner as to maximize incentives to explore for domestic oil and gas. In conjunction with its need for tax incentives, the API also argues for elimination of all price controls in order to increase profitability and give industry more incentive to explore for more supplies. Successful in getting petroleum prices decontrolled in the Carter and Reagan administrations, the industry now presses for full deregulation of the natural gas market.

API couches its arguments for tax relief and price freedom in national security terms. API reported with alarm the increasing dependence on foreign sources and the resultant decline in domestic exploration and production in the 1980s. It argues against utilizing foreign sources and conserving domestic supplies on the grounds that it will take considerable time to gear up to explore for oil in a military emergency. It also advocates filling and increasing the strategic petroleum reserve (SPR) for security reasons, a government policy that would increase the sales of the oil industry.

Generally, API supports government policies that will maximize production and sales of domestic supplies. In 1987 it joined with the American Gas Association* and other trade associations in urging Congress to repeal the 1978 Powerplant and Industrial Fuel Use Act (PIFUA), because the law reduced sales of oil and gas to utilities and some other industries that had been forced to switch to coal, a more abundant domestic fuel. API also advocates repeal of the Petroleum Marketing Act, also passed in the oil crisis of the mid–1970s, forcing producers to guarantee a supply to their fanchisers at a modest price in order to keep the supply distributed throughout the country.

### DEVELOPMENT OF PUBLIC RESOURCES

In order to bolster production and remedy the disastrous decline in the industry that API reported in the mid–1980s, it advocates opening up most federally held lands to oil and gas exploration. API sees the exploration of the Arctic National Wildlife Refuge (ANWR), located next to the Prudhoe Bay area which has been producing the largest single amount of domestic oil in recent years, as critical to increasing domestic oil production. The oil industry was successful in convincing the Reagan Departments of Energy and Interior to advocate opening all federal lands to oil exploration, but it has been less successful with Congress, where it continues to wage a concerted campaign to get enabling legislation to open the wilderness.

One of the other major areas that the industry hopes to open to oil exploration is the outer continental shelf off California and other areas where Congress has imposed a moratorium on drilling for some years. In 1985 a compromise was worked out between the California congressional delegation and the Department of the Interior to open up 150 tracts of land in the outer continental shelf to oil exploration, but later the industry was successful in convincing Secretary of Interior Donald Hodel to withdraw administrative support on the grounds that the industry needs a much larger percentage of the potential oil fields open to exploration. After the *Exxon Valdez* ran aground in Prince William Sound in March 1989 and spilled 11 million gallons of crude oil into the coastal waters of Alaska, opposition to further drilling in coastal areas hardened in Congress. API argued that this was wrong-headed because increasing domestic production of oil would decrease the number of tankers that would be needed to bring imported foreign oil into domestic waters. It also coordinated an industry-wide Petroleum Industry Response Organization (PIRO) designed to fund a network of 5 oil spill response centers around the United States to contain and clean up future spills. API, however, acknowledged that "rebuilding public trust will be a long and arduous process" (API, 1989).

## ENVIRONMENTAL CONTROLS

In addition to taxing, pricing, and natural resource development policies, the petroleum industry places high priority on reducing the cost to industry of safety and environmental regulations. One of the major new regulatory initiatives in the 1980s has been the effort to define and control hazardous wastes separately from other solid wastes in the United States. The industry has testified often concerning the Resource Conservation and Reclamation Act (RCRA), arguing against EPA's defining hazardous wastes to include exploration wastes and muds from wells. API's members have developed a technique of disposing of drilling wastes by injecting them into deep wells, and they feel this is an environmentally safe method of disposal and oppose regulation of it. API also testifies that many petroleum wastes may be safely disposed of by spreading them on land surfaces and discing them into the earth. Congress nevertheless amended RCRA in 1986 to control land application, and industrial spokesmen now concentrate on convincing EPA not to define certain kinds of industry wastes as hazardous in order to prevent their being banned from land disposal. API spokespeople also argue that RCRA should supplant federal common law so that no one can sue for nuisance or damages if injured by a waste disposal method that was defined as safe under RCRA regulations.

The petroleum industry has been hard hit by Superfund legislation that placed a tax on the chemical and petrochemical industries in order to fund the cleanup of abandoned hazardous waste dumps that constitute a threat to human health. It argued successfully when Superfund was up for reauthorization in 1986 to have the tax extended to other types of industry. It was not successful, however, in having the amount of tax reduced to what it considered a reasonable level. It also argued unsuccessfully that the courts' use of joint and several liability to allow the government broad discretion in seeking reimbursement for its cleanup efforts from all those involved in creating the dumps was excessive and should be modified by the statute law. It also advocated turning over to the states more responsibility for enforcing Superfund rather than allowing the U.S. Environmental Protection Agency (EPA) to control it, and opposed the inclusion of a private right to sue for individuals who feel injured by leaking hazardous waste dumps.

Another federal regulatory statute of importance to API is the Clean Air Act (CAA). In 1977 API representatives testified during the reauthorization of the CAA, arguing that national ambient air quality standards were already excessive and should not be increased. Nevertheless, the Congress in 1977 did increase the restrictiveness of the law. Throughout most of the 1980s, API joined the Reagan administration's EPA in advocating radical changes in the CAA. Together they argued there was sufficient protection of vistas around national parks and historic places to preclude any further visibility requirements. API advocates eliminating the requirement that industry seeking to locate new plants in dirty-air areas find old sources of emissions to reduce before new sources can be sited there. Otherwise, the industry argues, there will be no growth in industrialized areas, which need expansion in order to survive economically. API's health and environment division does research to demonstrate that EPA's standards concerning ozone are excessive and can be reduced without any deleterious effect to public health. It also conducts research that opposes the control of certain types of pollutants, such as trichloroethylene, as toxic emissions under the CAA. Its federal government affairs division argues that gas vapors should be controlled through modifying automobile canisters rather than by reducing the volatility of gasoline. In this it is opposed by the auto manufacturers who prefer to see the volatility reduced by refining.

In 1989, the Bush administration introduced several suggested amendments to the CAA to Congress, including a recommendation that a percentage of cars be produced to burn alternative fuels (such as methanol or ethanol) in the 1990s. Many petroleum companies, such as ARCO, countered with the argument that it would be more environmentally sound to reformulate gasoline to burn more cleanly because this could be used in old as well as new cars. They began a cooperative research endeavor with automotive manufacturers to produce such a fuel, although some gasoline companies continued to advocate blending alcohol with gasoline. It was not possible for API to coordinate all its members in presenting a united front on this issue to Congress, but API opposed any mandate that would impose a government-determined percentage of methanol-fueled cars by a certain date. Concerning global warming, its researchers argue that there is so much uncertainty about the impact of increased carbon dioxide emissions that it is premature to propose solutions in the CAA based on today's limited understanding of the issue.

The API's environmental division also does research on water pollution control and groundwater protection. It opposes amending the Safe Drinking Water Act to force industry to reinject the brine produced as a by-product of its drilling operations below the level of the water table. It attempts to influence state governments in their actions controlling the leaking of underground storage tanks for gas. Its industry affairs division advocates changing the CAA to permit more dredging and filling of wetlands. It also objects to many Occupational Safety and Health Act regulations and state fire and safety laws on the grounds of excessive cost to industry. It argues to change the method of measuring crude oil withdrawn in order to minimize the severance taxes it has to pay to state governments, and for defining more pipelines as intrastate rather than interstate in order to minimize the length of line regulated by the federal government. It opposes the Coast Guard's application of user fees to barges hauling petroleum products on U.S. waterways.

## TACTICS

The federal government affairs division of API regularly informs its membership about legislative hearings, markups, and other events in Congress. It also testifies and submits statements at congressional hearings. It sends out research monographs API publishes to members of Congress and their staff, including *Two Energy Futures*, which argues for increased domestic supply. API also makes formal presentations to federal agencies such as EPA and OSHA. API is by far the largest of the energy lobbies; its budget and number of employees enables it to launch the most comprehensive program for influencing public policy in the area of energy development and environmental controls.

Each one of its major members, however, also maintain extensive public relations operations in the Washington area. Whenever API testifies before Congress or the agencies, its efforts are supplemented by the professional staff of individual petroleum corporations. API and corporations such as Mobil Oil also devote considerable resources to drafting press releases, writing articles and advertisements for editorial pages, producing video tapes and books for educational institutions, and fielding a major speakers' bureau to address groups around the country about the industry's point of view. In 1989 Mobil Oil launched a major campaign against substituting methanol for gasoline in automobiles, a policy that some oil corporations such as Texaco had embraced through their membership in the Council on Alternate Fuels.* At least one observer of the lobbying scene in Washington believes that API's efforts are eclipsed by the individual lobbying programs of specific oil corporations, which are difficult to coordinate because of their conflicting views on policy (Soloman, 1987).

API runs a regular tour program designed to show members of Congress, staff, and opinion leaders some oil production rigs in offshore locations that it feels are environmentally benign. Its representatives have been effective in influencing U.S. Department of Interior and Forest Service officials to give greater consideration to mineral exploration in planning for wilderness areas during the Reagan administration. It has not been so successful in convincing the relevant congressional committees, and it now focuses its efforts there.

API has an extensive research program. It publishes a yearly report to its membership concerning its lobbying activities and an extensive research monograph series on such issues as marketing techniques and technical problems of the industry including drilling and fire-control problems. It also publishes a number of monographs on health and environmental issues that generally play down the problems of air and water quality problems in the United States and emphasize how effective industry controls on such phenomena are.

In addition, each major oil corporation publishes very professional bimonthly magazines available to the public, especially educators, at no charge. In 1918 the Standard Oil Company of New Jersey published the first issue of *The Lamp*, directed toward its employees to present management's point of view about employment policies. After World War II, however, it changed its editorial thrust to present industry's perspective to a broader audience. In 1988 *The Lamp* celebrated its 70th anniversary with a circulation in excess of 700,000, including stockholders, libraries, educators, and government officials.

## FURTHER INFORMATION

American Petroleum Institute (1986). *Myths and Misperceptions*. Washington, D.C.: API.

———— (1986). *Two Energy Futures: National Choices Today for the 1990s*. revised ed. Washington, D.C.: API.

———— (1989). *Report to the Membership*. Washington, D.C.: API.

Blair, J. (1977). *The Control of Oil*. New York: Pantheon.

Chubb, John E. (1983). *Interest Groups and the Bureaucracy*.    Stanford, Calif.: Stanford University Press.

Davis, David Howard (1982). *Energy Politics*. 3d ed. New York: St. Martin's Press.

Downs, Matthews (1988). "Producing Oil on Public Lands." *The Lamp* 70: 6–11.

Exxon Corporation (1988). *The Lamp* 70.

McFarland, Andrew (1984). "Energy Lobbies." *Annual Review of Energy* 9: 501–527.

Mobil Oil (1989). "More Problems with Methanol." *The New York Times*, September 23, p.22.

Oppenheimer, Bruce (1974). *Oil and the Congressional Process: The Limits of Symbolic Politics*. Lexington, Mass.: Lexington Press.

Soloman, Burt (1987). "Measuring Clout." *National Journal*, July 4, pp.1706–1711.

Stanfield, Rochelle L. (1986). "Alaska Face-Off: Crude Oil v. Habitat." *National Journal*, December 13, pp. 3028–3029.

———— (1987). "Another Oil Crisis?" *National Journal*, January 17, pp.131–133.

Stobaugh, Robert, and Daniel Yergin, eds. (1983). *Energy Future*. 3d ed. New York: Vintage Press.

## AMERICAN PUBLIC HEALTH ASSOCIATION (APHA)
1015 15th St., N.W.
Washington, D.C. 20005

### ORGANIZATION AND RESOURCES

In 1872 the American Public Health Association (APHA) was founded by health professionals to represent their interests and promote and protect the public health. In the late 1980s it had over 31,000 individual members as well as 47 state and local affiliates that represent about 20,000 additional health professionals. Individuals pay dues of $60 a year and affiliates from $100 to $750. It has an annual budget of $6.5 million; 30 percent comes from government funding, 30 percent from publications, 15 percent from its annual membership meeting, 19 percent from dues, and 5 percent from investments.

APHA is divided into 24 sections representing different specializations in the profession of public health from community health planning, administration, nursing, social work, to mental health, occupational health, and epidemiology. Each of these is represented in proportion to its respective membership on a 200-person governing council, where each of the states is represented as well. At the annual meeting to which all professional members are invited, the governing council elects a 20-member board of directors. A nominating committee, consisting of the president, the chair of the executive board, and 6 members of the governing council, submits nominees for each of the offices at that meeting. The council is divided into several committees, such as membership and bylaws. Its action board has responsibility for formulating, planning, and implementing association policies and positions on which the whole council votes each year.

### POLICY CONCERNS

APHA has a wide range of priorities in public policy at both federal and state levels, including increased funding for Medicare and Medicaid to provide for treatment for the aged and indigent population in the United States, and provision for prenatal care and child health programs, including improved early childhood nutrition, by all levels of government. It opposes legislation that would restrict teenagers' access to contraception and abortion counseling unless they obtain parental consent. It opposes discrimination by insurance companies against clients testing positive for the AIDS virus. It supports restrictions on the export of drugs not approved for sale in the United States. Together with the American Medical Association, it attempts to increase the tax and reduce sales of tobacco products because of their deleterious effect on human health. It supports the 55 mph speed limit because of its role in decreasing the number of fatal traffic accidents. It supports gun control legislation and ratification of nuclear test ban treaties and other means by which human exposure to radiation can be decreased.

APHA joined with several environmental groups to support passage of the Superfund and Reauthorization Act (SARA) Amendments in 1986 to increase funding to clean up toxic waste dumps around the United States. Its position is that such concentrations of chemical contaminants increase health risks to nearby human populations. It advocates increased epidemiological research on the causes of cancer and other diseases. The Association also joined environmental groups in arguing for more-restrictive controls over the use of pesticides and other toxic substances controlled by the U.S. Department of Agriculture and the U.S. Environmental Protection Agency (EPA). It generally assumes a more restrictive position regarding the use of commercial poisons and toxic air pollutants than does the more business-oriented American Medical Association. Its representatives have testified before Congress for increasing the restrictiveness of the Clean Air and Clean Water acts as well as the Safe Drinking Water Act.

*TACTICS*

The executive director of APHA administers a fifty-four-person professional staff in Washington who testify before congressional committees, monitor the voting record of Congress, inform their membership of crucial issues before the legislature, and encourage them to write their representatives. It estimates that it spends only 3 percent of its annual budget on governmental relations, as most of its revenues go toward educating the public and its membership on professional and public health developments and issues. Its highest priorities are placed on such issues as funding medical research. Its interest in environmental policy concern issues of air, water, and land pollution and chemical contaminants that have been linked to cancer and other human disease. Less than 30 percent of its public policy resources are devoted to environmental issues. It tends to coordinate its efforts on these matters with such environmental groups as the Environmental Defense Fund,* Environmental Action,* and Friends of the Earth.*

APHA publishes the *American Journal of Public Health*, a monthly scientific, refereed journal with authoritative articles about the practice of public health and specialized areas of science, which has wide distribution in the profession. It also publishes *The Nation's Health*, a newspaper distributed to its membership ten times a year on policy issues of interest to the profession, explaining how individual representatives and senators have voted on proposed legislation in the public health field, and what actions have been proposed and taken by the regulatory agencies, especially EPA, Occupational Safety and Health Administration, and Health and Human Services. The Association also publishes monographs on specific public health issues, such as *Standard Methods for the Examination of Water and Wastewater* and *Public Health Law Manual*.

*FURTHER INFORMATION*

*American Journal of Public Health* (1989). Washington, D.C.: APHA, March.
*The Nation's Health* (1989). Washington, D.C.: APPA, February.

**AMERICAN PUBLIC POWER ASSOCIATION (APPA)**
2301 M Street, N.W.
Washington, D.C. 20037

## ORGANIZATION AND RESOURCES

There are some 2,200 publicly owned utilities in the United States, supplying electricity, irrigation water, and other public services to customers. These companies service the power needs of 35 million Americans, 13.6 percent of the market. Of these, about 1,500 belong to the American Public Power Association (APPA), founded in 1940 to represent the interests of publicly owned power suppliers. Policy is set for APPA by a 35-member board of directors elected at its annual meeting for 3-year terms. The executive director, Lawrence S. Hobart, selected by the board, oversees a staff of 60 professionals who represent APPA before Congress and administrative agencies, including the Federal Energy Regulatory Commission (FERC) and the Interstate Commerce Commission.

Its budget of about $5 million a year is derived primarily from dues from its member utilities, ranging from $250 to $1,250 a year, depending on their kilowatt hour sales and annual revenues. Other sources of revenue are fees earned from conferences, workshops, and other services provided to the membership. Approximately 30 percent of its annual budget is used for governmental relations.

## POLICY CONCERNS

Throughout its history APPA has defended the small segment of the electricity industry that is publicly owned against takeover threats from investor-owned giants such as Commonwealth Edison. Its representatives argue that among the benefits to be gained from a publicly owned sector are lower rates for consumers and continued competition in the industry which has become increasingly consolidated. APPA argues that the Federal Energy Regulatory Commission (FERC) should prevent further mergers among the giants, but at the minimum it should condition any mergers on the provision of access to facilities and power produced by the corporation.

Many of APPA's members obtain their electricity from federal power generators, and the association defends against any proposal to sell off such facilities to the private sector. The Reagan administration continually tried to raise revenues without raising taxes by selling off federally owned power generating facilities, including the Tennessee Valley Authority and the Bonneville Power Authority, in the 1980s. This was rejected both the 100th and 101st congresses under considerable pressure from APPA and continues as an issue in the 1990s. APPA also advocates making a distinction between costs of constructing public hydroelectric facilities and the costs of mitigating environmental impacts. It believes the public at large should share the costs of such mitigation with the beneficiaries of the projects, such as the Central Utah Project.

Another contributing factor to APPA's members' low rates is the ability of state and municipal governments to issue tax-free revenue bonds to finance publicly owned utilities. APPA regularly defends its members against proposals to change the federal tax law to their disadvantage. APPA joined with privately owned utilities to oppose the ban on using natural gas to generate electricity from its imposition during the energy crisis of the 1970s. This was accomplished in 1987 when the Powerplant and Industrial Fuel Use Act (PIFUA) was repealed.

APPA members purchase much of their electrical power from investor-owned utilities whose rates are regulated by FERC. APPA advocates changes in the Federal Power Act to facilitate its members' access to transmission services from all power sources. It also urges FERC to investigate rates of return on power purchased from investor-owned generators in order to adjust prices to reflect decreases when costs of producing electricity fall. It argues that there is lack of parity in FERC's treatment of requests for increases in rates (which are handled expeditiously) as opposed to requests for rate decreases.

Legislative representatives from APPA regularly testify about proposals to reduce acid rain, arguing that a tax on kilowatt-hours is unfair, and that a least-cost cleanup program should be funded by a national emission tax on all polluters. APPA supported the National Appliance Energy Conservation Act passed in 1987 to establish national standards for household appliances. It also argues before the Interstate Commerce Commission against allowing railroads to charge monopoly prices for the shipment of coal on which much power generation depends.

Although there was some difference of opinion expressed among its membership, APPA leadership supports the expansion of nuclear power. It advocates allowing the federal Nuclear Regulatory Commission to determine when and where nuclear plants may be located and to stop localities and states from preventing their operation by refusing to participate in plans for evacuation in case of an emergency. It also supported reauthorizing the Price-Anderson Act in 1988 to limit liability for nuclear accidents and to include the Shoreham, N.Y., and Seabrook, N.H., plants in this coverage. It also advocates solving the nuclear waste storage problem by allowing the national government to determine the location of such a facility. It has officially recognized the concern about global warming by resolving that the federal government should do further research on the issue.

Some of APPA's members obtain their electricity from coal-fired generators. APPA, therefore, supports the National Coal Association's* drive to expand the market for coal fly ash by eliminating the definition of ash as a solid waste under the Resource Conservation and Recovery Act (RCRA). It argues that ash can be used beneficially if it is not identified as hazardous in the public's mind. It opposes the creation of a tax incentive to encourage private companies to invest in clean coal technology because, it argues, it gives the private sector an advantage over the public sector.

### TACTICS

In addition to representing its membership before Congress and the regulatory agencies, APPA also provides other services. It produces and markets video cassettes and computer applications for planning and operating public power systems. It produces manuals concerning cogeneration and environmental regulation compliance and runs seminars on managerial techniques for managing and evaluating public power systems. It publishes the *Public Power Weekly*, *Public Power Quarterly Communication*, and *APPA Washington Report* to keep its membership abreast of developments on power issues in Washington and around the nation, and runs an annual convention. APPA organizes Public Ownership of Electric Resources Political Action Committee (POWERPAC), to funnel voluntary contributions to electoral campaigns of office seekers who support public power.

### FURTHER INFORMATION

*Annual Report* (1987–88). Washington, D.C.: APPA.

Chubb, John E. (1983). *Interest Groups and the Bureaucracy*. Stanford, Calif.: Stanford University Press.

Davis, David Howard (1982). *Energy Politics*. 3rd ed. New York: St. Martin's Press.

McFarland, Andrew (1984). "Energy Lobbies." *Annual Review of Energy* 9: 501–527.

*Public Power* (1989). Washington, D.C.: APPA, May-June.

*Public Power Weekly* (1988). Washington, D.C.: APPA, April 27, May 11, 18, 25.

Rosenbaum, Walter A. (1987). *Energy, Politics, and Public Policy*. 2d ed. Washington, D.C.: Congressional Quarterly Press.

Rudolph, Richard, and Scott Ridley (1986). *Power Struggle: The Hundred-Year War over Electricity*. New York: Harper and Row.

Stobaugh, Robert, and Daniel Yergin, eds. (1983). *Energy Future*. 3d ed. New York: Vintage Press.

## AMERICAN RECREATION COALITION (ARC)
1331 Pennsylvania Avenue, N.W.
Washington, D.C. 20004

### ORGANIZATION AND RESOURCES

The American Recreation Coalition (ARC), founded in 1979 to represent the interests of the recreation industry, consists of 100 recreation-related associations and companies selling outdoor equipment and recreational vehicles, and park and marina operators. Among its members are the American Fishing Tackle Manufacturers, American Motorcyclist Association, Conference of National Park Concessioners,* International Snowmobile Industry, Kampgrounds of America, National Marine Manufacturers Association, and Winnebago Industries. Membership groups, representing such interests as campers, boat owners, bicyclists, recreational vehicle owners, and skiers also belong.

Dues are based on the income of the industry or organization involved. ARC's budget at the end of the 1980s was about $300,000, 95 percent of which came from dues of its corporate members. ARC has a four-person professional staff in Washington, headed by president Derrick Crandall.

## POLICY CONCERNS

In the 1980s Mr. Crandall testified before the Senate Committee on Energy and Natural Resources that user fees for national parks might be increased as proposed by the Reagan administration, but that funds should be used to improve park facilities, not put into general revenues to reduce the national deficit as proposed. ARC also advocates federal and state government expenditures for increasing the availability of sport fishing and hunting on publicly owned lands.

Two of ARC's priorities are the expansion of the energy supply and the use of public lands for outdoor recreation. In 1985, a representative from the California Travel Parks, a Coalition member, testified on the need to drill for offshore oil in California to provide a sufficient gasoline supply in the United States for recreational vehicles. Generally the Coalition favors opening up more federally owned lands and waterways to motorized off-road vehicles and motorboats and opposes attempts by conservation groups such as the Sierra Club to keep wilderness areas roadless and inaccessible to large motorized campers.

Its interests occasionally coincide with environmental goals of expanding public land holdings for recreational use. More often, however, the Coalition favors greater economic development rather than conservation. It would prefer less-strict government control of resources and greater autonomy for states in making environmental decisions.

## TACTICS

ARC issues press releases occasionally and attempts to educate the public to its concerns. It publishes an annual report, *Recreation Industrial Forum Proceedings and Conclusions*, and *Who's Who in Recreation*. Its professional staff testify before congressional committees and provide members of Congress, their staffers, and the media with information about the recreation industry. It sponsors an annual convention.

## AMERICAN RIVERS CONSERVATION COUNCIL
*See* American Rivers, Incorporated.

## AMERICAN RIVERS, INCORPORATED
801 Pennsylvania Avenue, S.E., Suite 303
Washington, D.C. 20003

## ORGANIZATION AND RESOURCES

In 1973 a group of river activists banded together to form the American Rivers Conservation Council, a name later changed to American Rivers, Incorporated, dedicated to preserving outstanding free-flowing rivers and their landscapes. In the late 1980s American Rivers reported 9,000 members, paying dues of $24 yearly, and some corporate members, primarily outdoor recreational industries and outfitters, paying between $100 and $10,000. It is governed by a 25-member board of directors, who recruit their successors, chaired by Rafe Pomerance. President W. Kent Olson heads a staff of 8 in Washington.

American Rivers has an annual budget of nearly $1 million; 41 percent comes from foundations, such as the American Conservation Association, the New-Land Foundation, the Rockefeller Family Fund, and the Harold Wiley Trust; 25 percent comes from member dues; 16 percent from large gifts; 9 percent from fund-raising from members; and 9 percent is earned through river trips, publications, and interest. Its expenditures are spent on developing new members, 23 percent; public education, 20 percent; preservation and conservation of rivers, 18 percent; fund-raising, 15 percent; member services and communications, 12 percent; and administrative services and events, 12 percent.

## POLICY CONCERNS

The Wild and Scenic Rivers Act was passed in 1968 through the efforts of other conservation groups such as the Sierra Club.* Since its creation in 1973, American Rivers has monitored the implementation of this law, urging Congress to designate additional rivers as wild and free-flowing. It opposes building dams on waterways that its board of directors considers to be ecologically important. It argues that it seeks to protect only the most ecologically sensitive and important waterways, not to halt all economic development. It estimates that there are 3.5 million miles of rivers in the United States, of which 17 percent are already behind dams, whereas only 7,300 miles have been protected by the Wild and Scenic Rivers Act and 17,000 by state laws.

Its officers and staff urge the Department of Interior, U.S. Forest Service, and various state departments of conservation to study significant rivers under their jurisdiction for possible inclusion in the wild and free-flowing rivers category. They then testify before Congress and state legislatures for laws that will provide protection for these rivers. American Rivers sponsored an Omnibus Rivers bill in 1987, passed by Congress, that added twenty-one miles of the Black Creek in Mississippi and seventy-seven miles of the Cache La Poudre River in Colorado. American Rivers also uses the Federal Land Management Policy Act to urge Congress to designate various reaches of rivers as National Scenic Areas, which are protected from hydroelectric development. In 1987, parts of the Columbia River in Washington and Oregon, the Farmington River in Connecticut and Massachusetts, Great Egg Harbor River in New Jersey, Henry's Fork of the Snake River in Idaho, and the Hood River in Oregon received such protection.

American Rivers also influences Congress and state governments to purchase riverside acres to preserve as wildlife and recreation areas. Money from the Federal Land and Water Conservation Fund, raised from user fees from the national parks, are used for this purpose as well as some state conservation funds. Whenever possible American Rivers attempts to save important riparian lands itself through direct purchases, or through work with other conservation organizations, such as The Nature Conservancy.* It hopes to incorporate these lands later into state or federal park systems.

One of American Rivers' policy priorities is to modify the Federal Power Act and the Energy Supply and Environmental Coordination Act and the Public Utilities Regulatory Policy Act to make them more responsive to ecological and environmental demands.

## TACTICS

American Rivers tries to work directly with both conservation groups and government agencies. It fosters the formation of local citizen groups and has succeeded in states as different as Vermont and Texas. It seeks to cooperate with any local or statewide group that is striving to preserve individual stretches of rivers.

American Rivers publishes an annual report as well as a quarterly newsletter, *American Rivers*. It informs its membership about threats from dams and other water projects to specific rivers and encourages them to write their congressional representatives and state representatives when needed. It holds an annual conference in Washington, D.C. each spring.

## FURTHER INFORMATION

*1988 Annual Report* (1989). Washington, D.C.: American Rivers, Inc.


## AMERICAN SOCIETY FOR THE CONTROL OF CANCER
*See* American Cancer Society.


## AMERICAN TEXTILE MANUFACTURERS INSTITUTE (ATMI)
1801 K Street, N.W., Suite 900
Washington, D.C. 20006

## ORGANIZATION AND RESOURCES

The American Textile Manufacturers Institute (ATMI) was formed in 1949 from a merger of the American Cotton Manufacturers Association, founded in 1897, and the Cotton Textile Institute, founded in 1926. It absorbed the National Federation of Textiles in 1958, the National Association of Finishers of Textile Fabrics in 1965, and the National Association of Wool Manufacturers in 1971. ATMI now represents the combined interests of the wool, cotton, and apparel industries, including such corporations as J. F. Stevens, Milliken, Dan River, and Pendleton Woolen Mills. It has an elected board of directors of thirty and a forty-person staff. It has an annual budget of about $3 million. Its dues are $1,000 a year for individuals; they vary, depending on the percent of value added, for corporations.

## POLICY CONCERNS

The primary policy of concern for textile manufacturers in recent years has been how to control the flow of imported fabrics and garments from overseas. ATMI has focused most of its lobbying efforts on convincing Congress to pass a restrictive trade bill, accomplished in the 99th and again in the 100th Congress. However, President Reagan vetoed that legislation, and Congress failed to override despite bipartisan support from the states where the textile and apparel industry is concentrated.

On environmental matters, representatives of ATMI testified on the Resource Conservation and Recovery Act (RCRA), urging that the U.S. Environmental Protection Agency (EPA) should have more time to develop a hazardous waste list, because it is difficult to determine what the risks of each substance are. It also argued unsuccessfully to extend the small generator exemption rather than to reduce it, as the 1986 amendments did. ATMI also opposes most community and worker right-to-know laws about the dangers of substances in the workplace and communities.

ATMI testified against having Congress determine what constitutes a hazardous air pollutant, preferring to leave this decision to EPA which was slow to act under the Reagan administration. Congress did assert its legislative authority to define automotive emissions in 1970, but it has not taken steps so draconian regarding any other parts of the Clean Air Act. This policy stance was common among trade associations, including ATMI, through the 1980s because they preferred administrative rather than congressional decision making. ATMI argues that any government agency should be required to prove that any proposed new regulation will have greater benefits to the public than costs to industry before it can be enforced, an attitude that reflected the philosophy of the Office of Management and Budget in the 1980s. This position was not accepted by the courts, for in 1981 ATMI lost a major law case in which the Supreme Court refused to rule that a cost/benefit analysis was necessary for the Department of Labor to set a cotton-dust standard for workers in the textile mills.

## TACTICS

ATMI publishes an annual report, an annual directory, and the weekly *Textile Trends*. It sponsors an annual meeting and maintains a 1,200 volume library at its headquarters. It provides statistical services for its membership on production and sales of textiles in the United States. It also sponsors a safety contest among textile mills each year.

## FURTHER INFORMATION

*Annual Report* (1989). Washington, D.C.: ATMI.
*American Textile Manufacturers Institute v. Donovan*, 452 U.S. 490 (1981).

## AMERICAN TRUCKING ASSOCIATIONS (ATA)
2200 Mill Road
Alexandria, Virginia 22314

### ORGANIZATION AND RESOURCES

The American Trucking Associations (ATA) was founded in 1933 and today represents over 3,500 member firms organized into 50 state organizations. Dues for member firms, which range from $60 to $6,000 a year depending on the volume of business, raise a budget of about $30 million a year, which includes some foundation grants. President Thomas J. Donohue oversees a staff of 280 in Alexandria, and is directed by a 150-person board of directors selected from various trucking firms.

### POLICY CONCERNS

ATA and its affiliates have a number of policies of primary concern to them, especially the carrier rates regulated by the Interstate Commerce Commission (ICC). ATA opposes deregulation of the trucking industry's rates because it has benefited over the years by the rates set by the ICC.

ATA also has a number of interests in energy and environmental laws. ATA opposes the use of tax exemptions in order to give incentives to the development of fuels that are alternatives to gasoline, such as the reduced tax on gasohol. It feels this removes too much revenue from the federal highway trust fund, which maintains the nation's interstate highway network. While ATA supports the concept of alternative fuels, it does not want them used until they can be guaranteed to cause no damage to vehicle engines. ATA also opposes any diversion of highway trust fund moneys to any other purpose such as mass transit construction advocated by the governments of many metropolitan states. It opposes raising the gasoline tax on the grounds that the highway trust fund already has an unspent balance, despite environmental arguments for conservation of energy and reduction of the federal deficit through such a tax. It supports keeping the trust fund separate from general revenues of the federal budget in order to prevent misuse of fund moneys. ATA opposes any oil import fee for fear it will increase the cost of fuel for the trucking industry.

ATA also claims to support a ban on asbestos materials for use in brake linings as long as there is a cheap, effective substitute that is sufficiently available to do the job. Until then, it does not believe the risk to health is sufficient for EPA to stop asbestos use in truck brakes.

One of the trucking industry's primary objectives is to increase the size of trucks and to have double trailers admitted to all state roads. It argues that the Federal Highway Administration (FHA) ought to preempt any states that attempt to regulate large trucks because of the congestion on their roads. ATA opposes any attempts by states to keep trucks off main commuter routes during certain times of day. ATA also opposes any state restrictions on the transport of hazardous materials through highly populated areas.

ATA opposes emission standards mandated by the Clean Air Act (CAA) for diesel trucks. It argues that the trucking industry should not be regulated to any greater degree than air freight, railroad freight, and water barge traffic are, because this gives its competitors a major advantage. It argues, as do other motor vehicle polluters, for extension of the deadlines under the CAA for areas not in compliance with air quality standards. But it supports the reduction of sulfur content in diesel fuel in order to avoid adding particulate trap oxidizers to 1994 trucks. The petroleum refining industry opposes having to reduce sulfur content of the fuel and wants it controlled by emission control devices. ATA also opposes having canisters installed on trucks to reduce hydrocarbon vapors during refueling. It prefers to have the petroleum refiners reduce fuel volatility but opposes a proposed law to make tank carriers responsible if they haul fuel that does not meet specifications.

ATA has long opposed any state, local, or federal laws recognizing communities' right to know what chemicals are being stored and moved through them. It succeeded in getting transportation exempted from the Superfund Amendments and Reauthorization Act (SARA) of 1986, although chemical spills do come under SARA. It argues that any federal law that affects the community's right to know about chemicals, such as the Hazardous Materials Act of 1974, overrides any state laws, which cannot be stricter.

ATA agrees that the Department of Transportation's emergency response guide should be available to drivers of trucks with hazardous materials. But it opposes the distribution of highly technical material on all hazardous materials being transported. On this issue it differs with the Teamsters' Union, which agrees with the National Highway Safety Board that complete information should be made available to everyone who might come into contact with hazardous materials in case of an accident.

## TACTICS

Generally the ATA and truckers' unions are in coalition in opposing any strengthening of the CAA or SARA regulations that would increase costs for the trucking industry. On these issues they tend to agree with both the automotive industry and the unions there as well. However, on occasion, when the issue is one of safety for workers on the job, the unions and management may be on opposite sides.

ATA has a political action committee that raises money each year for distribution in political campaigns. It publishes *American Trucking Trends* annually, *Transport Topics* weekly, and several technical reports for its membership, and sponsors an annual meeting.

## FURTHER INFORMATION

American Trucking Associations (1988). *Congressional and Regulatory Issues*. Alexandria, Va.: ATA.
———(1989). *Report to Members*. Alexandria, Va.: ATA.

## AMERICAN WILDLIFE INSTITUTE
*See* National Wildlife Federation.

## AMERICAN WIND ENERGY ASSOCIATION (AWEA)
1730 North Lynn Street, Suite 610
Arlington, Virginia 22209

### ORGANIZATION AND RESOURCES

The American Wind Energy Association (AWEA) is a trade association founded in 1974 to represent the interests of companies engaged in the business of producing energy from wind. In the late 1980s it had 100 corporate members (including all major manufacturers of wind machines), about 100 associate members, and 200 individual members. Its dues vary from $500 to $5,000 for corporate members, depending on the size and number of employees of the company. Associate dues are $250, individual dues $35 a year. Altogether, these produce a budget of about $250,000 a year. It operates with a staff of 3 from Arlington, Virginia.

### POLICY CONCERNS

Two major legislative issues have engaged most of the resources of AWEA since its inception. The Public Utilities Regulatory Policy Act (PURPA) requires major utilities to purchase electricity from small generators at a price commensurate with the cost to the utility of replacing that power with its own generating capacity. The wind energy industry has benefited from this legislation and has grown because of it. A primary goal of AWEA is to keep this legislation in force. Public utilities, however, continually attempt to have the law modified to allow them greater discretion in purchasing power, arguing that the transmission of small amounts is uneconomic. Thus far, AWEA, together with other small generators and cogenerators, have been successful in blocking these attempts to modify the law.

AWEA has been less successful in convincing Congress to reestablish federal tax credits for investments in wind energy. During the heyday of the energy crisis when conservation was in vogue, a tax credit was instituted for solar, wind, and other renewable energy sources. During the Reagan administration, however, this tax credit was removed, and AWEA has been unsuccessful in having it reinstated, although it continues to advocate renewal. It has been more successful in preventing the Treasury Department from classifying commercial wind projects as public utility property for tax depreciation purposes. AWEA also advocates more federal government investment in wind energy research.

State public utility or service commissions are primarily responsible for implementing parts of PURPA for determining how much power public utilities must buy from small generators and transmit over their distribution systems. AWEA attempts to keep abreast of state regulations concerning power production, taxation, and zoning for wind farms, especially in such states as California where alternative energy sources are relatively common. AWEA argues that renewable energy sources are less damaging to the environment than such hard technologies as nuclear and fossil fuel–fired plants.

## TACTICS

AWEA sponsors an annual national conference and trade show devoted to displaying the industry's wares to investors, component suppliers, dealers, utilities, and state regulators. It also works with the U.S. Department of Commerce to try to promote U.S. exports of wind energy technology. It cosponsors international conferences on renewable energy resources and provides information to the World Bank, the Agency for International Development, and other international financing agencies. It belongs to the U.S. Export Council for Renewable Energy,* an umbrella organization dedicated to exporting renewable technologies.

The Association publishes its conference proceedings each year and *Wind Energy Weekly* to keep its membership informed about developments in the industry as well as events in Washington and state capitals that may affect its business. *Windletter* is published eight times a year and covers issues of concern to the industry in greater depth than the weekly newsletter. In addition, AWEA sells books about wind power published by organizations that advocate renewable energy resources, such as Worldwatch Institute.*

## FURTHER INFORMATION

Flavin, Christopher (1981). *Wind Power: A Turning Point.* Washington, D.C.: Worldwatch Institute.

Nosburgh, Paul V. (1983). *Commercial Applications of Wind Power.* Alexandria, Va.: AWEA.

*Wind Energy Weekly* (1988). Alexandria, Va.: AWEA, April 26, May 19, 26, June 3, 10.

## AMERICANS FOR ENERGY INDEPENDENCE (AEI)
1629 K Street, N.W., Suite 500
Washington, D.C. 20006

## ORGANIZATION AND RESOURCES

Admiral Elmo R. Zumwalt founded Americans for Energy Independence (AEI) in 1975 during the energy crisis in order to generate public support for making the United States independent from foreign oil. In the late 1980s AEI had about 100 corporate and union members primarily from the oil and nuclear industries. Hans A. Bethe, nuclear physicist and Nobel prize winner, is chair of the twenty-four-member board of directors. Such well-known individuals as former president Gerald Ford and Endicott Peabody, former governor of Massachusetts, belong. Elihu Bergman is executive director of a four-person staff in Washington.

It raises approximately $300,000 a year, primarily from corporate and union donations. It spends approximately 63 percent of its income on broadcasting "American Energy Update," a public affairs radio program, holding meetings, and issuing news releases about the crisis in American energy supply; and 37 percent on management and fund-raising.

### POLICY CONCERNS

AEI is primarily concerned with American dependence on foreign oil sources for its primary fuel, which it believes is as great in the late 1980s as it was before the energy crisis of the mid 1970s. The United States obtains more of its energy supply from the western hemisphere now and should continue to do so both to bolster the economies of countries such as Mexico and to ensure American independence of Middle Eastern oil, according to AEI. It also argues that all potential domestic supplies should be explored, including wilderness areas, especially in Alaska.

AEI advocates continued expansion of the electric generating system in the United States, including nuclear power plants and those using fossil fuels. It encourages "realistic conservation" measures to increase energy efficiency. AEI believes in a balance between energy and environmental values through streamlined procedures for permitting energy facilities, thus avoiding environmental disputes. It also advocates filling the strategic petroleum reserve as a stopgap measure against any interruption in supplies from abroad. In 1986 its representatives testified against Ford and General Motor's petition to reduce corporate average fuel economy (CAFE) standards for motor vehicles.

### TACTICS

AEI's activities are primarily directed toward convincing public opinion that the United States is in a precarious situation regarding its fuel supply and should impress upon Congress the need to develop a comprehensive energy policy. It publishes a newsletter twice a year and produces a weekly public affairs radio program, "American Energy Update," which it distributes to public broadcast affiliates around the United States. It also issues news releases and editorial comments to the print media and sponsors education activities designed to keep energy issues on the national agenda.

### AMERICANS FOR NUCLEAR ENERGY (ANE)
2525 Wilson Boulevard
Arlington, Virginia 22201

### ORGANIZATION AND RESOURCES

Americans for Nuclear Energy (ANE) was founded in 1978 as a membership organization that advocates the use of nuclear power. It publishes the *Nuclear Advocate* bimonthly which addresses such issues as the safety of U.S. nuclear power plants, which it argues are much safer and more contained than the Soviet plant at Chernobyl. ANE asks for donations of from $15 to $100 from its 18,000 members from which it derives a budget of $200,000 a year.

### POLICY CONCERNS

ANE argues that radical groups, which it identifies as the Government Accountability Project of the Institute for Policy Studies in Washington, give out false and misleading statements about nuclear energy, which it seeks to counter. It notes that the electronic and print media have been too receptive to the arguments of nuclear critics such as Ralph Nader groups and Jane Fonda.

After the Chernobyl accident in the USSR, it argued that the Soviet Union is unconcerned about its citizens' safety and therefore invested nothing in containment vessels. ANE emphasizes the differences between U.S. and Soviet technology and attributes them to the indifference of a totalitarian regime to its citizens' well being. Its publications argue that antinuclear activists in the United States want to return the U.S. economy to a preindustrial time.

### TACTICS

ANE sponsors prominent nuclear physicists to educate the public about the need for nuclear power. They also testify to Congress and government agencies. It publishes the *Nuclear Advocate* monthly.

### FURTHER INFORMATION

*The Nuclear Advocate* (1988, 1989). Washington, D.C.: ANE, April-May, September-October.

## ASSOCIATED GAS DISTRIBUTORS (AGD)
1001 Pennsylvania Avenue, N.W.
Washington, D.C. 20004

### ORGANIZATION AND RESOURCES

The Associated Gas Distributors (AGD) is a trade association of approximately 100 gas pipelines and retailers on the east coast. Its members include many members of the American Gas Association,* such as the Baltimore Gas and Electric Company. It is, however, a much smaller organization, begun only in 1963, with particular concerns about the costs of obtaining a natural gas supply for customers in the northeastern part of the United States and problems of sustaining a constant supply. It has a 16-member board of directors, elected by the membership in their annual meeting, and a staff of 5. AGD has an annual budget of less than $1 million, collected entirely from corporate member dues, which depend on the volume and profitability of the individual companies.

### POLICY CONCERNS

Like the larger American Gas Association,* Associated Gas Distributors are concerned with providing gas to their customers at the lowest possible cost with the highest possible profit for themselves. Hence, AGD advocates tax breaks for gas producers, but also control on wellhead prices. The northeastern United States is particularly disadvantaged in that it has little in the way of supply but much demand for natural gas. It is dependent on the southeast and southwest for its supplies. Hence, AGD is more eager than the AGA to see wellhead prices controlled.

It too worked for the 1987 repeal of the Powerplant and Industrial Fuel Use Act (PIFUA) restrictions on the uses to which natural gas could be put in industry, including electric power plants. It promotes the use of gas in all sectors of the economy and opposes take-or-pay contracts that prevent its members from negotiating more-favorable prices whenever possible. It seeks to open up the outer continental shelf to oil and gas exploration and generally searches for more supplies closer to its market.

## TACTICS

AGD produces an annual report and holds an annual meeting and trade fair for its members. It does some research of its own, but like the AGA it tends to rely on the Gas Research Institute* for most of its information about new technology and marketing techniques. As a small trade association, it calls on CEOs from its member corporations to make representations to Congress and on cooperation with its allies, the AGA and American Public Gas Association, for its major lobbying efforts.

### FURTHER INFORMATION:

Davis, David Howard (1982). *Energy Politics*. 3rd ed. New York: St. Martin's Press.
McFarland, Andrew (1984). "Energy Lobbies." *Annual Review of Energy 9*: 501–527.
Oppenheimer, Bruce (1974). *Oil and the Congressional Process: The Limits of Symbolic Politics*. Lexington, Mass.: Lexington Books.
Soloman, Burt (1986). "Ganging Up." *National Journal*, July 19, pp. 1778–1781.
——— (1987). "Measuring Clout." *National Journal*, July 4, pp. 1706–1711.
Stanfield, Rochelle L. (1986). "Reaching a Compromise." *National Journal*. July 26, pp. 1829–1831.
——— (1987). "Another Oil Crisis?" *National Journal*, Jan. 17, pp. 131–133.
——— (1987). "Paying for Nothing." *National Journal*, April 4, pp. 812–814.
Stobaugh, Robert, and Daniel Yergin, eds. (1983). *Energy Future*. 3d ed. New York: Vintage Press.

## ASSOCIATION OF CASUALTY AND SURETY COMPANIES
*See* American Insurance Association.

## ASSOCIATION OF LICENSED AUTO MANUFACTURERS
*See* Motor Vehicle Manufacturers Association of the U.S.

## ASSOCIATION OF LOCAL AIR POLLUTION CONTROL OFFICIALS
*See* State and Territorial Air Pollution Program Administrators.

## ASSOCIATION OF METROPOLITAN WATER AGENCIES (AMWA)
477 H Street, N.W.
Washington, D.C. 20001

## ORGANIZATION AND RESOURCES

The Association of Metropolitan Water Agencies (AMWA) was formed in 1981 to represent the interests of large metropolitan public agencies that supply water to their populations. There are 48 members: cities such as New York, Los Angeles, Chicago, and Houston, and some counties with populations over 150,000. There is an elected board of directors of 15 people, who set policy for the association. Dues are assessed according to population served and vary from $1,000 to $7,000 a year. Associate members with service areas under 150,000 population may join for $500. Dues produce an annual budget for AMWA of about $100,000, less than 20 percent of the revenues raised by the National Association of Water Companies* (NAWC), the trade association for privately owned water utilities.

## POLICY CONCERNS

AMWA is primarily concerned about the Safe Drinking Water Act (SDWA) and the standards it imposes on suppliers of potable water. It agrees with the NAWC that standards need to be set for various water contaminants, but these should be based on real health risks and not rushed. When the SDWA was first passed in 1974, the U.S. Environmental Protection Agency (EPA) investigated the presence of toxins such as chloroform in the nation's drinking water supply. As a result, in 1977 EPA proposed regulations to require water supply systems to adopt activated carbon filtration in place of chlorination in water treatment. However, both AMWA and NAWC opposed this regulation vehemently and were successful in preventing its promulgation. In 1986 amendments to SDWA gave EPA authority to set standards for eighty-three additional substances. AMWA argues that each of these needs to be studied extensively before standards are established, and local and state governments should be involved in this process.

AMWA also urges all states to take primary authority for administering the SDWA because state governments are closer to local governments and are in a position to consider the financial resources of various public water suppliers and set deadlines accordingly. Economic costs should be carefully considered as well as health effects when setting standards.

AMWA is enthusiastic about the provisions of the SDWA that protect public water supplies by controlling sources of contamination, such as industrial plants, that are located above water aquifers. Other federal legislation, the Clean Water Act (CWA), Comprehensive Environmental Response, Compensation, and Liability Act (CERCLA, or Superfund), and Resource Conservation and Recovery Act (RCRA), also have potential power to protect surface and groundwater supplies. AMWA has supported amendments to the CWA that provide for controlling agricultural and urban runoff into surface water. It also approved EPA's ban on hazardous wastes in landfills under RCRA and the reauthorization of Superfund in 1986 to extend cleanups of leaking toxic dumps. It also approves of imposing strict liability and joint and several liability on users and owners of disposal sites in order to allow potential injured parties, including water supply companies, to sue and obtain compensation for their losses.

On the whole, most requirements of pollution control laws help public water suppliers provide safe, clean water to their customers. AMWA is especially enthusiastic about federal funding for research on protecting aquifers, building sewage treatment plants, and finding new cost-effective methods of treating finished water. It also approves of additional efforts to control sulfur dioxides under the Clean Air Act (CAA) in order to reduce the acidity of surface waters. However, it opposes any EPA regulation or control of dams which some believe contribute to surface water contamination. AMWA argues that the seventy water-supply dams used by its members have had no adverse effect on water quality, and EPA could determine this through research without any regulations.

AMWA is also concerned about the availability of capital to publicly owned utilities. It supported continuing tax-exempt bonds to finance publicly owned water supply facilities under the 1986 tax reform law. In most matters involving protection of water supplies, AMWA works with the NAWC. However, the two diverge on the issue of financing, as NAWC advocates greater privatization of water supplies while AMWA prefers public sector ownership.

### FURTHER INFORMATION

*AMWA Resolutions* (1987). Washington, D.C.: AMWA.
Hays, Samuel P. (1987). *Beauty, Health and Permanence: Environment Policies in the U.S. 1965–1985*. Cambridge, Eng.: Cambridge University Press.
*Monthly Report* (1989). Washington, D.C.: AMWA, May.

## ASSOCIATION OF PETROLEUM REFINERS (APR)
1915 I St., N.W. Suite 600
Washington, D.C. 20006

### ORGANIZATION AND RESOURCES

The Association of Petroleum Re-Refiners was founded in 1950 and changed its name to the Association of Petroleum Refiners (APR) in 1987. It is a modest trade association of fifty companies that specialize in rerefining used oil, such as Breslube Enterprises. Dues vary between $300 and $3,000 a year, producing an annual budget of over $50,000. There is an elected six-person board and three professional staff persons in Washington.

### POLICY CONCERNS

APR has only one public policy of concern, namely how the government treats used oil. Since its members specialize in removing contaminants from used oil, it urged the U.S. Environmental Protection Agency (EPA) to list used oil as hazardous waste, which would prevent its being used as a fuel or spread along rural roads to keep down dust. In 1985 EPA proposed to list used oil as hazardous waste, but was inundated with complaints from the petroleum industry, and especially the Service Station Dealers of America,* which argued that if used oil were so labeled this would lead to illegal disposal of oil into sewers rather than to recyclers.

In 1986 EPA decided not to list recycled oil as toxic, but the U.S. Circuit Court of Appeals for the District of Columbia ruled in 1988 that this decision should be reconsidered because of the toxic materials contained in some used oil. This suit was brought jointly by the Natural Resources Defense Council* and the Hazardous Waste Treatment Council,* combining the arguments of environmentalists and the industry that would benefit from having recycled oil defined as hazardous because of increased business to them. The APR supported this action, as its business also depends on obtaining used oil from recyclers.

*FURTHER INFORMATION*

*APR Review* (1989). Washington, D.C.: APR, January.
"Labeling of Safe on Recycled Oil Upset by Court" (1989) *The New York Times*, October 8, p. 3.

## ASSOCIATION OF PETROLEUM RE-REFINERS
*See* Association of Petroleum Refiners.

## ASSOCIATION OF STATE AND INTERSTATE WATER POLLUTION CONTROL ADMINISTRATORS (ASIWPCA)
444 North Capitol Street, N.W., Suite 330
Washington, D.C. 20001

*ORGANIZATION AND RESOURCES*

In 1961 the Association of State and Interstate Water Pollution Control Administrators (ASIWPCA) was founded to represent and coordinate the activities of the fifty state administrators of water pollution control programs. In 1979 a Washington office was established to keep in close contact with the federal government. Although many states had such departments within their governments in the past, others created such offices only because of the incentives written into the federal Clean Water Act (CWA) which supplied some grants to state governments during the 1950s. By the end of the 1980s, all fifty states belonged to ASIWPCA along with the District of Columbia and eight interstate agencies, including the Ohio River Valley Commission. It is funded entirely by state government payments according to a formula that depends upon the population and revenues of states. Its executive director heads a professional staff of three in Washington. ASIWPCA has a board of directors of ten people, representing the ten regions into which the U.S. Environmental Protection Agency (EPA) is broken down. Board members serve two-year terms, and half are elected from their region each year. The board elects the president yearly at the first board meeting. Appointed task forces develop policy positions and present them to the membership at the annual meeting. They must later be considered and approved by the state officials responsible for their own law enforcement program.

## POLICY CONCERNS

ASIWPCA's primary goal is to assist states in coordinating their role in implementing the CWA with each other and with the federal government. The clean water law is the major reason for ASIWPCA's existence; hence its representatives advocate its continued funding and support from Washington. At the same time, it is the legislation to which they must respond. Hence, ASIWPCA attempts to retain as much autonomy for the states as possible in administering the law. The 1987 amendments to the CWA called for control of toxic pollutants. ASIWPCA agrees with this goal, but argues that states should have discretion in deciding how to control them in individual waterways in order to avoid excessive costs to publicly owned treatment plants.

ASIWPCA opposed the reduction in federal aid for sewage treatment plants in the CWA during the 1980s, but supported the 1987 amendments to the law with the highest level of funding possible under the new federally guaranteed loan program. It also opposed the 1986 Tax Reform Law which reduced the benefit that taxpayers could obtain from investing in municipal bonds used to fund sewage treatment plants, arguing that this had a deleterious effect on the water pollution control effort cities could afford.

It argues for delay in the deadline for municipalities to achieve secondary treatment of their sewage. It also advocates flexibility in requirements for industrial treatment of effluents as well as pretreatment of discharges industry makes to municipally owned treatment plants. ASIWPCA argues that individual states should be able to set their own requirements for pretreatment under federal guidelines and to control the National Pollutant Discharge Elimination System effluent permits.

ASIWPCA argues that states should be free to set their own water quality standards, and the burden of proof should be on EPA to show they are not appropriate. It argues states should control permits to industry and the kinds of limits placed on these permits. It seeks to avoid EPA civil penalties imposed against permittees while the states are undertaking enforcement.

One major challenge facing water pollution control administrators in the 1990s will be how to control nonpoint sources of water pollution. ASIWPCA argues that much of the challenge of controlling point sources, such as sewage outlets, has been met in the 1980s. However, surface and groundwater continue to be contaminated from a variety of nonpoint sources such as agricultural and urban runoff, leaking landfills, septic tanks, underground storage tanks, dams, and other water resource management projects. ASIWPCA would like states to retain as much authority for controlling nonpoint sources as possible on the grounds that various regions have different problems and should be allowed to address them in their own way. ASIWPCA recognizes groundwater contamination as one important problem in the United States. It also argues for adequate federal financial and technical assistance to address this problem, but it argues against a goal of no degradation of groundwater because of the costs involved in controlling all sources of contamination.

ASIWPCA is generally ambivalent in its relationship with the federal government, as is the Water Pollution Control Federation.* It must cooperate closely with the regional EPA offices, and finds the federal government useful as a threat when trying to convince industry to comply with the law. State governments are closer to local industry than are federal officials and are often more sympathetic to its economic arguments. Under the fiscal constraints of most state governments, in the 1980s which experienced reduced federal aid, ASIWPCA argued the federal government should reduce its demands on compliance dates.

*TACTICS*

ASIWPCA represents its membership before Congress regarding the Clean Water Act. It also serves as the technical arm to the National Governors' Association,* and serves on many workgroups of the EPA, such as the nonpoint source workgroup. It also provides technical symposia to its members; one such program was held in 1988 to introduce state officials to the financial ramifications of changes from a federal grant to a revolving loan program for funding sewage plants. It publishes *Washington Update* to keep its members apprised of developments in the capital and the *ASIWPCA Quarterly* to highlight state activities and advancements.

*FURTHER INFORMATION*

*America's Clean Water* (1985, 1987). Washington, D.C.: ASIWPCA.
*Annual Report 1987–88.* (1989). Washington, D.C.: ASIWPCA.
*Position Statement 1988–89* (1989). Washington, D.C.: ASIWPCA.
*ASIWPCA Quarterly* (1988, 1989). Washington, D.C.: ASIWPCA, Fall, Spring.

**ATOMIC INDUSTRY FORUM**
*See* U.S. Council for Energy Awareness.

**AUDUBON SOCIETY**
*See* National Audubon Society.

**AUTOMOTIVE PARTS AND ACCESSORIES ASSOCIATION (APAA)**
5100 Forbes Boulevard
Lanham, Maryland 20706

*ORGANIZATION AND RESOURCES*

The Automotive Parts and Accessories Association (APAA) is a trade association for some 2,050 companies that manufacture and sell, wholesale and retail, auto parts. It was formed in 1967 and has an annual budget of about $3 million. Corporate dues range up to $1,500 a year and are supplemented by trade shows and other money-raising events. Members may be specialty companies such as Champion Sparkplug or major retailers such as Sears, for whom auto products are only one part of a major retail industry.

There is a board of directors of twenty-seven people, who are elected by the member companies. There are forty professional staff people who represent the association's interests from headquarters in Maryland, near Washington.

### POLICY CONCERNS

One issue of major concern to auto parts makers are the various laws that control disposal of solid wastes because waste oil and other lubricants from vehicles are controlled under these laws. Representatives of APAA testified in congressional hearings on Resource Conservation and Recovery Act (RCRA) amendments in the early 1980s that small generators of hazardous wastes should not be regulated until research proves that hazardous wastes are more dangerous than has yet been shown. They were not successful because in 1986 RCRA was amended to tighten the definition of small generators and bring many more companies under the control of the regulations requiring waste oil to be disposed of in secure landfills.

Another concern is the Clean Air Act (CAA), which mandated devices to reduce auto emissions in 1972. APAA is concerned because the CAA orders manufacturers to guarantee their emission control devices for 5 years or 50,000 miles, and legislation introduced in 1987 would have extended that guarantee to 10 years. APAA argues that giving extended warranties for automotive parts forces car owners to return to their dealers for most repair work, and this greatly reduces the market for independent automotive parts to be substituted for the original devices. It would prefer to maintain competition in the auto parts business by giving customers warranties that would enable them to contract with anyone they choose for the parts.

### TACTICS

APAA allies itself on most issues with independent service stations and the Automotive Service Association* that also want to maintain their share of the auto repair market. APAA has many other policy concerns such as the tax structure and trade laws that are more important to it than are pollution control issues. It publishes *APA Report* eight times a year and *APA Governmental Affairs Report* bimonthly to keep its membership up to date with Washington events. It has an annual meeting and trade show in Chicago.

### FURTHER INFORMATION

U.S. Congress. House Small Business Committee (1983). *Hearings on Hazardous Waste and Enforcement Act*. Washington, D.C.: Government Printing Office, July 26.

## AUTOMOTIVE SERVICE ASSOCIATION (ASA)
P.O. Box 929
1901 Airport Freeway, Suite 100
Bedford, Texas 76095

### ORGANIZATION AND RESOURCES

The Automotive Service Association (ASA) was formed in 1986 from a merger of the Automotive Service Councils, Inc., founded in 1955, the Independent Automotive Service Association, founded in 1949, and the Independent Garagemen's Association, founded in 1979. ASA represents some 10,000 independent auto repair shops in the United States. Dues are $150 a year; its budget is about $4 million. Its executive vice-president has a staff of twenty-five in Texas and is represented in Washington by a professional lobbyist.

### POLICY CONCERNS

The main policy that concerns ASA is competition in the auto repair industry. On this issue it takes a position similar to that of the Automotive Parts and Accessories Association.* ASA argues that competition in this service industry prevents car manufacturers and their dealers from charging customers any price they choose for repairs after purchase. It believes that car owners prefer to use independent repair facilities both because of lower price and greater reliability of repairs.

ASA's representative testified before the U.S. Senate concerning the Clean Air Act (CAA) in 1987. He argued that the warranty required by law should not be extended from 5 to 10 years because this would force car owners to return to their dealers to have work done on emission control devices, and they would end up having other repair work done as well. ASA argued that this would push up costs for owners of cars and drive independent repair servicers out of business. ASA argued for withdrawal of the 5-year or 50,000-mile warranty that diverts business from independent repair shops to the dealerships. In place of the mandatory return to the dealership for emission control repairs, ASA argued for a warranty contract in which the owners of the vehicles could choose which repair shop to use for repairing their vehicles.

ASA also advocates a mandatory policy to force owners of vehicles to have their cars periodically inspected for safety. In 1966 the Federal Motor Vehicle and Highway Safety Act empowered the U.S. Department of Transportation (DOT) to require periodic safety inspections, but this was never enforced at the federal level. In 1976 Congress eliminated DOT's power to withdraw highway construction money from states that fail to comply. ASA advocates reinstating safety inspections because of the business it would generate for its members. Some states do have compulsory inspection programs, and ASA believes that accidental death tolls are lower in those states. It also advocates inspection and maintenance programs under the Clean Air Act for emission control devices. It advocates both types of inspections in all states, and tries to influence the federal government to reinstitute its sanction, the withdrawal of federal highway funds, to states without such programs.

## TACTICS

ASA publishes *ASA Update* and *Auto Inc.* monthly, covering technical problems for its membership. It sponsors an annual convention and produces video tapes of automotive repair techniques.

## FURTHER INFORMATION

*A Study Regarding the Addition of Motor Vehicle Safety Inspection to Motor Vehicle Emissions Inspection* (1984). Compiled by Donald A. Randall, Washington, D.C.

U.S. Congress. Senate Committee on Environment and Public Works (1987). *Hearings on Clean Air Act Enforcement*. Washington, D.C.: Government Printing Office, June 16.

Washington office: 321 D Street., N.E., Washington, D.C. 20002

## AUTOMOTIVE SERVICE COUNCILS, INC.

*See* Automotive Service Association.

# B

**BUYERS UP**
*See* Public Citizen.

# C

—————— / ——————

## CARRYING CAPACITY
1325 G Street, N.W., Suite 1003
Washington, D.C. 20005

### ORGANIZATION AND RESOURCES

Carrying Capacity was founded in 1981, dedicated to the proposition that the United States needs to develop a sustainable economy. By the late 1980s it had about 800 members, paying dues of $15 a year. Its budget of $75,000 is derived mostly from individual contributions. Carrying Capacity has a board of 3 people who select their successors. Dr. Edward Passerini is president; and the executive administrator, Linda Kovan, is its only paid staff in Washington.

### POLICY CONCERNS

The board of directors of Carrying Capacity concentrates on doing research on natural resources in the United States and publishing this information for the education of its members and the public in general. In 1986 it published a summary report of *Beyond Oil: The Threat to Food and Fuel in the Coming Decades*, a study written by researchers at the Complex Systems Research Center at the University of New Hampshire. That report emphasized the dependence of the United States economy, including agriculture, on a diminishing petroleum supply. It advocates that population be brought under control and balanced against natural resources; that conservation, cogeneration, and renewable energy resources replace dependence on finite fossil fuels; and that agriculture emphasize organic sustainable farming with less dependence on insecticides and fertilizers.

## TACTICS

The board of Carrying Capacity provides information to members of Congress on issues with which it is concerned. It does not litigate, fund candidates, testify before committees, or have a network of activists to influence Congress.

## FURTHER INFORMATION

Carrying Capacity (1986). *Beyond Oil: The Threat to Food and Fuel in the Coming Decades*. New York: Ballinger.

## CENTER FOR AUTO SAFETY (CAS)
2001 S Street, N.W.
Washington, D.C. 20001

### ORGANIZATION AND RESOURCES

The Center for Auto Safety (CAS) was founded in 1970 by Ralph Nader and the Consumer's Union to work on behalf of the consumer for improved auto and highway safety and quality. CAS became an independent membership organization in 1979; in the late 1980s its membership was about 14,000, up substantially from before President Reagan took office. Its revenues and expenditures more than doubled in the period from 1982 to 1985. Its annual revenues at the end of the 1980s were about $650,000, derived mostly from membership dues of $15 a year, grants, and contributions, supplemented through sales of its publications. It spent most of its income on research and advocacy regarding highway and vehicle safety.

The Center for Auto Safety's board of directors include the chief executive officer and a representative of Public Citizen,* the original Ralph Nader group. Three other members are lawyers in the Washington area. It has a staff of fifteen including the executive director, Clarence M. Ditlow III, who is selected by the board of directors.

### POLICY CONCERNS

The primary policy concerns of CAS are to reduce the toll of injury and death due to vehicle defects and highway design problems. It interacts mostly with the National Highway Traffic Safety Administration (NHTSA), insisting on stricter rules for vehicle design. It pressures the NHTSA to investigate dangerous vehicles and to force the manufacturers to recall those found to have defects for repairs. Its second emphasis is on convincing public authorities to improve the design and maintenance of public highways, roads, streets, and bridges to reduce the traffic death rate.

Its third policy priority is energy conservation. It advocated the 55-mph speed limit and considered the passage of the 1987 law permitting states to raise the speed limit to 65-mph on certain roads a defeat for safety and energy conservation. In 1975 it was active in the passage of the Energy Policy and Conservation

Act which set corporate average fuel economy (CAFE) standards at 27.5 mpg by 1985. The Environmental Protection Agency later adjusted its method of measuring whether auto manufacturers had met the standards at the request of General Motors and the Ford Motor Corporation. The Center for Auto Safety sued and won in federal court, arguing that EPA had no right to change the measurement technique. Later, when the NHTSA reduced the standards to 26 mpg for 1986 cars, the Center for Auto Safety protested and testified against this action in congressional hearings and in court.

The Center also urged EPA to recall cars that failed to meet the auto emission standards created by the Clean Air Act. When EPA refused to do so, allowing General Motors to offset its failure to meet emissions standards in 1979 with increased reduction in subsequent years, the Center sued and won in federal court. Later this decision resulted in GM's contributing some methanol buses to replace high polluting diesel buses in New York City.

### TACTICS

CAS issues two newsletters to members, the *Lemon Times* and *Impact*, which report to consumers on actions the Center has taken before agencies, Congress, and the courts. It also maintains a computerized data base of consumer complaints about various cars. There is an annual membership meeting in Washington each spring.

### FURTHER INFORMATION

*Impact* (1986). Washington, D.C.: CAS, vol. 13, no. 1.
*The Lemon Times* (1988, 1989). Washington, D.C.: CAS, vol.6, nos. 1, 2; vol. 7, no. 2.

## CENTER FOR DEVELOPMENT AND ENVIRONMENT (CDE)
1709 New York Avenue, N.W.
Washington, D.C. 20006

### ORGANIZATION AND RESOURCES

The International Institute for Environment and Development was established in 1971 to advocate the productive use of natural resources and to stress the linkage between human needs, economic development, and the limits of the physical environment. Barbara Ward, an English economist, founded the organization which today has offices in London, Washington, and Buenos Aires. This international organization changed its name to the Center for Development and Environment (CDE). It has a board of directors of fifteen individuals from various countries, including Robert S. McNamara, former president of the World Bank. CDE has a professional staff of about forty in Washington headed by an executive director.

Its budget of approximately $3 million derives primarily from government agencies (58 percent), foundations (15 percent), corporations (14.2 percent), international agencies (8.5 percent), and publications (4.3 percent). It expends its resources on developing individual programs for third world countries, such as improving living conditions in shantytowns in Latin America or finding energy supplies for households in South Asian countries. It attempts to influence policy makers in all areas of the world to adopt ecologically sensitive development policies and aid missions. It is a member of the Global Tomorrow Coalition.*

## POLICY CONCERNS

CDE does research on sustainable development programs for the third world and searches for ways of implementing solutions at the local level. Its sustainable agriculture program emphasizes local involvement, cultural sensitivity, equity, and environmental protection. Its publications tend to criticize existing priorities and programs of international aid organizations as too concerned with massive programs not designed to create a sustainable economy. It maintains Earthscan, an information unit providing books on environmental problems. It publishes an annual, *World Resources Report*, and monographs on specific conservation issues.

## FURTHER INFORMATION

*Africa in Crisis* (1984). Washington, D.C.: International Institute for Environment Development.
*Natural Resources and Economic Development in Central America* (1986). Washington, D.C.: International Institute for Environment and Development.

## CENTER FOR ENVIRONMENTAL EDUCATION
*See* Center for Marine Conservation.

## CENTER FOR MARINE CONSERVATION (CMC)
1725 DeSales Street, N.W., Suite 500
Washington, D.C. 20036

## ORGANIZATION AND RESOURCES

The Center for Environmental Education was founded in 1972 as a tax exempt foundation devoted to the conservation of marine life and its habitat. It absorbed the Whale Protection Fund, founded in 1976, the Marine Mammal Conservation Fund, founded in 1979, and the Sea Turtle Rescue Fund, founded in 1980, and changed its name to the Center for Marine Conservation (CMC) in 1988. CMC has a board of directors comprised of 11 members. Its executive director, Roger E. McManus, formerly with the U.S. Fish and Wildlife Service, heads a professional staff of 17. It has a membership of 110,000 and a budget of around $2 million a year, derived 88 percent from contributions and grants, 4 percent from merchandise royalties, 2 percent from publication sales, and 6 percent from other sources.

*POLICY CONCERNS*

CMC is dedicated to the conservation and protection of the oceans and the species that live in them, such as whales and sea turtles. It opposes the capture of sea turtles in shrimp nets; it advocates the use of turtle excluder devices to keep sea turtles out of fishing nets. In 1986 CMC considered it a major victory when Brevard County, Florida, passed an innovative ordinance to regulate the lighting of beaches in order to protect sea turtles' nesting areas and urged other jurisdictions to follow suit. CMC's staff also monitors the activities of the International Whaling Commission (IWC), which regulates the killing of various endangered whale species around the world. It opposes the U.S. government's position before the IWC that the Eskimo quota of bowhead whales should be increased. It also opposes Japan's and Norway's insistence on their populations' needs for conducting "subsistence" and "research" whaling. Other marine species that CMC attempts to aid are manatees, dolphins, porpoises, and fur seals.

CMC advocates managing marine resources internationally to promote conservation of endangered species and seeks to prevent human activities that will lead to their extinction. CMC advocates controls on plastic debris and fishing gear that are discarded by ships into seas and lakes, harming marine life and later washing up on beaches. It also opposes the fishing industry's use of gill nets and drift nets that entangle and kill many marine creatures. Because of the coincidental killing of marine life it opposes the oil industry's method of dismantling old oil platforms by blowing them up.

*TACTICS*

CMC seeks to educate the public and its membership about the threat to endangered sea life from commercial fishing and pollution of the high seas. It has established a sanctuary for humpback whales in the Caribbean. It monitors the regulations of the National Marine Fisheries Service and the National Oceanic and Atmospheric Administration, in the Department of Commerce, which are responsible for enforcing the major U.S. laws regarding conservation of marine life, such as the Marine Mammal Protection Act.

*FURTHER INFORMATION*

*Marine Conservation News* (1989). Washington, D.C.: CMC, May.

**CENTER FOR RENEWABLE RESOURCES**
*See* Renew America.

**CENTER FOR SCIENCE IN THE PUBLIC INTEREST**
*See* Resource Policy Institute.

**CHEMICAL MANUFACTURERS ASSOCIATION (CMA)**
2501 M Street, N.W.
Washington, D.C. 20037

## ORGANIZATION AND RESOURCES

Founded in 1872, the Chemical Manufacturers Association (CMA) was known as the Manufacturing Chemists Association until 1979. Seventeen charter members, primarily producers of sulfuric acid, began the CMA, but it has expanded to include about 175 member corporations in the 1980s, including all of the major American and Canadian chemical and petrochemical companies.

CMA represents over 90 percent of the producers of industrial chemicals in the United States, including Chemdyne, Monsanto, Du Pont, and Dow Chemicals. It has an annual budget of over $15 million, 95 percent of which is obtained from corporate dues which vary according to the individual company's share of the market. There are also some 20 independent state chemical groups in those states where the industry is most important. CMA has a 49-member board of directors, which meets 5 times a year. Robert A. Roland is president and head of a professional staff of about 200 in CMA's national headquarters in Washington. There are 12 committees that help make policy for the association, including energy, environmental management, government relations, and health and safety.

## POLICY CONCERNS

Nearly all environmental control laws concern the chemical industry intimately, and CMA and its corporate members have had a considerable amount of influence in their formulation and implementation. Generally CMA's position on all pollution control issues is that there has been over zealous regulation in the 1970s without appropriate concern about the costs of regulation. It was generally more satisfied with the Reagan administration's enforcement of all regulations than it had been of earlier administrative and congressional actions.

CMA testified every time the Clean Air Act (CAA) was amended throughout the 1970s and 80s, generally arguing that the law should not be made stricter. One especially important part of the CAA for CMA is the authority given the U.S. Environmental Protection Agency (EPA) to regulate toxic gaseous emissions from industrial plants. EPA has been slow to define what toxic emissions are and even slower in setting standards for these emissions.

CMA has taken the position that EPA has all the authority it needs to control toxics, and much more study is needed on each substance before any should be listed as toxic. EPA is not only acting fast enough for the chemical industry, but, in its view, EPA should acknowledge that it is impossible to achieve zero risk in an industrial society and so inform the public. EPA should have the courage to declare some substances riskless and refuse to list them. CMA is also concerned about the possibility that Congress may amend the CAA to reduce acid rain; it is worried about the increased cost of electric power if that were to occur and it generally supports the power industry's position that enough is already being done to control sulfur emissions.

CMA's position on the Clean Water Act (CWA) and the Safe Drinking Water

Act (SDWA) are similar to those on the CAA. CMA has testified against tightening CWA and SDWA standards each time they came before Congress. Its representatives have been influential with EPA officials in getting effluent guidelines and pretreatment standards for chemical pesticides reduced. It has also argued successfully before EPA that chemical plants should get credit in their pretreatment plans for any reduction in pollutants that can be achieved by municipal treatment plants where effluents are later sent. CMA opposes any attempt to regulate runoff from farm fields that contain pesticides and fertilizer residues. CMA takes the position that groundwater should be protected by the states rather than the federal government, but it also opposes any stringent state guidelines that list a large number of carcinogens such as those that California proposed to prohibit any industry from discharging.

Under the terms of the Toxic Substances Control Act (TSCA) all commercial chemicals on the market must be tested for toxicity in humans. However, EPA has never had the resources to review all the chemicals coming onto the market in a given year, let alone the backlog of untested chemicals already in commerce. The burden of actual testing falls on the industry, and CMA and its members complain regularly about the information collection and reporting requirements which they consider excessive. The industry's effective control on information has made it highly influential in helping EPA to determine how to make exposure and risk assessments.

One public policy innovation, at the state and federal level, that CMA defended its members against for many years was the community's right to know what chemicals are stored in its jurisdiction. This provision was finally included as Title III of the Superfund Amendments Reauthorization Act (SARA) in 1986 despite CMA's argument against it on the grounds it would be too expensive for the corporations to provide this information to local fire and police forces, and too difficult for emergency response officials to understand and use. After passage of the law, CMA claimed that the chemical industry had complied with it more completely than any other industry. It points to the National Chemical Response and Information Center as the industry's primary facility for storing information and assisting local emergency crews during crises. It also argues that the information furnished to the public thus far about chemicals stored in communities has only served to inflame public opinion about the need for stricter controls on toxic emissions from plants.

One policy that has involved a considerable amount of CMA's congressional liaison resources has been the disposal of hazardous waste materials. In 1976 Congress passed the Resource Conservation and Recovery Act (RCRA), designed to track hazardous waste from cradle to grave. CMA has been active in all the hearings about RCRA through the 1980s and all the hearings over regulations proposed by EPA to implement RCRA. Its representatives have opposed most measures to tighten RCRA's requirements, including requiring liners for hazardous waste sites, sampling groundwater near dump sites, and banning the disposal of liquid hazardous wastes in landfills.

One extremely controversial issue has been the definition of what constitutes a hazardous waste and how it differs from ordinary solid waste (garbage and trash). Generally the chemical industry has resisted broadening the definition of hazardous wastes, as it has the definition of toxic chemicals. CMA expects amendments to RCRA in the 1990s, and it stands prepared to argue against such government-imposed solutions as product bans and binding quotas on waste minimization. It does, however, agree with the concept of source reduction for all solid wastes and hopes to achieve this through voluntary actions of the industry. It also hopes to avoid further state legislation by convincing Congress to preempt state regulations that are more restrictive than RCRA's.

One suggestion made by environmental groups concerning RCRA regulations was that injecting hazardous wastes, especially wastes associated with the petrochemical industry, into deep wells should be stopped because of the threat to groundwater that such injections pose. CMA resisted this requirement on behalf of its many member corporations that form part of the highly influential petrochemical industry. It argues for site-specific variances to almost all of RCRA's requirements for liners and technology designed to make landfills more secure. It also argues that the deadlines suggested by EPA or environmental groups are unrealistic because they do not allow sufficient adjustment time for industry.

In 1980, the Comprehensive Environmental Response, Compensation, and Liability Act (CERCLA, or Superfund) was passed to help the federal government clean up abandoned leaking toxic waste dump sites. CMA was highly successful in preventing any victim compensation clause from being included within this law. Hence its title is somewhat deceptive as there is no liability clause in the law to provide compensation for neighbors of toxic waste dumps. The only funds that have been used to move residents away from such sites are government funds. The industry's constant position has been that not enough information has yet been developed about the real risks from chemical contamination, and more research needs to be done to prove the desirability of such a costly program. In Times Beach, Missouri, a number of families were evacuated from a dioxin-contaminated area at government expense. However, CMA continues to maintain no causal connection has been made between disease and dioxin exposure.

Superfund has been financed from its inception by a tax on the chemical and petrochemical industries, despite their objections that the tax ought to be extended to industry generally and/or especially the waste disposal industry, which has benefited from Superfund by being paid to clean up sites but has not been willing to share the burden of paying for the cleanups. In 1986 Congress amended Superfund to provide a new tax of $12 for each $10,000 of taxable income from corporations earning more than $2 million a year in response to this demand. Superfund was extended for 5 years with an authorized budget of $2.5 billion a year.

During hearings over reauthorization of Superfund in 1986, chemical companies argued for their being giving a right to judicial review of every waste site before cleanup is ordered. One of the major issues facing courts has been how to assign liability for the costs of cleaning up sites. The chemical industry has argued in many court cases that precedents of joint and strict liability are unfair because complete liability may force one company to pay the entire bill if other equally guilty parties cannot be located. CMA officials have agreed Superfund may be needed for another five years, but to institutionalize it on a permanent basis is unwarranted. It also believes that the level of funding is too high, and states should pay more than 50 percent of the cost of cleaning up sites it now owns regardless of who may have disposed of their wastes in them earlier.

One major issue that undergoes continual discussion is the issue of ozone depletion caused by chlorofluorocarbons (CFCs). Generally manufacturers that produce and sell these substances oppose any regulation of them. In recent years, however, there has developed a considerable competition among corporations seeking to discover a viable substitute for them. The company that succeeds in finding such an alternative will be in a position to increase its profits, and this may change its perspective on the need for such regulation.

There are a number of public policies that concern CMA in addition to pollution control statutes, especially tax incentives for investment in industry. In addition CMA testified in 1986 against an import tax on foreign oil, which would increase the price of energy, as most energy intensive industries did.

## TACTICS

The CEOs of such corporations as Dow and Du Pont Chemicals testify both for their own companies and for CMA to Congress and the regulatory agencies; they also provide other access points in the executive branch such as the Office of Management and Budget and the White House. CMA's own professional staff provides expertise to Congress and the agencies. They also have a wide-ranging public relations program designed to influence public opinion concerning the risks of chemicals in society and the environment. They have an extensive media campaign, meeting regularly with the editorial boards of the nation's major electronic and print media. CMA also provides free educational programs for high schools, colleges, and civic organizations. CMA seeks to "put into perspective" the information that the public may receive from other sources about the toxicity of some chemicals by preparing video tapes on the health effects of different chemicals and making these available to its membership.

Despite general agreement within the chemical manufacturing industry that pollution control efforts have been too zealous and too hurried, in some instances individual chemical corporations have developed specific techniques for reducing certain kinds of chemical contaminants. Some of the largest chemical firms have developed environmental control divisions within their corporate structures and have succeeded in selling some of their own discoveries and methods of reducing pollution to other corporations. Hence there are within certain manufacturers of chemical products some officials who view environmental control regulations as a potential market rather than a burden. It is certainly true of the waste control industry that has grown up in the last decade, but it is also true of some members of CMA. Hence the trade association may find it difficult to reach consensus among all its members on every policy stance it assumes.

After the accidental release of deadly chemicals by a Union Carbide Company in Bhopal, India, in December, 1984, CMA initiated a program to respond to the public's nervousness over its ignorance about chemical materials that may be stored in or shipped through their communities. The community awareness and emergency response (CAER) program is a program by which some chemical plant managers help community groups and officials plan for emergency responses to accidents involving chemical plants or trucks hauling hazardous chemicals. Since the passage of SARA and the community right-to-know law, this program has been increased and emphasized in CMA's public relations releases. CMA also produces brochures and video tapes, explaining to its members how to allay the fears of emergency response officials and average citizens and public interest groups such as the League of Women Voters* in areas where chemical manufacturing plants are located.

CMA produces an annual report for its members, numerous research reports of use to all chemical corporations, and three monthly newsletters, including *Chemecology*, which addresses environmental issues. CMA holds an annual meeting in White Sulphur Springs, West Virginia, each June.

*FURTHER INFORMATION*

*Annual Report 1988–89* (1989). Washington, D.C.: CMA.
*Chemecology* (1989). Washington, D.C.: CMA. September, October.
Epstein, Samuel, Lester O. Brown, and Carl Pope (1982). *Hazardous Wastes in America*. San Francisco, Calif.: Sierra Club Books.
Wishart, Ronald S. (1988). "The Lessons of Bhopal." *The Woodlands Forum* 5:1–3.

## CHEMICAL SPECIALTIES MANUFACTURERS ASSOCIATION (CSMA)
1001 Connecticut Avenue, N.W., Suite 1120
Washington, D.C. 20036

*ORGANIZATION AND RESOURCES*

Founded in 1914, the Chemical Specialties Manufacturers Association (CSMA) is a trade association of some 400 companies that produce specialty products such as cleansers, disinfectants, and pesticides. It includes such giants of the industry as Union Carbide, Dow, Du Pont, Monsanto, and Velsicol, as well as the chemical companies that are part of Texaco, ARCO, Exxon, and other oil companies. Its membership overlaps to a large degree that of its larger sister trade association, the Chemical Manufacturers Association (CMA).* CSMA has a board of directors of 24 people to direct policy. Ralph Engel is president of the association, and he has a staff of 28.

CSMA has annual budget of about $2 million, 68 percent of which comes from corporate dues, 24 percent from meeting fees, 5 percent from publications, and 3 percent from investments. Its expenditures include 23 percent for legislative representation, 20 percent for legal services, 16 percent for scientific and technical services, 14 percent for public relations, 12 percent for member services, and 15 percent for meetings. It has 6 divisions: detergents, industrial and automotive specialty chemicals, aerosols, pesticides, polishes and floor maintenance products, and antimicrobial products.

## POLICY CONCERNS

Like CMA, CSMA is primarily concerned about pollution control regulations that affect the chemical industry. It opposes any increased stringency of the Clean Air and Water Acts and a broader definition of what constitutes hazardous wastes and toxic materials. In the states it operates to water down community and worker right-to-know laws which would inform workers and the public about the hazards of the chemicals they work with and live near. CSMA credited itself with preventing New Jersey from imposing hazard communications requirements that would have exceeded federal standards by arguing in court that federal laws such as the Occupational Safety and Health Act preempt any state standards.

CSMA's legislative affairs division testified often in the 1980s against amending the Federal Insecticide, Fungicide and Rodenticide Act (FIFRA) to make it more difficult to register new commercial poisons. In 1988, however, FIFRA was reauthorized requiring the reregistration of about 600 active ingredients, establishing new fees for registration, and nearly eliminating the previous custom of compensating manufacturers of suspended pesticides. However, several provisions were included that were favorable toward industry, including a fast-track consideration of products similar to those already registered with the U.S. Environmental Protection Agency (EPA). The new law was a stand-off between those who sought a stronger and those who wanted a weaker law.

Another concern of CSMA is the proliferation of product liability laws in several states. It seeks to obtain uniform standards throughout the nation rather than having individual state standards that may conflict and cause hardship for the industry. Along with CMA, it succeeded in preventing any victim compensation clause from being included in the Comprehensive Emergency Response, Compensation, and Liability Act (CERCLA, or Superfund). It was less successful in preventing right-to-know legislation from being passed in 1986 under the Superfund Amendments and Reauthorization Act (SARA).

Supporting their opposite numbers in CMA, representatives of CSMA have testified that the major hazardous waste disposal law, RCRA, is too strict in its demands on industry. It opposed amendments to remove the exemption for small generators of wastes. This was, however, changed to redefine the term *small generator* more stringently. CSMA also believes that most of RCRA's deadlines are unrealistically short and cannot be achieved by industry.

CSMA also is concerned about new moves to protect groundwater in the United States through Clean Water and Safe Drinking Water Act amendments. It opposes any controls over stormwater runoff from agricultural fields and chemical plant sites, and believes that the present pollutant discharge permit system is sufficient to protect groundwater. It argues that the marginal costs to increase controls far outweigh any additional benefits to public health, as does CMA.

The aerosol division of CSMA is particularly protective of the industry's interest in continuing to manufacture products that are dispensed through aerosols, such as hair spray, underarm deodorant, and household cleansers. Nevertheless, some of its members are now trying to find chemical compounds that will release fewer photochemically reactive organic compounds at the same time that CSMA itself argues the danger from aerosols is exaggerated by a "hysterical press". However, it has published *Fight Back: Helping Young People Kick the Sniffing Habit*, which recognizes the misuse of some aerosols.

## TACTICS

CSMA publishes a quarterly journal, *Chemical Times and Trends*, for its membership which is also circulated to government decision makers to keep them up to date with the industry's needs. It produces a weekly publication, *Executive Newswatch*, for its members to keep them abreast of regulatory developments in Washington. It sponsors semiannual conferences and trade shows. CSMA is especially concerned about public reactions to such issues as how safely to dispose of household chemicals, and it has launched a major public relations project to inform the media about the safety of chemical products. It also emphasizes the excellent worker safety record that the industry has had.

Individual corporations that make up the membership of CSMA and CMA are even more active in influencing Congress, the agencies, and the public about the benign nature of the chemistry industry than are the trade associations, however. Dow Chemicals, for example, with sales over $10 billion a year, has several political action committees that raise funds to contribute to political campaigns each year. It has a multimillion dollar advertising campaign, part of which is spent convincing the public that Dow "does good things" for them. E. I. Du Pont, with sales around $30 billion a year, has many more experts than does either CMA or CSMA to send to Congress and EPA to testify, for example, that the United States will be put at an economic disadvantage if it should unilaterally discontinue using chlorofluorocarbons. European and Japanese products would soon replace United States products in the international marketplace with the same net result for the ozone layer.

## FURTHER INFORMATION

*Annual Report* (1989). Washington, D.C.: CSMA.

U.S. Congress. Senate Committee on Environment and Public Works (1987). *Hearings on Ozone Reduction*. Testimony of Elwood P. Blanchard, Group VP. E. I. Du Pont, March 9, May 13.

**CITIZEN'S CLEARINGHOUSE FOR HAZARDOUS WASTES (CCHW)**
P.O. Box 926
Arlington, Virginia 22216

## ORGANIZATION AND RESOURCES

In 1977, toxic wastes long buried in an area known as Love Canal began to make their way to the land surface in Niagara Falls, New York. A group of homeowners there, led by Lois Marie Gibbs, began a campaign to have the city, New York State, and the federal government recognize their plight. In 1980 the Comprehensive Environmental Response, Compensation, and Liability Act (CERCLA, or Superfund) was passed in order to clean up such sites with public funds to be recovered from the former and present owners, operators, and users of such abandoned dumps.

In 1981 Lois Marie Gibbs founded the Citizen's Clearinghouse for Hazardous Wastes (CCHW). In the late 1980s CCHW had about 13,000 individual members who paid $15 a year in dues. It also was supported by a few companies that provide environmental services through contracts with the Environmental Protection Agency (EPA) to clean up such sites. Its total budget is approximately $500,000, about 50 percent of which come from foundation grants from such organizations as local churches in communities with toxic waste dump problems.

CCHW has a professional staff of six in Arlington, Virginia, whose primary activity is making contacts with local groups attempting to address specific problems in their areas. In 1986 it opened two additional offices, CCHW/Appalachia in Charleston, West Virginia, and CCHW/South in Harvy, Louisiana, to reach grass-roots organizations in those areas. CCHW provides them with information about how to organize and get their demands met at the local and state government levels.

## POLICY CONCERNS

CCHW has been involved in some national legislation, notably the Comprehensive Environmental Response, Compensation, and Liability Act, the Resource Conservation and Recovery Act (RCRA) and their amendments, including the Superfund Amendments and Reauthorization Act of 1986 (SARA), which gives communities the right to know what toxic chemicals are stored in their jurisdictions. Its representatives also argued for inclusion of a victim compensation section to CERCLA, but industry's arguments about the costs of such a program convinced Congress not to pass it.

## TACTICS

CCHW's primary emphasis is on the implementation of such laws at the local level. It specializes in direct political action against particular dump sites, both proposed and active, and provides information to 72,000 grass-roots organizations. CCHW publishes *Action Bulletin* four times a year to inform its membership about local events in other parts of the country. It also publishes *Everyone's Backyard*, a quarterly, with feature stories about hazardous waste problems. It also publishes occasional monographs on subjects such as those listed below. Lois Gibbs wrote a personal memoir of the Love Canal story, dealing with her fight to organize the residents and to force the federal and New York State governments to purchase some of the residents' homes around the Love Canal site. CCHW holds a triennial conference.

### FURTHER INFORMATION

*Deep Well Injection: An Explosive Issue* (1985). Washington, D.C.: CCHW.
*Fight to Win on Hazardous Waste: A Leader's Manual* (1986). Washington, D.C.: CCHW.
Gibbs, Lois Marie (as told to Murray Levine) (1982). *Love Canal: My Story.* Albany: State University of New York Press.
*Incineration: Burning Issue of the Eighties* (1986). Washington, D.C.: CCHW.
*Love Canal: A Chronology of Events that Shaped a Movement* (1985). Washington, D.C.: CCHW.
*Victims' Compensation: What Do People Want?* (1987). Washington, D.C.: CCHW.

## CLEAN SITES, INCORPORATED
1199 North Fairfax Street
Alexandria, Virginia 22314

### ORGANIZATION AND RESOURCES

In May 1984, a consortium of industrial and environmental leaders created Clean Sites, Incorporated as a nonprofit corporation with tax-exempt status designed to facilitate voluntary cleanup of chemical dump sites in the United States. Clean Sites does not attempt to influence public policy. Rather it developed out of one policy, the Comprehensive Environmental Response, Compensation, and Liability Act (CERCLA, or Superfund), under which the U.S. Environmental Protection Agency (EPA) can clean up abandoned chemical dumps and force their owners and former users to pay the costs. Under the auspices of The Conservation Foundation*, and the leadership of Dr. Louis Fernandez, chair of the Monsanto Company, a task force of environmental and industry representatives agreed to cooperate in a private endeavor to attempt to clean up in the private sector, rather than relying on government controls. Environmentalists were dissatisfied with the slow pace of cleanup under CERCLA, and industrialists were concerned about the costs of the cleanup.

Its nineteen-person board of directors is composed of environmental organizations' representatives, such as A. A. Berle, president of the Audubon Society, and Russell Train, chair of the board of Clean Sites and the World Wildlife Fund*; industrial executive officers, such as Edwin A. Gee, of International Paper, and H. E. McBrayer of Exxon Chemical Company; and public officials, such as Douglas Costle, formerly administrator of EPA, and Donald Kennedy, formerly Food and Drug commissioner. Its president and treasurer is Thomas P. Grumbly, former executive director of Health Effects Institute of Washington, D.C. It has a staff of fifty-four professionals: chemists, engineers, lawyers, business managers, and scientists.

In its first year of operation, 1985, Clean Sites had revenues of over $2.4

million, funded primarily by corporate donations, although foundations such as the Andrew Mellon Foundation contributed also. In 1987 its revenues peaked at just over $7 million; in 1988 its revenues were about $4.9 million. This decline was due to the deliberate effort to reduce start-up contributions from the chemical industry which had assumed most of the burden in the early years. Funding in 1988 came 51 percent from reimbursement for services, 33 percent grants from the chemical industry, 8 percent contributions from other industry, and 8 percent grants from foundations, government, and individuals.

## POLICY CONCERNS

Clean Sites does not advocate specific changes in public policy, although its own goal is to privatize solutions to one of the major environmental problems of the 1990s. It does not lobby Congress or other parts of the government, but it cooperates with EPA in its cleanup activities. It focuses exclusively on one public policy, the cleanup of abandoned leaking chemical dumps, and it would not exist but for the passage of the Comprehensive Environmental Response, Compensation, and Liability Act in 1976. Given the mixed composition of its board, it recognizes that national legislation such as Superfund is necessary for giving an impetus to private actions. Superfund provides that EPA can insist that parties responsible for contaminating a site pay for its cleanup. Without EPA enforcement of this part of the law, however, there is no incentive for industry to ask Clean Sites for its assistance in reaching agreements over sharing costs.

## TACTICS

Clean Sites represents a new trend in environmental policy, that of accommodation among the major proponents of formerly contending forces. It facilitates negotiations between owners of dump sites, residents near those sites, and environmental groups in several regions of the United States and oversees cleanup of hazardous disposal sites. In 1988 Clean Sites' settlement division served as mediator at 16 sites, and its technical staff gave advice about cleaning up 8 sites. Two-person teams, representing both the public and private sector of the economy, typically work together with the owners of leaking dump sites that have been placed on the national priority list of sites needing cleanup by the EPA. At the end of the 1980s EPA had identified 1,177 such priority sites in the United States. Through negotiation, Clean Sites attempts to settle disputes about how much cleanup is needed and how the costs of such cleanup are to be distributed among the various past and present owners and users of the site. Representatives of Clean Sites help draft the technical review and compliance plan and then follow up by monitoring the actual cleanup operations by the responsible parties.

## FURTHER INFORMATION

*Clean Sites and Private Action* (1984). Washington, D.C.: Steering Committee convened
   by The Conservation Foundation, May.

*Clean Sites Annual Report* (1988). Washington, D.C.: Clean Sites, Inc.

*From Concept to Reality* (1986). Washington, D.C.: Clean Sites, Inc., January.

Kosowatz, John J. (1988). "Mediating Toxics Responsibility." *Environment and Natural Resources*, May 26.

Rikleen, Lauren Stiller (1985). "Superfund Settlements: Key to Accelerated Waste Cleanups." *The Environmental Forum*. Washington, D.C.: Environmental Law Institute, August, pp. 51–54.

# COGENERATION AND INDUSTRIAL POWER COALITION OF AMERICA (CIPCA)

Two Lafayette Centre, Suite 500
Washington, D.C. 20035

## ORGANIZATION AND RESOURCES

In 1980 twelve companies interested in cogenerating electricity with their process steam energy founded the Cogeneration Coalition of America (CCA), which changed its name to Cogeneration and Industrial Power Coalition of America (CIPCA) in 1987. CIPCA consists of twenty industrial users of electricity, including paper and pulp, steel, aluminum, petroleum, coke, and equipment producers. It has a budget of about $75,000 a year derived entirely from corporate dues. There are three professional representatives in Washington. It has a six-person board of governors who meet once a year to make policy.

## POLICY CONCERNS

There is only one major policy with which CIPCA is intimately involved, which overlaps with one of the major interests of the Electricity Consumers Resource Council (ELCON)*: the creation and maintenance of the 1978 Public Utilities Regulatory Policy Act (PURPA). Under that law, electric utilities are obligated to buy power from cogenerators of electricity at a price no higher than the marginal cost to the utility if it were to produce that energy itself. CIPCA argues that PURPA has introduced some much-needed competition into the electric utility business and has thus brought down the cost to all ratepayers who otherwise would have been forced to pay whatever price the monopoly company in their area could convince the state regulatory body to agree to.

CIPCA disagrees with the Edison Electric Institute (EEI)* that cogenerators have an unfair advantage over utilities. It argues that cogenerators have sprung up in areas where there is overproduction of electricity by power companies because the latter have overextended their ratebase and are charging exorbitant fees for electricity. It argues that PURPA should continue to prevent utilities from owning more than a 50 percent interest in a PURPA-qualifying facility;

otherwise the production of electricity might return to a monopoly industry. It did agree, however, with EEI that the Powerplant and Industrial Fuel Use Act should be amended to allow gas and oil to be used freely in generating electricity.

CIPCA allies itself with the National Hydropower Association and the National Wood Energy Association in arguing that all companies able to generate electricity should be tied into the grid that the local distributor has developed and allowed to compete for customers.

*TACTICS*

CIPCA issues *Cogeneration Action*, a monthly newsletter. It also encourages its members to testify before congressional committees and the Federal Energy Regulatory Commission about PURPA regulations.

*FURTHER INFORMATION*

U.S. Congress. Senate Committee on Energy and Natural Resources (1986). *Hearings on PURPA*. Washington, D.C.: Government Printing Office.


**COMMON CAUSE**
2030 M Street, N.W.
Washington, D.C. 20036

*ORGANIZATION AND RESOURCES*

In 1970 John W. Gardner, former Secretary of Health, Education, and Welfare under President Johnson, founded Common Cause, a mass-membership organization, whose primary goal is to reform the processes of government through government in sunshine acts, freedom of information acts, increased public participation, and public funding of political campaigns. At the end of the 1980s it had a membership of 285,000, who pay $20 each year. Its budget is over $12 million, collected primarily from dues and other contributions from the same members. Of that amount, it spent approximately half on support services: developing membership and administration; and half on programmatic concerns: lobbying and communicating.

It employs seventy-eight professional staff in Washington and sixty-five additional staff in state offices around the forty-eight states in which it has affiliated groups. It has a sixty-person board of directors, twenty of whom are elected each year at large from its membership by mailed ballot for a three-year term. Members are forbidden to serve more than two consecutive terms, and an effort is made to bring in new directors through a nominating committee. However, only 15 percent of the total membership voted in the 1987 election. The president of Common Cause is Fred Wertheimer, and the chair of the board is Archibald Cox, former Watergate special prosecutor.

## POLICY CONCERNS

Common Cause makes a concerted effort to involve its membership in policy selection and positions. It polls the membership regularly, and about 25 percent returned polls in 1987. It generally focuses on good government issues, such as openness in government and public funding for political campaigns. Another important issue in the 1980s was the government deficit and priorities for spending. Most Common Cause members support reduced military spending and efforts for an international nuclear freeze and oppose the strategic defense initiative. However, they also support environmental legislation, such as the Clean Air and Water acts and reduction of toxic waste disposal in the earth. Generally, Common Cause members approve of more government spending for and attention to environmental issues.

## TACTICS

The journal *Common Cause* is issued every other month and features articles on military spending, health care, and other policy issues as well as political campaign contributions and spending. In 1987 it won a National Magazine Award for excellence in magazine reporting, sponsored by the American Society of Magazine Editors.

### FURTHER INFORMATION

*Common Cause* (1987). Washington, D.C.: Common Cause, May-June.
McFarland, Andrew (1984). *Common Cause*. Chatham, N.J.: Chatham House.

## CONFERENCE OF NATIONAL PARK CONCESSIONERS (CNPC)
1901 North Fort Myer Drive
Arlington, Virginia 22209

## ORGANIZATION AND RESOURCES

The Conference of National Park Concessioners (CNPC) was founded in 1919 to represent the interests of businesses with concession contracts in the national parks. These companies range from small local businesses to major hotel and restaurant chains such as Fred Harvey's or Howard Johnson. Dues range from $500 upward depending on the size and profitability of the company. The annual CNPC budget is modest, under $300,000, derived 90 percent from corporate dues. There is a twelve-person board of directors elected by the membership each year, as well as a professional staff person in Washington.

## POLICY CONCERNS

CNPC is primarily interested in keeping private businesses located in the national parks. It argues against any takeover by the National Park Service of lodges and accommodations in such scenic areas as Yellowstone National Park. The National Park Service (NPS) in the Department of Interior negotiates contracts with such concessioners, and it is the purpose of CNPC to obtain the most profitable deals for its members with the government. NPS also keeps up the parks, provides naturalists to give talks and develop educational exhibits for the parks, as well as provides roads into the parks and sells camping and hiking permits in the parks. The CNPC would like to take over many of these activities in order to profit from the thousands of tourists who visit the national parks each year. During the Reagan administration it was successful in arguing for the privatization of many activities in the parks. However, congressional agreement was not always forthcoming.

In 1986 the CNPC's representative testified to the Senate Committee on Natural Resources in favor of new fees for national park use by tourists. However, he stipulated that such fees should be used to acquire new parklands and provide for the upkeep of present facilities, rather than placed in the general revenue fund of the treasury. Generally the CNPC favors preserving wilderness areas in the United States and additional acquisitions of national parklands in order to expand tourism. It does not, however, favor wilderness preservation, but advocates having the NPS increase access for motor vehicles into all parts of the public lands in the United States.

## TACTICS

On some issues, such as park expansion and prevention of clear-cutting national forests and mineral exploration in the parks, the CNPC agrees with environmental and conservation groups and joins with them in lobbying Congress. In other instances it agrees with other business and trade associations that access should be increased and more uses made of the parks rather than preserving them in a wilderness state accessible only to backpackers. It publishes a periodic newsletter and a semiannual membership roster and holds a semiannual conference in March in Washington and in October elsewhere.

## CONGRESS WATCH
*See* Public Citizen.

## THE CONSERVATION FOUNDATION (CF)
1250 24th Street, N.W.
Washington, D.C. 20037

## HISTORY AND DEVELOPMENT

In 1948, Fairfield Osborn, then president of the New York Zoological Society, founded The Conservation Foundation (CF), arguing that the basic natural resources—air, water, energy, land, and animal and plant life—are finite and must be conserved by humankind if it is to survive. In collaboration with four associates, George E. Brewer, David H. McAlpin, Samuel H. Ordway, Jr., and Laurance Rockefeller, Mr. Osborn stated that the purposes of the new organization were to be the "conservation of the earth's life-supporting resources—animal life, forests and other plant life, water sources, and productive soils—

and to advance, improve, and encourage knowledge and understanding of such resources, their natural distribution and wise use, and their essential relationship to each other and to the sustenance and enrichment of all life'' (certificate of incorporation of The Conservation Foundation, 1948).

## ORGANIZATION AND RESOURCES

CF's forty-two-member board of directors comes from a variety of professions—politicians, such as former Governor Richard Lamm of Colorado and Thomas Kean, governor of New Jersey; executive officers of major corporations, such as H. Eugene McBrayer, president of Exxon Chemical Company, John Dorrance, Jr., Campbell Soup, Richard Ruckelshaus, CEO of Browning-Ferris Industries; academics, including Professor Raymond F. Dasmann, of the University of Southern California; conservationists, including Christine Stevens, president of the Animal Welfare Institute; and major foundations, notably George H. Taber, vice-president of the Richard King Mellon Foundation. The board represents a broad range of opinion and seeks to balance developmental and conservation values and to find consensus on these issues. It selects the president of CF and its own successor board members.

In 1985 CF joined with the World Wildlife Fund* to share facilities, staff, and a chief executive officer, William K. Reilly, president of both organizations. He remained in that position until late 1989 when President Bush selected him to head the EPA. At that time Katherine Fuller, formerly a vice-president of WWF, was selected to succeed him. CF's professional staff of over fifty is engaged in research and communication of findings in areas of concern to conservationists. It is exempt from federal income tax under Section 501(c)(3) of the Internal Revenue Code and has no official lobbying activities.

CF is not a membership organization. It derives its support from foundations and corporations such as the Arco, Charles Stewart Mott, Andrew Mellon, William and Flora Hewlett, VIDDA, H. J. Heinz, Gaylord and Dorothy Donnelley, Howard Phipps, and James and Marshall Field foundations; and the Eastman Kodak, Exxon, Standard Oil, U.S. Steel, Union Carbide, Procter and Gamble, Aluminum Company of America, Du Pont, Dow Chemical, and Monsanto corporations. In 1988 its revenues totaled over $5 million, up from nearly $4 million in 1987. Over $2 million came from foundations and corporations, much of it earmarked for particular projects. Government contracts and grants for specific projects totaled over $1.5 million. The remaining revenues derived from investments, sales of publications, and individual contributions.

General administrative, communications, and support activities, including fund-raising, consume 20 percent of the budget. The remainder is divided into program areas: 15 percent land and wildlife, 19 percent environmental quality, 15 percent environmental dispute resolution, 16 percent international environment, 8 percent general programs, and 7 percent communications. In 1977 there were six areas of concentration: public lands management, coastal resources management, land use and urban growth, economics and the environment, pollution control and toxic substances, and energy conservation. By 1989 the emphasis had shifted somewhat away from land-use issues to greater focus on consensus building and international affairs.

## POLICY CONCERNS

The largest single program concerns environmental quality and trends. In 1982 CF issued its first *State of the Environment*, a comprehensive look at all environmental issues from natural resource management to pollution control and the public policies that have been adopted to address them. In 1984 it issued its second volume, and its third appeared in 1987. In some ways these volumes replaced the *Annual Reports* of the Council of Environmental Quality, whose budget was severely restricted during the Reagan administration. CF also focused attention on the need to develop public policies that emphasize the interrelatedness of different kinds of pollution, from air to land to water, and the need to find solutions that will recognize the cross-media nature of pollution control. In keeping with the renewed interest in federalism, it worked with state governments on the need for integrated programs, and with the U.S. Environmental Protection Agency (EPA) on the need for a comprehensive pollution control statute. In 1988, at the request of the Council on Environmental Quality and the National Science Foundation, CF drafted a handbook describing the uses of risk assessment in setting standards for environmental quality.

The land and wildlife program remained CF's second largest program in 1988 with specific projects on the national parks, forest management, agricultural lands, urban growth, historic preservation, protection of barrier islands, and outdoor recreation. In 1986 CF issued a report on the national parks in which it proposed a ten-year program to improve the condition and management of national park resources. President William Reilly testified before Congress on the need for new legislation to strengthen the national park system and to retain the integrity of the Land and Water Fund for improving facilities in the parks rather than allowing fees obtained from park users to be funneled into the general revenue fund. Foundation staff have also given advice directly to the National Park Service in the U.S. Department of Interior, running a course for natural resource management trainees on natural resource law. In 1986 the Foundation also ran a forum on funding state parks, initiated a study of policies governing timber sales by the U.S. Forest Service, and published a book on agricultural patterns in the South.

Water is both a natural resource and a part of environmental quality. CF has specific projects to prevent the contamination of groundwater, to protect surface water against nonpoint sources of pollution such as agricultural runoff, and to improve management of water as a natural resource. CF released proposals for dealing with groundwater contamination in November, 1985, and staff members testified before Congress on the need to reauthorize the Safe Drinking Water Act, which passed in 1986. In 1987 it ran a forum in cooperation with the

National Governors Association* to promote cooperation between the federal and state levels of government for controlling groundwater contamination. The foundation also focused on soil erosion, as both a natural resource depletion and water pollution problem. Its 1985 report on erosion influenced the drafting of Clean Water Act amendments dealing with nonpoint sources of pollution, which were approved and passed over the president's veto in early 1987.

## TACTICS

In 1988 CF and WWF founded the Osborn Center for Economic Development in order to help developing nations devise sustainable economic programs. In so doing they joined many other environmental organizations in their concern for the way in which international banking institutions and the U.S. government, through its Agency for International Development, have encouraged Third World countries to invest in massive irrigation and power projects. The latter have put these nations into debt which influences them to sell off their natural resources, such as timber, at rates that cannot be replaced and to clear-cut large areas of tropical forest in order to find land to grow crops for export to the United States and other markets. Through the Osborn Center CF hopes to develop pilot projects that will enable developing countries to find ways of sustaining their populations without destroying their natural resource base through soil erosion, chemical contamination of land and water, and loss of biological diversity. In cooperation with the Biomass Users Network in Costa Rica, CF hopes to promote use of agricultural and forestry by-products in order to make traditional commodities, such as tropical fruit and rubber, more profitable.

One of the most important programs on CF's agenda in the 1980s was its dispute resolution program. Since its inception the Foundation has attempted to bring together environmentalists and members of the business community as well as government officials and academics in cooperative endeavors. In 1977 it published *Business and Environment: Toward Common Ground*. In the 1980s this effort achieved its own program. Since 1982 the Foundation has conducted an Agricultural Chemicals Dialogue Group in which it attempts to facilitate consensus among chemical corporations and church and environmental groups about various ways of reducing the misuse of agricultural chemicals in developing countries.

It obtained a contract in 1986 from the Council on Environmental Quality to mediate rule-making by the Environmental Protection Agency and other federal agencies. Its first task was to help EPA negotiate rules regarding underground injection of hazardous wastes and procedures for modifying hazardous waste facility permits with industry and environmental groups before the rules were published as proposed regulations.

Staff members of CF testify before congressional committees about issues under review there, run and participate in conferences, and organize and conduct symposia. Their primary activity, however, is research and writing of reports. A selected bibliography of their publications is given below.

## FURTHER INFORMATION

*Annual Report, 1988* (1989). Washington, D.C.: CF.

Bingham, Gail (1986). *Resolving Environmental Disputes: A Decade of Experience.* Washington, D.C.: CF.

Liroff, Richard A. (1986). *Reforming Air Pollution Regulation: The Toil and Trouble of EPA's Bubble.* Washington, D.C.: CF.

Miller, Taylor O., et al. (1986). *The Salty Colorado.* Washington, D.C.: CF.

Osborn, Fairfield (1948). *Our Plundered Planet.* New York: Pyramid Books.

Rabe, Barry G. (1986). *Fragmentation and Integration in State Environmental Management.* Washington, D.C.: CF.

Reilly, William K. (1987). "Shaping an Environmental Policy for the 1990s." *The Woodlands Forum.* Houston, Tex.: Center for Growth Studies, Fall, pp. 6–7.

*Resolve: Newsletter on Dispute Resolution (1989).* Washington, D.C.: CF, May.

*State of the Environment* (1982, 1984, 1987). Washington, D.C.: CF.

Waddell, Thomas E., ed. (1986). *The Off-Site Costs of Soil Erosion.* Washington, D.C.: CF.

## CONSULTING ENGINEERS COUNCIL OF THE U.S.A.

*See* American Consulting Engineers Council.

## CONSUMER ENERGY COUNCIL OF AMERICA (CECA)

2000 L Street, N.W., Suite 320
Washington, D.C. 20036

### ORGANIZATION AND RESOURCES

The Consumer Energy Council of America (CECA) was founded in 1973 and was originally known as the Energy Policy Task Force of the Consumer Federation of America. It represents consumer points of view on energy supply and pricing. It has no individual members but fifty-two member organizations: publicly owned power systems, rural electric cooperatives, governmental groups such as the U.S. Conference of Mayors,* and senior citizen, urban, labor, and minority groups. Headed by a 15-member board of directors elected from among the corporate members, CECA's policies are set by this board, the executive director, Ellen Berman, and its other 5 professional staff in its Washington headquarters. Dues for corporate members range from $500 to $10,000 per year. Its annual budget averages around $320,000, 60 percent of which comes from government funds. It also obtains some funds from foundations and from fees for services.

### POLICY CONCERNS

CECA conducts research on such issues as the relative economics of using heat pumps as opposed to traditional heating and cooling systems and disseminates information to its membership. It has also developed a method for calculating the lifetime operating costs of appliances such as room air conditioners.

It collaborated with the American Council for an Energy Efficient Economy* on a compendium of appliance efficiency rebate programs. It established a clearinghouse to inform oil consumers, municipalities and schools, for example, on how to obtain part of settlements by oil companies for overcharges in the 1970s for heating fuel.

CECA advocated uniform national energy efficiency standards for major household appliances, which constitute the National Appliance Energy Conservation Act passed in 1987. It opposes administration cutbacks in funding for conservation research and development in the U.S. Department of Energy's budget. It opposed selling off publicly owned power companies, such as the Tennessee Valley Authority, as proposed by the Reagan administration to Congress in the 1980s. CECA supported the 1987 repeal of the Powerplant and Industrial Fuel Use Act, passed in the middle of the 1970s energy crisis, giving a preference to home and institutional heating plants for obtaining natural gas supplies. This repeal allowed utilities to obtain natural gas for generating electricity, thus cutting generating costs.

## TACTICS

CECA supplies congressional representatives and their staff with needed information about energy policy proposals, but it concentrates its energies on conducting and publishing research for its own members and the public. The Council seeks to bring together community organizations and utilities in cooperative endeavors to conserve energy and to find ways to mitigate the impact of energy pricing on low-income families.

## FURTHER INFORMATION

Consumer Energy Council of America (1983). *Equity and Energy: Rising Energy Prices and the Living Standard of Lower Income Americans*. Boulder, Colo.: Westview Press.

*Heat Pumps Versus Alternative Space Conditioning Systems* (1985). Washington, D.C.: CECA, September.

## CONSUMER GAS ASSOCIATION
*See* American Gas Association.

## COTTON TEXTILE INSTITUTE
*See* American Textile Manufacturers Institute.

## COUNCIL OF INDUSTRIAL BOILER OWNERS (CIBO)
5817 Burke Center Parkway
Burke, Virginia 22015

## ORGANIZATION AND RESOURCES

The Council of Industrial Boiler Owners (CIBO) was formed in 1978 to represent the interests of boiler manufacturers and non-utility boiler operators such as steel companies, petroleum refiners, auto manufacturers, chemical corporations, and breweries. Its fifty corporate members pay dues of $7,500 a year, which, along with investments and income from meetings, produces a budget of about $300,000 a year. CIBO has a board of directors of seven persons.

## POLICY CONCERNS

CIBO was founded in response to the Clean Air Act (CAA) amendments of 1977 and the National Energy Act of 1978. Its representatives have argued against elements of those laws ever since. CIBO argues that its members should be treated differently from electric utilities under both these laws. Industrial boilers are smaller on average than are those in powerplants and they contribute only a minor percentage of the air pollutants, especially sulfur oxides. Because of their size, the cost per unit of pollutant reduced is much higher for industrial boilers than that for electric utilities. CIBO feels that this is unfair and that the CAA should be amended to reduce the burden on industry. Therefore CIBO argues that the CAA restrictions should not be applied to industrial boilers because to do so would cause some plants to go out of production and others to delay or abandon plans to replace outmoded boilers with new ones that would have to be fitted with desulfurization systems.

There is considerable difference of opinion between CIBO and the electric power industry about who should pay the costs of cleaning up sulfur emissions and other air pollutants under the CAA. However, CIBO is in complete agreement with the utilities and such groups as the Electricity Consumers Resource Council* about the need to reduce the cost of electricity to its end users. In the late 1980s CIBO representatives argued consistently along with other industries, including electric utilities, that not enough is yet known about acid deposition to enable Congress to pass legislation designed to restrict sulfur emissions further than the CAA does now. They argue for more government and private research on the issue first.

Another federal law that CIBO members strenuously objected to until it was amended in 1987 was the Powerplant and Industrial Fuel Use Act (PIFUA), which restricted the types of uses to which gas and oil could be put. In the mid–1970s the energy crisis caused Congress to become concerned about whether there would be a sufficient supply of gas to heat homes and businesses. It therefore prohibited powerplants and other industrial boilers from using gas and ordered them to switch to coal, a more abundant fuel in the United States. While CIBO wants its members to be able to use coal whenever it is the cheapest fuel available, it advocates no government regulation of the kinds of fuels that can be used in different sectors of the economy. It believes that there are sufficient gas supplies to permit industrial uses of them, and that the increased price will be sufficient incentive for industry to switch to coal whenever gas becomes scarce. CIBO, together with the gas and powerplant industries, was successful in getting the gas-use ban lifted in 1987.

CIBO argues that government should stay out of the market relationship between suppliers of natural gas and end users by not controlling the price of gas. It believes that by allowing the price to react to the market there will be greater competition and lower prices in the long run. However, it does advocate government intervention to force pipelines to transport gas to end users who have bought natural gas in the field. CIBO also agrees that the Public Utilities Regulatory Policy Act (PURPA) should be kept because it requires electric utilities to serve industries that cogenerate their own electric power and buy back unused portions of that energy.

CIBO also advocates allowing use of solid wastes to generate heat in industrial boilers. In this endeavor it is opposed by the waste treatment industry, which argues that there are not sufficient controls on industrial boilers to prevent exposure of the population to toxic emissions that may be given off from waste materials. CIBO representatives have consistently testified against Resource Conservation and Recovery Act (RCRA) amendments in the 1980s that restrict the burning of industrial wastes in boilers. As do chemical manufacturers, CIBO believes that dioxins have not yet been linked to real health effects in humans and that there is little risk to humans from exposure to emissions coming from industrial boilers. Generally, CIBO argues that the government has been too eager to list industrial wastes as hazardous, and that risk assessment needs to be done more carefully before any further controls are placed on solid and liquid wastes.

## TACTICS

CIBO issues an annual report for its members as well as a quarterly newsletter in order to keep them abreast of developments in Washington. As do other trade associations, it uses the considerable lobbying capacities of its individual member corporations to make its points before Congress and the agencies.

## FURTHER INFORMATION

Epstein, Samuel, Lester O. Brown, and Carl Pope (1982). *Hazardous Wastes in America*. San Francisco, Calif.: Sierra Club Books.
U.S. Congress. Senate Committee on Environment and Public Works (1983). *Hearings on Solid Waste Disposal Act Amendments of 1983*. Washington, D.C.: Government Printing Office.

## COUNCIL OF PETROLEUM MARKETERS ASSOCIATION
*See* Petroleum Marketers Association of America.

## COUNCIL OF STATE GOVERNMENTS (CSG)
Iron Works Pike
P.O. Box 11910
Lexington, Kentucky 40578

## ORGANIZATION AND RESOURCES

The Council of State Governments (CSG) was organized in 1933 during the depression in order to combat problems facing the states at that time. It was originally called the American Legislators Association, as the National Governors Association* already existed. Today all fifty states and the territories and commonwealths are represented. The governor of each state and two legislators serve on the governing board. An executive committee is made up of governors, legislators, attorneys general, chief justices, and other elected officials of state government. It is divided into four regions in order to take up issues of special interest to specific regions of the country.

CSG also provides associate membership to business corporations and trade associations such as Union Carbide and the Tobacco Institute. It has an annual budget of approximately $4 million assessed primarily from member states according to a formula based on population. Carl S. Stenberg is executive director of a staff of 100.

## POLICY CONCERNS

The Council of State Governments is concerned about the reduced level of revenue sharing from the federal to state governments during the 1980s. It has seen its responsibilities for many government programs gradually increased over this decade and fewer resources made available for dealing with these increased responsibilities. Generally the states were united in seeking more help from Washington with fewer controls attached, but were unsuccessful.

One issue that most of the coastal states were united on was that the states should have greater input into policies controlling exploration and development of oil and gas resources in the outer continental shelf owned by the federal government but having impacts on the adjoining states' coastlines. Despite the Reagan administration's asserted commitment to states' rights, it opened up leasing to oil companies, and the governors asked Congress to prevent the leasing of all such tracts of land.

The Clean Air Act (CAA) affects the states also, and state representatives have testified before Congress that the states should have more autonomy over the state implementation plans (SIPs) that constitute the main program for achieving air quality standards set by the Environmental Protection Agency (EPA). At the same time states want federal aid for states to administer the law increased.

One major concern of CSG in the 1990s is groundwater quality, as the states' water supplies come increasingly from wells rather than surface water. Withdrawals of groundwater have grown immensely in the 1980s, and the aquifers are not being replenished as fast as they are being used up. Hence, the states, especially in the west, are concerned about adequate supplies for the future. Quality of groundwater is also a concern, as contaminants from agriculture pesticides, leaking toxic waste dumps, septic systems, and other sources increase. The states are reluctant to accept more federal controls over their autonomy, however, and seek to solve their groundwater problems through regional co-operation based on watersheds such as the Delaware River Basin Compact.

CSG was enthusiastic when Congress refunded Superfund to clean up abandoned dumps in 1986. However, they hope to increase their own discretion to determine which sites are designated for cleanup and what the definition of cleanliness should be. They seek to avoid responsibility for paying for the cleanup and to relieve their municipalities of liability for the sites that they own. For many urban states the major crisis of the 1990s will be finding sufficient land space to dispose of solid wastes as well as hazardous wastes. Typically, solid waste managers are turning more to recycling and incineration as alternatives to landfills.

Western states rebelled in the late 1980s over the issue of storage for the nation's radioactive waste and challenged the federal government's exclusive right to determine where to locate these facilities. They hope to be able to veto any decision in the future.

## TACTICS

The governing board meets annually and can call special conferences to take up particular issues of interest to the states. CSG publishes many research studies that discuss problems common to all state governments, including the biennial *Book of the States*. It also publishes *State Government News* monthly and *The Journal of State Government* bimonthly in order to keep its members informed about developments around the states and in Washington. Its national offices remain in Kentucky, although it has a substantial staff in Washington to communicate its concerns to the national government.

## FURTHER INFORMATION

*1988 Year in Review* (1989). Lexington, Ky.: CSG.

Washington Office: Hall of the States, 44 North Capitol Street, Washington, D.C. 20001

## COUNCIL ON ALTERNATE FUELS (CAF)
1225 I Street, N.W., Suite 320
Washington, D.C. 20005

## ORGANIZATION AND RESOURCES

A number of energy corporations founded the Council on Synthetic Fuels in 1980 to advance their interest in obtaining government funding for synthetic fuels and methods of converting one form of energy to another. In 1987 it changed its name to the Council on Alternate Fuels (CAF) because of public disenchantment with the expenditure of government funds on the U.S. Synthetic Fuels Corporation, designed to do research on converting coal and oil shale into liquid and gaseous fuels. In the last decade CAF has worked to involve other corporate organizations, especially major users of energy such as chemical companies, to join them in influencing the federal government to focus on energy supply problems because of national security arguments.

CAF has twenty-eight regular and associate members interested in developing synthetic fuels and manufacturing equipment to use them. They include such industry giants as Amoco, Ashland, Occidental, Shell, and Texaco oil companies, as well as Air Products and Chemicals, Bechtel, Burns & Roe, Dow Chemical, Fluor Corporations, Airco Energy, Ingersoll-Rand, Japan Australia, KRW Energy, Mitsubishi, Sasol, South Pacific Petroleum, and Southern California Gas companies. Its president is Michael S. Koleda, who heads a small staff in Washington. Dues are assessed according to the corporations' profitability and volume of business.

## POLICY CONCERNS

CAF representatives focus on influencing the U.S. Congress to fund synthetic fuel research at a higher level than it has thus far. It also attempts to influence the Department of Energy (DOE) to request more money. The Reagan administration significantly reduced the synfuels portion of the federal research and development budget, but Congress roughly doubled the amount requested from DOE each year. This can be viewed as a partial victory for CAF. Generally energy trade associations such as CAF avow support for free enterprise and market mechanisms to determine prices and drive development of new technology. They make exceptions in cases where industry does not wish to invest its own funds because of the size of the risk involved. They argue that government needs to take a longer-term view of the marketplace than corporations, responding to immediate demands for profitability, can afford to do.

Among the projects for which CAF seeks federal government funding are methods of converting tar sands and oil shale to liquid fuel, techniques for converting coal to liquid and gaseous fuels, and new engine technologies that will enable motor vehicles to use more alcohol as a petroleum substitute. Government support for all of these new technologies is sought on the grounds of national security, arguing that imports from abroad are again rising and that the United States needs to be independent of foreign suppliers.

Because of its massive investment in coal fields, the energy industry also advocates increased government experimentation with methods of using high sulfur coal to generate electricity. CAF argues that government should find ways of burning coal cleanly in old and new boilers. In this policy area it is allied with environmental groups that also want government to find environmentally acceptable methods of using the United States coal supply. They divide on most other issues, however, especially whether such environmental controls were necessary in the first place. CAF regularly testifies to Congress that it must not impose deadlines to reduce sulfur emissions in proposed acid rain legislation until technology is found for electric utilities to reduce sulfur economically. It advocates opening up vast amounts of public lands for mineral exploration to find new supplies of fossil fuels.

## TACTICS

CAF representatives frequently testify before Congress about funding from DOE for research on fossil fuels, but they also call upon executive officers of their respective member companies. CAF puts out *Alternative Fuels News* biweekly for its members, apprising them of developments in Washington. It also sponsors semiannual meetings to keep members abreast of the latest developments in the technology of interest to them, as well as inviting influential members of Congress and officials in DOE to attend. Mobil Oil and other members of the American Petroleum Institute* oppose CAF on the issue of substituting methanol for gasoline in cars, thus creating a rift in the powerful energy lobby.

## FURTHER INFORMATION

*Alternate Fuels News* (1988–89). Washington, D.C.: CAF.

McFarland, Andrew (1984). "Energy Lobbies." *Annual Review of Energy* 9: 501–527.

Mobil Oil (1989). "Problems with Methanol." *The New York Times*, September 23, p. 22.

Stobaugh, Robert, and Daniel Yergin, eds. (1983) *Energy Future*. 3d ed. New York: Vintage Press.

## COUNCIL ON SYNTHETIC FUELS
*See* Council on Alternate Fuels.

## CRITICAL MASS ENERGY PROJECT (CM)
215 Pennsylvania Avenue, S.E.
Washington, D.C. 20003

## ORGANIZATION AND RESOURCES

In 1971 Ralph Nader, a consumer activist, founded Public Citizen,* a nonprofit, citizen research, lobbying, and litigation organization based in Washington. From this organization evolved a number of affiliated groups, including Congress Watch, which monitors consumer legislation on Capitol Hill, and the Health Research Group, which focuses on unsafe foods, drugs, and workplace hazards. Buyers Up is a cooperative that buys fuel oil for the northeast and attempts to keep prices down for low-income consumers. The Citizens Utility Board Campaign (CUB) is a clearinghouse for voluntary citizens' confederations around the United States that provide citizen oversight of utilities and the state commissions that regulate them. In 1974 Ralph Nader convened the first national conference of safe energy activists, and Public Citizen began its Critical Mass Energy Project (CM). Three additional conferences have been held in 1975, 1978, and 1983 to motivate the antinuclear movement.

Critical Mass's goal is to end reliance on nuclear power in the United States and "promote safe, economical, and environmentally sound energy alternatives." It has a budget of about $1 million a year, part of Public Citizen's $3 million. It accepts no funding from government, but does receive some money from foundations. Ralph Nader appoints a board of directors of three for CM. He also hires an executive director, who heads a staff of four in Washington who set policy for the organization, do research on nuclear power, and issue monthly reports to its membership.

## POLICY CONCERNS

Critical Mass has one issue position: all nuclear plants should be phased out and replaced with energy saving technology, small locally based power systems, and renewable energy resources, notably wind, hydropower, and solar projects. Its publications argue that the Price-Anderson Act, which relieves the nuclear industry of much of its financial liability in the event of a catastrophic accident, should be eliminated. In 1987, however, Congress reauthorized Price-Anderson while increasing the liability of industry.

CM also opposed the passage of the Nuclear Waste Policy Act of 1982, which provides for nuclear waste that has been accumulating from power plants around the United States to be buried; no suitable site has been selected yet, and this remains an important unresolved problem that bolsters CM's position. CM opposes industry's desire and NRC's agreement that some radioactive wastes can be classified as "below regulatory concern." It also argues that NRC should increase its control over the radiation exposure of nuclear power plant workers. It opposes any increase in coal- and oil-fired generating capacity to replace the nuclear capacity on the grounds that conservation and renewable sources of energy should be sufficient for the nation's electricity needs.

In 1986 the Senate Committee on Energy and Natural Resources held hearings on industry's proposal to standardize nuclear plant design and speed up the licensing process. Critical Mass, together with the Union of Concerned Scientists,* opposed it, and no action was taken. During the lifetime of CM the nuclear industry has suffered a considerable decline with no new nuclear plants ordered. Some advocates of nuclear power argue this was primarily due to the public relations success of such organizations as CM (Cook, 1980). However, a number of incidents, such as the accidents at Three Mile Island in Pennsylvania in 1979 and Chernobyl in the USSR, have been instrumental in these developments. It would be difficult to separate the impact of Critical Mass on public opinion from external factors.

## TACTICS

Critical Mass publishes an annual survey of nuclear power plant safety violations and accidents and occasional research reports on such topics as the cost of decommissioning nuclear plants and least-cost alternative energy planning. It seeks to reach state government officials and candidates for office with these publications and argues for state autonomy regarding nuclear plant siting in order to slow development further. While the staff of Critical Mass does testify before Congress, its primary focus is on educating the public about the economic, safety, social, and environmental problems of nuclear power.

*FURTHER INFORMATION*

Cook, Constance Ewing (1980). *Nuclear Power and Legal Advocacy*. Lexington, Mass.:
     D. C. Heath.
Gordon, Joshua (1986). *Nuclear Power Safety Report 1979–1985*. Washington, D.C.:
     Public Citizen CM, May 3.
*Public Citizen* (1988, 1989). Washington, D.C.: Public Citizen, March-April.
*See also* Public Citizen.

# D

/

## DEFENDERS OF FURBEARERS
*See* Defenders of Wildlife.

## DEFENDERS OF WILDLIFE
1244 19th Street, N.W.
Washington, D.C. 20035

### HISTORY AND DEVELOPMENT

The Defenders of Furbearers was founded in 1947 by seven naturalists, including Lloyd Symmington, in order to raise public consciousness about the suffering of animals killed for their pelts. In 1959, it was renamed the Defenders of Wildlife and expanded its goals to preserve, enhance, and protect the natural abundance and diversity of wildlife including the integrity of natural wildlife ecosystems for all species. Its most important success was the passage of the Endangered Species Act (ESA) in 1973, although it also considers the Land and Water Conservation Fund (1964), Wildlife Refuge (1966), Marine Protection, Research and Sanctuaries (1972), and Alaska National Interest Lands Conservation (1980) Acts as major landmarks in its fight to prevent humankind from intentionally or inadvertently eradicating other species from the earth.

Joyce M. Kelly became president of the Defenders of Wildlife in May 1986 after serving as the head of the wilderness program in the U.S. Department of Interior's Bureau of Land Management (BLM). During her tenure in BLM, she resisted the asserted plan of its director, Robert Burford, for increasing the amount of wilderness area open to mining and mineral exploration, timber harvesting, and cattle grazing. For her efforts, she won the 1985 Mid-Atlantic regional Stephen T. Mather award presented by the National Parks and Conservation

Association* to federal government employees who "have risked their careers for the preservation of America's environmental integrity."

## ORGANIZATION AND RESOURCES

Defenders of Wildlife has around 80,000 members, from whom it obtains dues of $20 a year; this represents an increase of over 50 percent in membership from the beginning of the Reagan administration. The 24 members of its board of directors are nominated by their predecessors and are elected by the membership. Together with the president, whom it selects, the board sets policy for the organization. Dr. M. Rupert Cutler, an assistant secretary of agriculture in the Carter Administration and former executive director of Population-Environment Balance,* became president in 1988. Defenders has a headquarters staff of 30, who are primarily wildlife biologists and refuge specialists. It also maintains 5 regional offices—the northern Rockies, Southwest, Great Basin, California/Nevada, and Great Lakes—to address area-specific problems.

Its revenues in the late 1980s were around $4 million; 39 percent came from membership dues and 36 percent from contributions from individual conservationists and foundations and corporations such as the Aldermere, Helen V. Brach, Burlington Northern, and the New York Times foundations. The remainder came from individual bequests (18 percent) and investments and merchandizing (7 percent). After expenditures for fund raising (10 percent), membership development (9 percent), communication (8 percent), and general management (15 percent), it spends 36 percent of its budget on educational programs and 22 percent on action programs.

## POLICY CONCERNS

Defenders' major goals are to defend and expand the ESA and other laws passed by Congress to help preserve plant and animal life in the United States and to monitor the administration of those laws. During the late 1970s and throughout the 1980s, it argued against weakening the law to accommodate public works projects such as the Tellico Dam, which had been stopped temporarily by a law suit over the endangered snail darter. For four years it testified before Congress about the need to reauthorize the ESA without weakening its provisions; the new law was signed into law October 7, 1988 by President Reagan.

One of Defenders' most important action programs has been to protect predator species, such as wolves, coyotes, and grizzly bears against ranchers and farmers who argue that they should be hunted and poisoned to reduce the killing of domestic stock. It has attempted to reduce the hunting of wolves in Minnesota and Alaska by educating the public about the habits of wolves through school programs, library exhibits, and publications. In the late 1980s it spearheaded a move to restore the Rocky Mountain gray wolf to Yellowstone National Park to help cope with oversized elk and bison populations, but this proposal met with considerable resistance from local ranchers and Wyoming politicians. Defenders joined with other conservation organizations, including the Natural Resources Defense Council,* suing to stop wolf trapping in Minnesota. They also convinced the Fish and Wildlife Service (FWS) of the U.S. Department of Interior to reintroduce the red wolf into the Alligator River National Wildlife Refuge in North Carolina and resisted local hunters' pressure to allow hunting in the refuge. They also resist attempts by the U.S. Environmental Protection Agency (EPA) to authorize the use of poison against coyotes in areas where ranchers complain about the predators' killing domestic stock.

Defenders also strive to increase the pace at which new species are added to the endangered list. In the late 1980s over 4,000 species of plants and animals were under consideration for listing. Many of these will become extinct before effective action is taken at the government's present rate of listing about 60 species a year, according to Defenders. A campaign initiated in 1978 to have the National Marine Fisheries Service (NMFS) in the U.S. Department of Commerce list the Gulf of California harbor porpoise as an endangered species was finally successful in 1985. This was the first and only species the NMFS agreed to list in the 1980s. Throughout the Reagan years, Defenders argued in Congress against the administration's efforts to reduce funding for the act and the Fish and Wildlife Service budget.

Defenders also protest against the U.S. Forest Service's efforts to increase clear-cutting that destroys the habitat of bears and other threatened species. In 1986 Defenders helped to create Ash Meadows National Wildlife Refuge in Nevada. When the FWS announced it was opening the refuge to hunters, the Defenders and the Sierra Club threatened to sue and succeeded in getting parts of the refuge closed to hunting and camping.

Defenders argue against many oil company requests for drilling permits in various areas in the coastal zone and in wilderness areas, especially in Alaska because of the impact on whales and other wildlife. In 1989 after the disastrous 11 million gallon oil spill in Prince William Sound, it stepped up efforts to prevent exploring for oil in Alaska wildlife refuge areas. In 1987 it worked to convince the Senate to ratify an international treaty prohibiting ocean dumping of plastics that can entangle marine life.

In the late 1980s Defenders expanded its efforts to protect endangered wildlife overseas such as the African elephant that has been decimated by ivory poachers. It urges its members to boycott ivory products and other artifacts from endangered species, as well as wild birds for pets. In 1988 Defenders sued to force the Reagan administration to include overseas actions under the Endangered Species Act requirement that FWS be consulted before any U.S. government action can be taken. It attempts to force the Department of State to reduce Japan's fishing rights in U.S. waters and to penalize Iceland for their defiance of the International Whaling Commission's ban on killing certain endangered whale species. It tries to reduce the number of North Pacific fur seals that can be killed and argues that any animals killed by Pribiloff Island Aleuts for subsistence should be consumed.

## TACTICS

Defenders of Wildlife is a tax-exempt, non-profit corporation that does not contribute to elected officials or parties, but it does seek to influence Congressional representatives and agencies through information and testimony at various hearings. It also educates its own membership and the public through its research and publications efforts and has a 9,000 member network of activists whom it encourages to write elected officials and agency personnel about crucial national, state, and locally important issues. In 1988 Defenders experimented with raising funds from its Montana members to compensate stockmen who lost livestock to wolves reintroduced into Glacier National Park. They hope to be able to reduce rancher resistance to the proposal to add wolves to Yellowstone National Park by defusing the confrontation between stock raisers and conservationists in this manner.

Defenders regularly seek national media attention to their causes and were successful in getting the *Smithsonian, Newsweek, The New York Times,* and TV news programs to cover such issues as aerial wolf killing and the decline of the black-footed ferret population in Wyoming. At the end of the 1980s Defenders joined a coalition of California conservationists to place Proposition 70 on the ballot, a bond issue to acquire state parklands and wildlife habitats in California. Its publication *Defenders* is published every two months. Articles in *Defenders* cover controversial issues such as whether the remaining California condors should be captured in order to breed them in captivity or whether they should be allowed to roam free with the government increasing its efforts to preserve the condors' natural habitat.

### FURTHER INFORMATION

"Annual Report 1988" (1989). *Defenders* 64, no. 4 (July-August): 20–22.
"Defenders Welcomes a New President" (1986). *Defenders* 61, no. 4 (July-August): 6–7.
Fisher, Hank (1989). "Restoring the Wolf." *Defenders* 64, no. 1 (January-February): 9.
Frome, Michael (1988). "Needed: Higher Expectations." *Defenders* 63, no. 4 (July-August): 6–7.
*Saving Endangered Species: Amending and Implementing the Endangered Species Act* (1986). Washington, D.C.: Defenders of Wildlife.

## DUCKS UNLIMITED (DU)
One Waterfowl Way
Long Grove, Illinois 60047

## ORGANIZATION AND RESOURCES

Ducks Unlimited (DU) was founded in 1937 by businessmen who enjoyed duck hunting and feared that dust-bowl conditions in North America would quickly deplenish the duck population. It absorbed a previous organization, More Game Birds, which was started in 1936. Since then, it has grown to 550,000 members. Although founded in Washington, it moved its national headquarters to Illinois. It has focused its attention on conserving wetlands in order to maintain breeding grounds for waterfowl in order to provide an ample supply of ducks to hunt during their annual migrations.

In the late 1980s Ducks Unlimited had revenues of about $60 million a year. Forty-six percent of this came from fund-raising events, such as dinners, golf outings, and clay target shooting, sponsored by local committees; 17 percent came from membership dues; 21 percent came from sponsors such as manufacturers of guns, ammunition, beer, trucks, outboard motors, and other outdoor equipment; 3.4 percent came from advertising in *Ducks Unlimited*; 7.7 percent came from interest; and 5.5 percent came from state governments. The money raised was used primarily (77 percent) to inventory marshland and birds, to buy and develop wetland habitat for waterfowl, and to manage those refuges in Canada, the United States, and Mexico. In addition, 3.2 percent went for fund-raising, 16.4 percent for field operations, and 3.1 percent for administration.

Ducks Unlimited has a 260-member board of trustees, thirteen vice-presidents, nineteen regional vice-presidents, and fifty state committee chairs, as well as presidents from Canadian, Mexican, and New Zealand affiliates. There is a professional staff of twenty-five in Illinois headed by Matthew B. Connolly, Jr., executive vice-president. In addition there are over ninety personnel in the field for various regional flyways.

## POLICY CONCERNS

Ducks Unlimited's main priority is to preserve and protect wetland habitat and upland nesting areas for waterfowl and other wildlife. It cooperates with state conservation departments to inventory and set aside certain areas for wildlife refuges. Its local members frequently object to filling in and using wetlands for new development projects as well as agricultural development. Its biologists estimate that the United States has witnessed a decline from 216 million wetland acres in 1700 to about 92 million acres in the 1980s and that the United States loses about one-half million acres each year. DU argues that any additional loss to housing, shopping malls, or agriculture must be avoided. Since its beginning in 1937, DU has preserved over 4 million nesting/breeding acres in Canada. Since initiating its preservation program in Mexico in 1974 to protect waterfowl wintering areas, DU of Mexico (DUMAC) has placed over 750,000 wintering acres under management in Mexico. Since starting a Matching Aid to Restore States Habitat (MARSH) program in the United States in 1984, DU has placed over 300,000 acres under protection in the most critical areas identified by data from a Landsat satellite.

## TACTICS

Ducks Unlimited concentrates on private solutions to the problem of a diminishing supply of wetlands, but it is not adverse to joining with other wildlife organizations, such as the National Audubon Society,* in advocating preservation of wildlife habitat in the Department of Interior and in the halls of Congress. DU biologists reported that in the 1980s, the duck and geese populations suffered a dramatic depletion similar to that in the dustbowl of the 1930s. The situation was exacerbated by the 1988 summer drought. In 1986 the U.S. and Canadian governments signed the North American Waterfowl Management Plan (NAWMP) designed to restore the duck and geese populations to 1970s levels, and DU, in collaboration with other conservation organizations, undertook to implement this plan. In 1988 it combined forces with The Nature Conservancy* to convince private landowners in the farm belt of the Midwest to leave wetlands unfilled and to create additional small ponds in the flyways. It publishes a bimonthly *Ducks Unlimited* and holds an annual meeting.

## FURTHER INFORMATION

*A Living Legacy* (1989). Long Grove, Ill.:DU.
*Annual Report, 1988* (1989). Long Grove, Ill.: DU.
Ducks Unlimited (1989). Long Grove, Ill.: DU, May-June
*The Duck Depression of the 1980s—An Agenda for Recovery* (1989). Long Grove, Ill.: DU.

# E

---- / ----

**EARTH FIRST! (EF!)**
P.O. Box 5871
Tucson, Arizona 85703

*ORGANIZATION AND RESOURCES*

Earth First! (EF!) is a radical environmental group started in 1980 by Howie Wolke, Dave Foreman, Mike Roselle, Bart Koehler, and Ron Kezar. They were former members and staffers of such organizations as the Wilderness Society* and the Sierra Club,* who consider such large groups too conservative and willing to compromise with industry. EF! has no organizational headquarters nor any lobbying office in Washington. Instead, it has several post office box addresses around the country: New Mexico, California, Oregon, Washington, Texas, Colorado, Florida, and Arizona, where *Earth First!* is published. Each of these locations is autonomous, locally organized, and dependent on the enthusiasm and program of individuals there. There is no governing board nor are there officeholders in the group; there is a conscious effort to keep the group grass-roots oriented, decentralized, and nonhierarchical. There are approximately seventy local groups listed in the EF! directory, most of which are in western states. There are, however, groups in Vermont, Virginia, Wisconsin, Massachusetts, Maryland, and Ohio. In addition, there are some twenty-five local contact persons listed for those states that have no groups.

The organization has no official dues. It publishes *Earth First!* eight times a year out of Tucson, Arizona, and asks individuals to contribute $15 to defray costs. It charges government and business organizations that want to subscribe $50 a year. In 1989 an EF! treasurer's report indicated that the foundation had collected a little over $109,000 in 1988; 65 percent came from earmarked contributions and 33 percent from unrestricted contributions. EF! spent $55,607 in the same year; nearly $50,000 on such projects as an Alaska roadshow, the biodiversity project, and the grizzly bear task force. The remaining funds were spent on meetings and postage. Its members come from the ranks of disaffected environmental organization members, former staffers of such groups, former (or current) employees of government bureaucracies that may be involved in natural resource management, and individual citizens who do not care for hierarchically organized groups, especially those who were involved in social movements such as the civil rights and antiwar movements of the 1960s.

Dave Foreman, one of the founders of EF!, worked for the Wilderness Society from 1973 to 1980 when he resigned because of his belief that the mainline conservation organizations had been co-opted by the Carter administration. He argued that, although many of the officers and staffers in such groups had occupied positions of authority in government during those years, policies coming out of such agencies as the Departments of Interior and Agriculture and EPA had not favored environmental/conservation groups.

Foreman and others attribute this to the fact that these former interest group members adopted conciliatory, moderate stances regarding these issues, but were met with adamant, unrelenting positions by industry. Hence, in such policies as the designation of areas for wilderness review, most of the victories were won by industry and most of the acreage remained open to development. This will remain true, according to EF!, as long as mainstream conservation organizations continue to make arguments based on economic reasoning, such as the importance of tourism and fishing in the Alaskan economy or the failure of the Forest Service to recover costs for building timber roads into national forests for industry to cut old growth. Foreman is a forceful speaker who travels the United States inspiring new environmentalists to activism with his talk on biodiversity, deep ecology, and the need for people to turn away from a homocentric worldview.

*POLICY CONCERNS*

EF!'s groups adopt specific positions regarding particular local problems, and normally take direct action to promote them. In 1981, 75 members of Earth First! demonstrated for the destruction of Glen Canyon Dam by draping 300 feet of black plastic down the side of the dam to resemble a crack. In 1987, 8 members of an Arizona group protested the mining of uranium in the vicinity of the Grand Canyon and were arrested by National Park rangers. Throughout the 1980s EF!'s naval affiliate, the Sea Shepherd, has attempted to protect Canadian Harp Seal pups, dolphins, and whales by interfering directly with hunts. The California group has attempted to reduce the hunting of mountain lions by buying up some of the permits issued by the California Fish and Game Department. In 1984 Earth First! launched a campaign against Burger King and other fast-food chains because of their use of imported Latin American beef that is grown on former rain forest areas that have been clear-cut to make more room to produce beef. It also opposes killing dolphins by tuna fishing boats using drift-nets and advocates boycotting canned tuna.

EF! believes that the U.S. Forest Service is simply an extension of the demands of the timber industry in the United States. It refers to forest rangers as FRED-DIES (Forest Rape Eagerly Done and Done in Endless Sequence), and declared April 21, 1988, the National Day of Protest against the Forest Service, whose only function that EF! sees is to build roads into otherwise roadless areas to facilitate harvesting of timber. Other major targets of Earth First! are the use of off-road vehicles in desert areas, over grazing public lands in the west under the auspices of the Bureau of Land Management, and opening the Alaska Arctic National Wildlife Refuge to oil drilling.

*TACTICS*

One major goal of Earth First! is to stop clear-cutting in the national forests. In June 1985, Howie Wolke, a founding member, was arrested by an employee of Chevron Oil for pulling up survey stakes for a road being laid out in Bridger-Teton National Forest in Wyoming. He was forced to pay Chevron $2,554 in damages and assessed a $750 fine and sentenced to six months in jail by the court. He served all six months because of his refusal to demonstrate remorse for his actions. Other tactics designed to stop timbering in national forest are blockading logging roads and conducting sit-ins in eighty-foot high trees about to be cut down. Another is to spike trees designated for cutting with twenty-penny nails which chew up the blades of saws in the mill. Sometimes the timber companies are warned about the spikes and then have to try to find them with metal detectors before cutting down the trees.

In 1976 the iconoclastic writer and godfather of EF!, Edward Abbey (1927–1989), wrote a novel, *The Monkey Wrench Gang*, which fictionalized the kind of direct actions that have since been adopted by many members of Earth First! Differences of opinion exist about how widespread such activities are. Some Earth Firsters believe that victimized companies fail to report instances of sabotage to police and the authorities do not inform the media because of fears of copycat reactions. A guide to monkey-wrenching was written by Dave Foreman in 1985, which depicts various methods of slowing development of areas, including spiking roads to give flats to logging trucks or off-road vehicles, removing markers from snowmobile trails, using syrup, water, dirt, and carborundum to disable bulldozers and other machines, and burning down billboards. EF! does not have a regular presence in Washington for lobbying purposes, although individuals may testify at departmental hearings on issues such as the designation of areas as wilderness.

On May 30, 1989, four Earth Firsters, Kate Millet, Marc Baker, Mark Davis, and Dave Foreman, were arrested by the FBI and charged with conspiracy to damage power lines leading into the Palo Verde nuclear plant and pylons supporting a cable chairlift at Fairfield Snowbowl ski resort in Arizona. According to *Earth First!*, this happened as a result of infiltration by the FBI of EF! groups in order to gather intelligence about planned activities.

EF! holds an annual rendezvous each summer, at which workshops about various kinds of national and international issues are conducted. Stories about particular local campaigns are carried in the regular issues of *Earth First!* For the most part, individual groups act independently in devising methods of addressing issues in their own areas. Conservative environmental groups have denounced the tactics of Earth First! Jay Hair, president of the National Wildlife Federation,* said, "They are outlaws; they are terrorists; and they have no right being considered environmentalists." However, some groups may regard Earth First! as useful since by comparison their stands are less radical (Steinhart, 1987).

## FURTHER INFORMATION

Abbey, Edward (1968). *Desert Solitaire*. New York: Ballantine Books.
——— (1975). *The Monkey Wrench Gang*. Philadelphia: Lippincott.
Brower, Kenneth (1988). "Mr. Monkeywrench." *Harrowsmith* 40 (September-October): 40–51.
*Earth First!* (1987, 1988, 1989).Tucson, Ariz.: Earth First!, vols. 7, 8, 9.
Fergus, Jim (1988). "The Anarchist's Progress." *Outside*, November, pp. 51–129.
Foreman, Dave (1981) "Earth First!" *The Progressive* (October): 39–42.
——— (1985). *Ecodefense: A Field Guide to Monkeywrenching*. Tucson, Ariz.: Ned Ludd Books.
Malanowski, Jamie (1987). "Money-Wrenching Around." *The Nation*, May 2, pp. 568–570.
Russell, Dick (1987). "The Monkeywrenchers." *The Amicus Journal* 9, no.4 (Fall): 28–42.
Steinhart, Peter (1987). "Respecting the Law." *Audubon*, November, pp. 10–13.

## EARTH ISLAND INSTITUTE (EII)
300 Broadway, Suite 28
San Francisco, California 94133

## ORGANIZATION AND RESOURCES

David Brower established Earth Island Institute (EII) in 1982 as an alternative and more radical ecological group than Friends of the Earth (FOE).* He chairs the fifteen-member board of directors, which in 1986 broke with FOE when it decided to move its operation from San Francisco to Washington. Policy is set by the board, which selected David Phillips and John Knox, former FOE staffers, as coexecutive directors for the ten-person professional staff in San Francisco.

Earth Island Institute is headquartered in San Francisco and claims a membership of 20,000 people who pay $15 a year or more to belong and receive the quarterly *Earth Island*. In the late 1980s it had a budget of $250,000, of which half came from foundation grants and the remainder from dues and other membership fund-raising. One major policy difference David Brower had with other directors of FOE was budgeting and fund-raising strategy. He maintains that "any conservation organization that is not in debt is not doing its job," (Brower, 1984) while his opponents prefer a more conservative fiscal strategy.

## POLICY CONCERNS

The leadership of EII is particularly concerned about the dangers of nuclear power, the devastation of tropical rainforests, the need to preserve endangered species, problems of Indians and natural resource development, pesticide use, and destruction of ecological systems through warfare in southeast Asia and Latin America. They view their concerns as international, convinced that international organizations such as the World Bank, through its loan policies, are destroying the resources of developing nations it is attempting to assist. EII argues that major issues of poverty of the people of Latin America, Asia, and American Indians must be solved if the depletion of natural resources in their homelands is to be halted. Its members have attended conferences on how to put sufficient pressure on international corporations such as Coca-Cola and Burger King to stop destroying rainforests to provide space for growing citrus fruits and cattle.

EII argues that the problems of natural-resource depletion, destruction of ecological systems, and endangered species can only be addressed if human populations can be controlled and destructive international competition over development of new nuclear weapons can be halted. It sees continued warfare in Central America as one of the major challenges to ecologists in the 1990s, and argues for halting development of Star Wars weapons to free funds for education, health, housing, and environmental protection.

## TACTICS

EII does not focus its efforts on lobbying Congress but on educating the public and encouraging them to put pressure on their representatives. It publishes a quarterly, *Earth Island Journal*, which includes reports on ecological disasters around the world. It also belongs to a computer network, Econet, designed to move articles of general interest to various organizations around the world for publication. In 1986 it sponsored a Fate and Hope of the Earth conference in Canada and in 1988 in the Soviet Union. In 1989, in Nicaragua, David Brower met with Daniel Ortega, the Sandanista leader, to discuss a proposed international restoration center for healing the wounds of industrialization in Central America. At that meeting David Brower urged the delegates to "move from global pillage to global tillage" (Russell, 1989).

## FURTHER INFORMATION

Brower, David (1984). "In Wilderness Wanders David Brower, Still Seeking to Preserve the World." *California Magazine*, September, pp. 115–167.
*Earth Island Journal* (1986). San Francisco: EII, vol. 1, Fall.

McPhee, John (1971). *Encounters with the Archdruid*. New York: Farrar, Straus and Giroux.

Russell, Dick (1989). "Nicaraguan Journey." *The Amicus Journal* (Summer): 32–37.

Sale, Kirkpatrick (1986). "The Forest for the Trees." *Mother Jones*, November, pp. 25–58.

## ECOLOGICAL SOCIETY OF AMERICA
*See* The Nature Conservancy.

## EDISON ELECTRIC INSTITUTE (EEI)
1111 19th Street, N.W.
Washington, D.C. 20036–3691

### ORGANIZATION AND RESOURCES

The Edison Electric Institute (EEI) was founded in 1933; in 1975 it absorbed the Electric Energy Association and in 1978 the National Association of Electric Companies. Today it is the trade association for 190 electric utilities, owning 97 percent of the market for electricity in the United States. EEI has a yearly income of about $70 million and expenditures of a similar magnitude. Over $20 million has been devoted each year since 1985 to cleaning up the Three Mile Island nuclear plant in Pennsylvania, an expenditure likely to continue into the 1990s. This is done through voluntary contributions from electric utilities to the General Public Utilities Nuclear Corporation. About $6 million is expended each year through EEI's Media Communication Fund to present the industry's position on energy issues through the mass media. About $3.5 million is used to address regulatory issues that have resulted from the Clean Air Act (CAA). Nearly $6 million is used to address other special issues such as nuclear waste management, relicensing hydroelectric facilities, and utility line problems. Normal activities that consume over $30 million include energy and environmental concerns (22.5 percent) and governmental affairs (20.4 percent), but only 1.5 percent of EEI dues are devoted to lobbying under the Federal Regulation of Lobbying Act.

EEI has a board of directors of 45 representatives from various member companies, including Northeast Utilities, Hawaiian Electric Company, Ohio Edison, South Carolina Electric and Gas Company, and Commonwealth Edison; there are 19 vice-presidents. Thomas R. Kuhn is executive vice-president with a staff of 300.

### POLICY CONCERNS

The most important policy concerns of EEI and its companies are tax and rate regulation and environmental controls. It argues regularly for tax breaks for people investing in electric utilities and for accelerated depreciation of the equipment of the industry. It also lobbies state regulatory commissions that regulate the rates that utilities can charge for such matters as construction work in progress. In 1988 EEI succeeded in getting the U.S. Department of Interior to rule that federal black-lung taxes, abandoned mine land fees, and state severance taxes can all be deducted from royalties on coal produced from federal lands.

One policy on which EEI believes it was outmaneuvered was the passage in 1978 of the Public Utilities Regulatory Policy Act (PURPA). This law forces electric utilities to buy power from cogenerators at a price at or below the replacement cost of that power. EEI argues that this law has had the effect of encouraging large industries to build their own power plants, using gas and oil which were prohibited to electric utilities for years under the Powerplant and Industrial Fuel Use Act (PIFUA), and to avoid purchasing power from the utilities. It argues that PURPA discriminates against utilities that also want to be licensed as qualified cogenerating facilities. It hopes to influence Congress to amend PURPA to redress this imbalance. In 1987 EEI helped get the end-use restrictions that had been placed on gas and oil under the PIFUA rescinded. Residential and commercial heating plants are no longer favored by the law; powerplants may use gas and oil also.

In 1986 it lobbied effectively to achieve passage of a law that specifies that relicensed hydroelectric projects do not have to prefer municipally owned utilities when selling their energy. The energy generated can be sold to any willing buyer, whether public or private, whereas in the past municipally owned utilities were preferred. It also lobbies the Interstate Commerce Commission to set rail rates that do not discriminate against power plants dependent on railroads to transport coal for use in generating electricity.

EEI advocates increasing the number of nuclear power plants and argues that the Soviet Chernobyl power station was different from U.S. commercial nuclear plants. The industry worked to get the Price Anderson Act extended in 1988 for fifteen years to protect the nuclear industry from liability for nuclear accidents. This was successful, but the liability limit was extended to $64 million per reactor per accident. In 1986 EEI argued for a standardized nuclear power plant design that would reduce costs and also for consolidating licensing to speed the process. It advocates that the U.S. government speed the process of finding a solution to the nuclear waste problem which it perceives would greatly reduce public opposition to siting new nuclear plants. It 1989 EEI was successful in delaying implementation of a Nuclear Regulatory Commission rule that would require the industry to maintain $1.06 billion in nuclear property insurance with decontamination costs given higher priority than property repair or replacement.

EEI representatives were successful in convincing the Senate Committee on Energy and Natural Resources that the commercial and residential energy audit program mandated by the National Energy Conservation Act of 1978 should be eliminated. They argued that there is no need to regulate, as the marketplace can produce energy conservation without government mandate. They argued both that there was little response from the residential sector and that poor residents end up subsidizing the middle-class consumers who take advantage of it. EEI also supported appliance manufacturers in modifying the law to reduce the strictness of national energy efficiency standards for appliances.

The EEI has what it calls a "balanced approach" to air and water quality, solid waste disposal, and other environmental regulations that it argues add greatly to the costs of doing business. Representatives of EEI have testified that the idea of preventing significant deterioration under the CAA in clean areas of the country is unrealistic and that buffer zones around national parks and other protected places are not useful for visibility. It urges all government agencies to consider costs and to do outside studies of the utility of all regulations. EEI representatives testified against reducing sulfur oxides to control acid rain on the grounds that such a strategy might actually increase carbon dioxide emissions, and that clean air issues must be considered as a whole. They argued that too much money has already been expended on controlling sulfur oxides, that we know very little about the benefits of this program, and that the global warming issue must be addressed comprehensively.

EEI and its research associate, the Electric Power Research Institute,* have done many studies of the costs of present sulfur oxide reduction technology, and both argue that any further reduction would put an undue burden on midwest utilities which are already hard pressed. In addition, sulfur oxides have already been reduced considerably as old plants are being phased out, and the present regulations should be given a chance.

In Superfund amendment discussions EEI has argued effectively to prevent Congress from defining fly ash from power plants as hazardous waste. It has urged the Federal Highway Administration to designate coal fly ash as safe for fill in highway projects. It seeks to reduce the costs of disposal of fly ash wherever possible by influencing government to define it as useful construction material rather than dangerous waste material. EEI also has argued before Congress that the Clean Water Act should be relaxed to be less concerned with storm water runoff from waste disposal sites near electric generating plants. It also opposes any proposal by the Environmental Protection Agency to regulate power plant sites as potential contributors to groundwater contamination.

## TACTICS

EEI is one of the most powerful lobbying organizations in Washington. Like the American Petroleum Institute,* it uses the executive officers of many of its member corporations to plead its case before the Federal Energy Regulatory Commission, the Environmental Protection Agency, and Congress. It spends much of its budget communicating directly with the public through the mass media and through its own publications and educational films it makes for schools and public service organizations. It also publishes *Electric Perspectives* quarterly for distribution throughout the industry.

## FURTHER INFORMATION

*Acid Rain: The Sensible Strategy* (1986). Washington, D.C.: EEI.
*EEI 1986–87 Annual Report* (1988). Washington, D.C.: EEI.
McFarland, Andrew (1984). "Energy Lobbies." *Annual Review of Energy* 9: 501–527.

Rosenbaum, Walter A. (1987). *Energy, Politics, and Public Policy*. 2d ed. Washington, D.C.: Congressional Quarterly Press.

Stobaugh, Robert, and Daniel Yergin, eds. (1983). *Energy Future*. 3d ed. New York: Vintage Press.

U.S. Congress. Senate Committee on Energy and Natural Resources (1986). *Hearings on PURPA*. Washington, D.C.: Government Printing Office.

## ELECTRIC ENERGY ASSOCIATION

*See* Edison Electric Institute.

## ELECTRIC POWER RESEARCH INSTITUTE (EPRI)

3412 Hillview Avenue
P.O. Box 10412
Palo Alto, California 94303

### ORGANIZATION AND RESOURCES

The Electric Power Research Institute (EPRI) is the research arm of the electric power industry, serving the same function as the Gas Research Institute* does for the gas industry. It is not a trade association as is the Edison Electric Institute,* but it derives it revenues from the same sources, namely, the major suppliers of electricity in the United States. In 1972 many of the investor-owned utilities decided to band together to conduct cooperative research into the production, transmission, and use of electric energy that it was unlikely they could accomplish on their own.

Since that time about 500 electric utilities have joined and contributed to EPRI's research mission, ranging from such important private corporations as Commonwealth Edison and Northern States Power, to major federal industries such as the Tennessee Valley Authority and Bonneville Power, to small rural electric cooperatives. Over 70 percent of investor-owned electric capacity is represented in EPRI, and over 30 percent of both cooperative and municipal utilities, and fully 100 percent of federally generated power.

Floyd Culler served as president from 1978 to 1988, but he retired in 1988 and was replaced by Richard E. Balzhiser. There is a twenty-four-person board of directors; a twenty-six-person advisory council including William Ruckelshaus, former administrator of the U.S. Environmental Protection Agency (EPA), and Stewart Udall, former secretary of the interior; and a thirty-four-person research advisory committee, all from power companies.

In the late 1980s about $350 million was raised and expended yearly by EPRI, 100 percent from electric utilities or interest on investments. Administrative expenses and cost of distributing information represented about 7 percent of the budget, and 94 percent went to funding research. Of the program funds, 85 percent went to outside contractors and 15 percent remained for in-house research. EPRI employed 725 individuals in its headquarters in Palo Alto, California, and its Washington office. In addition, many executive officers of EPRI's members are available for testifying before congressional committees and agencies such as EPA.

## POLICY CONCERNS

EPRI's research and development program is divided into four major parts: generation, environment, utilization, and delivery. The most important, technologies for generating power, account for nearly half its budget. Under this part of its research EPRI focuses on finding new ways of burning fossil fuels and extending the life of present fossil fuel–fired plants. One technology it has developed is atmospheric fluidized-bed combustion which enables utilities to burn coal without costly flue gas scrubbing to reduce pollutants. EPRI also works on methods for converting coal to gas and on potential economic uses of the sulfur oxides removed from the coal in the gasification process. It has focused on standardizing nuclear plant design in order to reduce the costs of nuclear power and environmental objections and fears about nuclear safety. EPRI has also worked on improving hydroelectric generation and the technology of photovoltaic cells to produce electricity from the sun at a cost competitive with other sources.

EPRI uses 27 percent of its R&D budget on environmental problems generated by electric power. It has studied methods for removing sulfur oxides from coal and emissions from coal-burning plants. It has also worked on disposal methods for by-products from treating coal. It and its contractors also search for technologies to reduce nitrogen oxides from combustion and is seeking cost-effective methods of treating the emissions. EPRI has also devoted resources to studying the effects of electric magnetic fields on human health because scientists outside the industry have suggested that this technology may have detrimental side effects. It has also studied ways of making the nuclear power industry safer and more cost-effective to increase reliability and improve maintenance processes.

EPRI devotes 12 percent of its research resources to methods of delivering electricity to customers, looking for new ways to protect high-tension wires, and developing new methods of transforming power and repairing lines through robots. It devotes 10 percent to finding new ways to utilize electric power and promoting them. These include extending the range and speed of electric cars by developing better batteries, and more uses for electricity in computer-controlled residences of the future.

## TACTICS

EPRI does not officially lobby, but it maintains a presence in Washington. Employees of EPRI have testified about acid deposition before the Senate Committee on the Environment, arguing that not enough is known about the effects of acid rain to justify more controls on sulfur oxides. EPRI also produces dozens of research reports yearly that are widely distributed in government agencies and before Congress, to universities, as well as throughout the utility industry. This information may find its way to Congress and the agencies when experts who are funded by EPRI testify about the energy supply and the latest technology and any problems it may be generating. It also publishes the *EPRI Journal* eight times a year to report about the latest research that it has funded, including articles about waste-to-energy plants, superconductivity, and other recent developments in the industry.

## FURTHER INFORMATION

Chubb, John E. (1983). *Interest Groups and the Bureaucracy*. Stanford, Calif.: Stanford University Press.
*EPRI Journal* (1989). Palo Alto, Calif.: EPRI, January-February.
McFarland, Andrew (1984). "Energy Lobbies." *Annual Review of Energy* 9: 501–527.
Rosenbaum, Walter A. (1987). *Energy, Politics, and Public Policy*. 2d ed. Washington, D.C.: Congressional Quarterly Press.
Stobaugh, Robert, and Daniel Yergin, eds. (1983). *Energy Future*. 3d ed.
New York: Vintage Press.
Washington office: 1800 Massachusetts Ave., N.W., Suite 700 Washington, D.C. 20036

## ELECTRICITY CONSUMERS RESOURCE COUNCIL (ELCON)
1707 H Street, N.W., Suite 1050
Washington, D.C. 20006

### ORGANIZATION AND RESOURCES

The Electricity Consumers Resource Council (ELCON) was established in 1976 by industrial consumers who wanted a guaranteed adequate power supply and low prices. Twenty corporations belong to ELCON: Air Products and Chemicals, Anheuser-Busch, Armco, Bethlehem Steel, Cone Mills, Corning Glass, Diamond Shamrock, Du Pont, Dow Chemical, FMC, General Motors, Hercules, Hershey Foods, Kaiser Aluminum, Olin, Owens-Corning, PPG, A. E. Staley, Staufer, and Union Carbide. All contribute according to their volume of business, which produces an annual budget for ELCON of about $650,000. There is a five-person staff in Washington.

### POLICY CONCERNS

One policy of particular interest to industrial consumers of electric power is the issue of cogeneration of electricity by large users. Since the nineteenth century some industries have generated part of their own electricity and used the waste heat from the turbines in other industrial processes. Until the passage of the Public Utilities Regulatory Policy Act (PURPA) in 1978, however, electric utility companies were not obligated to supply supplemental power to such companies nor to purchase any excess electricity that such cogenerators create. PURPA requires state regulatory commissions to allow—indeed, to favor—cogeneration. In addition, the Federal Energy Regulatory Commission (FERC), which administers PURPA, has also ruled that utilities must provide for moving electric power through nationwide grids, which allow large customers to shop for suppliers of energy on a competitive basis. ELCON takes the position that such regulations enable large industrial electricity users to compete in the market with the utilities that formerly had a monopoly on the supply, and this can only be good for the general ratepayer.

ELCON's representatives also argue that industrial users are charged higher prices than are other consumers in order to subsidize residential customers who are more numerous and therefore more influential with state rate control commissions. ELCON argues, along with other users of electricity, that construction work in progress should be paid for by the utilities and not put into the rate base and charged to end users. In these policies the interests of industrial users diverge from those of the suppliers of energy. The Edison Electric Institute* takes a much different view of such issues.

Other issues of interest to ELCON also center around its desire to keep down electricity costs, but in these policies ELCON's interest coincides with that of its suppliers. In 1986 representatives of ELCON testified to the Senate Committee on Energy that nuclear plants should be standardized to facilitate licensing so as not to close out the nuclear option for electricity. ELCON members felt that having many different sources would increase competition and lower prices in the electric industry. ELCON also argues against Clean Air Act acid rain amendments that would increase costs to electric plants. Like the producers and sellers of electricity, ELCON argues government should study the problem rather than take action against sulfur or nitrogen oxide emissions on the ground that pollutants have been reduced already and no further efforts are needed.

## TACTICS

ELCON holds a convention every three years in Washington. It also issues the *ELCON Report* to its members quarterly to keep them abreast of developments in the nation's capital. ELCON representatives testify before the Federal Energy Regulatory Commission (FERC) along with other major electricity consumers such as the American Iron and Steel Institute,* and representatives of many of ELCON's individual member corporations. ELCON generally prefers that FERC make decisions about what costs are permitted into the electricity generators' rate base, but it also lobbies state regulatory agencies and Congress for changes in federal laws.

### FURTHER INFORMATION

*ELCON Report* (1988; 1989). Washington, D.C.: ELCON, first quarter; last quarter.

## ENERGY CONSERVATION COALITION (ECC)
1525 New Hampshire Avenue, N.W.
Washington, D.C. 20036

## ORGANIZATION AND RESOURCES

The Energy Conservation Coalition (ECC) is a group of nineteen environmental, consumer, church, and scientific organizations: American Association of Retired Persons, Citizen/Labor Energy Coalition, Environmental Action,* Environmental Policy Institute,* Federation of American Scientists, Friends of the Earth,* Renew America,* International Institute for Energy Conservation, Jobs in Energy, League of Women Voters,* National Consumers Law Center, National Consumers League, National Wildlife Federation,* Natural Resources Defense Council,* Public Citizen,* Sierra Club,* United Methodist Church, Union of Concerned Scientists,* and U.S. Public Interest Research Group.

It was founded in 1981 in order to increase public awareness of energy conservation methods and to find ways of obtaining low-cost energy for the poor. It was a two-person operation until 1986 when ECC joined with Environmental Action (EA) to share staff and office space in Washington. In the late 1980s ECC had a annual budget of $73,000, 90 percent of which came from grants from its member groups; the remainder came from publication sales.

## POLICY CONCERNS

ECC advocates reducing our reliance on nuclear power and additional fossil fuel–fired power plants. It argues that electric utilities already have excess capacity in most regions of the country and that additional construction can be avoided through energy conservation techniques. It supports the concept of energy audits supplied free by utilities to property owners in order to encourage conservation, a measure opposed by electric utilities and independent engineering firms alike. ECC believes that if all consumers learned to conserve energy, it could be provided for all segments of the population at less cost.

ECC has long advocated increasing the 25 mpg corporate average fuel efficiency standard for passenger cars. Congress initially established a 27.5 mpg standards for model year 1985, but this was postponed several times during the Reagan administration. It was finally declared the Bush administration's official goal for 1990, and ECC began a new campaign to have this increased to 45 mpg for cars and 35 mpg for light trucks. It also advocated passage of the National Appliance Energy Conservation Act, passed in March 1987, which established minimum appliance efficiency standards for all major household appliances.

ECC opposed the passage of the 1982 Nuclear Waste Policy Act, and has proven an active critic of the Department of Energy's attempts to implement the law by locating a site for a permanent nuclear waste deposit facility. In 1987 it pointed out the possibility that a temporary monitored retrievable storage facility might become a *de facto* permanent solution if all states refuse to host a permanent site. It also opposed the extension of the Price-Anderson Act, which absolves the nuclear industry of most liability in nuclear accidents. In 1987 this law was extended, but the industry's liability was increased.

## TACTICS

ECC conducts workshops at the state level for consumer and environmental groups interested in reducing reliance on increased power plant capacity. ECC, in cooperation with Environmental Action, publishes *Power Line* quarterly to inform the public about developments in energy policy, including actions regarding nuclear waste policy at the national level, as well as state rate regulations. In it, ECC and EA seek to counter the arguments of the utility industry for building additional capacity. It also argues that the Nuclear Regulatory Commission, as presently constituted, is in the pocket of industry and fails to perform its public safety function adequately.

### FURTHER INFORMATION

*Least-Cost Electrical Strategies* (1987). Washington, D.C.: ECC.
Noogee, Alan (1987). *Gambling for Gigawatts.* Washington, D.C.: Environmental Action.
*Power Line* (1987). Washington, D.C.: ECC, January-February-March.
Rudolph, Richard, and Scott Ridley (1986). *Power Struggle: The Hundred Year War Over Electricity.* New York: Harper and Row.

## ENERGY POLICY TASK FORCE OF THE CONSUMER FEDERATION OF AMERICA

*See* Consumer Energy Council of America.

## ENVIRONMENTAL ACTION (EA)

1525 New Hampshire Avenue, N.W.
Washington, D.C. 20036

### ORGANIZATION AND RESOURCES

In Spring 1970, Earth Day was celebrated on many college campuses around the United States, sponsored by local environmental activists. The national organizers of the event founded Environmental Action (EA) that year in order to keep alive the spirit and goals of the movement. By the late 1980s, EA had 10,000 members, who pay $25 in dues each year. The professional staff in Washington number twenty, headed by Ruth Caplan, who replaced Alden Meyer as executive director when he moved to the League of Conservation Voters* in 1986. The staff and executive director reach policy decisions by consensus. In 1986 the Energy Conservation Coalition* merged with EA to streamline operations, and in 1988 the Environmental Task Force joined with the Environmental Action Foundation.

In the late 1980s EA had an annual budget of a little over $400,000. Forty-seven percent of its revenues came from dues, and 42 percent from contributions from the same members in special appeals. The remainder came from grants from its affiliated Environmental Action Foundation, which raises tax-deductible money for research under Section 501(c)(3) of the tax code. EAF raises over

$500,000 a year from contributions, bequests, and foundation grants. Grants came from the Beldon Fund, Compton Foundation, Joyce Foundation, and the McIntosh Foundation, among others. Both EA and EAF spend approximately 56 percent of their budget on programmatic matters and devote about 20 percent each to fund-raising activities and general administration of their programs.

## POLICY CONCERNS

EA is concerned with all environmental issues, but its staff focused on two major projects in the 1980s. One of its priorities continues to be toxic substances and waste disposal. Its representatives argued for the Superfund Amendments and Reauthorization Act (SARA) which was passed by Congress in October 1986, and signed into law by President Reagan. EA attributed the president's agreement to grass-roots pressure placed on Republican senatorial candidates up for reelection in November 1986. EA worked to include a community right-to-know provision in SARA, which provides that chemical companies must inform public safety officials in communities of the nature of the chemical hazards stored there. It is now concerned that the U.S. Environmental Protection Agency (EPA) intends to water down this law by exempting all firms with less than 10,000 pounds of toxic materials stored on site from this requirement and is working to prevent this. One provision that EA was not successful in getting in SARA was a provision for parties injured by toxic dumps that would have enabled them to sue in federal court for damages. It has launched a Toxics Liability Campaign to work with victims of pollution and encourage them to take their cases to state courts, including the publication of *Making Polluters Pay: A Citizens' Guide to Legal Action and Organizing*.

In the 100th Congress, another EA goal that failed was reauthorization of the Clean Air Act (CAA), and increased controls on toxic emissions and sulfur oxides to reduce acid rain. EA hopes to remedy this, however, in the 1990s.

EA also advocates bottle bills and deposit laws in the various states which would force consumers and producers to recycle glass and other materials. It seeks to reduce the amount of landspace used for solid waste disposal, but EA does not consider incineration as the solution because it considers this an unproven technology that has many environmental problems of its own, especially air pollution. One of the major objectives for EA in the 1990s is to reduce the use of plastics for packaging and to emphasize the need to develop alternative degradable materials.

EA's second priority after waste disposal is energy conservation, and it has merged with the Energy Conservation Coalition.* EA opposes nuclear energy and considered it a victory when the utilities' proposal to streamline nuclear licensing by standardizing nuclear plant design failed passage. However, a defeat was suffered in 1988 when the Price-Anderson Act that protects the nuclear power industry from liability for accidents was reauthorized for another fifteen years. The liability was increased from $700 million to $7 billion, which EA supported. EA was particularly disturbed by the proposals to find sites for permanent storage of nuclear wastes that are presently stored temporarily near nuclear reactors and on Department of Energy (DOE) weapons manufacturing sites. Revelations about leaks from several weapons plants run by DOE contractors in the late 1980s gave EA reason to hope that Congress will halt its efforts to force one of the scarcely populated western states to accept a nuclear storage facility.

Another legislative victory came in 1986 with the passage of the tax reform bill which included the closing of several tax loopholes EA staff considered to be tax subsidies to the electric utility industry. EA advocates reducing the number of nuclear and fossil fuel–fired plants and recovery of energy through conservation methods instead. It argues that twenty-two large power plants could be avoided through better use of the energy we have. In 1986 it worked for the passage of the National Appliance Energy Conservation Act, establishing energy efficiency standards for all major household appliances, which was signed into law in March 1987. During the heat wave of the summer of 1988 EA emphasized the threat to the world's climate from the greenhouse effect and increased its efforts to convince Congress, the media, and the public that it is crucial to reduce the amount of fossil fuels burned and to increase conservation efforts instead. After the Exxon *Valdez* 11-million-gallon oil spill in March 1989, EA redoubled its efforts to prevent drilling for oil in Alaska's Arctic National Wildlife Refuge and argued Exxon should continue its cleanup efforts that it terminated in September 1989.

## TACTICS

EAF concentrates on doing research and publications, whereas EA itself lobbies Congress and the agencies and develops media and public information. EA also has an Environmental Action Political Action Campaign, EnAct/PAC, which raises money from the membership and makes contributions to individual congressional campaigns. Each year it publishes the Dirty Dozen, a list of twelve senators and representatives with the most antienvironmental voting record. EA organizers also go into some congressional campaigns where environmental supporters face difficult reelection battles or where there is a chance to defeat an antienvironmental member of congress. It publishes lists of members of Congress who receive the most campaign contributions from petrochemical and nuclear PACs. In the 1988 election thirty-nine of fifty-one EA-endorsed congressional candidates were elected, including three opponents of the dirty dozen incumbents targeted by EA. It also endorsed the presidential candidacy of Michael Dukakis on his environmental record in Massachusetts.

EA publishes a bimonthly report for its members entitled *Environmental Action*, in which it urges its members to write their members of Congress about environmental issues and reports on developments in Washington on these matters. Its staff also write longer pieces on such controversial issues as acid rain, mothballing nuclear plants in the northwest, and food preservatives. Within each issue there is a special section, *Re:Sources*, that is produced by the Energy

Conservation Coalition within EA. EAF also publishes a bimonthly energy news-journal entitled *Power Line* and several monographs.

### FURTHER INFORMATION

Audette, Rose Marie (1989). "The Greenhouse Effect." *Environmental Action*, January-December, pp. 17–19.

*Environmental Action* (1987, 1988). Washington, D.C.: EA, March-April, May-June, September-October.

Ledbetter, Sandra (1988). "Environmental Action's Dirty Dozen of 1988." *Environmental Action*, September-October, pp. 10–15.

Millar, Fred (1988). "Every Towns Needs a Hazard Analysis." *Environmental Action*, (September-October): 22–23.

Moore, A. (1986). *Making Polluters Pay: A Citizen's Guide to Legal Action and Organizing.* Washington, D.C.: EA.

Nogee, Alan (1987). *Gambling for Gigawatts.* Washington, D.C.: EA.

"Recycling Plastics: A Forum" (1988). *Environmental Action*, July-August, pp. 21–25.

The Role of Energy Conservation in Acid Rain Control in the Midwest (1987). Washington, D.C.: Environmental Action.

## ENVIRONMENTAL ACTION FOUNDATION
*See* Environmental Action.

## ENVIRONMENTAL DEFENSE FUND (EDF)
257 Park Avenue South
New York, New York 10010

### ORGANIZATION AND RESOURCES

In 1966 a Long Island attorney, Victor Yannacone, filed a lawsuit on behalf of his wife against the Suffolk County Mosquito Control Commission to stop its spraying of DDT which was killing fish and wildlife in the area. To substantiate his charges Mr. Yannacone sought expert help from scientists who could furnish facts about the impact of DDT. His search for scientific talent led him to the Brookhaven Town Natural Resource Committee, some of whose members later helped found the Environmental Defense Fund (EDF). Encouraged by their successful lawsuit, the Yannacones and eight scientist friends incorporated EDF on October 6, 1967, without capital, members, or officers, and filed suit to stop DDT and dieldrin spraying in Michigan and Wisconsin. Ultimately these suits had the effect of getting the U.S. Environmental Protection Agency (EPA) to ban DDT in the United States.

The founding members of EDF included ten environmental scientists, conservationists, and attorneys, including Arthur Cooley, a high school science teacher, and Charles F. Wurster, professor of Marine Sciences, who remained members of the board of trustees in 1989. Three other founding members continued as honorary trustees. The board, which sets policy for EDF, numbered thirty-six in 1989 and was headed by Frank E. Loy, who is also president of the German Marshall Fund of the United States. Other trustees include Dr. Irving Selikoff of Mount Sinai School of Medicine, Richard B. Stewart of Harvard Law School, and several partners in major law firms. The executive director, Fredrick D. Krupp, heads a staff of about 100, including 17 attorneys and 29 scientists and economists. EDF's headquarters are in New York City, but it has opened additional offices in Oakland, California; Boulder, Colorado; Richmond, Virginia; Raleigh, North Carolina; Austin, Texas; and Washington, D.C. where it represents environmental causes before Congress and the administrative agencies as well as the courts.

EDF's revenues in 1989 were over $12 million, of which about 57 percent came from dues of $35 from its 100,000 members, plus other contributions. The remainder came from foundation grants, 27 percent; investments, 5 percent; government grants, 3 percent; bequests, 7 percent; and attorney's fees obtained from opposing litigants in successful law cases, 1 percent. In 1987 EDF recovered 6 percent of its income in attorneys' fees, but this was due to the conclusion of some large cases, and by the end of the 1980s attorneys' fees had returned to their normal 1 percent of revenues. EDF spends 80 percent of its budget for program activities. These are divided into energy and air quality, 11 percent; toxic chemicals, 18 percent; wildlife protection and water resources, 24 percent; education, 13 percent; membership information, 6 percent; and legislative action, 1 percent. Support services take up the remaining 20 percent, including general administrative expenses, fund-raising, and membership development. In addition to its $12 million budget, EDF also has set a goal to raise $5 million for future work, and by the end of 1989 it had topped the $3 million mark.

## POLICY CONCERNS

In the 1980s EDF concentrated on four major program areas: energy, toxic chemicals, wildlife preservation, and water and land resources. It conducted research on acid rain and argued for increasing limits on sulfur oxides and other emissions under the Clean Air Act (CAA). Representatives of EDF have testified before Congress each time the CAA was under review, and they have also argued before state legislatures including Wisconsin's and Massachusetts', to increase state control over sulfur oxides. An EDF study of Chesapeake Bay revealed that nitrates in acid rain cause algae blooms that deplete oxygen in seawater, suffocating sea life. In the late 1980s EDF turned its attention to two major air pollution problems: depletion of the ozone layer in the upper atmosphere and global warming due to the greenhouse effect caused by accumulated carbon dioxide. In September 1987, EDF helped to secure an international protocol signed in Montreal freezing the use of chlorofluorocarbons (CFCs) at present levels and seeking to halve use of the chemicals by 1999 in order to slow the ozone depletion problem.

Another EDF priority is its desire to reduce human exposure to toxic materials, such as asbestos, through strict air pollution standards and by keeping hazardous wastes out of landfills and the water supply. From 1983 to its amendment in 1987, EDF representatives testified in hearings before Congress to reauthorize and amend the Resource Conservation and Recovery Act (RCRA), which controls the disposal of hazardous wastes. It argued to ban land disposal of liquid hazardous wastes, to eliminate the exemption for small generators, for more inspections by EPA, for controlling exports of hazardous wastes, and to allow intervention by citizen suits and to award attorney's fees for successful interventions.

EDF also testified in favor of the Superfund Amendment and Reauthorization Act of 1987 (SARA), and for a victim compensation fund, which Congress did not pass. It argued against excessive use of pesticides, which run off into the water table, and for tighter controls over underground storage tanks for gasoline and other hazardous materials.

Under its water and land resources program EDF staffers have argued for eliminating the need for more dams and irrigation projects through conservation and more efficient use of water. Its Rural Economy and Environment Program promotes water conservation by arguing that farmers with irrigation rights should sell some of their water rights to cities, thereby reducing the pressure for new expensive water reclamation projects, such as the Two Forks Dam in Colorado. In 1989 EPA administrator William Reilly vetoed this project after much lobbying by EDF. EDF staffers have also helped facilitate an agreement between the Los Angeles Metropolitan Water District and the Imperial Irrigation District by which the water district pays for water-saving measures in the nearby irrigation district in order to obtain water from it instead of building a costly canal project to bring northern California water to the south.

In recent years EDF has expanded its activities into the international arena and has joined the ranks of environmental groups seeking to make the U.S. government and international lending institutions such as the World Bank more sensitive to the ecological impacts of their fiscal policies in developing nations. It argues against clear-cutting tropical rain forests in order to raise cattle for sale abroad because of the resulting desertification of sensitive areas in developing areas. EDF also opposes the forced resettlement of populations in tropical countries such as India and Brazil to newly clear-cut areas. Instead it seeks to substitute solutions to overpopulation through creating sustainable yields in such commodities as nuts and rubber. In February 1989, a rubber tapper and leader of Brazilian conservationists, Francisco "Chico" Mendes Filho, was killed after organizing peasants against landowners who favor burning and clearing the tropical rain forest. EDF had worked with him and made his death a rallying point for stepped-up efforts to internationalize its activities.

In the field of wildlife protection EDF in 1972 advocated and obtained a ban on the use of DDT in the United States mainly because of its threat to endangered species. It has argued for the inclusion of many species of both flora and fauna under the Endangered Species Act, and in 1988 successfully testified in favor of the reauthorization of that law. It attaches high priority to protecting sensitive habitats, and was instrumental in convincing Congress to reverse the Department of Interior's decision in the early 1980s to open parts of the National Wildlife Refuge System to oil and gas leasing. EDF also was instrumental in the passage of the Marine Mammal Protection Act which reduced the toll of dolphins killed each year in fishing nets. Its staff has watchdogged the implementation of this law and now seeks to extend protection to endangered turtles that perish in shrimpers' nets. In 1988 it worked for U.S. ratification of Annex V of the Marpol Convention requiring oceangoing vessels to dispose of plastic debris, which can kill or injure marine species, on shore rather on the high seas. EDF wildlife scientist Bruce Manheim served for most of the 1980s as a U.S. delegate to the convention on the Conservation of Antarctic Marine Living Resources to secure concessions from fishing nations to protect Antarctic marine life. He argues against opening this last wilderness to mineral development and against the discharge of raw sewage and open burning by the scientific research stations there.

## TACTICS

In its early years, EDF concentrated on bringing together environmental attorneys and natural scientists to pursue law cases primarily against government agencies in order to force them to become more environmentally aware of the consequences of their actions. It began its history with litigation forcing the federal government to write environmental impact statements about such projects as highways and dams and eliminating such pesticides as DDT from use in the United States.

In the 1980s, EDF added a number of economists to its staff and sought to find innovative solutions to problems of unemployment and water and energy supply that are less ecologically damaging than traditional ones. While continuing to advocate strong laws and to go to court to have them enforced, it has sought to cooperate with former antagonists such as major utility companies and convince them to invest in conservation and alternative energy supplies. EDF leadership perceives this as the "third stage of environmentalism" after the initial consciousness-raising and confrontation stages.

EDF staff, for example, developed a computer model to compare the cost-effectiveness of traditional utility investment in generating plants with alternatives such as conservation through insulation, cogeneration, load management, and energy-efficient appliances. It tackled this problem by direct negotiations with large utilities such as Pacific Gas and Electric in California and argued that it could save PG&E's consumers money while increasing the utility's own profit margin.

EDF publishes a newsletter five times a year for its membership to inform them of recent court victories as well as other developments in the environmental field. It also publishes an annual report as well as occasional research reports and books on specific ecological topics.

### FURTHER INFORMATION

*Annual Report 1989–1990* (1990). New York: EDF.

*EDF Letter* (May, October, December 1986; March, June, November 1987; January, April, June, September, December 1988; February, May, August, October 1989). New York: EDF.

*Environmental Defense Fund 20th Anniversary Report 1967–1987* (1988). New York: EDF.

Udall, Stewart (1988). *The Quiet Crisis and the Next Generation.* Layton, Utah: Gibbs Smith.

Washington Office: 1616 P Street, N.W. Washington, D.C. 20036

## THE ENVIRONMENTAL FUND
*See* Population-Environment Balance, Incorporated.

## ENVIRONMENTAL LAW INSTITUTE (ELI)
1616 P Street, N.W., Suite 200
Washington, D.C. 20036

### ORGANIZATION AND RESOURCES

The Environmental Law Institute (ELI) was founded in 1969 by a group of attorneys associated with The Conservation Foundation* as a national nonprofit research and educational institution to fill a need for information about statutes, regulations, and court decisions in the new area of environmental law. With financial support from the Ford Foundation, ELI was created to conduct research and to publish *The Environmental Reporter*, a compendium of legislative and regulatory developments, which includes full texts of recent federal and state trial and appellate court decisions.

In the late 1980s it had a thirty-person board of directors, including advocates of environmental causes and representatives of industry. There is a fifty-member professional staff directed by J. William Futrell, president of ELI, consisting of lawyers, economists, scientists, and journalists.

In the late 1980s ELI had a budget of over $3 million, derived partly from dues of between $25 and $50 from its 800 individual members, and $1,000 from its eighty corporate members. The largest percentage of its budget, 35 percent, is derived from sales of publications and conference fees; 30 percent comes from foundation grants and 25 percent from government funding. The remainder is raised from corporate dues, individual dues, and additional fund-raising from members.

Corporate members include General Electric Corporation, Minnesota Mining and Manufacture, and the University of Pittsburgh. It has received research support from the Ford, Richard King Mellon, William and Flora Hewlett, Rockefeller, and Alvord foundations, and program support from Gulf Oil, Exxon Corporation, and Armco Steel. It has done research sponsored by the U.S. Environmental Protection Agency (EPA), the National Science Foundation, the

Congressional Office of Technology Assessment, the German Marshall Fund, and the Fish and Wildlife Service of the Department of Interior. ELI actively seeks the expertise of corporate officers and environmental professionals inside corporations and government agencies.

## POLICY CONCERNS

Some of the issues in which ELI has done research and held workshops in recent years include EPA's bubble policy under the Clean Air Act, which develops market alternatives to regulation by permitting the trade of emission rights for air pollutants. ELI has also studied the acid rain issue as one of several transboundary problems among nations as well as between states in the United States.

In the area of toxic torts, ELI has conducted research sponsored by the Library of Congress into the impact of compensation for toxic tort victims. It brought together representatives of industry, insurance companies, state officials, and environmental groups to discuss the need for legislation about responsibility for compensating people injured by exposure to toxic materials. The conference focused on innovative strategies for controlling hazardous substances and avoiding contact by the public through greater knowledge of chemical hazards.

ELI has increased its expertise in economics in the 1980s, emphasizing the need to use benefit/cost analysis in examining environmental issues and to promote both increased productivity and environmental protection. It has investigated the relative merits of using economic incentives as opposed to regulation to control environmental risks to society.

## TACTICS

ELI does no advocacy work; it neither litigates cases nor lobbies Congress or administration agencies. It publishes *The Environmental Law Reporter*, which tracks developments in Congress, the agencies, and federal courts on environmental law, and also prints in-depth analyses of these developments. The twenty-five members of its editorial advisory board work for government agencies such as EPA, major industries such as the Olin Corporation, and environmental litigators such as the Environmental Defense Fund.* In addition to its publications, ELI sponsors conferences, seminars, and workshops for environmental professionals from all three sectors (government, industry, and environmental organizations) to study cooperatively critical environmental issues. Between 1971 and 1985 over 11,000 professionals took part in conferences on air and water pollution control, energy and public lands, wetlands policy, recycling, toxic torts, and other topics sponsored by ELI.

ELI publishes books, periodicals, and newsletters which it sells to its subscribers, primarily practitioners of environmental law in government agencies, industry, and public-interest law firms. In collaboration with the National Wetlands Technical Council, ELI publishes the *National Wetlands Newsletter*, a bimonthly information source for practitioners in wetlands and coastal resources management. In 1981 ELI began publishing *The Environmental Forum*, a journal of opinion pieces by writers from environmental groups as well as industry and government. It holds an annual conference in Washington.

### FURTHER INFORMATION

*Environmental Law Institute: The First Decade* (1980). Washington, D.C.: ELI.
*Environmental Law Reporter* (1987).Washington, D.C.: ELI, April.
*National Wetlands Newsletter* (1987). Washington, D.C.: ELI, vol. 9, no. 2, March-April.

## ENVIRONMENTAL POLICY CENTER

*See* Environmental Policy Institute.

## ENVIRONMENTAL POLICY INSTITUTE (EPI)

218 D Street, S.E.
Washington, D.C. 20003

### HISTORY AND DEVELOPMENT

The Environmental Policy Center was founded in 1972 by Joe Browder, Louise Dunlap, Brent Blackwelder, Barbara Heller, John McCormick, and David Zwick as an environmental organization designed to help citizens throughout the United States influence decision makers in Washington on environmental issues. In 1974 the Environmental Policy Institute (EPI) was established to provide research and educational leadership on the same issues; in 1982 the two organizations merged into one and kept the name Institute. Originally begun with funds provided by Arthur Godfrey and space donated by the Sierra Club,* the first president of EPI was Joe Browder, who served until 1977 when he became an official in Jimmy Carter's Department of the Interior. At that time Louise Dunlap became president of EPI and served until 1986.

In July 1986 the board selected Michael S. Clark to be president of EPI. Immediately before going to EPI, Clark had served as director of the Northern Lights Institute, a research center serving grass-roots groups in Montana, Idaho, and Wyoming; before that he had worked in the Highlander Center in Tennessee on problems of strip mining and poverty in Appalachia.

In January 1989 the board of EPI voted to merge with Friends of the Earth (FOE),* the FOE Foundation, and the Oceanic Society (OS). Like the FOE Foundation, EPI is eligible to receive tax-deductible contributions under 501(c)(3) of the tax code. FOE remained the 501(c)(4) group with an active membership and lobbying mission. Michael Clark became executive director of all four groups.

### ORGANIZATION AND RESOURCES

EPI policy is formulated by a twenty-one member board of directors, including Robert Redford, actor-environmentalist; David Zwick, former Nader raider; and

Marion Edey, former head of the League of Conservation Voters.* In the 1980s EPI reported receiving 55 percent of its income from foundations, 23 percent from individual donations, 12 percent from corporate grants, 8 percent from earned income, and 2 percent from churches and civic organizations. Its reported expenditures were for the following research programs: nuclear waste, insurance and weapons, 22 percent; agriculture, 12 percent; toxic chemicals, 8 percent; international development, 9 percent; oceans, coasts, and estuaries, 12 percent; water resources and groundwater protection, 14 percent; energy conservation, 5 percent; strip-mining, 7 percent. Policy development accounted for 3 percent; communications, another 3 percent; and other, 5 percent. In 1989 the combined budget for EPI, FOE, and OS was estimated at $2.5 million. In 1989 FOE/EPI/ OS had a thirty-three-member staff and a separate nine-member *Not Man Apart* newsmagazine staff in its Washington office.

EPI is not a membership organization, but it does request donations from interested individuals and foundations. Its primary purposes are to provide information to grass-roots organizations throughout the United States, the news media, government agencies, and industry, and to lobby in Washington for environmental policies.

## POLICY CONCERNS

One of EPI's major priorities concerns U.S. nuclear programs; it seeks to phase out U.S. dependence on nuclear power, to end worldwide production and testing of nuclear weapons, and to protect the environment and people from the nuclear fuel cycle. It has worked to remove the limitation on liability for the nuclear industry (the Price-Anderson Act) and to increase public participation in determining how to dispose of nuclear wastes and where to site such disposal facilities. It argued against the Department of Defense's acquisition of plutonium produced from U.S. nuclear power plants and for greater worker protection against radiation in weapons production. It supports states and cities in their efforts to control the transportation and storage of nuclear and other hazardous materials through their jurisdictions.

From its inception EPI argued for passage of a strong Surface Mining and Reclamation Act, which was signed into law by Jimmy Carter in 1977. Since that time, EPI has advocated strong enforcement of the law. It has been disappointed by the success of mining companies in avoiding strict enforcement of the law by taking advantage of a loophole that allows for exemption of small strip mining sites of less than two acres. During the Reagan Administration EPI worked with citizens groups in Appalachia to attempt to get state enforcement of the law; however, these efforts met with limited success.

EPI also advocates increased safety regulation of chemical plants to reduce worker exposure to hazardous materials as well as leaks to the environment such as happened in Bhopal, India, in 1984. It advocates closer government supervision of chemical production and argued for amendments to Superfund legislation to increase individual communities' rights to know what is stored and transported through their jurisdictions in order to prepare for emergencies. It advocates moving the regulatory process to the federal level because localities generally lack expertise in judging chemical hazards and tend to be dependent economically and politically on large employers in their communities.

EPI began work in 1982 against foreign development assistance that encourages large dams and other projects that spread disease, eliminate fish and wildlife habitat, and sterilize the land. It argues that destruction of tropical forests will eventually result in desertification of lands and loss of biological diversity that will lead to greater economic deprivation for the developing nations involved. EPI advocates projects by international banks and aid organizations to restore degraded watersheds and encourage conservation of energy and rehabilitation of forests and grasslands that will result in a sustainable economy for developing countries.

On the domestic front, EPI offers citizen groups assistance in arguing against proposals for additional U.S. Army Corps of Engineers (COE) and Bureau of Reclamation water projects. It believes that it has helped to halt 150 water projects by helping local groups argue for less expenditure of taxpayers' moneys to fund the projects and more recovery of the costs from the beneficiaries of the projects. It hopes eventually to phase out the Bureau of Reclamation and to shift the COE into nonstructural water projects.

One area in which EPI would like to see more government research and projects is to protect the quality of groundwater in the United States. In 1984 it held a citizens' conference on groundwater to increase public awareness of the dangers to their drinking water supply. Representatives of EPI have testified before Congress about strengthening the requirements of the Safe Drinking Water Act and before EPA in setting drinking water standards.

EPI has an agricultural project which seeks to ensure the survival of U.S. family farms. It argues against overuse of pesticides and fertilizers that increases individual farmers' dependency on chemical corporations. While acknowledging that biotechnology may improve the profitability of farming in some ways, EPI researchers are skeptical about the potential damage to the environment from genetically altered microbes. In 1985 one of EPI's staff, Jack Doyle, who runs the agricultural project, published a book, *Altered Harvest*, warning against the impact biotechnology may have on both the U.S. farm system and the food consumers eat.

EPI has been concerned since 1973 with the profligate development of oil and gas resources on public lands, especially in the outer continental shelf. It argues against drilling in fragile areas of the coastal zone and against use of deep ocean waters for disposal of toxic, nuclear, and other wastes. In 1989, after the catastrophic 11 million gallon oil spill in Prince William Sound, FOE/EPI/OS called for a boycott of all Exxon products until the corporation agrees to pay for all cleanup costs and damages resulting from the spill, establishes a $1 billion annual trust fund for environmental protection, conducts no oil drilling in the Arctic

National Wildlife Refuge, pays for safe oil tankers, and rolls back gasoline price increases made after the spill.

## TACTICS

EPI publishes *Environmental Update*, a bimonthly newsletter which keeps contributors informed about projects EPI is doing and solicits donations. It also publishes monographs from time to time. In 1989 FOE/EPI/OS testified against the confirmation of Secretary of the Interior Manuel Lujan, former congressman from New Mexico, because of his long record of anti-environmental votes in the House.

## FURTHER INFORMATION

Doyle, Jack (1985), *Altered Harvest*, New York: Viking.
*Environmental Policy Institute 15th Anniversary Report* (1987), Washington, D.C.: EPI.
*Environmental Update* (April-May 1987; January, February 1989), Washington, D.C.: EPI.
"FOE Family Grows: New Head Named" (1988), *Not Man Apart* 18, no. 6 (November).
Kehoe, Keiki (1980), *Unavailable at any Price: Nuclear Insurance*. Washington, D.C.: EPI.
"Michael S. Clark Interview" (1988–89), *Not Man Apart* 18, no. 6 (November-January): 4–5.
Roach, Robert, and Rick Young (1982), *Distant Dreams*. Washington, D.C.: EPI.
*See also* Friends of the Earth.

## ENVIRONMENTAL TASK FORCE
*See* Environmental Action.

# F

/

## FOUNDATION ON ECONOMIC TRENDS (FET)
1130 17th Street, N.W., Suite 630
Washington, D.C., 20036

### ORGANIZATION AND RESOURCES

Jeremy Rifkin started the Foundation on Economic Trends (FET) in 1977 in order to counter arguments that the biotechnology revolution is entirely benign. FET obtains funding of about $400,000 a year from individual contributions and from such funds as Mary Ann Mott's C. S. Fund and from Rifkin's own income from lecturing on college campus and royalties from his books. Edward Lee Rogers, a former counsel for the Environmental Defense Fund,* does much of the litigation; Andrew Kimbrell, policy director, does much of the lobbying in Congress and elsewhere in Washington.

### POLICY CONCERNS

The major focus of FET is against biotechnological innovations such as germ warfare, DNA manipulation, and surrogate motherhood. Its representatives have been successful in slowing the discoveries of such scientific discoveries as Frostban, a synthetic microbe that protects plants from frost, on the grounds that experimenting with Frostban in fields could release the organism throughout the plant world without knowing what the consequences will be.

FET has also objected to the use of human genetic material in other species in order to discover methods of treating genetically transmitted diseases. In this it has been joined by certain religious groups that object on ethical grounds. It also opposes manipulation of the genes of farm animals such as the creation of a "superpig." In this campaign it has been joined by farmers' organizations who object to biotech corporations being granted patents to these organisms, which may someday control the kinds of animals farmers can raise.

## TACTICS

FET generally objects to the lack of government regulation of many biological developments in the last two decades. It has generally had little influence within the Food and Drug Administration, whose scientists tend to regard its members as unscientific zealots, and within the National Institutes of Health, which is responsible for much of the funding of biotechnology. Its major opponents are in the biotechnology industry, especially pharmaceutical companies hoping to profit from new inventions. FET has been somewhat more successful with Congress, gaining entry to and testifying before several committees on biotechnological innovations. Its representatives also make many appearances on college campuses and have written several books attempting to reach and affect public opinion to demand more public participation in scientific decision making.

## FURTHER INFORMATION

Jeremy Rifkin (1980). *Entropy.* New York: Viking
Edward Tivnan (1988). "Jeremy Rifkin Just Says No." *The New York Times Magazine*, October 16, pp. 38–46.

## FOUNDATION ON EMERGING TECHNOLOGY
*See* Foundation on Economic Trends.

## FRIENDS OF THE EARTH (FOE)
218 D Street, S.E.
Washington, D.C. 20003

### HISTORY AND DEVELOPMENT

In 1969 David Brower, who had been executive director of the Sierra Club* for seventeen years, was asked to resign by the board of directors because of his "general intransigence, willful failure to follow board directives, unauthorized expenditures . . . and contemptuous disregard for club offices." (Rauber, 1986). He and several associates established Friends of the Earth (FOE) in San Francisco, at that time dedicated to a more militant activist environmental movement. For ten years Brower served as president of FOE, but in 1979 stepped down and became chair of the board. He was succeeded as president by Edwin Matthews who lasted one year, but who remains on the FOE board of directors.

Throughout its somewhat rocky history FOE has had financial troubles, having accumulated a debt of $700,000 by 1984. David Brower's philosophy is that an environmental organization not in debt is not doing its job properly. Edwin Matthews, Rafe Pomerance, and succeeding executive directors tried to reduce the debt by cutting back on staff and programs, but Brower and his allies on the board resisted these efforts, and much of the staff in San Francisco remained loyal to Brower. In 1984 Brower was expelled from the board by another faction, but he won his seat back through a court fight.

In 1985 the anti-Brower forces on the board voted to move headquarters to Washington, and after an unsuccessful attempt by Brower advocates to recall the majority on the board, the move took place in 1986, thus eliminating many of the Brower supporters on the San Francisco staff. The majority argued the move was made for budgetary reasons; the Brower minority, that it was orchestrated to strip power from the San Francisco loyalists, who went on to help Brower found the new Earth Island Institute.* Geoff Webb, FOE conservation director, became acting executive director. On October 1, 1986, Cynthia Wilson was named FOE's new executive director. Ms. Wilson had been a White House conservation aide to Mrs. Lyndon B. Johnson and in the Interior Department during the Carter administration, and had considerable administrative experience. She succeeded in reducing the $700,000 debt to a little over $400,000 by the end of 1987.

## ORGANIZATION AND RESOURCES

In January 1989 the FOE board voted to merge with the Environmental Policy Institute (EPI)* and the Oceanic Society for fiscal and administrative reasons. This also includes a sister FOE Foundation, which has IRS tax-exempt status and the authority to receive tax-exempt contributions. Michael S. Clark became executive director of all four organizations and now heads a thirty-four-person staff in Washington. Two branch offices are maintained in Seattle, Washington, and Manila, Philippines, but others in California, Michigan, Pennsylvania, and Alaska have been closed. There are several FOE organizations in other countries, such as Brazil, France, Britain, and Japan, affiliated with FOE U.S.A.

FOE membership increased in the early years of the Reagan administration until it achieved a high of about 30,000 in 1983. After James Watt resigned as secretary of interior in 1983, one of the most important money-raising symbols was removed from environmental groups, and FOE membership fell to about 20,000 in 1986. It charges $25 a year membership dues, and raises money from members and foundations through special appeals. Its 1988 budget of $447,000 was allocated in the following manner: 28 percent for membership services, 15 percent for debt retirement, 19 percent for administration, 12 percent for legislative work, 8 percent for public information, 7 percent for fund-raising, 9 percent for publishing *Not Man Apart*, and 2 percent, other.

## POLICY CONCERNS

FOE in its early years was the first environmental group to take on some of the major environmental issues of the 1970s. It argued that the Clean Air Act (CAA) must be strengthened to reduce acid rain, that nuclear war is an environmental issue, and that arms control should be a major goal of the movement. FOE campaigned for soft-energy alternatives to nuclear power; it fought against the Clinch River breeder reactor in Tennessee, plane, the supersonic transport and the leasing of coal and oil fields on public land. It advocated preservation of whales and other endangered species as well as preservation of the Alaskan wilderness. After the catastrophic 11-million-gallon oil spill in Prince William Sound in March 1989, FOE/EPI argued for sweeping oil-spill compensation and liability legislation, which came under consideration in the 101st Congress. FOE also advocates reintroducing wolves into the national parks and forests and keeping down their depredations on livestock through guard dogs, as does Defenders of Wildlife.*

FOE/EPI opposes the export of toxic wastes to third world nations and the burning of such wastes at sea. In 1988 Waste Management Inc. stopped its efforts to get a permit from the U.S. EPA to permit more experimental burns in U.S. coastal waters after European countries agreed to phase out their North Sea burns by 1994. In 1989 *Not Man Apart* wrote about the practice of using the same trucks that transport foodstuffs from the midwest to the east coast to haul garbage from eastern states that are running out of landfill space back to the midwest for burial. This was originally brought to public attention by two small Pennsylvania newspapers, but FOE was instrumental in forcing congressional representatives to offer legislation to correct it.

FOE/EPI also opposes clear-cutting in the United States and abroad and argues for reforestation both to reduce global warming and to provide a sustainable economic base for tropical countries. In 1988 FOE opposed amendments to the Federal Insecticide, Fungicide and Rodenticide Act (FIFRA), which other environmental groups endorsed, because it considered them too weak, labeling the new law "FIFRA Lite." It also called for stricter controls on chlorofluorocarbons to stop the depletion of ozone in the upper atmosphere in the 1990s.

During the 1980s FOE has become concerned about the new, highly controversial issue of biological engineering. Although most mainstream environmental groups have been reluctant to take a position on this important evolving issue, *Not Man Apart* has argued that many ethical questions about gene manipulation have not been resolved or even raised, and the unforeseen consequences of releasing new life forms into the environment should be carefully studied before any precipitous action is taken. The enormous stakes in the new field of bioengineering will doubtless make this issue an important one for future years. The potential for enormous profits has attracted many university researchers and administrators to this new field, and FOE/EPI has pointed up the difficulty of maintaining an independent critical research posture in the face of such opportunities.

## TACTICS

After FOE/EPI defines the problems, other more mainstream environmental groups have often taken up the same issues, and some establishment environmentalists believed that FOE/EPI serves a useful function as gadfly of the movement. After the move to Washington in 1986 some former staffers argued that compromise-oriented pragmatists would replace ideologues and convert FOE into another pale replica of the Sierra Club. The creation of Greenpeace* and Earth First!, * as well as its merger with EPI, may have indeed moved FOE/ EPI into a more centrist position among environmental groups.

One issue over which factions in FOE clashed in the 1980s was the endorsement of Walter Mondale for president in 1984. The majority of the board decided on this move before Mondale received the Democratic Party's nomination, while more-militant members wanted to support a more radical candidate such as Barry Commoner, who would better represent the movement. Thus the organization was divided over the issue of whether it was wiser to adopt a pragmatic stance and work within the system or to take a more radical ecological stance and remain better able to criticize the establishment. Brower loyalists argued that FOE will become similar to other environmental groups in Washington and will cease to act as the "early warning system" of the environmental movement. In 1988 FOE endorsed Michael Dukakis for president, and its political director, David Baker, appeared with him at rallies on campuses around the United States. FOE also endorsed 100 candidates seeking to retain or win seats in Congress and sent members into the field to campaign for them.

FOE publishes *Not Man Apart*, a newsmagazine on recycled newsprint every two months and distributes these to subscribers at $3.00 a copy or as part of the membership entitlement of $25 a year for members. In 1989 Paul McCartney, former Beatle, began a world tour in which he agreed to carry the message of FOE/EPI as his official sponsor.

### FURTHER INFORMATION

Brower, David (1990). *For Earth's Sake: The Life and Times of David Brower*. New York: Peregrine Smith.
Edwards, Rob (1985). "Friends of the Earth Cook Their Own Goose." *New Statesman*, August 23, pp. 11–12.
McPhee, John (1971). *Encounters with the Archdruid*. New York: Farrar, Straus and Giroux.
*Not Man Apart* (May-June, July-August 1987; January-February, March-April, August-September, October-November, 1988; January, June-September, 1989).
Rauber, Paul (1986). "With Friends Like These . . . " *Mother Jones*, November, pp. 35–49.
Russell, Dick (1987). "The Monkeywrenchers." *The Amicus Journal* 9, no. 4 (Fall): 28–42.
Sale, Kirkpatrick (1986). "The Forest for the Trees." *Mother Jones*, November, pp. 25–58.
*See also* Environmental Policy Institute.

### FRIENDS OF THE LAND
*See* Izaak Walton League of America.

### FUND FOR RENEWABLE ENERGY
*See* Renew America.

# G

—————————— / ——————————

## GAS APPLIANCE MANUFACTURERS ASSOCIATION (GAMA)
1901 North Moore Street
Arlington, Virginia 22209

### ORGANIZATION AND RESOURCES

The Gas Appliance Manufacturers Association (GAMA) began as the manufacturers' section of the American Gas Association.* However, in 1935 the manufacturers began their own separate trade association, calling themselves the Association of Gas Appliance and Equipment Manufacturers. In 1946 it changed its name to the Gas Appliance Manufacturers Association (GAMA), and in 1967 it acquired the Institute of Appliance Manufacturers which had been in existence since 1872.

GAMA's members are 225 corporations that manufacture over 90 percent of all residential, commercial, and industrial gas appliances in the United States as well as some equipment used in the production, transmission, and distribution of fuel gases. Dues vary according to the volume of business done by each company. GAMA is divided into 13 divisions representing different products: burners, controls (such as gas valves, thermostats, and filters), direct heating, domestic gas ranges, food service equipment, furnaces, gas boilers, general equipment for producing and distributing fuel gases, industrial forced-air heating, infrared heaters, outdoor grills and lights, water heaters, and general products.

GAMA has an elected board of directors, which includes a representative from each of the product divisions. The president heads a staff of nineteen in Arlington, Virginia.

## POLICY CONCERNS

GAMA has a legislative committee concerned about such issues as business taxation and product liability. It monitors government regulations at both state and federal levels. One of its primary concerns is the 1975 Energy Policy and Conservation Act which mandated efficiency standards for gas furnaces and other gas appliances. It argued against that law on the grounds that it was unnecessary as customers would become more interested in energy conservation because of the rise in fuel prices. However, its spokesmen also pointed out that the average efficiency of gas furnaces had increased by 20 percent from 1975 to 1985 while the law was in effect. The industry argues that manufacturers are uncertain about the requirements that the Department of Energy (DOE) will promulgate under the law, and this creates confusion in the minds of consumers.

GAMA has also argued that the industry must devote thousands of hours and travel expenses for company executives to participate in rule-making hearings generated by the new law. Much of the industry's research had to be redirected toward meeting efficiency standards after 1980. Of even greater concern to the industry, however, is the possibility that state governments might promulgate their own uncoordinated standards that might conflict with each other and cost industry more in increased manufacturing costs in the long run. Hence industry spokesmen were most adamant in their desire to have Congress modify the law to preempt all state standards once DOE reached a national standard.

## TACTICS

GAMA's professional staff keeps its membership informed about legislative and regulatory developments of interest in Washington. Like other medium-sized trade associations, its board members and the CEOs of member companies are the major spokespersons for its positions before Congress and the agencies. There is an annual meeting each spring where the board is elected and policies discussed. Its marketing council promotes the acceptance and use of gas appliances in general, although each corporation is in competition with each other for sales. Every other year GAMA sponsors an exhibit of products. It compiles statistics for the entire industry about sales of gas appliances.

## FURTHER INFORMATION

Chubb, John E. (1983). *Interest Groups and the Bureaucracy*. Stanford, Calif.: Stanford University Press.
*Interstate Gas Pipelines* (1987). Washington, D.C.: Interstate Natural Gas Association of America.
McFarland, Andrew (1984). "Energy Lobbies." *Annual Review of Energy 9*: 501–527.
Rosenbaum, Walter A. (1987). *Energy, Politics, and Public Policy*. 2d ed. Washington, D.C.: Congressional Quarterly Press.
Stobaugh, Robert and Daniel Yergin, eds. (1983). *Energy Future*. 3d ed. New York: Vintage Press.
U.S. Congress. House of Representatives Committee on Energy (1986). *Hearing on*

*National Appliance Energy Conservation Act*. Washington, D.C.: Government Printing Office.

## GAS INSTITUTE
*See* American Gas Association.

## GAS RESEARCH INSTITUTE (GRI)
8600 West Bryn Mawr Avenue
Chicago, Illinois 60631

### ORGANIZATION AND RESOURCES

Disappointed in individual corporations' abilities to conduct applied research, the gas industry founded the Gas Research Institute (GRI) in 1976 as the shared research arm of the gas industry. Its primary goal is to increase demand and consumption of natural gas as an energy source by increasing the number of end uses to which gas can be put and making these more efficient and less costly. Since its inception it has also focused on doing research into new technologies to enhance efficiency in its production, transportation, and delivery systems.

Its member companies include over 30 interstate pipeline companies, 150 intrastate and retail distributors, about 50 municipal utilities, over 40 gas producers, and 18 foreign gas suppliers in Europe and Japan. Its members and international affiliates are assessed dues in proportion to the volume of business they do. In addition, many manufacturers of gas appliances, commercial gas users, and pipeline and distribution companies have contributed directly to research on particular technologies in which they have a specific interest. During the first 10 years of operation, GRI estimated that it used $713 million to conduct research. The Institute contracts out its research to universities such as Columbia and Colorado School of Mines, and to engineering research corporations, such as Babcock & Wilcox and General Research Corporation, and even state and federal government agencies. GRI estimates that its research has had a 6:1 benefit-to-cost payoff to appliance manufacturers, end users, and pipeline companies.

Its president is selected by its twenty-seven-person elected board of directors. GRI also has four advisory bodies with members drawn from academia and governmental regulatory agencies as well as the gas industry, designed to assist GRI in selecting topics on which to concentrate its resources. In the late 1980s GRI had an annual budget of over $160 million, derived primarily from industrial contributions approved by the Federal Energy Regulatory Commission (FERC). A small amount came from interest on investments. It expended 95 percent of its funds on research projects and the remainder on administrative matters.

GRI maintains a staff of about 260 in its main Chicago office, which manages grants made to other institutions. Its Washington staff of over 20 people plans and manages the gas industry's research strategy and testifies before Congress on issues that concern it.

## POLICY CONCERNS

GRI focuses on three main topics in its research: increasing the efficiency of producing natural gas, reducing costs of distributing gas, and increasing end uses of natural gas. It has funded research designed to find gas zones in geological formations more easily; to coproduce gas and water in fields where companies had previously abandoned wells because of excessive amounts of water mixed with gas; to locate and produce natural gas trapped in coal seams; and to penetrate tight sand formations that contain abundant but difficult to recover natural gas. One of its most innovative production research projects is exploring methods of generating methane from chemical reactions between water and carbon dioxide and using photosynthesis to generate gaseous fuels from water.

GRI has reduced the costs of laying pipe to distribute natural gas by designing a guided horizontal boring system that reduces the amount of surface soil that has to be displaced. It has produced a soil additive that enables crews to backfill excavations almost immediately and to reduce settling. GRI also works on maintenance problems of the pipeline industry and has sought to find less-expensive ways to lay pipe under railroad track that will reduce the risk of rupturing pipe without having to encase it in double layers.

GRI has sought to find new uses for natural gas in all sectors of the economy. One of the first products of GRI's research efforts was the pulse combustion process for gas-fired furnaces, which use less fuel than previous models. GRI has worked on self-cleaning gas ovens, and continually attempts to increase the efficiency of gas appliances to meet federal standards and reduce the operating costs for the consumer. It has invented methods of using gas to both cool and dehumidify commercial and residential space. It researches the utilization of steam heat produced from gas in some industries to cogenerate electricity. It has worked on an engine usable in vehicles as well as industrial motors that can be fueled by gas rather than oil. It hopes to be able to sell such an engine to the auto and especially the truck industry as an efficient method of achieving emission limits on vehicles. It has created more-efficient griddles fired by gas for restaurants, as well as commercial hot water heaters and gas-fired heat pumps.

## TACTICS

The gas industry, through GRI, attempts to demonstrate how economical gas is as a fuel in competition with other fuels, especially electricity. It, therefore, investigates the costs of heat pumps and other electric appliances and stresses the efficiency of new gas appliances. It supports in principle the establishment of federal appliance efficiency standards because this is preferable to a variety of state standards, but it argues that there is a bias in these standards against small gas furnaces designed for starter homes.

GRI is a tax-exempt nonprofit organization, and as such is forbidden to lobby government officials directly. However, its research reports may be important in providing information for congressional committees as well as regulatory agencies such as FERC, and GRI representatives have testified before congressional committees. In all its endeavors it emphasizes the pollution-free nature of gas and the need to improve the environment through replacing dirty fuels with clean ones. In the 100th Congress, GRI testified in favor of acid rain controls because one way to control sulfur emissions is with gas-powered technology.

*FURTHER INFORMATION*

*Annual Report 1988* (1989). Washington, D.C.: GRI.

Washington office: 1331 Pennsylvania Avenue, N.W., Suite 730 North, Washington, D.C. 20004–1703

## GLOBAL TOMORROW COALITION (GTC)
1325 G Street, N.W.
Washington, D.C. 20005

*ORGANIZATION AND RESOURCES*

The Global Tomorrow Coalition (GTC) was founded in 1981 by a group of environmental and conservation organizations in order to emphasize the need for establishing a sustainable world economy not dependent on continuous population growth. Approximately eighty organizations belong, including population control groups, such as the Alan Guttmacher Institute, Planned Parenthood Federation of America,* Negative Population Growth, and Zero Population Growth;* agricultural organizations, such as the American Farmland Trust and International Alliance for Sustainable Agriculture; academic institutions, such as the Filene Center for Citizenship and Public Affairs–Tufts University and Linfield College; animal rights groups, such as the American Society for the Prevention of Cruelty to Animals, Defenders of Wildlife,* and the National Audubon Society;* international development organizations, such as CARE and the International Center for Development Policy; and mainstream conservation organizations, such as the Sierra Club* and The Conservation Foundation.*

Participating members pay $200 a year, or $300 if their annual budget exceeds $500,000, and are entitled to appoint a representative to the board of directors. Affiliate members, both individuals and organizations, may also join for $35 or $100 a year respectively. In 1989 GTC had a budget of over $600,000, which came from affiliated groups and some government sources, such as the Agency for International Development and Departments of Natural Resources in Wisconsin and Washington; and some corporate donors, such as the 3-M Corporation and Southern Pacific Railroad. Most of its expenditures, 62 percent, were used for training local leaders about global environmental issues; 16 percent went for education and information, 4 percent for public policy, 8 percent for membership and international liaison, and 10 percent for administration and fund-raising.

GTC's first chair of the board was Dr. Russell Peterson, then president of the National Audubon Society. In 1987 he was replaced by Dr. Fred O. Pinkham, president of the Population Crisis Committee. The eighteen members of the

board of directors are elected annually and include representatives of the World
Resources Institute, the National Wildlife Federation,* Worldwatch Institute,*
Planned Parenthood, Resources for the Future,* the U.N. Environment Pro-
gramme, Carrying Capacity,* and Zero Population Growth. Donald Lesh, the
original executive director, was elected president in 1989 and continues to head
GTC's five-person professional staff in Washington. It also maintains a West
Coast office in Portland, Oregon.

### POLICY CONCERNS

GTC's priorities in the 1980s included stopping the destruction of tropical
rain forests for the production of food exports to the developed world; preserving
the world's rapidly diminishing wetlands; halting the killing of endangered species such as certain species of whales and the destruction of dolphins in fishing
nets; and stopping the depletion of the ozone layer in the stratosphere. Its members considered it a major victory when an international treaty was drafted in
Montreal in 1987 by which signatories will seek to reduce the production and
use of chlorofluorocarbons in the 1990s. It seeks to influence major international
financial institutions to adopt projects for developing nations that do not deplete
the ecology of the country, and not to put emphasis on large industrial projects,
such as nuclear reactors, and to make developing nations less dependent on loans
and exports of their nonrenewable resources to industrialized countries.

GTC is concerned with all problems that affect the ability of Earth to sustain
its human population at a decent standard of living, including conservation of
natural resources with emphasis on renewable resources that will not become
depleted. Its major concern is to control the human population at a sustainable
level that will provide for a decent standard of public health for all inhabitants.
GTC became increasingly concerned about global warming in the late 1980s and
advocated increasing the miles per gallon standard for new cars in order to reduce
the amount of carbon dioxide put into the atmosphere by cars.

### TACTICS

GTC's emphasis is international, and its primary function is educational. It
seeks to expand its network of information to include educational institutions
whenever possible, and it sponsors international conferences and teacher workshops to inform local leaders of conservation organizations about global environmental issues. GTC sponsored six such Globescopes from 1985 through 1989;
Globescope Minnesota was held in June 1989 on ''Sub-National Policies and
Actions for an Era of Global Warming,'' and was cosponsored by the Hubert
Humphrey Institute of Public Affairs at the University of Minnesota.

GTC publishes *Interaction* from its Washington office every other month,
informing its members and affiliates about conferences on population control
and resource conservation, reviewing books on these subjects, and tracking policy
developments in Washington and on the international front. It gives awards to
politicians and other policy makers it perceives as adopting and supporting

ecologically sound policies. GTC notes when corporations and banks adopt conservation policies, such as when Amoco Corporation created an innovative man-made wetlands to treat refinery wastes in North Dakota oil fields, which can also be used as a wildlife sanctuary.

## FURTHER INFORMATION

*Globescope 89 An International Forum* (1989). Los Angeles, Calif., October 31–November 5.

*Interaction* (vol. 5, no. 2, June 1985; vol. 7, no. 1, April 1987; vol. 7, no. 3, August 1987; vol. 8, no. 1, 1988). Washington, D.C.: GTC.

*1988–1989 Program Overview and 1989 Budget* (1989). Washington, D.C.: GTC.

## GREENPEACE
1436 U Street, N.W.
Washington, D.C. 20009

### ORGANIZATION AND RESOURCES

Greenpeace was founded in 1971 in British Columbia, Canada, in order to oppose underground nuclear bomb testing on Amchitka Island in Alaska. Since that time it has grown to an international organization with headquarters in Britain, France, Germany, Holland, Australia, New Zealand, Denmark, and Canada, as well as six U.S. regional offices in Anchorage for Alaska; Cambridge, Massachusetts, for New England; Seattle, Washington, for the Northwest; Jacksonville Beach, Florida for the Southeast; and San Francisco, for the Pacific Southwest. The latest addition was the Great Lakes office which opened in Chicago in 1987. Greenpeace has a contributing membership of about 900,000 in the United States, but over 2.5 million internationally. It is governed by an elected board of directors, which represents each region. Voting members must have six years active involvement with Greenpeace, which includes not only contributing money but volunteering time to projects. Greenpeace, U.S.A. was originally organized regionally with complete autonomy for each regional office, which set its own agenda. In 1987, however, the board of directors decided to centralize with a national office in Washington, D.C., which now allocates funds to the six regions instead of allowing each to develop its own programs.

Dues are $25 a year for individuals, but donations of any amount are accepted. In the late 1980s Greenpeace had revenues of about $16 million per year, over 90 percent of which came from contributions from individuals. The remainder came from merchandise and publication sales, grants, and investments. Of the total budget, about 8 percent goes for general administration and nearly 23 percent for fund-raising. Greenpeace, U.S.A. donates a portion of its annual budget to Greenpeace International, which has a reported income of $28 million. The remainder is used for the following programs: disarmament, toxic wastes, whale campaign, ocean ecology, Antarctica expedition, dolphin campaign, seal campaign, kangaroo protection, outer continental shelf, and publishing *Greenpeace*. Greenpeace employs 400 full-time staffers whose work is supplemented by hundreds of part-timers and thousands of volunteers.

## POLICY CONCERNS

Originally organized around two major causes—the need to halt nuclear testing and the need to preserve the marine habitat and stop killing marine mammals— Greenpeace has expanded into the areas of toxic waste control, research on acid rain, and Antarctica. After atmospheric nuclear testing was halted, Greenpeace evacuated 308 residents of Rongelap Atoll which, it argued, had been contaminated by U.S. atmospheric nuclear tests in the 1950s. Greenpeace continues to protest underground testing by France, the United States, U.S.S.R., Britain, and China and urges all nuclear nations to negotiate a comprehensive nuclear test ban treaty. It opposes the proliferation of nuclear weapons around the world and tries to track the quantities of plutonium that are passed among nations. It also tracks ships that are armed with nuclear weapons and points these out to host nations when they dock in their ports.

Greenpeace opposes the continued killing of endangered whale and other marine mammal populations and urges boycotts of the fish caught by such nations as Iceland, Japan, and the Soviet Union that choose to ignore the international ban on whaling and continue to kill whales under the guise of research. It opposes the accidental killing of marine mammals such as dolphins and porpoises by entrapment in nets used to catch tuna and other commercial species. It supported the reauthorization of the Marine Mammal Protection Act in 1987 and urges the U.S. Department of Commerce to more forcefully implement its provisions.

In 1987 Greenpeace established a research station in Antarctica to investigate the condition of that subcontinent and the impact that human activities have had on the ecosystem there since 18 Antarctica Treaty nations agreed to allow development. Specifically, Greenpeace objects to national outposts (including the U.S. McMurdo run by the National Science Foundation) dumping sewage and garbage, a French airstrip being built in the Antarctic, over-fishing of the Antarctic waters, and the possibility now being discussed of mining there. Greenpeace volunteers believe that the Antarctic ecosystem is too fragile to sustain commercialization of the area and that the Convention for the Conservation of Antarctic Marine Living Resources is not sufficient to prevent endangerment of the exotic species that live there.

Greenpeace is also much concerned with present methods of disposing of toxic wastes. It has argued against land-filling these wastes in economically depressed areas in the United States, such as Emelle, Alabama. It also opposes incineration of such wastes because of potential air pollution and has intervened in the burning of toxics on the incinerator ships *Vulcanus I* and *II* operated by Waste Management, Inc. (WMI). In 1987 the North Sea Minister's Conference resolved that burning European toxic wastes in the North Sea should stop by 1995, and WMI announced it would abandon its efforts to obtain permits from the U.S. EPA to burn toxics in American waters. Greenpeace expects WMI to move its operations to waters in the southern hemisphere off developing nations and intends to oppose such operations there also.

## TACTICS

Greenpeace is one of the most militant groups presently active in the environmental movement. Its members are dedicated to direct action against governmental and private actions it perceives as environmentally damaging. However, it opposes any violence, unlike other militant groups such as Earth First!* and Sea Shepherd. Its founders were brought up in the tradition of the civil rights movement and it advocates direct, but not destructive, action against its opponents. Many of the activities its volunteers undertake are dangerous, and several Greenpeace members have been injured, but the organization subscribes to a philosophy of non-violence regardless of the response from the targets of its protests.

Greenpeace has a fleet of ships it uses to intercept whaling ships, to disrupt nuclear testing in the Pacific, and to protest the degradation of the marine environment through the dumping of toxic wastes into the oceans. Greenpeace crews use small rubber inflatable boats to place themselves between whales, dolphins, and other mammals it seeks to protect and whaling fleets from Japan, Spain, Iceland, Peru, and the Soviet Union. It also confronts seal hunters in Canada and in the Orkney Islands off Scotland and dumps green dye on baby harp seals to make their pelts less desirable for the international fur trade.

Greenpeace vessels have attempted to interfere with French and American nuclear tests in the Pacific by sailing into test sites in French Polynesia and the U.S. Marshall Islands. They also attempt to prevent the disposal of radioactive and other toxic materials in the oceans by sailing rubber rafts and diving directly into the path of British ships dumping the materials. Various governments have retaliated against Greenpeace protests. In 1980 Spain seized the *Rainbow Warrior* in international waters because it had interfered with whaling, and held it for five months before it escaped. British seamen attempted to sink the *Zodiac* while it protested dumping radioactive waste. The U.S.S.R. towed the *Sirius* out of Leningrad after Greenpeace members released balloons calling for a halt to nuclear testing. Greenpeace volunteers were beaten by French commandoes in 1974, and on July 10, 1985, members of the French Directorate General of External Security blew up the *Rainbow Warrior* in Auckland harbor, New Zealand, killing one Greenpeace photographer. Two French government employees were tried and sentenced to 10 years in jail by New Zealand, but they were later released to France after economic and political pressure was placed on New Zealand. The French government agreed to pay $7 million in compensation and apologize to New Zealand for interference with its sovereignty. New Zealand had opposed nuclear testing in the Pacific Ocean and the docking of American ships with nuclear weapons. In December 1989 a Greenpeace vessel was damaged off Florida by U.S. Navy ships that rammed it because it refused to leave an area where trident missiles were being tested from a nuclear submarine.

Greenpeace volunteers and employees attempt to influence regulatory agencies such as the U.S. Department of Interior's Mineral Management Service and the policy-making branches of government through direct lobbying and representation of its views. However, its primary focus is on educating the public concerning the issues of highest priority to it through direct protest activities and symbolic actions, such as hanging a banner from the U.S. Capitol in 1985 calling for a stop to nuclear testing. In 1988 members of Greenpeace dropped on ropes from the Golden Gate Bridge in San Francisco to hang a banner for "Nuclear Free Seas" and from the Triborough Bridge in New York City to protest ocean dumping of toxic sludge. In addition to such symbolic actions and the resulting media attention, Greenpeace also directly lobbies national legislatures and such international agencies as the World Bank. It has initiated some successful litigation and lobbying activities, as in the case of the Marine Mammal Protection Act.

As Greenpeace membership grows, the diversity of philosophy and discussion over tactics also expands. Some Greenpeace members are also adherents of Earth First! Others eschew the deep ecologists' distinction between themselves and the more pragmatic organizations' "shallow" commitment to ecological values. Its leaders disavow the more violent tactics of Sea Shepherd, but Mike Roselle, a founder of Earth First!, has participated in Greenpeace actions such as invading an underground nuclear site in Nevada in 1986.

Despite the recent centralization of its headquarters, Greenpeace, U.S.A., continues to be a highly diffused, grass-roots organization that relies on individual volunteer initiative to bring most issues to the attention of the public. It is committed to the idea that local participation in local problems, such as the siting of hazardous waste sites, is crucial. It publishes a quarterly, *Greenpeace*, formerly titled the *Greenpeace Examiner*, edited by Andre Carothers in Washington.

## FURTHER INFORMATION

*Greenpeace* (vol. 12, January-March, April-May, July-September 1987; vol. 13, January-February, March-April, May-June, September-October, November-December 1988; vol. 14, March-April, September-October, November-December, 1989). Washington, D.C.: Greenpeace.

Harwood, Michael (1988). "Daredevils for the Environment." *The New York Times Magazine*, October 2, pp. 72–75.

Russell, Dick (1987). "The Monkeywrenchers." *The Amicus Journal* 9, no. 4 (Fall): 28–42

# H

---------------------- / ----------------------

**HALOGENATED SOLVENTS INDUSTRY ALLIANCE (HSIA)**
1225 19th Street, N.W., Suite 300
Washington, D.C. 20036

## ORGANIZATION AND RESOURCES

The Halogenated Solvents Industry Alliance (HSIA), founded in 1980, represents the interests of companies that manufacture chlorinated solvents, substances that many toxicologists believe are carcinogenic in humans. This group of chemicals is used primarily for dry cleaning, degreasing industrial processes, aerosols, and paint stripping. With 200 members, it is a small trade association, compared to the Chemical Manufacturers* and Chemical Specialties Manufacturers associations.* Most of HSIA's members also belong to the larger chemical groups. It has seven members on its board of directors and a budget of about $1.4 million a year.

## POLICY CONCERNS

Members of HSIA are primarily concerned about the impact of the Toxic Substances Control Act (TSCA) and the Clean Air and Water acts on their part of the chemical manufacturing industry. Experts from various chemical corporations testify before the House and Senate, arguing that the Interagency Chlorinated Solvents Working Group, headed by the U.S. Environmental Protection Agency (EPA), is working as fast as it can on these problems. They urge Congress to leave the definition of toxic materials to EPA and to give the agency ample time to test each substance thoroughly before any regulations are issued.

HSIA representatives argue that the substances to be regulated are essential to the economy of the nation and the risks alleged by environmental and consumer groups are unproven. HSIA funds many studies that are designed to challenge the government's use of laboratory animal tests to predict risks to humans. HSIA experts argue that naturally occurring toxins cause more cancer in humans than do synthetic chemicals. Generally the 1980s have proved beneficial to the chemical industry, as few new initiatives have been made to control toxic materials, and EPA has taken a cautious approach to labeling substances as dangerous.

## TACTICS

HSIA issues a newsletter to its membership bimonthly and a monthly journal, *Solvents Update*. It combines strategies with the large chemical trade associations.

## FURTHER INFORMATION

*Chlorinated Solvents in the Environment* (1989). Washington, D.C.: HSIA.
*HSIA Newsletter* (1989). Washington, D.C.: HSIA, vol. 5, no. 3, May-June.

## HAZARDOUS WASTE TREATMENT COUNCIL (HWTC)
1440 New York Avenue, N.W., Suite 310
Washington, D.C. 20005

## ORGANIZATION AND RESOURCES

Founded in 1982 in order to oppose the Reagan administration's decision to allow disposal of liquid hazardous wastes in landfills, the Hazardous Waste Treatment Council (HWTC) is a trade association of companies treating hazardous wastes. Using landfills for the disposal of hazardous wastes had been banned by the U.S. Environmental Protection Agency (EPA) in 1980, and HWTC's founding members, such as ENSCO, Inc. and SCA Chemical Services, had invested in incinerators and high-technology methods of disposing of hazardous wastes, including chemical fixation, neutralization, and reclamation. The National Solid Wastes Management Association,* which represented these companies as well as many other waste disposal companies, was unwilling to support this position because of the interests of most of its members.

The HWTC consists of over sixty large and small firms that specialize in high-technology solutions to hazardous wastes. Its executive director is Richard C. Fortuna, a toxicologist formerly with the U.S. Congress House Energy and Commerce Committee Staff, who now heads a staff of seven. Dues are paid according to a sliding scale depending on the size of the firm.

## POLICY CONCERNS

Firms that belong to HWTC have devoted many of their resources to developing chemical fixation and incineration techniques for reducing hazardous wastes. They therefore oppose any relaxation of the requirements in the Resource Conservation and Recovery Act (RCRA) which would increase the landfilling of hazardous wastes. Representatives of HWTC testified in RCRA hearings before the House Committee on Science and Technology that the ban on land-filling hazardous wastes should be kept, that hazardous wastes should be reduced in volume and toxicity, and recovery implemented whenever possible.

HWTC was also instrumental in reducing the RCRA small generators exemption from 1,000 kilograms per month to 100 kilograms per month. Small generators make up most of the potential clients for commercial waste treatment companies, and this greatly expanded their market. HWTC also testified in favor of requiring double liners for any landfills accepting hazardous materials, mandatory cleanup of any leaks from landfills, and restrictions on the use of absorbents as solidification agents to allow liquids to be buried. It also opposes mixing waste materials with oil for use as an energy supply in industrial boilers. It argues that any hazardous wastes that are burned should meet incineration specifications under RCRA. It was successful in getting the ban on liquid hazardous wastes in landfills reinstated in 1982 and in closing other loopholes in RCRA amendments of 1984.

In 1986 and 1987 representatives of HWTC testified in favor of the Superfund Amendments and Reauthorization Act (SARA), arguing that more industries should be taxed to fund Superfund. They also advocated more extensive techniques for cleaning abandoned toxic sites, arguing wastes should not be reburied elsewhere, but should be treated and detoxified. If states choose more expensive methods of cleaning a toxic site than U.S. EPA recommends, under Superfund the state must cover 90 percent of costs. This, HWTC argues, is unfair. The federal government must provide funds, or states will choose the cheapest method, which will result in simply moving the problem to another site.

### FURTHER INFORMATION

Epstein, Samuel, Lester O. Brown, and Carl Pope (1982). *Hazardous Waste in America.* San Francisco, Calif.: Sierra Club Books.
*Proceedings from RCRA/SARA Conference* (1989). Washington, D.C.: HWTC.
U.S. Congress. House Committee on Science and Technology (1983). *Hearings on Hazardous Waste Disposal.* Washington, D.C.: Government Printing Office, March 30.

## HEALTH AND ENERGY INSTITUTE (HEI)
236 Massachusetts Avenue, N.E., Suite 506
Washington, D.C. 20002

### ORGANIZATION AND RESOURCES

The Health and Energy Institute (HEI) was founded in 1978 as the Health and Energy Learning Project to warn against nuclear hazards to public health in the United States. In 1989 it claimed approximately 7,000 members, who were asked to donate from $25 to $100. The Institute also obtained some funding from foundation grants and from sale of publications. The president of HEI is Kathleen M. Tucker, who cofounded the Karen Silkwood campaign to sue on behalf of a deceased former nuclear industry worker who claimed that her employer, Kerr-McGee Industries, had contaminated her and her apartment with radiation.

## POLICY CONCERNS

HEI's single purpose is to inform the public about radiation hazards, whether from nuclear power plants, weapons development and testing, X-rays for medical purposes, or irradiating food in order to preserve it. It is especially concerned about fetuses' and children's sensitivity to toxins and radiation and about worker exposure to radiation on the job. It has an advisory board of doctors who specialize in pediatric medicine, such as Helen Caldicott, founder of Women's Action for Nuclear Disarmament, or cancer, such as John Gofman, professor emeritus of medical physics, University of California, Berkeley, and physicists critical of the nuclear industry.

## TACTICS

HEI's executive director has testified before Congress about the dangers of ionizing radiation and has argued for increased government regulation of the levels of radiation to which workers in the nuclear and medical industries may be exposed. The Institute organizes conferences on the public health effects of ionizing radiation, such as the First Global Radiation Victims Conference in October 1987 in New York City. It also issues publications, such as those listed below, on the hazards of radiation.

### FURTHER INFORMATION

Kathleen Tucker (1979). *Uranium and the Nuclear Cycle*. Washington, D.C.: HEI.
*Food Irradiation Organization Packet* (1986). Washington, D.C.: HEI.
Stewart, Alice (1982). *Proceedings of a Seminar on the Health Hazards of Ionizing Radiation*. Washington, D.C.: HEI.

## HEALTH AND ENERGY LEARNING PROJECT
*See* Health and Energy Institute.

## HEALTH RESEARCH GROUP
*See* Public Citizen.

## HUMAN ENVIRONMENT CENTER (HEC)
1001 Connecticut Avenue, N.W. #827
Washington, D.C. 20036

### ORGANIZATION AND RESOURCES

The Human Environment Center (HEC) was founded in 1976 by Sydney Howe to provide a meeting ground for environmental and social justice groups that emphasize the needs of minority groups and the working class for employment. One of the main objectives of the organization was to stimulate conservation work programs that would provide training opportunities for the unemployed. It grew out of the work of the Urban Environmental Conference which was founded in 1972 to foster communication and develop cooperative programs between environmentalists and civil rights and labor groups.

The board of directors consists of eleven members. In the late 1980s it had revenues of about $250,000, derived entirely from grants from foundations such as Ford, and government funding. It spends about the same amount it takes in each year: 35 percent on general administration, 11 percent on minority internships in conservation work, 39 percent on dissemination of information, and 15 percent on youth conservation projects.

## POLICY CONCERNS

HEC offers technical assistance to states such as Maine, Maryland, and Wisconsin that have conservation corps programs and helps cities such as New York and San Francisco begin their own conservation corps. In 1985 a National Association of Service and Conservation Corps (NHSCC) was founded, and HEC serves as its secretariat. NHSCC provides information to all state and local conservation corps. HEC sponsored a 1986 bill in Congress to create a national youth conservation corps, which was passed by the Congress but vetoed by the president.

## TACTICS

The Center joins with environmental groups such as the Environmental Policy Institute* to oppose the commercial development of open spaces in cities that can be developed into parks and recreation centers for the urban poor. It joined the Committee for Washington Riverfront Parks in an unsuccessful lawsuit to oppose the Georgetown Waterfront development in Washington. HEC's twin goals of more equitable distribution of society's resources among its disadvantaged population and environmentally sound public policies have led to an emphasis on developing minority careers in environmental management. It publishes papers on these issues, and issues a quarterly *HEC Newsletter* to its affiliates and contributors.

## FURTHER INFORMATION

*HEC News* (1988). Washington, D.C.: HEC, Fall, December.
*Youth Can* (1985). Washington, D.C.: HEC.

# I

## INDEPENDENT AUTOMOTIVE SERVICE ASSOCIATION
*See* Automotive Service Association.

## INDEPENDENT GARAGEMEN'S ASSOCIATION
*See* Automotive Service Association.

## INDEPENDENT LUBRICANT MANUFACTURERS ASSOCIATION (ILMA)
651 South Washington Street
Alexandria, Virginia 22314

### ORGANIZATION AND RESOURCES

In 1947 the Independent Lubricant Manufacturers Association (ILMA) was founded by small manufacturers of lubricating oils. Today ILMA's members number about 265 small companies, but include the lubricating oil divisions of such giants as Chevron and Exxon Chemicals. ILMA is headed by a board of fifteen directors elected at their midyear meeting each April. The executive director heads a four-person staff in Alexandria, Virginia. Annual dues are $650; taken together with funds raised at the annual conventions and midyear meetings this provides about $700,000 for the annual budget.

### POLICY CONCERNS

ILMA is primarily concerned about government regulation of hazardous materials under Superfund and the Resource Conservation and Recovery Act (RCRA). It opposed the community right-to-know provision that was written into the Superfund Amendments and Reauthorization Act of 1986 (SARA). It has lobbied the U.S. Environmental Protection Agency (EPA) to set less stringent threshold levels for hazardous substances than EPA experts recommended. It also opposed the change in RCRA to include more small generators of hazardous wastes under its controls.

ILMA representatives generally agree with the large chemical manufacturers' trade associations in opposing any tighter controls on industry regarding clean air and water emission controls and on the definitions of hazardous wastes. It does so on the grounds that the health of the national economy should override public health considerations when the risks are not evident. However, ILMA's interests diverge somewhat on the subject of small generators of hazardous wastes. It feels that small businesses have been overregulated and that the larger corporations should be controlled first since they tend to generate a larger share of the problem.

## TACTICS

ILMA publishes a monthly newsletter for members, *Compoundings*, which keeps them up on events in Washington as well as changes in the industry. Its political action committee, ILMAPAC, collects funds to contribute for use in political campaigns. It also coordinates its activities with the major lobbying groups for the petrochemical industry such as the American Petroleum Institute* and the Chemical Manufacturers Association.*

### FURTHER INFORMATION

*Compoundings* (1987, 1988, 1989). Washington, D.C.: ILMA.
U.S. Congress. House Small Business Committee (1983). *Hearings on Hazardous Waste and Enforcement Act*. Washington, D.C. : Government Printing Office.

## INDEPENDENT PETROLEUM ASSOCIATION OF AMERICA (IPAA)
1101 16th Street, N.W.
Washington, D.C. 20036

### ORGANIZATION AND RESOURCES

Wirt Franklin, an independent oil entrepreneur, founded the Independent Petroleum Association of America (IPAA) in 1929 to represent the interests of independent businesses involved in the production of natural gas and oil. The American Petroleum Institute (API)* had existed for a decade, but smaller entrepreneurs felt a need to have their interests represented before government in addition to those of the major corporations. Although API and IPAA tend to agree on many issues, especially the need to keep taxes low and production high, over the years they often differed on such questions as what the appropriate mix of imported and domestic oil production should be, as small oil producers own no large foreign oil fields. In 1980 IPAA won major concessions from Congress by having most of the windfall profit tax burden put on larger producers, but during the Reagan administration this victory was reversed (Rosenbaum, 1987).

In the 1980s IPAA grew to a membership of 6,000 individuals. Dues range between $200 and $30,000, with an average of $357. In the late 1980s it had a budget of about $3 million, as contrasted with API's nearly $50 million. It derives 80 percent of these resources from membership dues and 20 percent from meeting registrations. A 42-member executive committee sets policy for the association and meets 4 times a year. Local and regional membership meetings are held throughout the year depending on the level of activity in particular regions. The membership elects a board of directors at the annual meeting held late each year. The directors select 34 area vice-presidents, representing every state in the United States, with several vice-presidents for a few of the major oil-producing states such as Texas and Oklahoma. H. B. "Bud" Scoggins, vice-president and general counsel since 1975, was elected president in 1987 and remains in that capacity in the 1990s. IPAA has a staff of 215 in Washington, which assists the officers and committees in tracking legislative and regulatory developments there.

IPAA has fourteen standing committees to discuss issues of importance to the membership: costs of developing oil and gas, crude oil pricing policy, economic policy, environment and safety, executive advisory, finance, membership, natural gas, nominating committee to suggest new officers and executive committee members and vice-presidents, oil recovery techniques, public lands, speakers bureau to educate the public on energy policies favorable to the oil industry, supply and demand for petroleum products, and taxation.

## POLICY CONCERNS

IPAA shares the perspective and many of the positions of its larger cohort, the American Petroleum Institute. Its representatives argue regularly before Congress for tax breaks for the oil industry in the form of depletion allowances for drilling oil wells and by writing off many of the operating costs of the industry. The tax committee believes that unique risks inherent in exploring for oil and natural gas need benevolent tax policies in order to promote production. Its energy price committee argues for no government controls on any prices of petroleum and gas products in order to encourage more domestic exploration. After the deregulation of all oil prices and the reduction in natural gas controls, a windfall profit tax was imposed by the Carter administration. IPAA opposes that tax in principle, as does API. IPAA also argues that most of the burden of that tax should fall on the larger producers of petroleum rather than its own members, and it was temporarily successful in this argument before Congress when the tax was first imposed. However, this changed in the Reagan administration, which tended to favor the major integrated companies over the smaller independents.

In the late 1980s IPAA was most concerned about the decline in domestic production of oil due to a drop in the price of foreign oil. IPAA advocates a significant import fee to bring the cost of importing foreign oil up to the costs of domestic production in order to encourage exploration for oil and gas in the

United States. Its representatives argue from a national security perspective that the United States is in a perilous position vis-à-vis its supply of oil and will be caught short again, as it was in the middle 1970s when a fuel supply crisis occurred in the United States.

IPAA also argues that "take-or-pay" contracts, which obligate distributors of natural gas or oil to buy a given amount of gas or oil from a particular field, are necessary in order to keep the industry viable. These contracts make it impossible for distributors and refiners to shift to a cheaper supply of fuel whenever the price in the international market shifts. This particular concern is not shared by the major producers that have significant foreign oil field holdings.

In most environmental and safety issues, however, the IPAA shares the perspective of the major corporations completely. The environment and safety committee follows developments in EPA and OSHA affecting the oil and gas industry and recommends association policy. IPAA believes that many regulatory programs are unnecessary, duplicative, and badly administered. Running at a generally lower profit margin than the major oil corporations, the independents tend to feel even more burdened by government controls than do their larger competitors.

The public lands committee studies and comments on legislation and regulations affecting exploration for and the development of oil and natural gas on government-owned lands. It argues for maximum use of publicly owned lands for energy development and believes that the Alaskan wilderness and continental shelf lands should be opened uniformly to exploration. Since many IPAA members do the initial exploration for supplies that the majors then purchase, they are particularly adamant about the need to use all domestic supplies, especially those on public landholdings.

## TACTICS

The staff of IPAA supplies congressional representatives, especially those from states where oil and gas production is important to the economy, with data to make the industry's case before Congress. Petroleum Independent Publishers, Inc., is a wholly owned subsidiary of IPAA that publishes *Petroleum Independent* monthly for its members; it keeps them informed about developments in the industry. The company also publishes *The Oil and Gas Producing Industry in Your State*, an annual compendium of statistics about domestic production. IPAA holds semiannual meetings in May and October.

IPAA communications department, in addition to keeping its membership informed, also attempts to reach the general public with information about the petroleum industry. It sponsors a syndicated radio program, "Energy Perspectives," heard over 300 stations in 50 states that presents the industry's perspective on energy problems. It also publishes books and brochures for public distribution and maintains contact with reporters and editors of the print media to give briefings and press releases on major issues concerning energy development. It began a speakers bureau in 1975 to train individual members in communication techniques. IPAA staff schedule events for these volunteer speakers around the country in order to improve the public's perception of energy producers.

In 1987 IPAA launched a fund drive for the Thomas Jefferson Energy Foundation to educate the public about the need for more domestic oil production. It raised $76,000, $130,000 in pledges, and a promise of a $100,000 grant from the Noble Foundation of Ardmore, Oklahoma. The Thomas Jefferson Foundation also accepts funding from API and the major oil corporations and intends to involve participants from other industries and from the academic and political areas. One of its divisions directs its activities toward raising funds for a permanent home for both the Foundation and IPAA.

### FURTHER INFORMATION

Blair, John M.(1976). *The Control of Oil*. New York: Pantheon.
Chubb, John E. (1983). *Interest Groups and the Bureaucracy*. Stanford Calif.: Stanford University Press.
McFarland, Andrew (1984). "Energy Lobbies." *Annual Review of Energy* 9: 501–527.
Oppenheimer, Bruce (1974). *Oil and the Congressional Process: The Limits of Symbolic Politics*. Lexington, Mass.: Lexington Books.
*Petroleum Independent* (1987, 1988, 1989). Washington, D.C., Petroleum Independent Publishers.
Rosenbaum, Walter A. (1981). *Energy, Politics, and Public Policy*. Washington, D.C.: Congressional Quarterly Press.
Stobaugh, Robert, and Daniel Yergin, eds. (1983). *Energy Future*. 3d ed. New York: Vintage Press.

## INDUSTRIAL GAS CLEANING INSTITUTE (IGCI)
700 North Fairfax Street, Suite 304
Alexandria, Virginia 22314

### ORGANIZATION AND RESOURCES

The Industrial Gas Cleaning Institute (IGCI) was founded in 1960 to represent manufacturers of air pollution control equipment for stationary (non-vehicular) sources of air pollution. Its members include corporations that produce flue gas desulfurization systems, electrostatic precipitators, fabric filters, wet scrubbers, gaseous emission control equipment, and mechanical collectors. It provides the same kinds of representational and information services that other trade associations provide for their members concerning profitability in the industry, marketing strategies, and research and development going on in the industry.

IGCI is a modest-sized trade association with approximately thirty-one member corporations and an annual budget of around $250,000. It derives most of its revenues from corporate dues that depend upon the sales volume of the individual companies. There is an assessment ceiling of $21,500 for any individual firm. It has a governing board of twelve members from some of its member corporations elected at the annual meeting. Two professional staffers provide information and legislative assistance from headquarters in Washington.

## POLICY CONCERNS

This is one trade association that benefits from increased strictness of pollution control laws, and it has argued for stricter air pollution control laws since its creation in 1960. It is unlikely that it would have come into existence had it not been for the rudimentary air pollution law that was passed in the 1950s. IGCI representatives testified throughout the 1980s for strengthening the Clean Air Act by forcing stationary sources to reduce their sulfur oxide emissions in order to reduce acid rain in the United States and Canada. Its representatives argued that Congress should give the U.S. Environmental Protection Agency authority over states that refuse to meet deadlines on sulfur oxides.

## TACTICS

IGCI holds an annual meeting for its members at which the latest techniques for reducing air pollution emissions are displayed. It also provides a bimonthly newsletter, *Clean Air News*, to members and research reports on market forecasts and statistical reports on production for the industry. As many small trade associations with modest staffs do, IGPA depends on the CEOs of its major members, and especially its board members, to testify before Congress and the agencies about its perspective on air pollution control policy.

## FURTHER INFORMATION

*The Clean Air People* (1987). Washington, D.C.: IGCI.
U.S. Congress. Senate Committee on Energy and Natural Resources (1986). *Hearings on the Clean Air Act*. Washington, D.C.: Government Printing Office.

# INSTITUTE OF GAS TECHNOLOGY (IGT)
3424 South State Street
IIT Center
Chicago, Illinois 60616

## ORGANIZATION AND RESOURCES

The Institute of Gas Technology (IGT) was established in 1941 to conduct research on all aspects of energy production, distribution, and use in order to promote the use of gas as a fuel. It is headquartered in Chicago, where it constructed its energy development center on the campus of Illinois Institute of Technology in 1950.

Approximately 200 U.S. firms in the business of producing, transporting, and selling natural gas belong to IGT and contribute regularly to its program of research. In addition, over 40 international and foreign corporations and governments in the energy supply business belong. It has a 41-person board of trustees, composed of executive officers of major gas production companies, pipelines, and distribution companies. Over 70 professionals conduct research at the Chicago location.

## POLICY CONCERNS

IGT does around $15 million worth of research in-house each year, one-third sponsored by the Gas Research Institute,* one-third by individual corporations, and one-third by government agencies at the state or federal level. Its officers deplore the reduction in basic research and development funds for nonnuclear energy sources appropriated by the federal government in the 1980s. It argues that R&D needs to be increased if the United States is to develop the alternative energy technologies needed when fossil fuels become less abundant. It attempts to obtain more funding from the industry itself, but argues that the plunge in oil prices in the 1980s has set R&D back as energy companies have been unable to invest in the necessary research.

IGT concentrates on applied research to develop new, less costly systems for producing gas from coal, shale, and biomass as well as transportation systems for natural gas. It also emphasizes innovative methods of using natural gas, such as gas-fired incineration systems for reducing toxic wastes, microbial methods of producing liquid fuels, production of electricity and chemicals from methane, and natural gas–fueled vehicles. Work is done starting with fundamental laboratory experiments and progressing all the way through development of scale models of new technology to testing commercial applications in the field.

## TACTICS

IGT's headquarters and laboratories are located in Chicago, but it maintains a Washington office with a small staff in order to testify before Congress and the Department of Energy (DOE) and other relevant agencies about development of gas technology and the need for more government investment in energy research. It supplies its members with research reports on its operations and sponsors workshops and symposia around the country on new technologies. It also issues *International Gas Technology Highlights* and *Energy Topics*, two newsletters, keeping the membership informed of current developments in research as well as in Washington.

## FURTHER INFORMATION

*Annual Report 1988* (1989). Chicago, Ill.: IGT.

Washington office: 1825 K Street, N.W., Suite 218, Washington, D.C. 20006

## INTERNATIONAL INSTITUTE FOR ENVIRONMENT AND DEVELOPMENT
*See* Center for Development and Environment.

## INTERSTATE NATURAL GAS ASSOCIATION OF AMERICA (INGAA)
555 13th Street, N.W., Suite 300 West
Washington, D.C. 20004

## HISTORY AND DEVELOPMENT

The Interstate Natural Gas Association of America (INGAA) was founded in 1944, separate from the American Gas Association (AGA)* which had been in operation since 1918. It is smaller than its sister association, having only interstate companies on its rolls. Known until 1974 as the Independent Natural Gas Association of America, INGAA originally claimed both producers and distributors of gas as members, but now it has only distributors. When technology made it possible to run pipelines across state lines, it became evident that the interests of the interstate pipelines were different from their intrastate competitors. When federal regulation became pervasive in the interstate market, the intrastate pipelines had less difficulty obtaining supplies, and their prices were allowed to rise. The Federal Energy Regulatory Commission (FERC) still determines the cost of service for interstate pipelines and the price that pipelines may charge for transporting gas. Hence interstate pipelines continue to have a separate interest from intrastate lines.

## ORGANIZATION AND RESOURCES

INGAA now has twenty-nine corporate members, including some of the largest and most-important members of the AGA, such as Transcontinental Gas Pipe Line and The Columbia Gas System of Wilmington, Delaware. It relies on corporate membership dues for the major part of its $3-million-a-year budget. Its policies are set by a twenty-one-member board of directors who come from its corporate members. It has a thirty-person professional staff in its Washington office.

## POLICY CONCERNS

As does the AGA, INGAA seeks to increase its own profitability by urging that Congress deregulate the wellhead price of natural gas for both old and new supplies. It opposes FERC's regulation that requires pipelines to take or pay for gas contracted for regardless of whether a market exists for the gas. From 1954 to 1978, when intrastate pipelines benefited from the control of price for interstate supplies and obtained most of the supplies of new gas, INGAA opposed the distinction made between intra- and interstate gas supplies.

Like AGA and gas producers, it opposed the Powerplant and Industrial Fuel Use Act (PIFUA), which required powerplants to use coal rather than gas to generate electricity because of the restricted supply of natural gas, which was reserved for residential and commercial heating plants. In 1987, however, this restriction was lifted after a compromise was reached with the coal industry to allow for new industrial boilers to be convertible to coal use.

Before a new interstate pipeline may be laid, an environmental impact statement must be written to discuss the disruption to the environment that will occur. INGAA argues that such restrictions are unnecessary because of the industry's willingness to restore the areas it disturbs in laying pipe and its concern for wilderness, agricultural, and residential areas. INGAA also argues that both its pipelines and compressor stations used to move the gas through the system are as secure as it is possible to make them and need no regulation.

## TACTICS

Despite its smaller size, INGAA is perceived as less effective than the larger AGA because its leadership is not so capable of resolving differences among its member companies (Soloman, 1987). This occurs despite the fact that the AGA has a much more diverse membership, consisting not only of interstate pipelines in various regions of the United States but also entirely intrastate pipeline systems. INGAA issues a weekly newsletter, *Washington Report*, to keep its members up to date with events in the regulatory world as well as research on market activities and productivity in the industry.

## FURTHER INFORMATION

Chubb, John E. (1983). *Interest Groups and the Bureaucracy*. Stanford, Calif.: Stanford University Press.
*Interstate Gas Pipelines* (1989). Washington, D.C.: INGAA.
McFarland, Andrew (1984). "Energy Lobbies." *Annual Review of Energy* 9: 501–527.
Oppenheimer, Bruce (1974). *Oil and the Congressional Process: The Limits of Symbolic Politics*. Lexington, Mass.: Lexington Books.
Rosenbaum, Walter A. (1987). *Energy, Politics, and Public Policy*. 2d ed. Washington, D.C.: Congressional Quarterly Press.
Soloman, Burt (1986). "Ganging Up." *National Journal*, July 19, pp. 1778–1781.
——— (1987). "Measuring Clout." *National Journal*, July 4, pp. 1706–1711.
Stanfield, Rochelle L. (1987). "Paying for Nothing." *National Journal*, April 4, pp. 812–814.

## IZAAK WALTON LEAGUE OF AMERICA (IWLA)
1401 Wilson Boulevard, Level B
Arlington, Virginia 22209

### HISTORY AND DEVELOPMENT

In 1922, 54 sportfishermen, concerned about the deteriorating quality of the streams they fished, met in Chicago and formed the Izaak Walton League of America (ILWA). They named their organization after Izaak Walton, a seventeenth-century English conservationist who wrote *The Compleat Angler*, and began a campaign to clean up the surface waters in the United States. Will H. Dilg was its first president; he began the monthly magazine *Outdoor America* which addressed all kinds of conservation issues from water pollution to disappearing marshlands. He developed the first mass membership conservation organization by using the techniques of fraternal organizations such as the Kiwanis to attract members. In the 1920s, while the Sierra Club* and Audubon Society* had fewer than 10,000 members, Izaak Walton claimed over 100,000.

Conservationists in the 1920s differed over whether game birds were disappearing because they were being overhunted or because they lacked appropriate breeding grounds due to civilization's encroachment on their habitat. The Izaak Walton League endorsed having the federal government regulate the number of fowl each hunter could bag and increase the number of federal wildlife preserves. Dilg personally convinced President Coolidge to sign a bill establishing 300 miles of river bottoms near the Upper Mississippi River as a new refuge when they were threatened with drainage and development. Like the early Auduboner, William E. Dutcher, however, Dilg overspent his treasury, and the other members of the board of directors deposed him in 1926.

The American Game Protective Association, which had numerous ties to the munitions and gun manufacturing industry, tried for many years to pass a refuge bill through Congress that would allow hunting on federal refuges. This was repeatedly stalemated by other elements of the conservation establishment, especially the Izaak Walton League, which took a more ecological approach to its conservationist efforts. Under Kenneth Reid's tenure from 1938 to 1949, the league made a coalition with the Audubon Society, although they differed over the use of wild bird plumage for fish flies. In 1961 ILWA absorbed Friends of the Land.

The League had its major strength in the Midwest, especially in Illinois and Oklahoma, but state chapters were also established in states farther east and west. Some Wyoming leagues attempted to interest the national leadership in stopping the abuse of western federal lands by stockmen, but found most Waltonians uninterested in the dry plains. The League was much more active on behalf of water pollution control, and in 1948 its lobbyists were successful in getting the first federal water pollution control law passed. Since that time, they have expanded their interests beyond water pollution to wilderness preservation and wildlife protection.

## ORGANIZATION AND RESOURCES

In the late 1980s the League claimed a membership of 50,000, distributed among 400 Izaac Walton League chapters throughout the United States, although the majority of its members reside in the Midwest. Of 57 national directors, 31 come from 8 middle-western states. The honorary president is William Ruckelshaus, former EPA administrator under presidents Nixon and Reagan, and general counsel for Weyerhaeuser Industries. The 22-member professional staff in Arlington, Virginia is headed by Jack Lorenz, executive director. In the late 1980s the Izaak Walton League had an income of over $1.5 million which came from membership dues, 40 percent; contributions and grants, 54 percent; and the remainder from sales and interest. Expenses amounted to over $4 million, distributed into conservation and education programs, 64 percent; membership services, 15 percent; administration and planning, 16 percent; and fund-raising and membership recruitment, 5 percent. Foundation grants came from both well-known foundations such as the Joyce Foundation as well as smaller, outdoors and sports-oriented groups such as the Easton Maryland Waterfowl Festival and the National Shooting Sports Foundation. Many corporations involved with sports equipment, such as Browning Firearms, Remington Arms, National Marine Manufacturers Association, and Shakespeare Tackle, contribute to the League, as well as other major industries, such as the American Gas Association, Chevron, USA, Duke Power, Du Pont, and Weyerhaeuser.

IWLA has been involved with Save our Streams, a grass-roots community program designed to clean up particular rivers and streams around the United States. Exxon Corporation has contributed to developing a citizen's guide to helping communities clean up streams by adopting specific rivers such as the Rappahannock in Virginia. The same technique has been used to preserve wetlands in various locations, such as Easton, Maryland, by the Waterfowl Festival there. In 1986 the League cosponsored with the Du Pont Company a conference on the Chesapeake Bay Region about how to involve industry and business in efforts to restore the Chesapeake.

In 1986 the staff of IWLA produced a brochure cosponsored by the fishing tackle industry entitled *Acid Rain Kills*, designed to be included in fishing gear packages to inform sportfishermen of the danger of acid rain to their lakes and rivers. The League also testified on behalf of strong acid rain control laws passed in Minnesota and Wisconsin. Staffers also testified for a national acid rain control bill which failed, and in favor of the amendments to the Clean Water Act and Superfund amendments which passed.

League spokesmen agreed with other conservation groups that soil erosion is one of the major sources of pollution to creeks and streams in the United States. They also argued against the Reagan administration's decision to extend its policy of below-market-value grazing fees and generous allotments to ranchers of public lands in the West. ILWA joined with other conservation groups to sue about the shortcomings of the Bureau of Land Management's control of federal rangelands. It also testified in favor of preserving public lands in Alaska for national parks and wildlife refuges and against the Reagan administration's plans to open wilderness areas there to oil exploration.

IWLA also lobbied Congress and the Federal Energy Regulatory Commission to impose larger fees on beneficiaries of electricity generated by federal hydropower projects and to require more consideration of the impact on fisheries of such public works. It advocated more federal expenditure on restoring and stocking federal fisheries. In 1977 it established an outdoor ethics program encouraging more responsible hunting use of the outdoors.

### TACTICS

The League publishes *Outdoor America*, a quarterly magazine with in-depth reports by major outdoor writers and naturalists. It also carries reports on issues such as groundwater contamination and the decline in population of ducks and the effects of acid rain on forests and lakes.

In the 1980s the League established a building fund to raise $2 million for a new national office and conservation center on forty acres owned by the League in Gaithersburg, Maryland.

## FURTHER INFORMATION

*1988 Annual Report* (1988). IWLA.

Steven Fox (1981). *John Muir and His Legacy: The American Conservation Movement.* Boston: Little, Brown.

# L

---- / ----

## LEAGUE OF CONSERVATION VOTERS (LCV)
200 L Street, N.W.
Washington, D.C. 20036

### ORGANIZATION AND RESOURCES

In 1970 some Friends of the Earth (FOE)* members who wished to become more directly involved in the political process founded the League of Conservation Voters (LCV) devoted to electing political candidates who support environmental legislation. The first steering committee consisted of the chair, Marion Edey, and seven others: David Brower, then president of FOE, Joe Browder, Gary Soucie, Douglas Scott, Michael McCloskey, Thomas Dustin, and George Alderson.

By 1990 LCV's board of directors had expanded to twenty-six, including representatives from Friends of the Earth/Environmental Policy Institute,* Environmental Action,* Environmental Defense Fund,* Natural Resources Defense Council,* National Audubon Society,* Sierra Club,* National Wildlife Federation,* Izaak Walton League of America,* and Clean Water Action Project.* Alden Meyer became executive director in 1986, replacing Marion Edey who had directed the League since its inception. He was in turn replaced by Jim Maddy in 1988.

LCV has six field offices in addition to the national office in Washington to help in political campaigns. These are located in: Philadelphia, Pennsylvania New Brunswick, New Jersey; Portsmouth and Manchester, New Hampshire; Portland, Oregon; and Seattle, Washington. LCV requests dues of $18 a year from members who receive its yearly *Congressional Report* and makes frequent requests for contributions, especially during election years in order to help fund individual campaigns. In 1988 it distributed about $3 million to congressional campaigns.

## POLICY CONCERNS

The 100th Congress voted in 1987–88 on numerous issues that the League had continually supported since its creation. It reauthorized the Clean Water Act over President Reagan's veto in 1987, including $18 billion in aid to states for constructing sewage treatment plants. It failed to pass an acid rain bill despite the best efforts of LCV and other environmental groups and postponed the sanctions that would have applied to areas not meeting clean air quality standards. The 100th Congress was essentially stalemated over the issue of clean air.

In 1987, also, Congress passed over the president's veto the Appliance Energy Standards Act, establishing federal energy standards for most major household appliances. However, in 1986, the Reagan administration reduced the corporate average fuel economy (CAFE) standards for automobile energy use from 27.5 mpg to 26, and the Congress did nothing to stop it. The Federal Insecticide, Fungicide and Rodenticide Act was reauthorized in 1988, and it was modified to some degree, but not to the extent LCV would have preferred.

The 100th Congress also reauthorized the Price-Anderson act in 1987, continuing the practice of absolving the nuclear power industry from full liability for any nuclear accident that might occur. It did raise the limit of liability from $700 million to $7 billion, but the environmental movement argued that even this amount was insignificant in comparison to the real potential damages. Throughout the 1980s LCV advocated reduced spending on public works projects that it considers ecologically damaging, especially massive water projects in the West constructed by the Bureau of Reclamation. It argued for various reforms such as making the recipients of this public largesse pay for more of the costs and refusing to pay farmers to take croplands out of production which are then replaced with lands irrigated by publicly funded projects. The 100th Congress eroded these reforms by spending more money on additional water projects.

The Endangered Species Act was reauthorized in 1988, and a law was passed banning U.S. ships from dumping non-degradable plastic debris, which often kills marine life, into the oceans. The secretary of commerce was also directed by Congress to study the impact of drift nets set out by the Japanese, many of which are lost and kill seabirds and mammals, as well as fish that are never harvested.

One of the major controversies in the 100th Congress was the Reagan administration's demands that the coastal plain of the Arctic National Wildlife Refuge be opened to exploration and development by the oil and gas industry. The issue was unresolved at the end of the 100th Congress, but promised to become a major priority in the Bush administration. In March 1989, when an Exxon tanker spilled 11 million gallons of crude oil into Prince William Sound in Alaska, the discussion of the wisdom of moving Prudhoe Bay oil by tanker rather than across

Canada by pipeline was once more opened. Environmental groups obtained new allies in their fight on Capitol Hill, but the Bush administration remained adamant in its support of the oil industry.

Throughout the Reagan administration the Department of the Interior expedited oil development in the outer continental shelf lands against the desires of some of the state governors in the coastal zone states, and a Senate attempt to make it harder for the department to ignore the states was defeated in 1986. An attempt to slow the Forest Service's expansion of roads in the national forests to accommodate timber cutting was also defeated. The state of Hawaii's Senate contingent succeeded in getting a new highway exempted from environmental impact requirements imposed by the federal courts, which the League and conservation-minded Senators opposed.

During the 99th Congress' Superfund reauthorization, LCV successfully supported the right of communities to know when hazardous chemicals are released into the community, but the right for those hurt by toxic waste to sue in federal court was rejected by the Congress. The Synthetic Fuels Corporation was eliminated with the President's approval.

The Westway Interstate Highway was eliminated after many years of debate over the feasibility of using the funds for other methods of transportation in New York City. The United States cut off all funding to the U.N. Fund for Population Activities that assists family planning programs in underdeveloped countries despite attempts by the LCV in Congress to retain some funding. A conservation corps plan to fund jobs for unemployed youths to work on public lands failed to pass the 99th Congress.

*TACTICS*

The League of Conservation Voters donates money to congressmen and senators of both parties who support environmental causes, especially those who are in danger of losing their seats. It also helps campaigns of challengers who compete for the seats of known opponents of environmental causes in both House and Senate. In 1988 it endorsed fifty-six candidates for the House of Representatives, and forty-two were victorious; similarly it won seventeen out of the twenty Senate races in which it became involved. Most of the victors were, however, incumbents. In the late 1980s it expanded its program by sending canvassers into the electoral districts of campaigns it deemed particularly crucial.

The League tracks how individual congressmen vote on environmental issues defined by the League each year as important to environmental causes. It publishes a chart on Senate and House votes each year and distributes these to subscribers who wish to track the behavior and response of individual policy makers to environmental causes.

During presidential campaigns LCV analyzes the environmental records of all candidates and publishes a report on all contenders for the nomination of both parties. It includes information on all actions taken by these individuals in their public lives on air and water pollution, toxic materials, wastes, pesticides and herbicides, worker health and safety, resource recovery, ocean, coastal and wetlands protection, water projects, public land management, wildlife conservation, agriculture and land use, stripmining, energy conservation and renewable energy resources, nuclear power, and synthetic fuel development. In 1988 it endorsed Michael Dukakis for president.

## FURTHER INFORMATION

Berke, Richard (1988). "How a PAC Chooses Its Candidates." *The New York Times*, July 8, 9.
*How Congress Voted on Energy and the Environment* (1970–89). Washington, D.C.: LCV.
*Presidential Candidates for 1988* (1988). Washington, D.C.: LCV.
*The 1988 National Election Report* (1989). Washington, D.C.: LCV.

## LEAGUE OF WOMEN VOTERS
1730 M Street, N.W.
Washington, D.C. 20036

### ORGANIZATION AND RESOURCES

The League of Women Voters (LWV) was founded in 1920 under the name National League of Women Voters, immediately after the women's suffrage movement had succeeded in obtaining the vote for women. Its founder, Carrie Chapman Catt, was dedicated to promoting women's participation in politics after the lengthy fight to obtain the vote. In 1987 it claimed 110,000 members, including a minority of men, in some 1,250 local and state leagues around the United States. Most members join at the local level, pay their dues of $30 to those leagues, and participate in consensus building at the local level. Its executive director heads a staff of 74 in Washington.

Local leagues collect dues from members annually and pay a per-member contribution to their state and national leagues. In the late 1980s the U.S. League of Women Voters had revenues of nearly $8 million, 35 percent of which came from per-member payments from local leagues and 6 percent came from direct-mail solicitation from individual members. The remainder came from sale of publications, registration and other fees from conventions, and investments. LWV solicits donations from unions such as American Federation of State, County and Municipal Employees and the International Ladies' Garment Workers; and from business organizations such as Exxon Company, U.S.A. It is a not-for-profit corporation under Section 501(c)(4) of the IRS code. However, it also has an education fund which has 501(c)(3) status, which enables it to accept tax-deductible contributions to be used for public information, not lobbying activities. Some of the corporations and foundations that have contributed to the League in the recent past are the AT&T Foundation, GTE Foundation, Sears Roebuck, Time, Inc. and IBM Corporation.

## POLICY CONCERNS

The League has been involved since its founding in major public policy issues, including voting and civil rights, the electoral process, and openness in government. It has added concerns over the years, including arms control, U.S. membership in the United Nations, equal access to housing and employment, income assistance, transportation, and urban and agricultural policies.

As early as the 1930s LWV became concerned about the depletion of natural resources and undertook a study of the Tennessee Valley Authority. In 1972 the League's national convention voted to evaluate land-use policies and procedures and their relationship to water, land, and air pollution. In 1975 LWV lobbied for passage of national land-use legislation in Congress that would have provided financial incentives for state and local land-use planning and management, but the proposed legislation did not pass. It has, however, successfully supported national laws concerning coastal zone management, open space preservation, wilderness designation, strip mining control, and air and water pollution control.

Between 1956 and 1958 the League undertook a water resources study throughout the country and advocated increasing the federal role in protecting water quality through amendments to the Federal Water Pollution Control Act. LWV representatives to Congress supported passage of the 1974 Safe Drinking Water Act (SDWA), and in 1986, expanded coverage to protect groundwater supplies. In 1987 it undertook an extensive study of groundwater quality throughout the United States with a grant from the Environmental Protection Agency (EPA). It both surveyed its membership about their perceptions of the quality of drinking water in their communities and asked local leagues to study the water treatment facilities that their communities depend upon.

Using its consensus on clean water as a model, LWV also advocated increasing the federal role in fighting air pollution in the 1960s. LWV staffers have traditionally testified before Congress each time the Clean Air Act has come up for reauthorization or modification. The League generally supports strengthening controls over pollution sources and tightening standards and setting new standards to include toxic pollutants. It opposed extension of deadlines for meeting ambient air quality standards and auto emission standards. The League has, since its first interest in natural resources, emphasized the interrelationship of air, water, and land resources and their contamination.

In the field of solid waste, the League advocates resource conservation, the reduction of volume of waste at the source, and recycling reusable resources to the maximum extent possible. LWV staffers testified before Congress in the 1980s about the reauthorization of both the Resource Conservation and Recovery Act and Superfund. They argued that liquid hazardous wastes should be banned from both landfills and injection wells, and exemption created for small generators of hazardous wastes should be eliminated. They also argued that EPA's review of permanent standards for hazardous wastes should be speeded up and no more interim permits issued.

Since 1974 the League has supported energy conservation as a primary focus for national energy policy. The League supports long-term government planning on energy supplies and the development of alternative energy resources, such as solar and other renewable resources. It advocates minimizing dependence on nuclear power and imported resources, and has testified in favor of commercial and residential energy conservation tax credits, decontrol of oil prices, and a windfall profits tax that was signed into law in 1980. It also supported decontrol of natural gas prices and mandatory conservation measures such as thermal standards for buildings and appliance standards.

LWV is committed to the notion of a strong federal role in formulating national policies regarding natural resource conservation and pollution control. It advocates national land-use planning and standards for air and water at the national level. At the same time, it is committed to maximum public participation and involvement at the grass-roots level, including state and local planning, and argues that enforcement should be carried out at the local level. It has traditionally supported all amendments to increase the public's right to know about toxic materials stored in local areas and for EPA to inform local and state governments about chemical hazards in their areas. It advocates notice to the public of any plants out of compliance with any pollution control standards.

## TACTICS

LWV is as nonpartisan organization devoted to openness in government and to promoting public participation in politics. It sponsors debates among political candidates at the national, state, and local levels. Local political chairpersons organize debates among candidates for office, from local school boards to mayors. They also attempt to register as many new voters as possible, and many members serve as volunteer registrars in states that permit this activity. The League's philosophy supports public education and public participation at all levels in all public policy issues.

Local leagues meet regularly to come to consensus on major issues that have been studied at the national and local levels. The national League's education fund regularly develops study guides and other information about controversial issues and distributes them to local leagues. These groups meet to come to consensus and report their opinions to the state level, which is later aggregated at the national level. Elected state delegates to the national League's biennial national convention develop policy positions on various issues based on studies conducted by local leagues based on information supplied through the national staff. This highly diffuse and decentralized system often results in moderate to liberal stances on particular issues. In the 1980s, LWV adopted a pro-choice position on abortion rights for women.

Members attending the biennial conventions in Washington are encouraged by the professional staff and national officers to visit their representatives and express their views to them while in the capital. The League rarely takes radical stands on any issue. It does not engage in direct action nor even support political candidates who support its position. It has a reputation as a cautious evaluator of issues; hence politicians and other policy makers at the national and state levels often turn to the League to help make up commissions formed to study environmental issues on which both industry and environmental groups are represented.

The League is often looked to as a neutral arbiter that can be relied upon to provide a forum for discussion of all sides of an issue. Its professional staff and elected officials frequently are asked to testify by congressional committee staff. Agencies that implement laws in the environmental and many other fields also call on them. Its membership is highly educated and, hence, reasonably affluent. Therefore, its stands are not often different from those of other mainstream groups. However, it is generally regarded as a proenvironmental force. Its membership is not motivated by personal profit, but rather by a desire to be involved in public affairs as well as to educate themselves. Its self-image is as an educational, public-regarding organization.

LWV publishes the bimonthly *National Voter*, which it distributes to its membership, in which its editors keep the membership abreast of political developments in Washington and include in-depth articles about major public policy issues. The Education Fund also publishes numerous research monographs on particular problems such as nuclear waste disposal which are available for purchase to local leagues. Local leagues publish their own community *Voters* on a semimonthly basis which keep individual members abreast of activities in their local leagues.

### FURTHER INFORMATION

*Annual Report, 1987–1988.* (1988). Washington, D.C.: LWV.
*Impact on Issues 1986–88.* (1988). Washington, D.C.: LWV.

## LIVING LAKES, INCORPORATED
1090 Vermont Avenue, N.W.
Washington, D.C. 20005

### ORGANIZATION AND RESOURCES

Living Lakes, Inc., is a not-for-profit organization established in 1985 to demonstrate that cost-effective techniques are available to restore acidified waters to a capacity to maintain fisheries for commercial and recreational use. It was created by the electric utility and coal industries in order to counter arguments made by ecologists that the problem of acid rain needs to be addressed at the source by reducing sulfur oxide emissions from industrial plants.

There is a thirteen-person board of directors consisting of CEOs and other officials from various electric utilities around the United States and the CEOs from Consolidation Coal Company and Peabody Holding Company. The six-person staff in Washington is headed by Dr. Robert W. Brocksen, executive director, who formerly was a senior program manager with the Electric Power

Research Institute (EPRI).* Living Lakes is funded entirely by contributions from its utility and coal members; it has an annual budget of about $3 million, 62 percent of which is spent on environmental services, 10 percent on professional services, and the remainder on administration.

## POLICY CONCERNS

Living Lakes is concerned with only one policy: the possibility that the Clean Air Act (CAA) will be amended at some time to increase mandatory controls of sulphur emissions from industrial and electric utility plants. It seeks to avoid this not by directly lobbying Congress but by proving the cost-effectiveness of alternative methods of solving the acid deposition problem.

## TACTICS

Living Lakes contracts out to two science and technology firms the tasks of testing lakes and streams for acidity and then dropping or injecting finely ground limestone into them in order to bring the water back into a sufficiently neutral pH to allow sport fish to reproduce. This technique was originally developed in Sweden, which has recognized its acid deposition problem for many years, and it was researched extensively by EPRI before being turned over to Living Lakes.

During 1986, Living Lakes' first year of operation, seven lakes in New York and eight in Massachusetts were studied and treated with lime. In some, fish were introduced and monitored in order to determine how effective the program had been. By the end of 1988 Living Lakes had treated twenty-eight lakes and eleven streams in New York, Massachusetts, Rhode Island, Pennsylvania, Maryland, Michigan, Minnesota, and West Virginia, some with the cosponsorship of the state's department of natural resources.

The sponsors of Living Lakes intend to continue the program for five years during which time they hope to identify more sites that are potential candidates for the mitigation treatment and to convince the relevant state departments of natural resources to take over maintenance of the program. In so doing Living Lakes hopes to convince governments and the public of the efficacy of mitigating the problem of acid waters rather than attempting to prevent it.

Included on Living Lakes' quality assurance and advisory board are representatives from various universities and wildlife groups, such as the Sport Fishing Institute and Trout Unlimited.* By inviting such organizations to participate and learn about the process, Living Lakes' sponsors hope to eventually turn over to such groups responsibility for continuing to ameliorate the various treatable sites.

In order to demonstrate the effectiveness of its program, Living Lakes and its contractors make presentations before industry, civic, conservation, and governmental organizations. It also produced a videotape, *Upon the Waters*, demonstrating its liming technique that it makes available to campgrounds, junior and senior high schools, colleges, and cable TV companies. In so doing it hopes to persuade the relevant state governments, and eventually the U.S. Department of Interior's Fish and Wildlife Service, to accept liming as the solution to acid deposition throughout the United States. It also publishes a newsletter for its membership to report on its progress.

## FURTHER INFORMATION

*Annual Report 1988* (1989), Washington, D.C.: Living Lakes.

# M

—————————— / ——————————

## MANUFACTURERS OF EMISSION CONTROLS ASSOCIATION (MECA)
1707 L Street, N.W., Suite 570
Washington, D.C. 20036

### ORGANIZATION AND RESOURCES

The Manufacturers of Emission Controls Association (MECA) is a trade association formed in 1976 to assist the new industry specializing in manufacturing catalytic converters and other emission control devices for the automotive industry. It now has eighteen corporate members, including Allied Signal Automotive Catalyst Company, Corning Glass Works, the 3M Company, Midas International, and Walker Manufacturing. Many of these companies have expanded into the business of providing air pollution controls for stationary sources as well as motor vehicles. It charges $3,500 for dues and produces an annual budget of about $60,000. It has three professional staff people in Washington, headed by Executive Director Bruce I. Bertelsen.

### POLICY CONCERNS

MECA was an unintended consequence of the Clean Air Act (CAA), one of the environmental initiatives undertaken by the U.S. government in the 1970s. By mandating a percentage reduction of hydrocarbons, carbon monoxide, and nitrogen oxide emissions from cars, Congress provided an incentive for entrepreneurs and established companies to devote resources to finding a method for reducing those substances. Motor vehicle manufacturers met the initial, rather low, standards by simply adjusting engines to perform less efficiently. However, in a few years the catalytic converter was developed as an add-on device for cars, which actually improved fuel efficiency. Originally, Congress had hoped to force the development of new clean-burning engines, but this has not happened, and we continue to rely on catalytic converters together with air/fuel metering systems for cars.

MECA continues to support the requirements of the CAA and argues before Congress that emission controls are necessary and should be strengthened. It argues that the U.S. Environmental Protection Agency (EPA) should ban all lead additives to gasoline, which would reduce the damage to catalytic converters caused when owners fail to comply with CAA requirements and refuel their cars with leaded gasoline. Increasing the price of leaded gas to more than that charged for lead-free gas would also solve the problem by eliminating the incentive for noncompliance. MECA also argues that gasoline-powered trucks and buses should meet the same standards as cars by using a three-way catalytic converter. MECA argued unsuccessfully in coalition with environmental groups against reducing the stringency of nitrogen oxide standards for both cars and light duty trucks.

One problem that remains to be addressed in the mobile-source area are particulates from buses and trucks. Although the CAA mandated controls, EPA has been slow in administering this part of the law, responding instead to demands made by the automotive manufacturing industry. MECA argues in favor of using trap oxidizers, filters located in the exhaust system, to control particulates emitted by diesel engines. Thus far, however, the truck and bus industry has been successful in getting delays for particulate standards which have been pushed into the 1990s. MECA also advocates incentives to force the petroleum industry to develop lower sulfur content diesel fuel, which would facilitate the development of trap oxidizers and reduce the load on the filters.

A significant percentage of MECA members also belong to the stationary source control committee, which produces similar kinds of control devices for stationary sources. MECA argues before EPA and Congress for more effective controls on all sources, especially those producing nitrogen oxide, which is one of the more difficult pollutants to control, and contributes to the ozone problem. MECA argues its catalytic converter technology, developed for mobile sources, could be effective in many industrial plants, and therefore favors increased stringency in the CAA to control acid deposition in the United States. It believes that the only way stationary sources will ever be cleaned up is to have Congress mandate percentage reductions there just as it did for mobile sources in 1970, rather than relying on state implementation plans as is done under the CAA now. MECA members argue they have selective catalytic reduction methods that could be used to retrofit power plants and industrial boilers to control nitrogen oxides now. It also argues that only if Congress increases the stringency of the law will more resources be put into reducing the costs of reducing emissions.

## TACTICS

MECA spends much of its resources in attempting to convince the public not to tamper with the catalytic converters on their cars and to use unleaded gasoline.

It argues before Congress and the states for more effective inspection and maintenance programs which would force car owners to have their cars tested for effective operation of the emission control devices. In so doing, MECA argues, the effectiveness of controls already in place would be greatly increased and air quality improved in most cities. EPA has been reluctant to impose inspection programs on states, although they are mandated by the CAA in those areas not meeting standards. On this issue MECA is in alliance with the auto repair industry. The resources of this coalition cannot begin to compare with those of the petroleum and auto industry, as well as industries such as the electric generating one that contribute to air pollution. However, it does send its representatives from individual companies belonging to MECA to Congress and EPA regularly. It also produces papers and press releases designed to improve the public image of the pollution control industry and to convince individual consumers not to tamper with their own emission control devices.

## FURTHER INFORMATION

U.S. Congress. Senate Committee on Environment and Public Works (1987). *Hearings on Acid Rain Legislation*. Washington, D.C.: Government Printing Office, June 17.

## MANUFACTURING CHEMISTS ASSOCIATION
*See* Chemical Manufacturers Association.

## MARINE MAMMAL CONSERVATION FUND
*See* Center for Marine Conservation.

## MEDIA RESOURCE SERVICE
*See* Scientists Institute for Public Information.

## MINING AND RECLAMATION COUNCIL OF AMERICA
*See* National Coal Association.

## MISSISSIPPI VALLEY ASSOCIATION
*See* Water Resources Congress.

## MORE GAME BIRDS
*See* Ducks Unlimited.

## MOTOR VEHICLE MANUFACTURERS ASSOCIATION OF THE U.S. (MVMA)
300 New Center Building
Detroit, Michigan 48202

## ORGANIZATION AND RESOURCES

The Motor Vehicle Manufacturers Association of the U.S. (MVMA) was founded in 1913 as a trade association to represent the interests of the young car and truck industry. It was created through the merger of the National Association of Auto Manufacturers, founded in 1900, and the Association of Licensed Auto Manufacturers in 1903. Until 1934 it was known as the National Automotive Chamber of Commerce, and as the Automobile Manufacturers Association until 1972. It now has 7 corporate members whose dues depend on the volume of their business on a yearly basis. Thomas H. Hanna is president of MVMA with about a $14 million annual budget and a 109-member staff in its headquarters in Detroit. It also maintains a lobbying presence in Washington.

The big three automotive engineering companies in the United States, General Motors, Ford Motor Company, and the Chrysler Corporation, form the heart of the MVMA. In addition, the major automotive corporations represent their own interests individually before Congress and the regulatory agencies. In the late 1980s General Motors (GM) had sales of over $100 billion, Ford Motor Company had sales totaling over $60 billion, and Chrysler, the smallest of the three, had sales of over $22 billion.

GM has 35 vice-presidents and employs some 876,000 people worldwide. Its corporate headquarters are in Detroit. Ford has 34 vice-presidents and employs over 382,000 people worldwide. Its corporate headquarters are in Dearborn, Michigan. Chrysler Corporation has 22 vice-presidents and employs over 115,000. Its headquarters are in Highland Park, Michigan. All three maintain major lobbying offices in Washington.

## POLICY CONCERNS

Corporate tax laws and worker/management relations are two issues that the motor vehicle manufacturing corporations and MVMA are primarily concerned about. However, they are also very involved in discussions of some pollution control and energy conservation issues. All three have consistently testified before Congress for the last three decades against the imposition of strict emission control devices on cars and trucks. They were singularly successful in preventing any major controls until 1970 when Congress, at the height of the environmental movement and despairing of administrative action against the automotive industry, mandated 90 percent reduction of auto emissions by 1975.

By the late 1980s, after many postponements of deadlines and setbacks in administration, the auto industry argued that this 90 percent reduction goal had been met for carbon monoxide and hydrocarbons, and 75 percent reduction for nitrogen oxides. Any additional controls would not be worth the marginal costs involved, according to representatives of the Ford Motor Company, because of adverse effects on the energy economy and the costly rhodium used in catalytic converters. Any further reduction in automotive emissions would have to await a long-term solution such as replacement of gasoline with methanol or some other fuel.

The Motor Vehicle Manufacturers Association of the U.S. argued before Congress during discussion of CAA amendments in 1984 that there is no need to control nitrogen oxide (NOX) emissions on diesel trucks because there is no technology known for accomplishing this. In addition, mobile sources are only responsible for a tiny part of the precursors of acid rain, and stationary sources should be reduced before any more draconian requirements are made on the automotive industry. Because most parts of the United States are not out of compliance with NOX standards, and EPA adopted a more relaxed method for measuring it in the Reagan administration, it should not be considered a crisis any longer. MVMA also believes that air pollution has been substantially reduced in the past two decades, and will go down further as old cars are phased out.

During 1989, the first year of the Bush administration, however, pressure increased to strengthen the CAA, and both administration and congressional actors vied to have their version of a new law enacted. States in the Northeast as well as California argued they could never meet ambient air quality standards without additional emission controls on the automotive industry. By the end of 1989 it was clear that some new regulations would be adopted in the 101st Congress. One suggested change was to require cars to have pollution controls that actually work for 100,000 miles rather than the 50,000 miles now prescribed under the CAA. Another possible change was to mandate that a certain percentage of cars run on alternative fuels rather than gasoline. The Bush administration actually suggested the latter change until convinced to remove it from their proposal by industry. MVMA and the big three auto producers admitted changes seemed to be inevitable but worked to keep them to a minimum. Parts of the oil industry and the auto industry combined to begin research on cars that would run on reformulated gasoline rather than switch to alternative fuels such as methanol. Other parts of the oil industry. however, began a campaign to gain acceptance for alcohol fuels, and business did not seem entirely united on a strategy to stop the impetus for a strengthened CAA in the 1990s.

Fuel economy is another policy issue that affects the motor car industry drastically. In 1975 Congress mandated a corporate average fuel economy (CAFE) standard at 27.5 mpg. In 1986, when the standard was due to go into effect, the Chrysler Corporation argued in favor of retaining this standard because it had retooled to produce small autos meeting the standard. However, Ford and GM, which had not managed to meet the standard, both argued for relaxing it because it was technologically impractical, and their demands were met by the Reagan administration (Rosenbaum, 1987). This was one of the rare instances in which the three corporate giants were not in agreement with each other on a major public policy issue affecting the environment. It is on such disagreements that the government must depend for information that contradicts the accepted wisdom about technological feasibility in an industry that normally presents a very solid front to government regulators.

In 1989, under pressure from environmental groups and some state and city officials, the Bush administration proposed new standards for cleaner cars that included reduced tailpipe emissions and some alternative-fuel vehicles to be produced by Detroit by the late 1990s. The Big Three lobbied heavily against these changes in the CAA, arguing that the alternative fuels, such as methanol, are not likely to be available in sufficient supply. Moreover, alternative fuels are less efficient, and cars using them would require larger fuel tanks in order to go the same distance as gasoline-fueled cars. The goal of clean air is therefore in direct competition with that of increased fuel efficiency, since the new cars would weigh more. All auto manufacturers are reluctant to produce such cars, which are likely to be more expensive than conventional models, until they have a proven market.

## TACTICS

All three major automotive manufacturers maintain their own governmental liaison departments in Washington. Each corporation sends its own representatives to persuade Congress about any legislation that affects them. Usually the Big Three are in agreement over such matters as the need for emission controls on cars. Indeed there was a major lawsuit in 1969 that was settled out of court in which the Justice Department argued that the Big Three had colluded to avoid producing any emission control devices for motor vehicles for many years preceding the 1965 CAA amendments that mandated reductions in emissions (Davies and Davies, 1975, p. 98). The Big Three have several political action committees that collect several hundred thousand dollars to donate to politicians for use in their campaigns.

Generally the MVMA and the three major auto manufacturers cooperate in their testimony before Congress and the agencies. In addition, certain members of Congress, such as John Dingall of Michigan, can be counted on to represent the industry's interest before his colleagues. This is true of any industry that is as geographically concentrated as the auto industry is in the United States.

## FURTHER INFORMATION

Davies, J. Clarence III, and Barbara S. Davies (1975). *The Politics of Pollution*. 2nd ed. Indianapolis, Ind.: Bobbs-Merrill.

Federal Election Commission (1987–1988). *Receipts and Disbursements*. Washington, D.C.: FEC.

Gold, Allan R. (1989). "Bush Proposal for Clean Air Is Dealt a Blow." *The New York Times*, October 12, p. 1.

Gold, Allan R. (1989). "Shift on Clean Air." *The New York Times*, October 5, p. 11.

Levin, Doron P. (1989). "Auto Makers' Plea on Pollution." *The New York Times*, July 21, p. 20.

Rosenbaum, Walter A. (1987). *Energy, Politics, and Public Policy*. 2nd ed. Washington, D.C.: Congressional Quarterly Press.

Washington Office: 1620 I Street, N.W., Suite 1000, Washington, D.C. 20006

# N

---/---

## NATIONAL AGRICULTURAL CHEMICALS ASSOCIATION (NACA)
1155 15th Street, N.W., Suite 900
Washington, D.C. 20005

### ORGANIZATION AND RESOURCES

The National Agricultural Chemicals Association (NACA) was founded in 1933 to represent the interests of the fourteen founding member corporations, all of which manufactured agricultural chemicals, such as fertilizers, insecticides, and fungicides. Its interests centered around developing markets for its members' products until the 1960s when some biologists such as Rachel Carson began to document the dangers of chemical contamination of the environment.

Congress passed the original Federal Insecticide, Fungicide and Rodenticide Act (FIFRA) in 1947 which authorized the Department of Agriculture to register commercial poisons for use in the agricultural industry, but this law had little impact on the development and marketing of new agricultural chemicals until after the U.S. Environmental Protection Agency (EPA) took over administration of the law in 1970 and Congress made substantial changes to it in the 1970s. During the 1970s NACA took on a defensive role for the industry in addition to its promotional role.

By the end of the 1980s NACA had increased its corporate membership to eighty-nine, including such giants of the chemical industry as Abbott Labs, American Cyanamid, BASF, Du Pont, Dow, FMC, NOR-AM, Velsicol, and Union Carbide. These same corporations also maintain membership in such other trade associations as the Chemical Manufacturers* and Chemical Specialty Manufacturers.* It has a board of directors of thirty-two major corporate executives. Dr. Jack D. Early has been president of NACA since 1976 and heads a staff of twenty-five in Washington. It has an annual budget of nearly $4 million generated by dues that vary according to individual corporations' volume of business.

## POLICY CONCERNS

The most important law from NACA's point of view is FIFRA. Although there are about 50,000 pesticides on the market in the United States containing more than 600 active ingredients, through 1989 EPA had canceled or suspended registration for only DDT, aldrin, dieldrin, kepone, chlordane, and heptachlor, and had certified the safety of 37 others. The rest remain to be reviewed. Nevertheless, the agricultural chemicals industry views FIFRA as an oppressive regulation, and many of NACA's members have initiated federal court cases since 1970 challenging the legitimacy of EPA's regulations. Many of these cases have revolved around the issue of whether EPA can legally use data provided by one chemical corporation to review the toxicity and possible harmful effects of another company's formulation of the same pesticide.

Throughout the 1970s FIFRA was gradually strengthened until it became mandatory for EPA to suspend registration of a chemical if it had evidence that a substantial safety question exists about its use. During the Reagan administration, congressional committees argued over suggestions by environmental groups to strengthen the law and other amendments by industry to reduce the law's requirements. Finally in 1985 representatives from NACA met with the Campaign for Pesticide Reform (CPR), a coalition of consumer, environmental, and labor groups, to discuss amending the law in a mutually acceptable manner. These negotiations were tied to a proposal by industry to increase the protection of proprietors of chemicals under the Patent Term Restoration Bill. Finally, in October 1988, Congress amended FIFRA to require that all pesticides be reevaluated within nine years, using a fund supplied by the pesticide industry. The new law lifted the former requirement that EPA purchase all stocks of pesticides that it banned, despite protests by the industry. It was, however, successful in preventing any groundwater protection provisions in the new law.

Under the Reagan administration, as regulation became looser, some states began to take up the slack in their own laws. NACA of necessity turned much of its attention to countering environmental initiatives at the state level. NACA estimates that there are 442 state legislative and 195 state regulatory proposals affecting the industry, concentrated in such states as California, Massachusetts, New York, and Wisconsin, and on such issues as community and worker right-to-know laws about the content of chemicals used near them, farm worker safety, liability insurance, and groundwater protection. In 1990 an environmental coalition put on the California ballot a proposal to ban all cancer-causing chemicals in the state's agriculture industry. Industry's response was to convince President Bush to propose modifying FIFRA to preempt any state standards.

Groundwater protection is an issue of major importance to NACA in the 1990s as environmental groups have brought to the public's attention the growing contamination of many water supplies due to residues of pesticides and fertilizers that leach through soil to the water table below. During 1988 EPA began planning to initiate a groundwater monitoring survey, and NACA responded with a briefing book on industry's position that the problem has been exaggerated. It also began a forum under the sponsorship of Georgetown University's Institute for Health Policy Analysis to discuss the problem with state and national regulatory officials as well as environmental groups.

## TACTICS

Like its sister associations, CMA and CSMA, NACA uses executive officers of many of its member corporations to testify before Congress and the agencies. It also forms coalitions with its sister trade associations. The wealth of individual companies' PACs outstrips any amount of money collected by the trade associations, but the latter make their own independent contributions to politicians' campaign funds as well. NACA concentrates on improving the public image of the agricultural chemical industry in general through media campaigns emphasizing the industry's contribution to increases in farm productivity over the years. It also serves as a forum in which its members can develop common strategies with others they are often in competition with in the marketplace. Arguing in court with one another about who owns the data concerning certain chemical formulations have in fact served to slow down EPA's ability to review the impact these chemicals have on the environment and human health.

One of NACA's major tactics in recent years has been to negotiate with its erstwhile opponents, such as the Environmental Defense Fund* and regulatory agencies rather than confront them in court. It has also launched a major educational campaign aimed at schools of journalism to inform students there of the industry's position on controversial issues and to defuse what the industry perceives as hysterical reporting on chemical hazards. To counter claims of toxicologists about widespread contamination from agricultural chemicals, NACA has established an applicator training program designed to inform farmers and farm workers of the need for wearing rubber gloves and washing their hands after applying some chemicals. It also warns individual members to mark their containers for safe disposal and urges landfill operators to take properly rinsed empty containers for disposal.

## FURTHER INFORMATION

*Annual Report 1987–1988* (1989). Washington, D.C.: NACA.

Epstein, Samuel, Lester O. Brown, and Carl Pope (1982). *Hazardous Wastes in America*. San Fransisco, Calif.: Sierra Club Books.

Reinhold, Robert (1989). "California Alliance Proposes Vote on Broad Environmental Measure." *The New York Times*, October 11, p. 1.

"Spokesman Sees Safer Pesticides in Industry's Future" (1987). *The Hartford Courant*, May 24, p. 5.

Stanfield, Rochelle L. (1987). "Legalized Poisons." *National Journal*, May 2, pp. 1062–
    1066.

## NATIONAL ASSOCIATION FOR THE STUDY AND PREVENTION OF TUBERCULOSIS
*See* American Lung Association.

## NATIONAL ASSOCIATION OF ATTORNEYS GENERAL (NAAG)
Hall of the States
444 North Capitol Street
Washington, D.C. 20001

### ORGANIZATION AND RESOURCES

The National Association of Attorneys General (NAAG) was organized in
1907 to foster communication and coordination among the chief legal officers
of the states. It is funded through appropriations from the state legislatures and
through revenue generated by publications and continuing legal education seminars. All fifty states' attorneys belong and elect a president each year at their
annual meeting. NAAG has a executive director, Christine T. Milliken, who is
also its general counsel. She heads a small staff in the Hall of the States in
Washington, where other state government associations are housed.

### POLICY CONCERNS

NAAG is concerned about all legal issues that confront state governments,
especially criminal law and problems of increasing crime rates, drug addiction,
and overcrowding in state prisons. It also has divisions concerned with antitrust,
consumer protection, and energy and environmental issues. In the latter category,
NAAG is particularly concerned about the implementation of the solid and
hazardous waste laws in the 1990s. One of the major issues that must be worked
out in the courts is the liability of owners and previous owners of abandoned
toxic waste dumps. States advocate strict liability for all groups that benefited
from use of these sites. Many law cases now in the courts involve state governments that are attempting to recover costs of cleaning up these dumps. NAAG
argues that the federal government should increase the pace of its cleanups under
Superfund and supported the 1986 extension of the law.

Another major problem for the states is the federal government's refusal to
allow its own facilities to come under the control of any of the federal pollution
control laws. Since the 1970s state governments have sued to force federal
facilities such as military installations to conform to the Clean Air and Clean
Water act's in the same manner that private corporations must conform. However,
the Justice Department has taken the position that sovereign immunity precludes
the states from enforcing these laws against federal institutions. Nevertheless
states have initiated many suits against federal agencies, and some have been
successful in federal court. The Justice Department refuses to allow the U.S.

Environmental Protection Agency (EPA) to initiate suits against its fellow executive agencies, and the president has refused to change this policy.

Individual state attorneys general have sued to force the Department of Defense to clean up various dumps, such as the Rocky Mountain Arsenal in Colorado and the Twin Cities Army Ammunition Plant in Minnesota, without success. NAAG argues that both the Resource Conservation and Recovery Act (RCRA) and Superfund should apply to federal facilities as they do to state ones. It also argues that the United States should spend money to dispose of its wastes safely and should serve as a model for other waste producers, rather than defend itself against state suits.

Federal government enthusiasm for enforcement of pollution-control laws decreased in the 1980s, and states have attempted to take up some of the slack by initiating more cases of their own against polluters. Hence, NAAG reports an increased number of state air and water pollution cases against private industry in the 1980s, and various states' attorneys have built up their prosecutorial staffs in this area of the law. In addition, states' legal officers must defend their own states in federally initiated suits against them. One common kind of suit comes through Superfund under which EPA attempts to recover costs for cleaning up dump sites that are now owned or were previously owned by municipal governments.

### TACTICS

NAAG publishes several specialized newsletters, including ones on consumer protection, medicaid fraud, and crime victims to assist its members in their research on what other states are doing on common problems. It also publishes the *National Environmental Enforcement Journal* eleven times a year in order to keep its members informed about developments around the states and in Washington. This journal accepts unsolicited contributions about environmental legal issues. State governments pay $95 a year to receive it, and nonmembers of NAAG can obtain copies for $195 a year.

### FURTHER INFORMATION

*National Environmental Enforcement Journal* (May 1987; January 1989). Washington,
    D.C.: NAAG.

## NATIONAL ASSOCIATION OF AUTO MANUFACTURERS
*See* Motor Vehicle Manufacturers Association of the U.S.

## NATIONAL ASSOCIATION OF COUNTIES (NACo)
440 First Street, N.W.
Washington, D.C. 20001

## ORGANIZATION AND RESOURCES

The National Association of Counties (NACo) was organized to represent counties' interests in Washington in 1946, later than either the state or municipal governments. It now represents most counties in the United States and serves as a liaison between the counties and all other levels of government.

It has an elected board of between 90 and 125 members: one from each state with at least one NACo member county; an additional representative from 10 states with the largest representation in NACo; an additional representative from each state with 100 percent of its counties as members; two members selected by the Western Interstate Region; and 10 at-large directors appointed by the president to balance race, sex, or urban/rural inequities. NACo's president is selected at the annual meeting by the membership present. It has a staff of 50 in Washington to represent its interests to the federal government.

Voting at the conference is weighted depending on the dues paid by each county, which in turn are based on population in the county. At the end of the 1980s its annual budget was around $7 million, and came 33 percent from individual member dues, 28 percent from fund-raising, 17 percent from contracts and grants, and 22 percent from meetings and publications. NACo has twelve steering committees that pass resolutions on policies of particular concern to the organization; these policies are later voted on by the board of directors and the annual meeting. Several of these committees emphasize economic development and employment problems as well as other social welfare issues such as education and health.

## POLICY CONCERNS

NACo has a steering committee on agriculture and rural affairs, which emphasizes the importance of rural counties in the organization. This committee advocates protecting agricultural land from development and from soil erosion. It has passed resolutions against acquisition by foreign investors, for tax policies that will keep land in agricultural production, and for the U.S. Department of Agriculture to assist in preventing soil erosion. It has also resolved that the federal government should ban importation of foodstuffs that have been treated with chemicals banned in the United States and that it accept no imports with higher residues of pesticides than those prescribed for American products.

NACo's committee on environment, energy, and land use generally supports the concept of improving the quality of life for citizens in counties, but emphasizes the need to develop resources for their economic prosperity. It views the federal government as responsible for research and technical and financial support and states as responsible for coordination, but the cities and counties as the primary service providers for citizens.

In the area of water pollution, NACo has supported amendments to the Clean Water Act (CWA) and Safe Drinking Water Act (SDWA). It urges the federal government to provide financial assistance to cities and counties for sewage treatment and for public water supplies. It opposed the elimination of construction grants for sewage treatment plants in the 1987 amendments to the CWA and urges Congress to appropriate more money for the revolving loan fund for this purpose. It argues that the requirement of secondary treatment for sewage treatment plants is unrealistic without federal funding. It supports protection of aquifers, but argues that SDWA standards for potable water may be too strict for counties to meet. NACo has agreed that sludge dumping in the coastal waters of the oceans and Great Lakes should be phased out, but only when practicable considering the impacts of on-land disposal of the same material, which may ultimately wash into the coastal waters even closer to shore.

NACo supports continued federal funding for coastal zone management by the states in order to plan development along the coasts. It argues county governments should obtain part of the revenues obtained by the federal government from leasing outer continental shelf lands to energy corporations for developing energy resources in order to mitigate the impacts from coastal zone drilling that fall on counties. It has supported the Great Lakes states in their demand that the International Joint Commission on the Great Lakes reduce the flow of water into the Great Lakes while water levels are high on the American side and threaten the property of beach front owners.

NACo accepts the basic goals of the Clean Air Act (CAA), but hopes the federal government will take into account trade-offs between quality of air for protection of health and costs of pollution control. It argues that local governments should have as much discretion as possible in setting secondary standards that can be more stringent than federal standards and in creating state implementation plans for achieving the goals. It seeks to have case-by-case extensions of clean-air deadlines for counties unable to meet the ozone or carbon monoxide standards. Sanctions against state and local governments should not be so severe, and the U.S. Environmental Protection Agency (EPA) should have discretion for incremental sanctions instead of taking away sewage treatment plant or highway funding.

NACo supports the need to reduce sulfur emissions because of acid rain and urges Congress to set new for limits for coal-fired electric utilities and for diesel exhaust emissions, which EPA has failed to set. However, it argues that utilities that have reduced their sulfur emissions should not be taxed to pay for this increased reduction. NACo also urges Congress to force EPA to accelerate its process of identifying toxic air pollutants and setting standards for them under the CAA. It also wants local jurisdictions to have the option of setting stricter standards if EPA's are too low for some areas. NACo also supports efforts on the international level to reduce synthetic chlorofluorocarbons that deplete the ozone layer and increase global warming.

Because of the crisis that faces many counties in finding new sites for disposing of their solid wastes, NACo advocates federal assistance in funding resource recovery and recycling alternatives for garbage disposal. It supported the highest level of funding during the debate over the Superfund Amendments and Reauthorization Act of 1986 (SARA). It also argued that local governments should be involved in the process of identifying national priority sites for cleanup under Superfund and that the fund should be used to pay the costs of cleaning up sites owned and operated by local governments. NACo also supported the community right to know about toxic chemicals stored in their jurisdictions that was contained in Title III of SARA, but would like federal funding to help local government prepare for emergencies.

NACo urges the United States to develop all domestic energy resources available to it in order to reduce dependence on foreign suppliers. It urged Congress to fund the superconducting super collider for research on high-energy physics, and it supports continuation of the nuclear option. It urges the deregulation of all natural gas prices in order to make gas producers more competitive. It also seeks to limit "take-or-pay" provisions in producer-pipeline contracts that it believes inflate the price to the consumer and seeks "contract carriage" provisions that will require interstate pipelines to transport natural gas between any producer and purchaser, including local governments. NACo opposed the Reagan administration's suggestion that federal power marketing agencies be sold to private investors on the grounds this would raise the price of energy to communities that are dependent on cheap power.

NACo also takes positions regarding the management of public trust lands in the western part of the United States that reflect the interests of the ranching community living near them. It advocates selling off federal lands wherever they can be used for industrial, commercial, or other purposes, in order to increase the county tax rolls. It also urges the federal government to build more roads into national forests and on grazing lands in order to accommodate private use of these lands. It urges greater payments in lieu of taxes for counties where federally owned lands are located. It argues against sacrificing local economic development to the establishment of integral vistas outside national parks by restricting emissions in those areas. NACo opposes any more designation of wilderness areas without the support of the counties in which the tracts of land are located. It opposes any change in the mining law that would make it more difficult to develop mineral resources on federal lands. It opposes any more acquisition by the federal government of inholdings in national parks owned by private citizens. NACo also opposes more autonomy for Indian tribes and urges the federal government to regularize relationships with the tribes to facilitate county control over hunting and fishing rights.

## TACTICS

Like other government lobbying organizations NACo depends on its staff to represent its membership's interests on a continuing basis in Washington. It also encourages its own members to lobby their national representatives while in Washington at annual meetings as well as back home when members of Congress return for town meetings. Unlike the National Governors' Association* and the National League of Cities*, few of NACo's members are such powerful politicians that they have immediate access to the White House and important agencies. However, NACo does attempt to use county board members whenever possible.

NACo issues an annual platform to all its county members and attempts to get their feedback about the resolutions passed by the annual meeting. It attempts to respond to all regional demands, especially from western and rural areas. It publishes a biweekly *County News* to keep its membership up to date on developments in Washington and news about developments in other counties around the nation.

### FURTHER INFORMATION

*The American County Platform and Resolutions 1988–89* (1989). Washington, D.C.: NACo.
*County News* (1989). Vol. 21.

## NATIONAL ASSOCIATION OF ELECTRIC COMPANIES
*See* Edison Electric Institute.

## NATIONAL ASSOCIATION OF ENVIRONMENTAL PROFESSIONALS (NAEP)
P.O. Box 9400
Washington, D.C. 20016

### ORGANIZATION AND RESOURCES

The National Association of Environmental Professionals (NAEP) was founded in 1975 as an interdisciplinary professional association for environmental management engineers, administrators, planners, environmental lawyers, researchers, and educators. Originally NAEP membership consisted primarily of individuals involved in writing environmental impact statements under the National Environmental Policy Act. Today anyone who has had three years' relevant experience working in some phase of environmental engineering, planning, or control is eligible for membership. NAEP certifies environmental professionals if provided with sufficient information about education and work experience in environmental policy. It draws its members from government, industry, research, consulting, and educational institutions, and therefore represents a diversity of points of view. Its membership has grown dramatically during the 1980s and stood at about 2,000 at the beginning of the 1990s.

Dues are $75 a year for general members, $65 for associates, and $45 for students. Corporations and institutions may join for $500 a year. NAEP's code of ethics includes reconciling societal and individual human needs with responsibility for physical, natural, and cultural systems. It seeks to promote policies that achieve complementary support between natural and man-made, present and future, components of the physical, natural, and cultural environment.

NAEP has a twenty-two-person board of directors representing government agencies such as the U.S. Environmental Protection Agency (EPA), the U.S. Bureau of Reclamation in the Department of the Interior, and various city governments, as well as engineering and consulting firms such as Dames & Moore.

### POLICY CONCERNS

NAEP is interested in all manner of environmental controls, including air and water pollution, solid and hazardous waste disposal, use and handling of toxic materials, and especially writing environmental impact statements for federal government projects. It is less concerned about natural resource management, as forestry and range managers have their own separate and older professional associations. Its members all earn their living in either regulating, consulting about regulations, or advising their corporations about how to conform with environmental regulations. This professional association provides a common ground for professionals on both sides of the regulatory process to meet and discuss technical problems. It is difficult for them to arrive at common policy stands, representing, as they do, both the regulators and the regulated.

### TACTICS

NAEP publishes a quarterly journal, *The Environmental Professional*, which is published in cooperation with the School of Engineering of the University of California, Los Angeles. It editorial board includes many academics in the fields of engineering, public health, law, public administration, and public policy. It also includes several representatives of the environmental community*, such as the Environmental Law Institute* and The Conservation Foundation*, as well as several industrial firms. It is a refereed journal and invites submissions of broad interdisciplinary articles with some public-policy implications. NAEP also publishes a quarterly newsletter for its membership with information about job opportunities and developments in various parts of the country and international events as well.

### FURTHER INFORMATION

*The Environmental Professional* (1989). Washington, D.C.: NAEP, vol 11, no. 2.

## NATIONAL ASSOCIATION OF FINISHERS OF TEXTILE FABRICS
*See* American Textile Manufacturers Institute.

## NATIONAL ASSOCIATION OF LOCAL GOVERNMENTS ON HAZARDOUS WASTES (NALGOHW)
1015 18th Street, N.W., Suite 1002
Washington, D.C. 20036

### ORGANIZATION AND RESOURCES

The National Association of Local Governments on Hazardous Wastes (NALGOHW) was founded in 1982 to represent the interests of cities with hazardous waste problems. It has about thirty members including such cities as Philadelphia and New Orleans, all of which also belong to the National League of Cities.* It has a board of directors of eleven, including representatives of Miami and New York. Dues come from members who are assessed in accordance with their populations. Its executive director heads a small staff in Washington.

## POLICY CONCERNS

There is one major issue on NALGOHW's agenda: the problem of treating and disposing of hazardous wastes which are becoming an increasing problem for many metropolitan areas. This issue is also on the agenda of the U.S. Conference of Mayors* and the National League of Cities.* However, the members of NALGOHW believe the issue is so important that it is necessary to have its own separate organization to address it.

NALGOHW hopes to convince the federal government that state and local governments have an important role to play in determining where any new treatment facility for hazardous wastes is to be located. It represents primarily the interest of residents who want to prevent any new facilities from being placed close to a large population base. It fears that by including regulation of hazardous wastes under the Resource Conservation and Recovery Act (RCRA) of 1976, the federal government will preempt any local control over this pressing problem for cities.

NALGOHW supported the reauthorization of Superfund in 1986 to help clean up abandoned toxic dumps around the United States. It felt that the original authorization of $1.6 billion in 1980 vastly underestimated the extent of the problem. It hopes that Congress will appropriate more funds in the 1990s for this urgent problem, but it also wants to increase local government participation in the implementation of the policy. It argues that since local governments are closest to the problem, they should have some voice in determining which sites are designated as national priority list problems that should be cleaned up first.

Many toxic dumps are now the property of city governments, and Superfund mandates that responsible parties pay for the cleanup of such dumps. NALGOHW argues that local authorities should be relieved of strict liability for their cleanup and that the federal government should share this responsibility. Yet it also argues that local governments should be able to recover costs and damages from other owners and users of leaking toxic dumps.

NALGOHW hopes that the Environmental Protection Agency (EPA) will provide technical assistance to local governments to enable them to cope with these problems. It has urged Congress to include funding for innovative technologies for treating hazardous wastes instead of consigning them to landfills and incineration. NALGOHW also argues for local governments to have some control over the hazardous materials that pass through their jurisdictions in addition to that provided by the federal Hazardous Waste Transportation Act.

NALGOHW is particularly concerned about the protection of groundwater resources from which many cities draw drinking water. Therefore, it argues before Congress that hazardous wastes should be prevented from entering the aquifers used by cities through preventive measures controlling land use on the surface of the aquifer.

## TACTICS

NALGOHW coordinates much of its lobbying efforts through the National League of Cities and the U.S. Conference of Mayors. However, its leaders feel that the variety of issues in which these larger groups are involved are so complex that it was necessary to form a separate organization designed to address the single issue of hazardous wastes. It is relatively small compared to the more comprehensive local government groups, but it provides an essential service to its members, serving as an information clearinghouse on how local governments respond to hazardous waste problems. It issues a weekly newsletter, *Washington Letter on Hazardous Waste*, to its subscribers.

## FURTHER INFORMATION

*Resolutions* (1988). Washington, D.C.: NALGOHW.

## NATIONAL ASSOCIATION OF MANUFACTURERS (NAM)
1331 Pennsylvania Avenue, N.W.
Washington, D.C. 20004–1703

### HISTORY AND DEVELOPMENT

The National Association of Manufacturers (NAM) was founded in 1895 by 600 businessmen who met in Cincinnati, inspired by an article in the *Dixie Manufacturer* which had suggested that a business organization was needed to help bring the economy out of a depression. The first focus of NAM was to expand exports in order to find new markets for American products. After the turn of the century, NAM came to focus primarily on preventing unionization of its work force and resisted for many years any welfare legislation such as child labor laws at the federal or state level. It also argued strenuously for the building of the Panama Canal and other public works that would benefit the manufacturing community in selling its goods.

NAM early in its history moved to New York City where corporate head-quarters for many companies, as well as major financial institutions, were located. In 1974, after federal regulation of business became more a focus of NAM's policy, it moved headquarters to Washington, where its staff could be close to Congress and regulatory agencies such as the Securities and Exchange Commission (SEC).

Through the 1960s NAM was known primarily for its stands against taxation on business, against unions, and against any welfare programs that smacked of socialism. Its attitude toward policy was ideologically based on such issues as free enterprise and anticommunism (Wilson, 1981). In 1963 when Bauer, Pool, and Dexter did their classic study on the influence of American business on public policy, they were able to conclude that the NAM and other business groups were unable to settle upon a unified stance to take on such issues as the tariff, because some were domestically based and others were partially dependent on foreign markets and suppliers.

Since that time there has been considerable revision in scholarly estimates of business influence on public policy. Today pluralists such as Charles Lindblom as well as academic critics of the capitalist system recognize the preeminent position that business groups play in the American pluralist system (Lindblom, 1977; Domhoff, 1967).

## ORGANIZATION AND RESOURCES

NAM's membership peaked at 22,000 during the 1950s and by the 1970s had declined to around 13,000. However, in the 1980s, its leadership began a campaign to revamp NAM's image from that of a representative of major corporations to a representative of all manufacturers, including small organizations. It claimed 9,500 small companies with fewer than 500 employees and 4,000 medium-sized to large companies. Many of its major contributors also belong to their individual trade associations such as the Chemical Manufacturers Association* and the Motor Vehicle Manufacturers Association.*

NAM's board of directors consists of 230 industrial leaders elected from the states in proportion to the number of NAM members in each state. The board elects a chair each year. Its president, Alexander B. Trowbridge, is a former Department of Commerce secretary who oversees a staff of 180 professionals, 66 of whom are located in the Washington office. There are also regional or area offices in San Fransisco, Los Angeles, Chicago, Detroit, Houston, Atlanta, New York, and Boston.

Annual dues range from $100 to $100,000, depending on the net worth of the company. Associate members include most of the major trade associations in the United States. Dues provide about 85 percent of the annual budget of around $13 million; convention registrations and publications provide the remainder.

## POLICY CONCERNS

NAM is divided into five major departments which represent its primary policy concerns. The taxation and fiscal policies department tries to convince all levels of government that keeping the corporate tax structure as low as possible will benefit the economy. The international economic affairs department attempts to coordinate business attitudes toward protective tariffs and foreign investment. The industrial relations department focuses on labor-management problems such as employee benefits and affirmative action programs.

Two departments, government regulation and natural resources and technology, deal with environmental and energy policies. NAM generally reflects industry's majority attitude toward most regulation: it seeks to minimize it. NAM representatives testified to House and Senate committees that small generators of hazardous wastes should not be regulated, and that the narrowest possible definition should be made for hazardous wastes. Despite its best efforts, however, the Resource Conservation and Recovery Act (RCRA) was amended in 1986 to reduce the exemption for small generators.

NAM testified against Clean Air Act (CAA) amendments throughout the 1980s on the grounds that the economic impact on business was excessive and not balanced by public health benefits. It opposed any suggestions to further control sulfur oxide emissions in order to reduce acid rain on the grounds that such regulations would greatly increase the cost of energy to all industry and have a direct impact on the costs for many manufacturing plants with their own boilers to control. Business representatives were successful in keeping any such changes from being made through the 100th Congress.

NAM also opposed reauthorization of the Clean Water Act (CWA) which was passed over President Reagan's veto in 1987 on the grounds that it was excessively expensive for both government and industry. Generally this goes along with NAM's policy to oppose government policies that would expend money on public health and welfare issues. There are, however, some exceptions, as some manufacturers earn a portion of their livelihood manufacturing such products as emission control devices and components of sewage treatment plants. Hence NAM's membership is not unanimous in its opposition to such government spending programs.

NAM does present a united front regarding exploration of public lands, whether wilderness or national forests, for mineral wealth. It advocates opening up all areas under the policy of multiple use and sees no conflict between recreation and conservation purposes and using the public lands to produce timber, stock, and fossil fuels, as advocated by the relevant trade associations. One of its major goals in the late 1980s was to see the Arctic National Wildlife Refuge opened up to exploration for gas and oil because of the need for more cheap energy supplies for all manufacturing and to keep the United States independent of foreign petroleum sources. This goal was not accomplished by the end of the 100th Congress.

NAM advocates total decontrol of all natural gas prices, whether old or new, despite the division within the gas industry. This is in line with NAM's general ideological support for free enterprise and freedom from government regulation. It also supports mandatory contract carriage, however, which favors the pipelines and distributors as well as end users of gas over the gas suppliers such as the American Gas Association.* It takes no stand on the take-or-pay controversy in that industry. It fully supported the gas industry's efforts to remove the prohibition against use of gas in industrial boilers which was accomplished in 1987.

NAM generally advocates expansion of all forms of energy in the United States and testified before the Senate Committee on Energy in 1986 that nuclear plants should be standardized in order to facilitate licensing and stop the moratorium on nuclear power in the United States. It advocates less-severe regulations for the nuclear power industry in general in order to increase development of the electricity supply.

## TACTICS

In the 1960s NAM was branded a "paper tiger" because of its unwillingness to lobby aggressively anyone other than its known friends. It was perceived as approaching only Republican probusiness representatives in Congress and simply reinforcing their own personal attitudes. In the 1970s with the proliferation of political action committees, NAM has become more active. Like other business groups, it contributes money to the campaigns of all powerful and strategically placed congressional incumbents, especially Republicans. Its Business Industry PAC collects several hundred thousand dollars in most political campaign years.

In the 1970s and 1980s NAM emphasized expanding its membership to include all businesses involved in manufacturing and in activating business people, whom it perceives as the silent, inattentive, hardworking majority, to become more personally involved in politics. NAM has also developed a nationwide grass-roots lobbying capability. With member companies in every state in the union, the national headquarters is able to launch a legislative alert to executives in states important to members of congress on the relevant committees for any policy.

NAM publishes a quarterly journal for its members, *Enterprise*, keeping them up with trends in business and events in Washington. It also produces weekly a much more detailed discussion of legislative developments, *Briefing*. It also produces a number of research reports on specific laws and regulations periodically.

## FURTHER INFORMATION

Bauer, Raymond, Ithiel de Sola Pool, and Raymond Dexter (1972). *American Business and Public Policy*. 2d ed. New York: Aldine-Atherton.

Domhoff, G. William (1967). *Who Rules America?* Englewood Cliffs, N.J.: Prentice-Hall.

*Enterprise* (1989). Washington, D.C.: NAM, Winter.

Lindblom, Charles E. (1977). *Politics and Markets*. New York: Basic Books.

Wilson, Graham K. (1981). *Interest Groups in the United States*. Oxford, Eng.: Clarendon Press.

## NATIONAL ASSOCIATION OF SOLVENT RECYCLERS (NASR)
1333 New Hampshire Avenue, N.W., Suite 1100
Washington, D.C. 20036

## ORGANIZATION AND RESOURCES

The National Association of Solvent Recyclers (NASR) was founded in 1980 by small businessmen who specialize in the recovery of solvents for reuse in industry. It is a trade association that probably would not have been created were it not for the 1976 Resource Conservation and Recovery Act (RCRA), which caused the U.S. Environmental Protection Agency (EPA) to ban the disposal of liquid hazardous wastes in landfills. Generally, RCRA was designed to encourage the formation of a recycling industry, which it has done.

NASR has a membership of 100 small companies whose average work force numbers fewer than thirty employees per company. It obtains dues of $900 to $1,200 a year from each, which produces an annual budget of about $100,000. It has a board of directors and a professional staff of 4 in Washington.

### POLICY CONCERNS

NASR's existence is due to environmental legislation, and its members generally support this type of legislation, especially such features as the 1986 amendments to RCRA, which reduced the small-generator exemption for hazardous wastes, and EPA's ban on hazardous wastes in landfills. This places it in opposition to such traditional business groups as the National Association of Manufacturers* and the U.S. Chamber of Commerce*; however, it links it to the Hazardous Waste Treatment Council.*

On other regulations, particularly those that apply to the recycling industry, however, NASR takes a defensive posture. It has argued to EPA that regulating volatile organic emissions from recyclers under the Clean Air Act (CAA) is unrealistic and unfair. NASR emphasizes that only about 15 percent of the solvents that recyclers accept fall into the halogenated category, and EPA has made unproven assumptions about the toxicity of emissions that come from waste treatment, storage, and disposal facilities. It also argues that the amounts of emissions from such facilities make up a minimal amount of emissions of halogens compared to those released from chemical manufacturing plants and gasoline filling stations.

NASR also opposes some of the regulations that apply to its members under Superfund Amendments and Reauthorization Act (SARA) of 1986. Under these regulations recyclers must alert community officials to the kinds of chemicals stored and disposed of on-site, and NASR is concerned that such right-to-know requirements will create so much fear among the public that recyclers will be driven out of communities. It also attempted, but failed, to have changed the judicial custom of assessing all contributors to an abandoned toxic waste dump for strict and joint liability. Under these terms, any one firm that used a dump at any time in the past can be assessed total liability for cleanup costs if no other participants can be located.

Under RCRA, NASR opposes regulations concerning incinerating bottoms, wastes left over after recovery of solvents. It believes that large corporations that dispose of their own solvents on sites are dealt with less stringently than are small commercial operations that handle wastes from small generators. It also opposes some of the regulations under the Hazardous Wastes Transportation Act.

## TACTICS

NASR coordinates its lobbying activities with the Halogenated Solvents Industry Alliance,* the Hazardous Waste Treatment Council, and other recyclers. It publishes *Flashpoint*, a biweekly designed to keep members informed on the latest developments in environmental regulations. It urges its members to contact their local congressional representatives whenever a major issue comes before one of the relevant committees. It holds semiannual conferences in April and October.

## FURTHER INFORMATION

Epstein, Samuel, Lester O. Brown, and Carl Pope (1982). *Hazardous Wastes in America.* San Francisco, Calif.: Sierra Club Books.
*Flashpoint* (1989). Washington, D.C.: NASR, April 15, May 1, 15.

## NATIONAL ASSOCIATION OF WATER COMPANIES (NAWC)
1725 K Street, N.W., Suite 1212
Washington, D.C. 20006

## ORGANIZATION AND RESOURCES

The National Association of Water Companies (NAWC) was formed in 1895 by 16 Pennsylvania companies that supplied water to towns; it was originally known as the Pennsylvania Waterworks Association. Later it assumed the name National Water Companies Conference, and in 1971 it took its present title. Today it represents about 500 privately owned water utilities that supply piped water to small and medium-sized towns in the United States, serving about 50 million people. Its board of directors has 102 members, distributed among the states according to the number of customers served by members, who set policy for the Association. James B. Groff is executive director of NAWC and heads a staff of 8 in Washington.

Dues are assessed according to water revenues earned by each member corporation and range from $25 to over $2,000. Its annual budget of nearly $1 million is derived 90 percent from corporate dues; the remainder comes from investments and dues paid by individuals who choose to become associate members.

## POLICY CONCERNS

NAWC is primarily concerned about the financial condition of its members; it disapproves of the tendency for large public agencies to buy up small financially troubled water utilities. One reason for problems in the utility industry is regulation of its rates by state public utility commissions, and NAWC attempts to influence these. It, like other industries, urges state governments to restrict the amount of damages injured parties can obtain through personal injury cases by restricting strict and joint liability laws.

Although it approved the 1980s' federal tax reductions generally, it opposed the 1986 change that requires privately owned utilities to pay federal taxes on contributions in aid of construction made by developers and others who will receive water service from the water company. NAWC also opposed the change in funding of the Comprehensive Environmental Response Compensation and Liability Act (CERCLA, or Superfund) made in 1986 which now imposes a tax on all corporations with alternative minimum taxable incomes in excess of $2 million.

Another policy that could affect the profitability of private water companies through adding to their costs of doing business is the Safe Drinking Water Act (SDWA). Under this law the U.S. Environmental Protection Agency (EPA) must set limits for eighty-three different constituents that appear in drinking water supplies in 1990. Because of the costs of treatment, NAWC opposes any tightening of regulations until studies have been completed that show that each of the substances needs to be controlled. It argues that uncertainty about the quality of piped water in the United States has been created by such zealous advocates as Ralph Nader and media hysteria. It argues that the costs for any additional treatment required by the federal law will have to be passed on to customers, and state regulatory commissions will have to acquiesce in this because there is no way for NAWC members to avoid these costs. However, NAWC did testify in hearings about the SDWA in favor of criminal penalties for people caught tampering with public water supplies.

During the late 1980s environmental organizations became concerned about the lead content of many public water supplies caused by the lead soldering in many distribution systems. NAWC argued this concern was overblown and any lead that might have accumulated in pipes could be avoided by running the water briefly after a night of disuse.

## TACTICS

NAWC coordinates much of its activities with the American Waterworks Association, and the Association of Metropolitan Water Agencies,* which is the trade association for publicly owned water suppliers in the United States. They are in agreement about the overzealousness of environmental groups that seek to increase the standards of the SDWA. NAWPAC distributes money to political candidates, and NAWC publishes a quarterly magazine, *Water*, for members. It also issues periodic governmental affairs newsletters, urging its members to contact their congressional representatives whenever any legislative action threatens their interests. It sponsors an annual conference in October.

## FURTHER INFORMATION

*Water* (1989). Washington, D.C.: National Association of Water Companies, Spring, Summer, Fall.

## NATIONAL ASSOCIATION OF WOOL MANUFACTURERS
*See* American Textile Manufacturers Institute.

## NATIONAL AUDUBON SOCIETY (NAS)
930 Third Avenue
New York, New York 10022

### HISTORY AND DEVELOPMENT

In the latter part of the nineteenth century a number of hunters and fishers became concerned about the rapidly diminishing supply of game, especially the destruction of many of the bird species on the North American continent. Among them was George Bird Grinnell, a Ph.D. from Yale in osteology and paleontology, who had grown up in Audubon Park, New York, named after the great bird painter, and had attended a school run by Audubon's widow. Grinnell's father was a successful investor who bought for his son *Forests and Stream*, one of many successful outdoor magazines at the time. In 1886, convinced that something must be done to stop the wanton destruction of bird life in America for sport and fashion, George Grinnell proposed in the editorial pages of his magazine:

The formation of an association for the protection of wild birds and their eggs, which shall be called The Audubon Society. Its membership is to be free to everyone who is willing to lend a helping hand in forwarding the objects for which it is formed. These objects shall be to prevent, so far as possible, (1) the killing of any wild birds not used for food, (2) the destruction of nests or eggs of any wild bird, and (3) the wearing of feathers as ornaments or trimming for dress.

In 1887 George Grinnell began *The Audubon Magazine* to keep the growing membership informed of developments in conservation. By 1888 membership had grown to 50,000, but the magazine was allowed to lapse in 1889.

In 1883 three New Englanders, Elliott Coues, J. A. Allen, and William Brewster, founded the American Ornithologists' Union (AOU) to study birds and to protect certain endangered species. They drafted a model law for states to adopt to conserve birds. In 1896 the Audubon movement was revived in Massachusetts, and Brewster was elected president of that state's Audubon Society. By 1898 there were fifteen state Audubon Societies which helped pass the first federal legislation for bird protection, the Lacey Act of 1900, which outlawed interstate sale of birds killed in violation of state laws.

William E. Dutcher, head of the AOU's protection committee, helped form the New York Audubon Society, and together with Frank Chapman of the American Museum of Natural History set out to see that the Lacey Act was enforced in New York. In 1901 Dutcher brought the existing state Audubon societies together, and in 1905 thirty-six state Audubon groups agreed to form the National Committee of Audubon Societies. Local game wardens were hired to protect endangered species. Dutcher, like David Brower of the Sierra Club,* proved to have little financial acumen, and the board of directors encouraged him to resign as president in 1908 and replaced him with T. Gilbert Pearson, a man with tremendous fund-raising abilities. In 1911 the Winchester Repeating Arms Company offered to double the Audubon income if they would protect game birds for hunting. The directors were divided on this issue with Pearson and Grinnell enthusiastic about the windfall, but Dutcher and others opposed. After first agreeing to the deal, the national committee eventually backed out, and Grinnell joined the American Game Protective Association which was organized by the hunting industry to compete with the Audubon committee. The two, however, cooperated to achieve passage of a law to conserve migratory game birds and prohibit hunting of some rare species.

By the 1920s Audubon's board of directors was controlled by professional conservationists who worked for the Agriculture Department or museums and were very much in agreement with many sportsmen's organizations. Some radicals within the organization, including Rosalie Edge, a suffragist, formed the emergency conservation committee to reform the association. She sued to obtain the 7,000-member mailing list in order to ask for proxies to vote at the next board of directors meeting, and succeeded in soliciting 1,646. She went through the association's financial records and revealed that it had received rents from hunters for trapping muskrats in a bird sanctuary. As membership plummeted in response to Edge's revelations, the board began to reform itself from within and in 1936 replaced Pearson as director.

In 1940 the Audubon Association officially changed its name to the National Audubon Society (NAS), and in 1941 its official publication *Bird-Lore* was changed to *Audubon*. John Baker became president and remained until his retirement in 1959 when Carl W. Buchheister, who had been a vice-president since 1944, took over. Buchheister proved to be more militant, hiring a lobbyist to present the Society's views in Washington and to write about developments in the national government for members. During the late 1970s and early 1980s, Russell Peterson, President Nixon's former chair of the Council on Environmental Quality, was president of NAS, and moved the organization into assuming a more active political role, attempting to affect more government policies.

## ORGANIZATION AND RESOURCES

Over the years the National Audubon Society has expanded its interests from protecting wild birds from feather hunters to protecting other wildlife, preserving wilderness areas and habitat, and supporting a myriad of other environmental causes. In the late 1980s it had 505 local chapters located in all 50 of the United States, with a total membership of about 550,000. It also had 9 regional offices in Alaska, Pennsylvania for the Atlantic Region, Indiana for the Great Lakes, New York for the Northeast, Colorado for the Rocky Mountains, Florida for the Southeast, Texas for the Southwest, Kansas for the West Central, and California for the West, in addition to its national headquarters in New York and its Washington office. In addition it maintains 6 environmental education centers,

4 ecology camps, 3 research stations, and 30 bird and wildlife sanctuaries around the United States.

At the end of the 1980s NAS had a professional staff of 291 in its Washington office and regional offices and centers around the country, including New York City where the editorial offices of *Audubon* are located. It has a 34-member elected board of directors, headed by an elected chair. The president since 1985 is Peter A. A. Berle, who is also publisher of the magazine.

Annual dues are $35, and contributions are collected for a number of special causes. At the end of the 1980s, revenues totaled over $32 million, of which 31 percent came from annual dues, 25 percent from grants and contributions, 8 percent from bequests, 32 percent earned from investments and mineral rights, and 4 percent earned from sales of property. It spent close to $31 million in the same time period, 21 percent on publishing, 12 percent on membership promotion, 8 percent on fund-raising, 10 percent on general administration, 20 percent on publications and education, 16 percent on wildlife preservation, 7 percent on science and field research, and 6 percent on chapter activities. Foundations making contributions included the Joyce, Mellon, Rockefeller, and Leonhardt foundations. Major corporations such as General Electric, Stroh Brewery, Chevron, U.S.A., and Waste Management, Inc., also contributed to Audubon.

## POLICY CONCERNS

The Audubon Society's main priority is the preservation of wildlife in the United States and throughout the world. It opposes all hunting, but it joins with groups of sportsmen such as the National Wildlife Federation* to advocate government preservation of wildlife habitat. While it continues to operate its own system of wildlife refuges, it also urges Congress to declare more areas in the United States wilderness areas and to restore endangered species such as wolves to the national parks and other public trust lands. Its local and state chapters regularly fight to preserve and increase national and state park holdings.

In 1986 the NAS began a campaign to save the Alaskan Wildlife Refuge against the Reagan administration's plan to explore and develop for oil rights there. After the Exxon oil spill in Prince William Sound in 1989, it stepped up its campaign to inform the public of the disastrous impact on seabirds and mammals from oil spills.

Throughout the 1980s the Society remained critical of the Forest Service's management of national forests and its emphasis on timbering off old growth and not paying sufficient attention to other multiple uses, especially wildlife habitat and watershed protection and recreation. In 1984 it criticized specifically the Forest Service's spotted owl management plan and insisted that the Service write another Environmental Impact Statement (EIS) about timber-cutting operations in the owl's habitat among old-growth forests on the west coast. In 1989 NAS sponsored a documentary on the "World of Audubon" narrated by Paul Newman, which spells out the destructiveness of timbering off the last uncut forests in the Pacific Northwest in order to improve our balance of payments by selling the logs to Japan. At that time Stroh Brewery and other corporate sponsors withdrew their support in the face of a threatened boycott by loggers who feel their jobs will be lost if any old growth is preserved.

Over the years, Audubon Society representatives have testified about numerous general environmental issues, including strengthening the clean air and water acts every time they came up for reauthorization and amendment. In 1986 representatives testified in favor of strengthening amendments for the Clean Water Act, which were pocket vetoed by President Reagan after being unanimously passed by Congress. In 1987 the same bill was reintroduced and passed over the President's veto with Audubon help.

NAS opposes the use of lead shot for hunting wildlife on the grounds that many waterfowl eat pellets and die from lead poisoning. The Fish and Wildlife Service agreed to ban lead for hunting waterfowl, effective in 1991, if lawsuits and other tactics by the National Rifle Association and other sportsmen's associations do not succeed. NAS also advocates eliminating all use of lead in gasoline which the Environmental Protection Agency has been phasing out for more than a decade.

In the late 1980s Audubon representatives also testified for amending the Resource Conservation and Recovery Act (RCRA) to increase funds for enforcement at both state and federal levels. They also sought to avoid groundwater contamination by ridding the law of loopholes that exempted small producers of hazardous wastes from the control of the law. They argued against a post-closure liability fund in RCRA, because it would absolve the chemical and hazardous waste industries of continuing responsibility after their disposal sites are closed, and would pay for potential cleanups from a public fund.

Audubon representatives also sought to change delisting procedures under the Toxic Substances Control Act to make it more difficult to take materials off the list. From 1984 through 1986, Audubon lobbyists testified to refund the Comprehensive Environmental Response, Compensation, and Liability Act (CERCLA or Superfund) and to increase the numbers of abandoned hazardous waste sites placed on the national priority list for cleanup. In 1986 President Reagan signed into law CERCLA amendments (SARA) after Audubon lobbyists and others had timed the passage to coincide with the election campaign in which many Republican Senate seats were in jeopardy. Among other things, these amendments gave local communities the right to know what toxic substances are stored and used in their areas in order to inform fire departments and other public safety officials of the hazards they may face.

NAS also lobbied for mandatory federal standards for energy-efficient household appliances, which its research staff argued would save the construction of ten large electric generating plants over the next decade. This conservation effort would reduce the sulfur and nitrogen oxides that help to form acid rain. After Reagan vetoed the bill, NAS urged state legislatures to pass their own acid rain control laws, which several, including New York and New Jersey, did. In the

1980s, Audubon's research staff produced a twenty-year energy proposal in opposition to that developed by the Department of Energy. Audubon's plan advocates extensive use of solar and other renewable forms of energy, much greater conservation of the remaining fossil fuels we have, and much less reliance on nuclear power.

### TACTICS

Audubon holds a biennial convention for all members at some location of particular ecological or wildlife interest, such as the Rocky Mountain National Park or the Everglades. It also runs bird-watching expeditions for members throughout the United States. It also runs workshops for American and foreign educators on teaching children about nature, and ecology camps for adults and children. It sponsors several Audubon television specials each year to bring information about conservation programs into the homes of millions of Americans.

Audubon operates 82 sanctuaries for birds and wildlife throughout the United States from Maine to California. It organizes an annual Christmas bird count in order to try to track as many species as possible and determine whether they are being reduced in numbers or recovering. Started in 1900, this annual census now includes over 40,000 human participants and has added substantially to our scientific knowledge about birds' migration patterns.

In 1987 *Audubon* magazine celebrated its 100th anniversary, although it did so in Volume 89, since the magazine counts its operation from the beginning of *Bird-Lore* which was started in 1908 by the ornithologist Frank M. Chapman. The name was changed officially to *Audubon* in 1941 and has been published six times a year ever since. It is a highly professional publication on wildlife and ecology that constitutes a major incentive to join Audubon for many members.

NAS began publishing the *Audubon Activist* in 1986 every other month at $6 a year, and 15,000 Audubon members subscribe to keep up with the latest legislative, administrative, and judicial actions taken by the Society and to learn of developments in Washington on issues of interest to the members.

The Washington office publishes frequent action alerts to members about issues that are coming to a vote in Washington or reaching some other crucial stage in development. These urge members to write or phone their representatives and/ or administrative agencies in a position to do something harmful or helpful to the environment. In addition the staff keeps a twenty-four-hour taped hotline available in Washington for members interested in learning the latest developments.

### FURTHER INFORMATION

*Audubon.* (March, September, November, 1987; January, March, September, November, 1988; March, May, September, November, 1989). New York: NAS.

*Audubon: Half a Million Strong Annual Report* (1988). New York: NAS, June 30, 1987–
   June 30, 1988.

Steven Fox (1981). *John Muir and His Legacy: The American Conservation Movement.*
   Boston: Little, Brown.

Mitchell, John G. (1987). "A Man Called Bird." *Audubon*, November, pp. 81–104.

Washington office: 654 Pennsylvania Avenue, S.E., Washington, D.C. 20003

## NATIONAL AUTOMOBILE DEALERS ASSOCIATION (NADA)
8400 Westpark Drive
McLean, Virginia 22102

### ORGANIZATION AND RESOURCES

In 1917 retailers of automobiles banded together to form the National Automobile Dealers Association (NADA) in order to represent their interests to the government and the manufacturers of autos. By the end of 1989 there were nearly 20,000 individual small businesses who belonged to NADA and paid dues ranging from $65 to $300 a year depending on the volume of business they do. It has a budget of about $10 million a year derived largely from services and publications it provides its membership. NADA has 104 state and local affiliates where many of its activities take place. It has a board of directors of 58 elected for 3-year terms by individual state affiliates. Frank E. McCarthy is executive vice-president in charge of the 320 professional staff people in Washington.

### POLICY CONCERNS

As is the Service Station Dealers of America,* NADA is largely concerned with protecting its members, who are small business people, against the major corporations with which they do business. As franchisees, the dealers need organization and sometimes government support to protect themselves from the business practices of their suppliers. However, NADA originated partly to defend against excise taxes on new cars in 1917, and the level of excise taxes remains an important policy issue for it at both the state and national levels.

In addition, the members of NADA share the concerns of the Motor Vehicle Manufacturers Association of the U.S.* about requirements under federal laws that raise the price of automobiles by mandating emission controls and safety equipment such as air bags. Suppliers call upon NADA members to testify before Congress and EPA against increasing limits on cars under the Clean Air Act (CAA). They also have argued against increasing the corporate average fuel efficiency (CAFE) standards for their cars on the grounds that they are unable to sell smaller, less-powerful cars. NADA generally opposes any policy that would increase the cost of driving cars and trucks, such as the suggested imported oil tariff. Like other small generators of waste oil and other potentially hazardous wastes, it opposed the 1986 amendments to RCRA that changed the definition of "small generator" to increase the number of businesses covered by RCRA.

### TACTICS

Because of the number of its members and their distribution throughout the United States, NADA is able to field a large grass-roots lobbying campaign whenever a policy of particular concern to it arises. Its Dealer Election Action Committee collects funds for distribution in political campaigns. It publishes a newsletter for its members to keep them up to date with the latest developments in Washington, as well as a monthly journal, *Automotive Executive Magazine*, and the *Official Used Car Book* (Blue Book) about the value of used cars.

### FURTHER INFORMATION

Federal Election Commission (1988). *Receipts and Disbursements*. Washington, D.C.: FEC.
*NADA Newsletter* (1989). McLean, Virginia, August 12.
*The NADA Report* (1989). McLean, Virginia, October, September.

## NATIONAL BOARD OF FIRE UNDERWRITERS
*See* American Insurance Association.

## NATIONAL CENTER FOR APPROPRIATE TECHNOLOGY (NCAT)
815 15th Street N.W., Suite 938
Washington, D.C. 20005

### ORGANIZATION AND RESOURCES

The National Center for Appropriate Technology (NCAT) was founded in 1976 by an act of Congress as a not-for-profit corporation designed to develop appropriate technologies and inform potential users about them. "Appropriate technology" is designed to match the needs and resources of the people who will use it, which means small scale, environmentally benign, labor intensive, and easily understood and controlled by users. NCAT was originally designed to benefit both low-income Americans and developing nations. NCAT has a board of directors of fifteen. Its president is Joseph F. Sedlak who heads a professional staff of fifty at headquarters in Washington and two technical offices in Butte, Montana, and Memphis, Tennessee.

In the late 1980s, NCAT had an annual budget of over $2 million, which came primarily from contracts it obtained from government agencies such as the Department of Energy (DOE) to do research on technology, as well as from sales of its publications. In the 1970s NCAT's primary source of support was the federal government; in the 1980s, with substantial cuts in U.S. support for energy conservation, it turned more and more to funding from local and state government as well as private industry.

## POLICY CONCERNS

During the Carter administration, when funding was plentiful from DOE, NCAT concentrated on assisting low-income communities to conserve energy through weatherizing homes and utilizing renewable energy resources such as the sun. It supported passage of the National Energy Conservation Act of 1978 which provided for free energy audits for residential buildings to provide information to owners and renters about how to conserve energy through such techniques as weatherization. This legislation was later rescinded by the Reagan administration in 1987 over NCAT's objections at the urging of the Edison Electric Institute* and other industrial groups. NCAT, however, continues to receive contracts from such government organizations as the Bonneville Power Administration to perform energy audits and prepare plans for conserving electricity in both residences and commercial buildings in its service area.

NCAT also opposed the withdrawal during the Reagan administration of energy tax credits for homeowners who invested in energy-conserving technology such as additional insulation and solar-powered devices such as hot water heaters. It contracts with the state of Montana to develop superinsulation plans for construction and to pass on this information through workshops for builders and buyers of housing. It also develops methods for weatherizing mobile homes which it recognizes as a primary source of shelter for low-income families throughout the United States and other countries.

## TACTICS

NCAT sees as one of its primary missions the transfer of information about conservation of energy to those who need it most. It publishes a number of papers about how to conserve energy and use renewable resources and attempts to tailor these publications to each audience such as builder/contractors and homeowners and renters. It contracted with DOE in 1984 to establish the National Appropriate Technology Assistance Service which answers questions directed to its Butte, Montana, office about engineering and technical problems.

In the 1990s NCAT intends to extend its efforts in non-energy-related appropriate technologies such as food production and land and water management. It has contracted with the U.S. Department of Agriculture's Extension Service to manage the Appropriate Technology Transfer for Rural Areas with headquarters in Memphis. Since NCAT is not a membership organization, it does not have any grass-roots organization to lobby Congress. It does attempt to influence policy decisions by discussing what its researchers have found with congressional staffers and by testifying at hearings on energy issues.

## FURTHER INFORMATION

*Moisture and Home Energy Conservation* (1985). Washington, D.C.: NCAT.
*Progress Report: Into the Nineties* (1989). Washington, D.C.: NCAT.

## NATIONAL CLEAN AIR COALITION (NCAC)
801 Pennsylvania Avenue, S.E.
Washington, D.C. 20003

### ORGANIZATION AND RESOURCES

The National Clean Air Coalition (NCAC) was founded in 1981 and dedicated to the reauthorization and strengthening of the Clean Air Act (CAA) which was last amended substantially in 1977. It consists of a number of environmental organizations, such as the American Lung Association,* Citizens for a Better Environment, Environmental Action,* Environmental Defense Fund,* Environmental Policy Institute/Friends of the Earth,* Izaak Walton League of America,* League of Women Voters of the U.S.,* National Audubon Society,* National Parks and Conservation,* National Wildlife Federation,* Natural Resources Defense Council,* Sierra Club,* and Wilderness Society.* In addition it has support from labor unions and other organizations that wish to see the Clean Air Act strengthened, such as the United Steelworkers of America, International Machinists and Aerospace Workers, Center for Auto Safety, National Association of Railroad Passengers, and the National Consumers League. It obtains funding from these organizations and is not a mass-membership group. It has a staff of three, directed by Susan M. Buffone, who do research on air pollution problems and testify before Congress on the act.

### POLICY CONCERNS

In the early 1980s NCAC testified against the Reagan administration's Environmental Protection Agency's proposal to weaken the CAA. It argued successfully that the provisions in the law protecting unpolluted areas (Prevention of Significant Deterioration) should be retained and that EPA should continue to monitor increments in air pollution in Class II and III areas. NCAC also argued that inspection and maintenance programs should be adopted for emission controls on vehicles and diesel standards should be adopted.

After Congress became more environmentally oriented and the EPA administrator was changed in the mid–1980s, NCAC became more aggressive and argued for changes in the law that would increase its strictness. Representatives testified that the Environmental Protection Agency needed to be forced to identify toxic air pollutants and set emission limits for them because it had listed only seven toxic gases in the fourteen years since 1970 when authority to do so was put into CAA. In 1990 the Bush administration made its own proposal to control half of the 191 toxics that have been identified, and the Senate countered with a proposal to control all 191. NCAC supported the Senate's version and argued that Congress should specify toxic emissions in the CAA as it earlier specified car emission control goals.

One of NCAC's primary objectives is to control acid rain, arguing before Congress that sulfur dioxide emissions must be reduced by 10 million tons by 1997. In 1990 the Bush administration agreed to the amount of the reduction, but by the year 2000, and the Senate revised this proposal to a compromise date of 1999. NCAC also argued to increase the strictness of nitrogen oxide and hydrocarbon tailpipe emission standards by 1993, and the Bush administration countered with a smaller increase by 1995. The Senate voted to accept the stricter controls for cars and trucks, and it appeared that the remainder of the 101st Congress would be spent arguing about the CAA.

*TACTICS*

NCAC has no regular publication program although it sends out alerts to its affiliated groups when developments occur regarding the CAA in Washington.

**NATIONAL COAL ASSOCIATION (NCA)**
1130 17th Street, N.W.
Washington, D.C., 20036

*HISTORY AND DEVELOPMENT*

Founded in 1917 to represent the interests of the coal mining industry, the National Coal Association (NCA) has been an active voice in Washington for over 70 years. In April 1987, the NCA merged with the Mining and Reclamation Council of America (MARC), which had for 10 years maintained a separate presence in Washington, representing primarily the small and medium-sized independent coal producers. With the merger, NCA came to represent more than 300 of the nation's leading coal producers, responsible for 70 percent of U.S. annual coal production as well as suppliers of goods and services to the mining industry.

The coal industry has been in decline for a number of years partly because of a fall in raw steel production in the United States that has resulted in a reduced demand for metallurgical coal and partly because of the increase in generation of electricity by nuclear plants in the 1970s that resulted in a decrease in coal-fired plant production. Despite the interruption of oil supply in the mid–1970s and the subsequent increase in oil and natural gas prices, the expected windfall to the coal industry did not materialize because of a subsequent decline in consumption of energy as well as a later glut of gas and oil that resulted in reduced prices for competing energy supplies.

The coal industry nevertheless believes that there will be substantial growth in coal consumption by the year 2000, an average annual increase of 1.9 percent. Much of this increase will be due to a projected net increase in electricity generation. The coal industry expects to recapture its 55.8 percent of that market by the year 2000, although there will be a drop-off in coal's share around 1990 because of increased use of nuclear plants. It also expects that U.S. coal exports will grow in the remainder of the twentieth century as markets both in Europe and Japan expand because of increased industrialization in those countries.

## ORGANIZATION AND RESOURCES

The National Coal Association (NCA) was headed by Carl E. Bagge from 1970 to 1987; in June 1987, the board of directors elected a new president, Richard L. Lawson, a retired four-star general of the Air Force. Included in the merger agreement was a commitment by NCA to include small operators in policy development and representation on the board of directors. Sixteen executives from small coal producers, former members of MARC, joined the NCA's board of directors in 1987, bringing the total board membership to sixty-six. NCA has an annual budget of $5 million and a staff of fifty.

## POLICY CONCERNS

The National Coal Association has taken stands on many energy and environmental policies. The ones most crucial to its profitability are the Clean Air Act (CAA) and the Surface Mining Control and Reclamation Act (SMCRA). NCA representatives have testified regularly before Congress concerning the CAA since its inception, but it particularly opposed the increase in standards in the 1970 amendments and the tightening of restrictions in 1977. It argues that the national ambient air quality standards that were set during the 1970s for particulates (suspended solids) and sulfur dioxide are too restrictive, and that the health benefits to be expected from these standards are not worth the cost to the industries regulated by them.

Specifically NCA submitted comments to the U.S. Environmental Protection Agency (EPA) that would change the standard for particulates to exclude all particles larger than ten micrometers on the grounds that it is only the smallest particles that can be inhaled and cause lung damage. It argued for the Reagan administration amendments to the CAA introduced in 1981 and 1982 that would have modified all ambient air quality standards to make them less restrictive and correct the lack of balance between the need for a livable environment and the need for energy production to meet the nation's needs. However, these standards were not changed; in fact, no significant amendments were passed by Congress through 1989. NCA has argued consistently that ambient air quality standards should be revised and should be based on scientific evidence from a panel of experts independent of the EPA.

One crucial amendment advocated by environmental groups is to increase the controls on sulfur dioxide emissions, a pollutant that is discharged by fossil fuel–fired power plants. Prior to 1977 electric generating plants could meet their obligations to reduce sulfur emissions in several different ways, including reducing the sulfur content of coal being burned in the plants. However, in 1977 Congress passed amendments to the CAA that required that all emissions from such plants be reduced by a percentage (90 percent for high-sulfur coal, 70 percent for low-sulfur coal). This requirement was supported by both environmental groups and the high-sulfur middle-western coal producers, who foresaw that their share of the market might be eliminated as electric plants switched to low-sulfur western coal to meet the requirements of the law. Hence the NCA could not take a united stand as part of its membership benefited from the change, while others were hurt by it. NCA's membership does agree on the need for more government research funding for ways of burning coal cleanly and for liquefying and gasifying coal.

In the 1980s, environmental groups began a legislative push to increase controls on sulfur oxides beyond what was required by the 1977 amendments, and the NCA was able to formulate a united policy against this initiative. Representatives testified against taking any precipitous action to reduce sulfur oxides further until scientific evidence proved conclusively that acid rain is indeed caused by sulfur emissions from fossil fuel plants. They also argued that the benefits from any sulfur reduction program should be subjected to rigorous cost/benefit analysis to demonstrate that the benefits will outweigh the costs to society. Their own testimony before Congress argued that health costs to the poor from not heating and air conditioning their homes sufficiently because of increased costs for power are much greater than any marginal impact on asthmatics from breathing sulfur dioxide.

In 1980 Congress authorized a decade-long study, the National Acid Precipitation Assessment Program (NAPAP), completed in 1990. In 1987 an interim report was issued. NCA used this report to argue that alternative ameliorative steps, such as liming lakes to offset acidification, should be emphasized, because it costs less than reducing acid precursors at their source. NCA takes the general position that sulfur emissions have been declining since 1973 at the same time that coal use has increased, demonstrating the effectiveness of the present law and the absence of need for additional controls. Through the Reagan administration its arguments were effective, as no legislative action was taken on acid rain controls. However, the Bush administration and the 101st Congress took demands for further controls more seriously, and it seems likely that CAA amendments will be made in the 1990s.

NCA has supported the electric utility industry's argument that tall stacks should be considered a legitimate treatment for sulfur emissions. However, the 1977 amendments to the CAA eliminated that possibility. In the 1990s NCA and other industries continue to argue that stack height should be given some credit for reducing air emissions. It also argues that new source performance standards are sufficient for all pollutants and such ideas as best available technology and lowest achievable emissions are excessive. It considers the discussion of a buildup of carbon dioxide in the atmosphere and a global warming pattern a hysterical reaction to an unusually warm dry summer in 1988.

NCA generally favors the rapid development of all mineral resources in the United States whether on private or federal land. Originally the Mineral Lands Leasing Act of 1920 favored industry over any environmental concerns when leasing federal lands to private developers such as coal companies to exploit the mineral wealth on them. However, this policy was changed in 1976 to require comprehensive land-use planning before leasing can be initiated. The Federal

Land Policy and Management Act was passed that year which mandates multiple land-use planning for all areas deemed suitable for leasing. The next year, the Surface Mining Control and Reclamation Act (SMCRA) was passed which regulates the way in which strip mining can be conducted even on privately owned lands.

NCA has been active in attempting to ameliorate the impact of these laws on the mining industry since their passage. Following a period of rapid leasing of federal lands for mineral development in the 1960s, the U.S. Department of Interior's Bureau of Land Management (BLM) called a temporary halt in 1971 in order to reassess the way in which leases were assigned. NCA argued throughout the 1970s for renewed federal leasing because of growing dependence on foreign oil. In 1981 when the Reagan administration entered office, policy changed drastically. NCA was so successful in convincing the BLM to lease new lands for exploration that several environmental organizations sued to stop the crash program, arguing that the government was not obtaining fair market value for its coal (Culhane, 1984). A congressional investigation and subsequent presidential commission slowed the sale of federal coal, but throughout the remainder of the Reagan administration, the NCA, like its sister oil and gas trade associations, had considerable influence in the BLM's leasing program.

NCA also lobbied the Office of Surface Mining (OSM) in the Department of Interior extensively when it set its regulations for enforcing SMCRA. Although during the Carter administration, rather stringent limits were placed on the areas that could be strip mined as well as the requirements for restoring the land after mining, these were changed drastically under President Reagan. The OSM itself was greatly reduced in staff and power, and most authority for enforcing SMCRA was turned over to the states, a change fervently desired by NCA which has considerable influence in the governments of such states as Kentucky.

One of the primary problems of the coal industry is the shortage of markets for its products. NCA urges the federal government to assist the coal industry in expanding foreign markets for its coal. It also lobbied for the Powerplant and Industrial Fuel Use Act (PIFUA) of 1978 which restricted the use of gas and oil in electric powerplants and other industrial boilers. However, it finally agreed to a compromise with the gas and oil industries in 1987 to withdraw this restriction in PIFUA as long as new boilers are constructed with the capacity to use coal as well as gas or oil.

NCA has several other policy concerns shared with other industries, such as tax rates, worker-manager relationships, especially safety for its workers, and the cost of shipping its products. The 1980 Staggers Rail Act, which decontrolled much of the rail industry, also generated tremendous increases in the costs of shipping coal by rail, and NCA has worked to have the Interstate Commerce Commission recontrol these rates ever since. NCA argues regularly before Congress that benefits for miners under the Black Lung Act are excessive and should be reduced.

## TACTICS

NCA coordinates its lobbying efforts about federal leasing laws with such organizations as the American Petroleum Institute,* the American Mining Congress,* and the Natural Gas Supply Association,* all of which share its interest in seeing wilderness areas opened up to exploration and development. Since many coal companies are now owned by energy conglomerates such as Exxon, Mobil, and Amoco, the CEOs of these individual corporations do much of the testifying before Congress and the BLM. In addition there are major corporate linkages between the petrochemical industry and mining, and these two types of trade associations often cooperate in doing research on reducing emissions from burning coal. Hence, for example, a representative of Consolidation Coal, a subsidiary of Du Pont Chemicals, testified in 1987 before the Senate about technologies for reducing sulfur oxides from coal (U.S. Senate, 1987).

NCA holds an annual convention for its members to demonstrate the latest technology in mining coal. It publishes a biweekly newsletter, *Coal News*, for its membership with information about developments in the agencies, Congress, and the courts. It also issues research reports on such issues as forecasts for coal consumption, coal transportation, mine safety and accidents, electricity utility coal stockpiles, and a weekly statistical summary on coal production and consumption.

## FURTHER INFORMATION

Culhane, Paul J. (1984). "Sagebrush Rebels in Office: Jim Watt's Land and Water Policies." In *Environmental Policy in the 1980s*, edited by Norman Vig and Michael Kraft. Washington, D.C.: Congressional Quarterly Press, pp. 293–317.
Mitchell, John G. (1988). "The Mountains, the Miners, and Mister Caudill." *Audubon*, November, pp. 80–102.
National Coal Association (1987). *Coal Policy Issues 1987*. Washington, D.C.: NCA.
————— (1989). *Coal News*, June 15, 29, July 6.
Rosenbaum, Walter A. (1987). *Energy, Politics, and Public Policy*, 2d ed. Washington, D.C.: Congressional Quarterly Press.
U.S. Congress. Senate Committee on Environment and Public Works (1987). *Hearings on the Clean Air Act*. Washington, D.C.: Government Printing Office, March 4.

## NATIONAL COALITION AGAINST THE MISUSE OF PESTICIDES (NCAMP)
530 7th Street, N.E.
Washington, D.C. 20003

## ORGANIZATION AND RESOURCES

In 1982 a group of environmentalists organized the National Coalition Against the Misuse of Pesticides (NCAMP) to serve as a national network for pesticide safety and to work for adoption of alternative pest management strategies to reduce dependency on toxic chemicals. Membership is open to individuals at

$10 a year and to organizations from $25 to $50 a year. Contributions are also solicited on a regular basis. Jay Feldman has been national coordinator since the inception of NCAMP in 1982; he has a staff of five in Washington. There is a sixteen member board of directors representing several farm workers' organizations, traditional environmental groups such as regional Audubon societies,* and local pesticide control groups.

## POLICY CONCERNS

The first objective of NCAMP in the 1980s was to prevent the Reagan administration from amending the Federal Insecticide, Fungicide and Rodenticide Act (FIFRA). One suggested change was to eliminate the states' authority to regulate pesticides beyond the level that U.S. Environmental Protection Agency (EPA) was willing to go—to collect additional data from chemical manufacturers about the contents of their pesticide compounds that EPA did not collect. Another proposal would have eliminated the public's right to know about the human health and environmental effects of pesticide products in the workplace and environment. Industry wanted a provision for greater secrecy for new formulations and was unwilling to share data developed to test one product with other companies which had developed similar products. All three proposals were defeated in the 100th Congress. However, in 1989 President Bush proposed that the federal law be changed to preempt any further state regulations in the face of a California ballot proposal that would phase out all agricultural chemicals that cause cancer or birth defects.

Since its inception NCAMP has advocated strict liability for victims of chemical poisoning against chemical corporations, closer controls by government of the conditions under which agricultural workers apply chemicals to crops and reduced reliance on chemical solutions to pests. Their research scientists have called for complete testing of toxic materials before they are released for commercial use and simple procedures for delisting compounds that have been accepted for use by EPA.

In September 1988, Congress passed amendments to FIFRA, requiring testing of all pesticides now on the market, and halting the practice whereby the government was obligated to buy all stocks of pesticides banned by EPA that were in existence at the time of the ban. Many other provisions advocated by NCAMP and other environmental groups, such as stringent groundwater protection requirements, were not passed. Altogether neither industry nor environmental groups were entirely satisfied with the new FIFRA, nicknamed FIFRA LITE by NCAMP. The 1990s are certain to produce more debate in Congress over pesticide laws.

In addition to testifying about FIFRA amendments, NCAMP representatives have advocated changes to the Toxic Substances Control, the Clean Water, and the Safe Drinking Water acts, designed to reduce contamination of groundwater by runoff from agricultural fields and residential areas sprayed with fertilizers and weed killers.

*TACTICS*

NCAMP advocates the formation of local grass-roots organizations designed to reduce chemical use at the state and local levels. It provides information about the dangers of all chemical contaminants and how-to-organize booklets for use by local groups. It has pushed for legislation requiring lawn chemical companies to post on the lawns they spray descriptions of the types of chemicals used and possible side effects and dangers from exposure to them. Such laws were passed in Rhode Island, Maryland, Minnesota, Iowa, and Massachusetts by 1987.

NCAMP publishes a quarterly newsletter, *Pesticides and You*, which it sends to subscribers to inform them about the latest research on side effects of chemicals and the efforts of various groups to reduce their use in particular states or towns.

*FURTHER INFORMATION*

"California Chides Bush on Pesticides" (1989). *The New York Times*, October 27, p. 1.
"Pesticide Reform Effort Moves Forward" (1988). Natural Resource Defense Council *Newsline* vol. 6, November-December, p. 1.
*Pesticides and You* (vol. 5, no. 4, December 1985; vol. 7, no. 2, June 1987; vol. 9, no. 3, August 1989). Washington, D.C., NCAMP.
Reinhold, Robert (1989). "California Alliance Proposes Vote on Broad Environmental Measure." *The New York Times*, October 11, p. 1.

## NATIONAL CONGRESS OF PETROLEUM RETAILERS
*See* Service Station Dealers of America.

## NATIONAL CRUSHED STONE ASSOCIATION
*See* National Stone Association.

## NATIONAL ELECTRIC RELIABILITY COUNCIL
*See* North American Electric Reliability Council.

## NATIONAL ENVIRONMENTAL DEVELOPMENT ASSOCIATION (NEDA)
1440 New York Avenue, N.W.
Washington, D.C. 20005

*ORGANIZATION AND RESOURCES*

In 1973 a coalition of industry, agriculture, and labor organizations organized the National Environmental Development Association (NEDA) designed to restore the balance between economic and environmental goals that its members perceived as having drifted too far in the ecological and conservation direction. Today NEDA has 305 members including many major corporations that also belong to their individual trade associations, such as Chevron, Dow Chemical, Consolidation Coal, General Motors, Kaiser Aluminum, and PPG Industries; labor union members include some of those affiliated with the American Federation of Labor and Congress of Industrial Organizations (AFL/CIO)*: building and construction trades, plumbing and pipe fitting, carpenters and joiners, and electrical workers.

## POLICY CONCERNS

NEDA is divided into four major projects, and individual members of NEDA can join one or more of these projects. The Clean Water Act Project (CWAP), which consists of twenty-two industries and six unions, takes positions close to some assumed by environmental groups. NEDA's CWAP advocated passage of amendments to the CWA in order to reauthorize and fund the water law over President Reagan's veto, which was accomplished in 1987. Under this law the federal government now provides loans as well as some outright grants to state and local governments to build and improve sewage treatment plants to reduce water pollutants discharged to surface waters. This was viewed by industry as a reform because it reduced the federal government's percentage of fiscal commitment but at the same time enabled state governments to continue building plants. It was supported by construction unions representing workers such as plumbers and electricians because of the jobs that it would generate. NEDA worked to reduce the strictness of the controls imposed on industry regarding its pretreatment of effluents sent to public treatment works and the permits issued to industry for direct dumping, but ended by being in a large coalition with environmental groups for final passage.

The Clean Air Act Project (CAAP) is a much different story. John Quarles, a former deputy administrator of the U.S. Environmental Protection Agency (EPA), and presently with the law firm of Morgan, Lewis, and Bockius, is the project director. He testified throughout the Reagan administration for relaxation of many of the requirements in the CAA. NEDA opposes the prevention of significant deterioration standards that are imposed on industry seeking to locate in clean areas on the grounds that this creates undue burdens on the industrial base of the country. In 1982 it opposed the bubble concept, through which trade-offs can be made in dirty-air areas to enable industry to expand or build new plants by obtaining reductions from older plants, on the grounds that not enough offsets could be found to site all the necessary expansion in noncompliance areas. Later, however, it embraced the idea of the bubble, as did the Reagan administration, while environmentalists objected to it on the grounds that it enabled some new industry to be located in dirty areas without the most up-to-date emission control equipment. NEDA now views this method as enabling the economy to continue to grow without making air quality worse.

It also argued for extending the 1987 deadline for ozone and carbon monoxide compliance by metropolitan areas that had not met standards on the grounds that the remedies imposed by the law, such as banning federal aid for sewage treatment plants, would only make the quality of life in such areas worse. NEDA also opposed the United States' unilaterally controlling chlorofluorocarbons in order to stop ozone depletion in the atmosphere on the grounds that foreign competitors would simply fill the gap if American industry reduced its output of the chemicals. It also opposes any efforts to control acid deposition through further reductions in sulfur oxides on the grounds that industrial boilers contribute only marginally to the problem and not enough is known about the impact of acidity on the ecosystem.

In 1984 NEDA initiated its third project, the groundwater project, chaired by Rober Strelow, a vice-president of General Electric. John Quarles is general counsel for the project, and Jeff Zimmerman of Occidental Petroleum chairs the project's technical committee for NEDA. Under this project NEDA takes the position that groundwater quality may be a problem in some areas of the United States, but it is not a national crisis and need not be dealt with through federal legislation. It argues that groundwater should be defined according to the uses to which it is put. In those areas where it supplies an aquifer used as a major water supply, it may be necessary to control the quality. This should be undertaken by state and local governments that can determine how they want to use groundwater and the quality that needs to be maintained. In other words, groundwater should be regulated in the manner that surface water was in the 1960s, according to local needs, not by national standards. Mr. Strelow testified to this effect to a Senate committee in 1987.

Finally NEDA formed a project on the Resource Conservation and Recovery Act (RCRA) in 1986. This project is designed to monitor any proposed amendments to RCRA that might make the law more severe. NEDA views any changes to RCRA as potentially dangerous to industrial growth in the United States which would create incentives to move business operations overseas to regulatory climates more responsive to industry needs. It sees as its primary goal in amending RCRA to gain governmental support for siting more facilities for disposal of hazardous wastes within the United States.

### TACTICS

NEDA believes that private enterprise must not be made a "victim of the war on pollution." Its officers argue the costs of unjustified controls could destroy industry's ability to provide the tax base for social progress and argue labor leaders should join them for this reason. It strives to reduce conflict with environmental groups and tries to negotiate with them and government agencies to speed up regulatory decisions.

NEDA's primary tactics are to cooperate with the relevant trade associations that are making the primary defense against environmental legislative proposals in Congress. It also provides expert witnesses, but it relies on the same CEOs that testify before Congress for the major industries that belong to NEDA. The unions that belong to NEDA agree with management on the basis of saving jobs for U.S. workers. NEDA publishes a quarterly, *Balance*, which keeps its members informed about threats of greater government control at the congressional or agency level.

## FURTHER INFORMATION

*Balance* (1989). Washington, D.C.: NEDA, nos. 131, 132, 133.

## NATIONAL FEDERATION OF TEXTILES
*See* American Textile Manufacturers Institute.

## NATIONAL FOREST PRODUCTS ASSOCIATION (NFPA)
1250 Connecticut Avenue, N.W., Suite 200
Washington, D.C. 20036

### ORGANIZATION AND RESOURCES

The National Forest Products Association (NFPA) was founded in 1961, replacing the National Lumber Manufacturers Association that had represented timber interests in the United States since 1906. There are now 500 corporate members of NFPA, including such giants of the industry as Georgia-Pacific, Boise-Cascade, International Paper, and Weyerhaeuser, as well as many smaller timber-cutting companies. NFPA is divided into four functional councils: international trade, public timber, market support, and American forest councils. Each of these councils provides different services for its members, and individual corporations may choose to pay dues to and belong to one or more of these councils in addition to its general membership. In the late 1980s, NFPA had an annual budget of around $6 million, derived over 80 percent from corporate membership dues that vary according to the number of board feet processed by the individual company. The balance is made up from additional fund-raising, publications, convention charges, and investments. In 1987 NFPA sold the Forest Industries Building, which realized a profit of over $6 million, and enabled NFPA to establish a trust fund account that generates revenues as well; it has a staff of 85.

### POLICY CONCERNS

One of NFPA's primary concerns is to expand the market for wood products both in the United States and abroad. The international trade council focuses on promoting U.S. wood and pulp products abroad. It urges Congress and the Commerce Department to influence foreign governments, such as Japan and Korea, to reduce trade barriers to U.S. wood products. Before the 1988 free trade agreement with Canada, NFPA was also active in attempting to protect American products from competition from Canadian imports. In 1987 it negotiated an agreement with the Canadian government to impose a 15 percent lumber export tax in exchange for the United States not exacting a tariff on Canadian wood.

The market support council focuses on increasing the domestic market for wood products by emphasizing the safety and energy-conserving qualities of wood construction products. It argues, especially before local zoning boards, to accommodate building codes to the needs of the wood products industry. It has been successful in convincing some states that the fire retardant treatment of wood studs makes some multiple-story buildings as safe during fires as is masonry construction.

The American forest council focuses on privately owned woodlots usually managed by farmers. Timber companies purchase some lumber from these small holdings, and NFPA has been successful in getting state and local governments to tax such woodlots favorably in order to keep up the supply. It argues that such small woodlots provide habitat for wildlife as well as prevent soil erosion in formerly cultivated areas and uses this program to improve its public image and gain favorable publicity as a conservation-minded organization. NFPA representatives argue before Congress that regulations regarding wetlands protection and pesticide use interfere with the independent management of such small woodlots.

The public timber council lobbies primarily the Forest Service to sell more timber from public lands, especially in the western United States, to timber companies. Since the 1960s, when the privately owned timber lands were cut so extensively that they could not keep up with the demand for wood, there has been increasing pressure on the federal government to sell off old-growth national forests for commercial use. Environmental groups have argued against many of these sales in the 1980s on the grounds that the price the government gets for its timber does not match the costs to the taxpayer of building roads into national forests and providing other services to the forest products industry.

NFPA counters these arguments before the Congress and executive branch on the grounds that it would stifle the construction industry to restrict the supply of lumber coming from public lands. NFPA regularly argues before Congress to increase appropriations for the Forest Service to build roads into national forests in order to facilitate timber cutting there. With a former lumber company executive as head of the Forest Service throughout the Reagan administration, the NFPA was highly successful in helping the Forest Service develop plans for the timberlands it manages. It has worked to minimize the number of acres of forest kept in wilderness and has gotten the Forest Service to extend roads into numerous forests designated for multiple use. Many timber companies have succeeded in getting permission to clear-cut large areas of national forest land despite court suits by conservation organizations that argue selective harvesting of mature trees should be used to preserve wildlife habitat.

NFPA argues that the Forest Service and the Department of Interior should have an active policy to prevent and halt the spread of forest fires in all national forests and wilderness areas. After the extensive burnover of parts of the national parks in the dry summer of 1988, NFPA argued that timber companies should be allowed to salvage the dead trees for consumption. At the same time, it argues that controlled prescribed burning is important for proper management of forests, and these burns should not be subject to regulation for smoke and particulates under the Clean Air Act.

Another environmental issue of importance to NFPA is the implementation of the Federal Insecticide, Fungicide and Rodenticide Act (FIFRA) by which the Environmental Protection Agency regulates the kinds of commercial poisons that can be sprayed on public and private woodlands. NFPA has been successful in the 1980s in getting the Forest Service to spray pests such as beetles that attack pine forests with pesticides that some toxicologists argue are detrimental to human health for nearby residents. It also opposes greater involvement of the federal government in groundwater protection on the grounds that any new regulations would interfere with appropriate management of pests on privately held lands. It opposes any more stringent limits on its members' discharge permits to surface waters because the industry has already invested over $7 billion on pollution control.

NFPA has also been active in resisting the control of wood dust in lumber mills under the Occupational Safety and Health Act (OSHA). It was successful in the 1980s in preventing the Consumer Product Safety Commission and EPA from regulating the content of formaldehyde in basic construction materials such as plywood and pressboard. Generally, NFPA argues that any regulations should be made more cost conscious and should balance the benefits of public health and ecological protection against the need for a strong economy.

Representatives of the NFPA and the American Paper Institute* regularly testify that there is no evidence man-made pollutants are causing acid rain or damaging forests. It believes it is unrealistic to expect industry to limit sulfur emissions from industrial boilers because there are no economic scrubbers for them. There is also no need to have emission offsets before siting new industry in dirty-air areas because of the need for economic growth. NFPA regularly testifies before both the House and Senate on Clean Air Act amendments, arguing that to prevent significant deterioration in clean-air areas is unrealistic, and EPA should go back to new-source performance standards for all areas.

In 1987 NFPA supported refunding Superfund, but it objected to the imposition of a tax on waste producers. It preferred to keep the feedstock tax, which affects only the chemical and petroleum industries, not the paper pulp industry. It argued that such a tax would simply increase imports of paper products since overseas producers do not have to dispose of wastes in the United States and therefore would not pay the tax. NFPA argued, along with other industries, that there should be no joint and several liability for toxic waste dumps, and that the time schedule for cleaning up is unrealistically fast.

## TACTICS

The congressional relations department of NFPA maintains regular contact with all congressional personnel from districts and states with important wood products industries. It was instrumental in starting the congressional Forestry 2000 Task Force, composed of 126 members of Congress with such interests.

NFPA has a political action committee (FIPAC) which distributes funds to political candidates during every election year. It has a computerized facility designed to inform members as well as key media in each district of the voting records of all congressional representatives. NFPA representatives also work within the Forest Service and Department of Interior where they had exceptional access in the 1980s with key industry representatives serving in such posts as director of the Forest Service.

NFPA coordinates all its actions with the American Paper Institute* with which it now shares office space in Washington. Each of NFPA's four councils issues a monthly or weekly update on news in Washington and state capitols for its members. There are local and regional organizations of timber companies throughout the United States that are active in influencing the Forest Service field representatives whose job it is to draw up plans for managing each publicly owned forest in the United States. As clear-cutting old growth forests increased in the 1980s, environmental and wildlife groups took legal action to slow leasing in such areas as the Tongass National Forest in Alaska. The timber industry responded by taking out newspaper advertisements in *The New York Times* and other papers arguing that "extremists who only talk about trees and owls" were trying to take away the jobs of mill workers and lumbermen.

### FURTHER INFORMATION

American Forest Resource Alliance (1989). "The Balance between Man and Nature."
    *The New York Times*, Op-ed advertisement, September 15, p. 23.
*Annual Report 1988* (1989). Washington, D.C.: NFPA.
Culhane, Paul J. (1981). *Public Lands Politics*. Baltimore, Md.: Johns Hopkins Press,
    Resources for the Future.
Grant, Wyn (1989). "Business Interest Organization and the Politics of Collective Consumption: An Analysis of the Forest and Forest Products Industry in the U.S.,
    Canada, and the U.K." Paper presented at the annual meeting of the American
    Political Science Association, Atlanta, Ga.
Luoma, Jon R. (1989). "Logging of Old Trees in Alaska Is Found to Threaten Eagles,"
    *The New York Times*, November 7, p. 19.

### NATIONAL GOVERNORS' ASSOCIATION (NGA)
Hall of the States
444 North Capitol Street
Washington, D.C. 20001

### ORGANIZATION AND RESOURCES

Governors in the United States first organized in 1908, and now the National Governors' Association (NGA) represents the governors of all fifty states and the territories and commonwealths. It meets twice yearly to discuss common problems and state-federal relationships. Bipartisanship is assured by its articles of organization which require that the position of chair of the NGA alternate annually between the two major parties, and that a majority of the members of the executive committee be of a party other than the chair's. It has an executive director, Raymond C. Scheppach, who heads a staff of eighty in the Hall of the States in Washington, which houses other state and local organizations. There are standing committees designated by the individual governors to deal with such problems as natural resources. Revenues come from all fifty-five members and create a budget of about $9 million annually.

## POLICY CONCERNS

The most important goal that all governors share is to see their state economies grow, and to this end they compete with each other in attracting industries, especially innovative high technologies, including biotechnology and computers. In keeping with this goal, NGA supports the rapid development of all domestic sources of energy in order to prevent the United States from becoming overly dependent on foreign sources. Different regions of the country are represented in this policy position, which advocates full exploitation of coal, oil, and gas resources, as well as developing synthetic fuels and keeping open the nuclear option. However, NGA also advocates that the federal government assume more responsibility for liability in case of nuclear accidents. NGA agrees with industry that the windfall profits tax should be taken off oil and new tax incentives given to energy developers.

Another issue on which the governors are able to find common ground is the general principle that state governments should have more control over public policies that affect them and their constituents directly. The Reagan administration said a great deal about passing control of policy from the national to the state and local levels of government. However, federal funds that had been used by state governments for programs ranging from social welfare to natural resource management were also systematically withdrawn. Hence the state governments ended with fewer resources and more responsibilities. Generally the governors were united in seeking more help from Washington with fewer controls attached, but were unsuccessful.

The Clean Air Act (CAA) is an example of a federal policy that affects states, and governors such as Jay Rockefeller of West Virginia have testified before Congress that the states should have more autonomy over the state implementation plans that constitute the main program for achieving the air quality standards set by the U.S. Environmental Protection Agency. At the same time states want increased federal aid to help states administer the law. Some governors have testified to increase the emission standards for cars and trucks, not to reduce them. Governors also argue, however, that new stationary sources of air pollution must be permitted in both dirty and clean areas, or states' economies will stagnate. They also lobby for eliminating the lowest achievable emission rates on industrial plants as too strict even for nonattainment areas. Acid rain is viewed by many governors as a major problem, but midwestern states fear losing a market for their high-sulfur coal unless new technologies are found to burn coal with lower emissions. They advise a five-year reduction program for sulfur oxides followed by a three-year study program before the next phase of reducing emissions is set, but they are unable to agree on how this program should be financed.

Another issue that most of the coastal states are united on is that states should have more influence on policies controlling exploration and development of oil and gas resources in the outer continental shelf owned by the federal government but affecting the adjoining states' coastlines. Despite the Reagan administration's claim to be committed to more states' control, it systematically tried to sell off such leases as rapidly as possible, and some governors turned to Congress for assistance to prevent leasing such tracts of land when it endangers other economic activities such as fishing and tourism. At the same time that states attempt to limit exploration in the most environmentally sensitive areas they also seek to increase their own share of the royalties from such projects.

The states were enthusiastic about the refunding of Superfund in 1986. However, they hope to increase their own discretion to determine which sites are designated for cleanup and what the definition of cleanliness should be. They seek to avoid responsibility for paying for the cleanup and to relieve their municipalities of liability for the sites that they own. The states are divided over the issue of the disposing of solid wastes. Some wish to export their problems, while other states seek to protect their dwindling landspace for landfills. NGA seeks to develop regional pacts among states that will resolve the problem of what to do with the nation's mounting garbage and hazardous waste problem. It recognizes solid waste disposal as one of the major issues of the twenty-first century and hopes to avoid federal preemption through state and regional initiatives. NGA also advocates federal research and assistance to states in this area.

Western states still advocate massive federal funding for water projects there, although there is resistance to this from other regions of the country. All states agree that groundwater needs to be protected, and NGA has urged EPA to speed up efforts to identify and set standards for all contaminants in drinking water. At the same time, NGA opposes federally mandated requirements for the quality of surface and groundwater, believing that local circumstances should dictate individualized standards.

## TACTICS

The NGA publishes a weekly *Governors Bulletin* for all its members. Its staff represents the governors' collective policy stands to Congress. Because it is self-consciously bipartisan, these policy preferences are perforce compromises. However, the bipartisan nature of the organization assures it of some influence in the national executive branch regardless of which party is in power. Governors also have excellent access to congressional committees and are able to present their views freely to the legislators and their staffs. The NGA's major problem is one of coordination among the members themselves, but once a common stand on the states' interests can be identified, it is easily communicated to the national level of government.

## FURTHER INFORMATION

*Policy Positions 1988–1989* (1989). Washington, D.C.: NGA.
*Restoring the Balance: State Leadership for America's Future* (1988). Washington, D.C.:
NGA.

## NATIONAL LEAGUE OF CITIES (NLC)

1301 Pennsylvania Avenue, N.W.
Washington, D.C. 20004

### ORGANIZATION AND RESOURCES

In 1924 ten state municipal leagues founded the American Municipal Association dedicated to improving the efficiency and effectiveness of city services.
In 1947 it began admitting as members individual cities as well as state associations. In 1964 it changed its name to the National League of Cities (NLC).
By 1988 its membership numbered over 1,300 cities and 49 state affiliates, which
in turn incorporated some 16,000 municipalities. Dues range from about $500
for the smallest towns to over $40,000 for major cities, with state leagues
contributing $20,000 each. In the late 1980s its operating budget was about $6.5
million, obtained almost equally from dues and additional fund-raising. Its
professional staff of about 50, headed by Alan Beals, executive director, represent
the interests of its members before Congress, administrative agencies such as
the Department of Housing and Urban Development, and the courts. It owns 10
percent of the equity in its headquarters in Washington, on which it has a 30-
year lease.

NLC holds an annual Congress of Cities after Thanksgiving each year at which
delegates from state leagues and city governments elect a president, two vice-
presidents, a thirty-five-member board of directors and adopt national municipal
policy positions.

### POLICY CONCERNS

NLC's policy interests have changed over the years. In the 1950s, it focused
on the interstate highway program and in developing legislation for the advisory
commission on intergovernmental relations. In the 1960s the League pushed for
general revenue sharing to replace many of the programmatic grants given for
specific types of projects in order to allow cities greater autonomy over their
programs. In the 1970s it argued for block grant programs for community development, employment and training, and law enforcement.

NLC supports policies on energy and environment designed to protect cities
against energy supply interruptions, to increase federal protection of the environment, and at the same time to preserve communities' prerogatives to impose
their own standards and penalties. Specifically, the League advocates that the
federal government develop an energy policy fair to all regions, sectors, and
income groups; that it fund research to promote conservation of energy, cogeneration, solar, wind, biofuels, hydro, and geothermal energy. In the late 1980s

it argued along with industry for repeal of the crude oil windfall profits tax, which was accomplished by the 100th Congress. Originally, NCL had supported the tax on the grounds it would produce funds that could be used to cushion the impact of high energy prices on low- and moderate-income families, support public transit systems, and develop alternative energy technology, including solar.

NLC is divided between the twin goals of conserving and developing more energy supplies and at the same time keeping the price low for its residents. To promote conservation of energy, the League urges federal and state regulatory agencies to encourage lower electric rates for customers at off-peak hours and for those who are willing to have service interrupted at peak demand times. It argues for federal assistance to weatherize houses for senior citizens and poor residents as well as for city buildings. In order to keep prices low for its residents, the League also urges that federal price controls on gas produced before 1977 be continued, but it does not advocate extending price controls to petroleum products. In order to reduce the price to the consumer, it also argues that gas pipelines should be allowed to renegotiate prices from gas field owners instead of being committed to take-or-pay contracts. NLC argues for increasing the supply of traditional fuels, including coal and nuclear, while alternative renewable fuels are being developed. But it also believes that siting decisions about new power plants should be left to the states and localities, and federal assistance should be given to neighboring communities to help them design emergency evacuation plans. The League also advocates a national emergency plan for distributing the strategic petroleum reserve and other supplies in case of an interruption in supply.

Regarding air pollution, NLC is also ambivalent about its desires to make air healthful for its residents and at the same time keep and attract industry to cities and retain local autonomy for controls. It advocates keeping air quality standards high enough to protect the health of even the most susceptible individuals and other standards for non–health related values. It also seeks to have the U.S. Environmental Protection Agency (EPA) permit construction of new sources of air pollution in nonattainment areas only if existing sources can reduce their emissions by twice the amount the new source would emit rather than having pollutants simply matched by offsets. It also argues that EPA should set standards for diesel vehicles which have been delayed for many years. It opposes industry's demand that the lowest achievable emission rates be relaxed in nonattainment areas. It also advocates keeping best available control technology strategy for new sources in clean areas in order to prevent the clean areas from drawing industry away from the dirtier, more metropolitan areas. NLC also testified for acid rain controls in 1986, advocating that sulfur and nitrogen oxides be reduced by 8 to 12 million tons by 1990. To fund this acid rain program it advocates a fee on all electric utilities that have not yet met emission standards for new plants.

While generally supportive of environmental values on clean air, NLC also recognizes the problems of its members in meeting standards. It also advocates allowing states to determine the level of emission controls under state implementation plans and to make revisions to the plans without extensive U.S. EPA oversight. It also advocates extending the period of time for nonattainment areas to reach the quality standards, and argues for using transportation control measures only as a last resort. Communities not meeting air quality standards should not be required to institute inspection and maintenance programs unless it is found to be cost-effective in the region. Despite these minor caveats, however, generally NLC supports environmental positions on the Clean Air Act.

Another major issue in the environmental area for NLC is disposal methods for solid waste, including hazardous wastes. It supported the reauthorization of the Resource Conservation and Recovery Act in 1987, urging the federal government to fund research on alternative methods of disposing of solid waste than landfills, especially resource recovery and recycling. It argued for strict controls on hazardous waste landfills, including liners and leachate collection systems, and opposed industry's demands that it be allowed to incinerate hazardous wastes at sea because of the lack of air pollution controls on the high seas.

NLC also supported the 1986 Superfund Amendments and Reauthorization Act (SARA), which extended Superfund to 1991 and to $9.5 billion in order to clean up abandoned hazardous waste dumps. It argued the fees on industry should be doubled in order to fund the program. But it also argued state matching requirements were too burdensome and states should be required to pay only 10 percent of costs involved at publicly owned or operated Superfund sites. It argued that owners of hazardous sites, including nuclear plants, should be held strictly liable to victims injured by a possible catastrophic accident. City officials were especially eager for the federal government to require industry to inform local police and fire departments about the chemical contents of wastes stored in their jurisdictions, which was included in SARA.

NLC also testified to the U.S. Congress about the reauthorization of the Clean Water Act. It advocated the continuation of federal funding of publicly owned municipal sewage treatment plants and was disappointed when this program was reduced by the 1986 amendments. It agreed that municipalities could reach the 1988 deadline for wastewater treatment facilities, but only if federal funding were increased. NLC argued for cities having autonomy for the way in which they charge industry for treating its wastes and the pretreatment they require for industrial wastes.

Cities want states to have the primary responsibility for enforcing the Safe Drinking Water Act, which requires municipalities to provide a potable water supply that meets national standards to their customers. Cities believe they should be able to differentiate between naturally occurring contaminants and man-made ones, and they also want financial assistance from the federal government to help defray the costs of the program.

Another issue that concerns the League and a few other groups is controlling noise from aircraft in metropolitan areas. NLC continues to urge the Federal

Aviation Administration to require state-of-the-art noise emission controls on all aircraft. It also seeks to maintain local options over whether supersonic transports should be permitted to overfly their areas. It argues that air carriers should retrofit their fleet to meet the 1977 noise control standards for planes. It argues that EPA and the Department of Transportation should establish noise levels for trucks, buses, automobiles, motorcycles, as well as railroad yard activities. In addition, it seeks to allow state and local government authority to add their own standards that may be stricter than federal standards.

For the most part, NLC supports strong pollution control programs to protect the health of their residents. When cities are the targets of national regulations the League argues for postponement of deadlines and federal financial assistance to help defray the costs of compliance. The League has been one of the most effective advocates of pollution control before Congress based on the rapport its members, who are also elective officials, have with the elected representatives from their areas. It has not, of course, focused singlemindedly on environmental and energy issues; rather, its primary concerns in recent years have been changes in the national tax code, reduction in revenues distributed to cities, and the social welfare problems of residents of metropolitan areas.

### TACTICS

NLC issues numerous research reports on subjects of interest to its members, such as waste-to-energy facilities, energy strategies for communities, and other policy issues. It also publishes directories of city officials and an annual policy position book. It keeps its members informed about developments in Washington through a weekly newspaper, *Nation's Cities Weekly*. It provides a local computerized information network in cooperation with Control Data Corporation, and it has a computerized data base of cities of various sizes. In March each year about 2,500 NLC members assemble from all over the country to hear from and talk to members of Congress, agency executives, and key staff people who write and administer the laws and regulations that affect cities. Five standing committees exist to develop policy on particular matters of concern to the League's members: finance, administration, and intergovernmental relations; energy, environment and natural resources; community and economic development; transportation and communications; and human development. These committees consist of about 200 members, appointed by the League's president in January, with 3 to 7 members from each state. These committees work all year on policy statements that are debated and voted on by the Congress of Cities in November. It publishes the proceedings of its two annual conferences and makes these available on audio cassette tapes as well.

### FURTHER INFORMATION

*National Municipal Policy* (1989). Washington, D.C.: NLC.

## NATIONAL LEAGUE OF WOMEN VOTERS
*See* League of Women Voters.

## NATIONAL LEGAL CENTER FOR THE PUBLIC INTEREST (NLCPI)
1000 16th Street, N.W., Suite 301
Washington, D.C. 20036

### HISTORY AND DEVELOPMENT

The National Legal Center for the Public Interest (NLCPI) was founded in 1975 by a group of lawyers who believe that the U.S. legal system should be devoted to the principles of free enterprise, private ownership of property, and limited government. It is opposed to the expansion of public law and the costs to industry of judicializing the administrative process. Its members believe activist judges have opened up to trial lawyers representing plaintiffs in personal injury cases excessive opportunities to overburden the judicial system. They also argue that trivial cases have been created by the liberal awards of attorney's fees to groups who wish to use rigid environmental laws for their own interests. NLCPI is part of the growing conservative criticism of expanding the use of courts to hear demands from interests other than business and industry.

### ORGANIZATION AND RESOURCES

NLCPI is a tax-exempt, nonprofit corporation, contributions to which are tax deductible. It obtains 52 percent of its funds from business organizations; another 28 percent comes from foundations, 14 percent from conferences, and the remainder from individual contributions and interest on investments. Its funds are used to litigate in the public interest (39 percent), educate the legal profession with research (32 percent), administration (20 percent), and communications (9 percent). It is affiliated with several regional legal organizations: the Pacific, Mountain States, mid-America, mid-Atlantic, Southeastern, Gulf, Great Plains, and Capitol Legal Foundations, which initiate law cases to reduce government interference with the economy, including pollution control regulations.

NLCPI has a twenty-eight-member board of directors elected by the previous board, including Joseph Coors of Adolph Coors Company, Robert J. Muth of ASARCO, Inc., V. J. Skutt of Mutual of Omaha Insurance Company, Irving Kristol of the American Enterprise Institute, and former attorney general William French Smith. The board's chair is John H. Bretherick, Jr., president of the Continental Corporation. NLCPI's president is Ernest B. Heuter.

### POLICY CONCERNS

NLCPI's primary focus is on litigating to reduce government interference with the private sector of the economy. It has published legal treatises on several topics of interest to its membership, such as its opposition to the American Law Institute's proposal to subject the boards of directors of U.S. corporations to outside oversight and extend liability of corporate directors for their companies' actions.

In 1986 Dr. Edward J. Burger of NLCPI testified before the Senate concerning reauthorization of Superfund to clean up toxic waste dumps. He argued that no link has yet been established between hazardous wastes and cancer, and more study should be done before any new legislation was enacted. Generally, the NLCPI opposes making industry liable for worker and third-party exposure to chemicals, and it opposes community right-to-know legislation. It points to the black lung legislation as one example of overcompensation of a few workers at the expense of stockholders and consumers.

### TACTICS

NLCPI sponsors an annual general counsel briefing designed to bring together corporate lawyers from various industries and government attorneys and judges to discuss topics of mutual interest. The keynote speaker at its 1986 meeting was U.S. Attorney General Edwin Meese III. Most of its efforts to affect public policy take the form of publications about legal issues such as *American Enterprise, the Law, and the Commercial Use of Space*, in which it argued that space should be privatized and government control minimized. Its staff, however, occasionally testify before congressional committees on issues. In 1987 NLCPI began its own law review, the *Public Interest Law Review*.

### FURTHER INFORMATION

*Annual Report 1987–88* (1989). Washington, D.C.: NLCPI.
Birrell, George A., et al. (1986). *The American Law Institute and Corporate Governance*. Washington, D.C.: NLCPI.
Meredith, Pamela Louise, et al. (1986). *American Enterprise, the Law, and the Commercial Use of Space*. Washington, D.C.: NLCPI.

## NATIONAL LIMESTONE INSTITUTE
*See* National Stone Association.

## NATIONAL LUMBER MANUFACTURERS ASSOCIATION
*See* National Forest Products Association.

## NATIONAL OCEAN INDUSTRIES ASSOCIATION (NOIA)
1050 17th Street, N.W., Suite 700
Washington, D.C. 20036

### ORGANIZATION AND RESOURCES

The National Ocean Industries Association (NOIA) was founded in 1966 to establish a voice in Washington for the offshore drilling industry. It was known until 1972 as the National Oceanography Association and in 1981 absorbed the Ocean Commercial Users Association. It began with 35 member companies but now has 350 members located in 33 states and representing other ocean industries as well as oil and other mineral production. Of 47 members of the board of directors, only 14 are not based in Texas, and these include the president of Amoco Production located in Chicago and a vice-president of Chevron based in California. Charles D. Matthews is president, heading an 8-person staff in Washington. NOIA has an annual budget of about $650,000.

## POLICY CONCERNS

The primary goal of NOIA is to open up all continental shelf lands to exploration and drilling by gas and oil companies. James Watt, while secretary of the interior, accelerated leasing of federal lands to oil companies, but Congress intervened to provide a moratorium on drilling off the California coast. Later a compromise was worked out between environmental groups and the U.S. Department of Interior (DOI) which opened some areas to drilling, but this was repudiated by Secretary of the Interior Donald Hodel in 1986 due to industry objections. NOIA prefers to work through the DOI because it has maximum influence there where it helped to draft the five-year leasing plan for 1987–1992. Congress, however, continued throughout the 1980s to prevent much offshore leasing through the appropriations process. NOIA objects strenuously to any control that local and state governments exert over the process of federal leasing through the Coastal Zone Management Act (CZMA), arguing that this is a national security matter that must be controlled in Washington.

NOIA also seeks to prevent any congressional amendment being attached either to the CZMA or the Outer Continental Shelf Lands Act to increase the discretion given to state governments concerning leasing federal land off their shores. NOIA representatives argue, as does the American Petroleum Institute,* that the United States needs to utilize every domestic source of petroleum in order to avoid becoming dependent on foreign suppliers. NOIA believes that economic considerations outweigh any environmental problems that might result. It also supports leasing the entire Alaskan wilderness area even though none of it is under water, as is consistent with its general philosophy.

NOIA is also concerned about the Clean Air, Clean Water, Resource Conservation and Recovery, and Endangered Species acts because of the implications these have for its operations. It opposes tightening regulations under any of these laws. It especially argues against giving the U.S. Environmental Protection Agency (EPA) control over outer continental shelf air quality, because authority presently resides with DOI, an agency much more sympathetic to industry needs. It regards EPA's standards regarding discharge of mining wastes from offshore operations as much too stringent and hopes to have them reduced through court action. It also defends the industry against the possibility that EPA might define such discharges as hazardous under RCRA.

NOIA has argued before several Congresses that the Endangered Species and Marine Mammal Protection acts (MMPA) need to be reformed to eliminate the protection of marine mammals against accidental killing by industry. In 1986 it succeeded in getting MMPA amended to allow for accidental killing of certain endangered species of whales. Drilling companies are under national and international obligation to remove drilling platforms that are no longer in use within a year after operations stop. They prefer to simply blow them up as the least expensive expedient. However, environmentalists object to this on the grounds that it also destroys marine life, and NOIA hopes to convince the International Maritime Organization that this is a trivial consideration.

### TACTICS

NOIA, as do other trade associations, depends primarily on the CEOs of its important members to make most presentations before Congress and the agencies. It organized a proleasing task force in 1987 chaired by John R. Huff, CEO of Oceaneering International and a NOIA board member, to coordinate appearances of officials from various companies before hearings held by the Department of Interior, Congress, and many state governments on the outer continental shelf issue. NOIA issues a bimonthly *Washington Report* to its members to keep them informed and holds an annual convention in April in Washington.

### FURTHER INFORMATION

*Annual Report 1989* (1990). Washington, D.C.: NOIA.
U.S. Congress. Senate Committee on Energy and Natural Resources (1984). *Hearings on Offshore Drilling Moratorium*. Washington, D.C.: Government Printing Office.

## NATIONAL OCEANOGRAPHY ASSOCIATION
*See* National Ocean Industries Association.

## NATIONAL OIL JOBBERS COUNCIL
*See* Petroleum Marketers Association of America.

## NATIONAL PAPERBOARD ASSOCIATION
*See* American Paper Institute.

## NATIONAL PARKS AND CONSERVATION ASSOCIATION (NPCA)
1015 31st Street, N.W.
Washington, D.C. 20007

### ORGANIZATION AND RESOURCES

Congress established the first national park, Yellowstone, in the United States in 1872, and passed the National Park Service Act in 1916. The first director of the National Park Service, Stephen Tyng Mather, founded the National Parks and Conservation Association (NPCA) in 1919, dedicated to defending, promoting, and improving the national park system and educating the public about the parks. By the end of the 1980s it had grown to 55,000 members who pay dues of $25 a year. A special rate of $18 is available for students and retirees.

Many members contribute higher dues, up to $250 a year, and life memberships are $1,000. The Stephen Tyng Mather Society consists of members who contribute $1,000 a year or more.

In the late 1980s it had an income of $3.8 million, 43 percent of which came from membership dues, 28 percent from additional fund-raising from members, 12 percent from foundation grants, 16 percent from investments, and 1 percent from bequests and miscellaneous sources. It spends 86 percent of its budget for programs, 8 percent for fund-raising, and 6 percent for administration. It also accepts contributions from major corporations such as Waste Management, Inc., Monsanto, Chevron Corporation, and the Santa Fe Southern Pacific Railroad, for helping to preserve national parks.

It has a thirty-seven-member board of trustees consisting of conservationists from around the country, including John B. Oakes of the *The New York Times*. The president of the twelve-person executive staff is Paul C. Pritchard.

## POLICY CONCERNS

Since its founding the NPCA has advocated acquisition of new parklands to accommodate a growing population and increased recreation demand by the public. Its land acquisitions fund is used to purchase inholdings (property owned by private citizens inside the national parks) and contribute or sell them to the federal government whenever Congress makes funds available. NPCA has supported the National Park Service (NPS) as a dedicated professional cadre that should be maintained and strengthened. Although it supports volunteers such as the Appalachian Trail Conference, a private citizens' organization that helps to maintain the trail, it argues that professional wildlife biologists are needed to manage the national parks properly. It has traditionally testified before Congress that the NPS needs more funds to conserve and protect the system of national parks as pressure from increased use has built.

Throughout the 1970s and 1980s, the NPCA argued that the National Park Service has too often bowed to pressure to provide more facilities within the parks for constantly growing crowds. It argues that areas around the periphery of the parks, both public and private, should be developed as resorts for recreation and housing, and the parks themselves should be preserved in their natural state for the people to enjoy. It opposes the encroachment of roads and concessions inside the parks that detract from their natural beauty and serenity. For example, it opposed the extension of the Jackson Hole Airport to accommodate large jets, a proposed parkway between the Grand Teton and Yellowstone parks, and drainage of the Big Cypress Swamp, which supplies the Everglades with water.

The NPCA argues that the NPS has not been in the forefront of many conservation battles, although it sympathizes with the Service's problems with recent administrations and tries to give it political support before Congress. In 1988 it testified before Congress in favor of creating a National Park Service review board and set a five-year term for the Service director, who would be appointed by the president and confirmed by the Senate. NPCA advocates separating the

NPS from the Department of the Interior in order to reprofessionalize the Service, but believes that any change that would protect the NPS from political pressures would be a step in the right direction. The Reagan administration vigorously opposed the bill.

NPCA faults the NPS for allowing grazing rights for private-property owners at Assateague National Seashore (Virginia), for not opposing development across the Potomac from Mount Vernon which destroys the vista from the park, and for planning monorails and railroads to supplement rather than replace the roads already built inside the parks. The Association advocates busing tourists from hotels and campgrounds outside the park system as a solution to the overcrowded conditions and traffic jams inside many of the most popular parks. It advocates more designation of wilderness areas inside the parks that will be accessible only by hiking. NPCA also opposes airplane overflights of such well-known parks as the Grand Canyon where several accidents have occurred because of the crush of air traffic. In 1987 President Reagan signed a law to protect some parts of national parks from overflights, but the Federal Aviation Agency interpreted it in favor of tour operators, and NPCA objected formally to the plan to implement the law.

The Association celebrated the creation of a 76,800 acre Great Basin National Park in eastern Nevada by the 99th Congress in 1986, although it would have preferred greater acreage. It was a compromise, as the Nevada senators sought a park of about half the size actually authorized by Congress. It supported the President's Commission on Americans Outdoors which supported the need for a trust fund to provide about $1 billion a year for acquiring a backlog of land designated for national parklands. However, these recommendations met with opposition from the Office of Management and Budget and the Department of the Interior's Bureau of Land Management. In the last days of the 100th Congress, NPCA and other conservation groups succeeded in getting several demands met that they had worked on throughout the Reagan administration. Congress added 8 new national park system areas to the system, and segments of 40 Oregon rivers to the wild and scenic rivers system.

NPCA is concerned about conservation of wildlife in parks and supports the reintroduction of wolves into such parks as Yellowstone, a position opposed by the Wyoming congressional delegation because of objections from ranchers in the area. It also argues for expanding the habitat of the grizzly bear in national parks, whose territory has been greatly reduced by visitors' increased use of areas where the bears previously roamed free. It also supported reauthorization of the Endangered Species Act in 1988.

In 1985 representatives of NPCA testified before Congress against development of geothermal energy resources near public parks unless industry can prove that this use will not affect the natural geysers in parks. In 1987 it succeeded in obtaining legislative protection for geothermal resources in the parks. When some parks, such as the Big Cypress in Florida, were purchased, the federal government did not buy the mineral rights there, and NPCA fights to prevent oil and gas exploration in those parks. In 1988 it joined other conservation groups in filing a lawsuit against the Interior Department for issuing a permit for Shell Petroleum to conduct seismic tests in the Big Cypress. Long before the 1989 massive oil spill in Prince William Sound, Alaska, NPCA deplored the 1988 spill off Washington state which fouled 300 miles of coastline, including Olympic National Park. It opposes the development of more offshore drilling because of the inability of the oil industry to prevent such accidents.

The Association also joined the National Clean Air Coalition* in arguing to strengthen the Clean Air Act (CAA) in order to preserve the vistas and air in and around the national parks that would deteriorate if the law were amended to drop the prevention of significant deterioration of clean areas requirement. In 1989 NPCA expressed disappointment with President Bush's proposals for amending the CAA because they allow clean-coal technology generating stations near the national parks to degrade the quality of air there. It considers acid rain a major threat to the ecology of the parks and advocates stricter controls on sulfur oxide emissions. It also opposes strip-mine development within view of the national parks and supports other conservation organizations' attempt to prevent mineral development in the Alaskan wilderness lands.

Throughout the 1980s the Reagan Department of the Interior proposed to increase fees for users of the national parks in order to reduce the federal deficit. NPCA testified repeatedly to Senate and House Committees that fees should be collected from users of parks, but that such revenues should be kept separate in a special treasury account for use in parks. It also argued that fees should be staggered according to the stress placed on the natural system. Hence, a nominal fee should be imposed for backpacking and proportionately more for campsites. Government charges nothing for industry to search for minerals on public lands, and this use also should be made to pay its fair share. NPCA believes that it is unrealistic to expect the national parks ever to become entirely self-sufficient and that they are worth some investment from the general revenue fund.

The Land and Water Conservation Fund (LWCF), created by Congress in 1965, primarily from oil and gas royalties from the outer continental shelf, has been the main source of funds for acquiring new park lands. Each year about $900 million is collected, but the Reagan administration used only about $220 million a year in the 1980s for parks. NPCA regularly urges Congress to allocate more of the LWCF for parklands. In 1988 it supported the American Heritage Trust Act that would have designated the trust fund for this purpose, but the bill failed to pass the 100th Congress. At the end of the Reagan administration Secretary of the Interior Donald Hodel moved to transfer many public lands and energy resources to the private sector, an action deplored by NPCA President Paul Pritchard.

During the summer of 1988 unusually hot, dry weather precipitated a rash of forest fires in the Yellowstone National Park area, and the NPS initially allowed them to burn because of its sixteen-year-old policy to allow natural fires to burn in order to clear out accumulated underbrush. The local tourist industry and state politicians put pressure on the NPS to fight the fires, and eventually they were suppressed. The NPCA supported the NPS's policy of allowing natural burns and argued that much of the vegetation had survived the fire and that previous policies of actively suppressing all fires had contributed to the problem. It opposes the Forest Service's willingness to allow clear cutting of old growth areas within national forests and especially its request to the NPS to truck cut trees through Yellowstone Park.

*TACTICS*

The NPCA sends *National Parks* to its members bimonthly. The magazine features stories on particular parks and keeps members abreast of legislative developments in Washington that affect the national parks and monuments. In addition it issues frequent alerts to its membership to write their congressional representatives about upcoming votes. In the late 1980s it established a network of citizen volunteers (park watchers) living near each of the national parks to alert the national headquarters whenever they perceive threats to the integrity of the park under their surveillance.

*FURTHER INFORMATION*

Fox, Steven (1981). *John Muir and His Legacy: The American Conservation Movement.* Boston: Little, Brown.
*National Parks* (vol. 63 March-April, May-June, July-August, September-October, November-December 1989). Washington, D.C.: NPCA.

**NATIONAL PETROLEUM ASSOCIATION**
*See* National Petroleum Refiners Association.

**NATIONAL PETROLEUM REFINERS ASSOCIATION (NPRA)**
Suite 1000, 1899 L Street, N.W.
Washington, D.C. 20036

*ORGANIZATION AND RESOURCES*

In 1902 leaders of the petroleum refining industry joined together to form the National Petroleum Association in order to represent their interests before the federal government and to exchange information about technical developments in the industry. In 1961 it merged with the Western Petroleum Refiners Association to form the National Petroleum Refiners Association (NPRA).

In the late 1980s NPRA had a budget of about $3 million derived from meetings, investments, and corporate membership dues ranging from $1,400 to $12,000, depending on the size of the company. The board of directors of NPRA includes representatives from such major corporations as Mobil, Phillips, Chevron, Shell, Amoco, and British Petroleum companies. President Urvan R. Sternfels heads a staff of twenty-five in the Washington office.

## POLICY CONCERNS

NPRA is concerned about both the Clean Air and Clean Water acts (CAA, CWA). Its member corporations seek to reduce the stringency of EPA regulations concerning the pollutants that can be emitted from cracking and refining plants either into the air or water. Throughout the 1970s and most of the 1980s NPRA was highly successful in postponing and diluting proposals to reduce or eliminate lead additives from gasoline.

In 1980 NPRA unsuccessfully resisted the move to create the Comprehensive Environmental Response, Compensation, and Liability Act (CERCLA, or Superfund) in order to clean up hazardous waste dumps in the United States. This fund comes from a tax levied against the petroleum and petrochemical industries, which, it argues, are not the only "culprits" and should not have to bear the financial burden alone. Nevertheless, Superfund was reauthorized in 1986 despite industry objections. NPRA also objects to regulations under the Resource Conservation and Recovery Act which controls how certain hazardous wastes may be disposed of in landfills. It argues that oily wastes can be safely spread on land and plowed into the earth. NPRA also resists the concept of designating certain industrial sites such as refining plants as hazardous to groundwater and has fought against amendments to the Safe Drinking Water Act that would control such sites.

NPRA shares the American Petroleum Institute's (API)* concern about falling gasoline prices and the increasing dependency of the United States on foreign imports in the late 1980s. Some members advocate imposing an oil import fee to protect domestic production, but this failed passage because of division in the industry. They argue that a certain minimum refining capacity needs to be retained in the United States for strategic defense purposes in the event that foreign sources are cut off.

NPRA members are united in supporting all possible incentives and tax breaks for the industry to produce more domestic oil and to open up all wilderness areas to oil exploration. NPRA also advocates filling the strategic petroleum reserve at taxpayers' expense, not, as was suggested by some congressional representatives in 1987, at the expense of oil importers. This back door import fee was criticized by oil importers as being discriminatory toward one part of the industry, and by domestic producers as too little to correct for their disadvantage in the market.

## TACTICS

NPRA coordinates its activities with API and the Independent Petroleum Association of America,* and many of its members are also active in these other trade associations. Like other trade associations, it utilizes its easy access to the White House through CEOs of major energy corporations, makes representations before Congress, and provides information to staffers; it comments on the many regulations that pertain to the petroleum industry, and litigates in the federal courts. NPRA publishes a variety of information for the use of its members, including the *Washington Bulletin*, a periodic summary of significant developments in Congress and the regulatory agencies; *Emergency Petroleum Digest*, a ready reference to activities of the Department of Energy including proposed rulemaking; an annual report of oil antitrust cases filed by the Justice Department; and various reports on production and sales in the refining industry.

NPRA also sponsors several annual meetings at which technical papers pertaining to the refining and petrochemical industries are presented. Together the petroleum and petrochemical industry represents one of the most powerful lobbying blocs in Washington.

### FURTHER INFORMATION

Oppenheimer, Bruce (1974). *Oil and the Congressional Process: The Limits of Symbolic Politics*. Lexington, Mass.: Lexington Books.

Rosenbaum, Walter A. (1987). *Energy, Politics, and Public Policy*, 2d ed. Washington, D.C.: Congressional Quarterly Press.

*Washington Bulletin* (1989). Washington, D.C.: NPRA, April, August.

## NATIONAL RECLAMATION ASSOCIATION

*See* National Water Resources Association.

## NATIONAL RIVERS AND HARBORS CONGRESS

*See* Water Resources Congress.

## NATIONAL SOCIETY OF PROFESSIONAL ENGINEERS (NSPE)

1420 King Street
Alexandria, Virginia 22314

### ORGANIZATION AND RESOURCES

The National Society of Professional Engineers (NSPE) is a professional association, founded in 1934 and devoted to advancing the interests of engineers. It is organized into 54 state and regional groups and 525 local organizations. Each state has representation on the 100-member board of directors in numbers proportionate to the number of individual state members. NSPE's executive director is Donald G. Weinert, who heads a professional staff of 25.

NSPE has some 75,000 individual members who pay dues of $60 a year, or $30 for members under 30 years old, to the national organization, as well as an equivalent amount to the state chapter. Members may also choose to join special interest groups within NSPE, including engineers in government, in private practice, in industry, and in construction. Each division has its own assessment of dues in addition to the main society's. NSPE has an annual budget of about $6 million, 65 percent of which comes from regular dues, and 17 percent from additional fund-raising among members. The remainder comes from interest on investments and sales of publications.

## POLICY CONCERNS

The official philosophy of NSPE resembles that of the U.S. Chamber of Commerce* and the National Association of Manufacturers,* namely that free enterprise and competition afford the best hope of finding technological solutions to all societal problems. It argues that governmental regulations stifle development of resources and advocates removing regulatory constraints on the marketplace. NSPE also believes that whenever possible state and local governments rather than the national government should make public policies.

Some of its individual policy stands are determined by this general philosophy. NSPE maintains a keen interest in pollution control acts, such as the Clean Air and Water acts because of the opportunities they provide for engineering firms. Representatives of the Society testified before Congress to pass amendments to the Clean Water Act (CWA) over President Reagan's veto in 1987 in order to make available more federal funds for the construction of new and improved sewage treatment plants. It also supported the change in funding to move from federal grants to guaranteed loans in order to increase state discretion over the way such funds are administered. It advocates more research by the federal government in ozone depletion, acid rain, and toxic air pollutants before any drastic actions are taken.

NSPE also regards laws regulating the disposal of all solid wastes, but especially hazardous waste materials, as affording the engineering profession considerable new markets. Therefore, representatives of NSPE have testified to amend the Resource Conservation and Recovery Act to reduce the small generator exemption and to find alternatives methods for disposing of toxic substances instead of using landfills. It advocates recycling, detoxification, and resource recovery of hazardous wastes, but also argues that only those materials that can be linked to real health risks to the public should be regulated. Generally it advocates extending deadlines and increasing flexibility and autonomy for state governments in implementing all environmental controls. One of its primary concerns about the hazardous waste business is to limit the potential damage suits that may be brought against its members. Hence it advocates before state legislatures changes in laws to eliminate strict and joint liability for users and operators of hazardous waste treatment facilities as well as other professional engineering projects.

One major policy concern of NSPE is the development and utilization of all American sources of energy in order to reduce dependence on foreign supplies. It argues for tax laws and utility rate structures that will encourage energy conservation, cogeneration, and small-scale power production and development of all our energy resources. It advocates the elimination of all price controls, especially those on natural gas, because they distort the marketplace by encouraging inefficient use of U.S. resources. It advocates use of federally owned resources in order to develop the country economically, and opposes set-asides for wilderness and other noneconomic uses. It seeks to modify mining restrictions in order to open up more land to development of the nation's coal supply. It also advocates the reevaluation of air pollution control emission standards in order to increase the use of abundant coal resources.

NSPE advocates constructing nuclear waste storage facilities immediately and wants government to launch a massive campaign to inform the public of the safety and efficiency of nuclear power. It advocates greater use of cost-effective nuclear power plants and more government research aimed at advanced nuclear technologies.

NSPE helped to convince Congress to eliminate from the energy conservation law the requirement that utility companies perform residential and commercial energy audits of buildings for their customers free of charge. It believes energy conservation may be achieved through developing new building construction standards by consensus in the profession.

NSPE has several other policy concerns that affect energy and environmental policies. It advocates maximum spending on the public infrastructure of the United States, and helped to pass over President Reagan's veto in 1987 a highway construction bill to increase spending on roads and bridges. It also advocates more appropriations for dams and other water projects sponsored by the Corps of Engineers and the Bureau of Reclamation that many environmental groups argue are ecologically damaging.

### TACTICS

NSPE's lobbying activities include donating money to congressional and other public officeholders, monitoring their activities in office, and testifying before congressional hearings as well as agency hearings. The NSPE political action committee disburses campaign funds to various congressional candidates each election year. It educates its membership and encourages them to write their congressional representatives. It coordinates strategies with business organizations such as the Associated General Contractors, Edison Electric Institute,* and the U.S. Chamber of Commerce.*

NSPE publishes *Engineering Times* monthly, and its divisions publish individual newsletters for their members, including one for engineers in government, in private practice, and in industrial firms.

### FURTHER INFORMATION

*Engineering Times* (1987). Alexandria, Va.: NSPE.

Federal Election Commission (1988). *Receipts and Disbursements 1987–88*. Washington, D.C.: FEC.

*Legislative Agenda of the Engineering Profession* (1987). Alexandria, Va.: NSPE.

*Policies: Professional and Administrative* (1986). Alexandria, Va.: NSPE.

## NATIONAL SOLID WASTES MANAGEMENT ASSOCIATION (NSWMA)

1730 Rhode Island Avenue, N.W.
Washington, D.C. 20036

## ORGANIZATION AND RESOURCES

The National Solid Wastes Management Association (NSWMA) was established in 1963 to represent the interests of private companies engaged in solid waste collection and treatment, including such giants of the industry as Waste Management, Inc. of Oak Brook, Illinois, and Browning-Ferris Industries of Houston, Texas. It now has over 2,500 member firms that provide a variety of services to their customers, including landfill operations, recycling, energy recovery, hazardous waste treatment, street sweeping, pavement maintenance, and snow removal.

NSWMA includes state chapters in almost all states and is divided into various specialized institutes and councils, including the chemical waste transportation council, the institute of chemical waste management, the institute of resource recovery, the sanitary landfill council, and the waste haulers council. The executive director is Eugene J. Wingerter. There is a forty-two-person board of directors that sets policies and includes representatives from the major corporations in this industry. There are ninety professional staff members in the headquarters in Washington.

## POLICY CONCERNS

One of NSWMA's goals is to convince state legislatures to allow waste haulers to carry more weight on the rear axles of their trucks than other commercial vehicles permitted on the roads of the states can. This keeps costs down, as refuse haulers can make less-frequent trips to landfills and other disposal sites if they are permitted to carry larger loads. Another cost-saving policy advocated by NSWMA is to force generators of dangerous, infectious, and hazardous wastes to contain their wastes more carefully in order to prevent injury to collectors and drivers. This has been accomplished partially through state legislation. NSWMA also argues that its insurance rates should be lowered because refuse management employees have good safety and health records.

Representatives of NSWMA have been active in all hearings about the Resource Conservation and Recovery Act (RCRA) initially passed in 1976. RCRA is in fact responsible for many changes in the waste control industry because it has imposed a number of requirements on disposal facilities, including segregating hazardous from other types of solid wastes, special liners to collect leachate (liquid that percolates through landfills and may contain toxic elements), and monitoring wells to detect hazardous leaks at landfills. The limits of RCRA and the state regulations that followed its creation have caused many small waste-hauling operations to go out of business or to be bought up by the major corporations in this business today, such as Waste Management, Inc. Many smaller operations simply could not afford to operate under the increased regulations.

One important innovation that RCRA made was to define hazardous wastes and mandate separate treatment for those kinds of refuse. Before 1986 plants that generated less than 1,000 kilograms per month were exempt from using hazardous-waste haulers. NSWMA has consistently testified for reducing the small generator exemption, and in 1987 it was reduced to 100 kilograms per month, which greatly increased the number of potential clients for NSWMA members' services. Although it advocated closing this loophole in RCRA, NSWMA has argued against tightening RCRA requirements for waste disposal companies themselves. Although it advocated banning the disposal of bulk liquids into landfills, in 1982 it agreed with EPA's decision to allow hazardous liquids contained in steel drums to be buried. It also argues that injecting certain hazardous wastes into deep wells is safe. Some members, including those with the most sophisticated methods for detoxifying and fixing chemical wastes disagree with this stand, and in 1982 formed a separate Hazardous Waste Treatment Council* in opposition to NSWMA.

One issue that NSWMA considers of extreme importance is the unwillingness of many communities to allow new waste disposal facilities of all kinds, but especially hazardous waste facilities, to be located in their area. It argues that unless some means is found to create new landfills, incinerators, and other disposal methods, all communities that need this vital service will suffer. Generally NSWMA state chapters advocate central state planning committees with authority to site and permit new facilities without allowing local governments to veto them. However, it opposes any plans that favor public over privately run disposal facilities or impose strict state controls over the operation of such sites.

While many of its members run recycling facilities and garbage-to-energy incinerators, NSWMA also represents firms that use landfills and other traditional methods. Hence its policies do not favor one kind of disposal technique over others, and sometimes its members' interests conflict with each other. It does, however, advocate a national plan under RCRA to control all infectious biomedical wastes in order to generate more demand for the services of its members and to prevent some hospitals and doctors' offices from avoiding control through the small generator exemption.

NSWMA has testified in favor of reauthorizing the Comprehensive Environmental Response, Compensation, and Liability Act (CERCLA, or Superfund) since many of its members obtain business by being hired to clean up some of the sites. Nevertheless, it opposes strict and joint liability of all users of abandoned leaking dump sites because many of its members also own and have used them. It seeks to limit its members' liability for cleaning up such sites and argues for states to underwrite insurance policies when the industry is unable to purchase liability insurance on the open market. It opposed the suggestion in 1986 that Superfund's tax on oil and chemical feedstock corporations be extended to the waste disposal industry. In addition, NSWMA also opposes strict bonding requirements of some states to guarantee that a site will not be abandoned after its useful life is over. It also urges states to permit mobile treatment units to operate at various sites being cleaned up in their jurisdictions.

NSWMA opposes the concept of treating ash produced from garbage-to-energy facilities as hazardous waste to be disposed of only in carefully guarded landfills. It also opposes "excessive" regulation of the emissions given off by incinerators and energy recovery plants.

## TACTICS

NSWMA fields a number of representatives to testify before Congress and the agencies involved in pollution control, and it also uses the services of the executive officers of major corporations that belong to the trade association, including Waste Management, Inc. (WMI) and Browning-Ferris. These individual corporations are better funded than the average trade association. During the 1988 campaign, for example, WMI PAC distributed $524,561 to political candidates; Browning-Ferris PAC used $205,267, according to the Federal Election Commission. NSWMA's PAC dispersed less than $20,000 at the same time (FEC, 1988).

In addition to testifying before government agencies and contributing to individual politicians' fund-rasing efforts, NSWMA plays a large role in raising the public image of the waste management industry by giving out press releases and developing publications that emphasize the industry's service orientation. In addition, individual firms such as WMI have an extensive advertising campaign that seeks to convince the public that the industry is part of the solution rather than the environmental problem.

With members scattered around the United States, NSWMA is able to mount an effective grass-roots campaign. NSWMA publishes a monthly, *Waste Age*, which keeps its members up to date with the latest technology, as well as frequent news briefs from Washington. It alerts members to the need to write or phone their representatives in Congress when a policy is before an important committee. *Waste Alternatives* is a quarterly journal on industry issues and federal, state, and local decision makers. *Newswatch* is NSWMA's monthly newsletter reporting on state chapter activities. There are also two specialized monthlies, *Just for Haulers* and *Just for Sweepers*, focusing on operational tips.

## FURTHER INFORMATION

*NSWMA 1988* (1989). Washington, D.C.: NSWMA.
U.S. Congress, House Committee on Energy and Commerce (1983), *Hearings on RCRA*. Washington, D.C.: Government Printing Office, March 23, 24, 25.
U.S. Congress, Senate Committee on Environment and Public Works (1984). *Hearings on CERCLA*. Washington, D.C.: Government Printing Office, June.

## NATIONAL STONE ASSOCIATION (NSA)
1415 Elliot Place, N.W.
Washington, D.C. 20007

## ORGANIZATION AND RESOURCES

In 1985, 2 trade associations that had represented the stone industry, the National Crushed Stone Association, founded in 1918, and the National Limestone Institute, founded in 1959, consolidated to form the National Stone Association (NSA) which today represents 425 companies that are in the business of quarrying and selling crushed and cut stone in the United States. Most of these are small locally owned quarries, but others are large, such as Genstar and the Koppers Company. There is a 44-member board of directors with representatives from around the United States. The president is Robert G. Bartlett who directs a staff of 18 professionals in Washington. It operates on a $2 million annual budget derived primarily from dues that depend on the volume and profit of the individual member corporation.

## POLICY CONCERNS

Like other trade associations, NSA is concerned about the tax laws and in keeping as many depreciation and deduction benefits as possible. It also lobbies heavily for increased federal highway construction and use of the trust fund for that purpose exclusively because its members sell much of their production to highway contractors to construct roadbeds. It opposes most union-supported labor-management initiatives and any safety regulations by the U.S. Labor Department's Occupational Safety and Health Administration (OSHA).

In the environmental area, NSA has been most active in opposing government standards under the Clean Water Act to control runoff from quarrying operations and to control effluents from stone-washing operations in gravel pits. It also opposes any regulations of the industry under the Surface Mining and Reclamation Act that seeks to force the mining industry to restore strip-mined areas to their previous condition.

## TACTICS

NSA combines with the American Mining Congress* and other trade associations to protect its interests against government regulations. StonePAC, the industry's political action committee, collects contributions for distribution to candidates in election campaigns. NSA also has developed a public relations program to improve the image of the stone and gravel industry. It has produced a film, "Crushed Stone: Our Most Basic Resource," for cable TV, libraries, and schools. It also has a video program "About Face" which publicizes industry efforts to beautify and reclaim quarries no longer in operation. NSA publishes a bimonthly magazine, *Stone Review*, and *NSA Digest* weekly for its members to keep them informed of events in Washington and the industry. It holds an annual meeting.

## NATIONAL TANK TRUCK CARRIERS (NTTC)
2200 Mill Road
Alexandria, Virginia 22314

## ORGANIZATION AND RESOURCES

The National Tank Truck Carriers (NTTC) was founded in 1945 to represent the interests of corporations in the business of transporting liquid and dry bulk chemicals, food, and petroleum products in tank trucks. In 1989 it had a membership of some 225 companies engaged in this business, who paid dues ranging from $250 to $6,000, depending on the size of the corporation. Their operating budget was about $1 million, 70 percent of which came from corporate dues and the other 30 percent from publications produced by the trade association.

Policy is set by the association's board of directors who are elected by the membership. Its president is Clifford J. Harvison who heads a staff of six in the national headquarters located in Alexandria, Virginia.

## POLICY CONCERNS

NTTC is primarily concerned with government regulation of trucks on highways, especially restrictions on size, speed, and the costs of fuel. In the early 1980s, it was concerned with the Resource Conservation and Recovery Act (RCRA), the Comprehensive Environmental Response, Compensation, and Liability Act (CERCLA, or Superfund), and the Hazardous Materials Transportation Act because of the impact these laws have on costs of doing business. Its members generally oppose provisions of Superfund that allow governments to recover costs from all contributors to hazardous waste dumps who profited from them in the past, including haulers. NTTC feels that these provisions are too generous to potential victims and increase the costs of carrying on business excessively. Generally it opposes industrial liability, but its primary public policy concerns are not with energy and environmental issues.

## TACTICS

The staff of NTTC testify before congressional committees and before the Federal Highway Safety Administration concerning these issues. It also publishes a monthly newsletter for its membership that keeps them informed about government regulations with which they should be concerned. NTTC also combines with other business and industrial groups to argue before Congress and the courts against provisions to increase industry's liability for damages from hazardous materials. It sponsors an annual conference each May.

## NATIONAL TRUST FOR HISTORIC PRESERVATION (NTHP)
1785 Massachusetts Avenue, N.W.
Washington, D.C. 20036

## ORGANIZATION AND RESOURCES

The National Trust for Historic Preservation (NTHP) was chartered in 1949 by the U.S. Congress as a private, not-for-profit corporation dedicated to preserving and restoring sites and structures of historic significance in the United

States. By the late 1980s it had a membership of over 220,000 people, divided into some 3,000 local and state affiliates. Dues for individuals are $15 to $20 a year, and affiliates contribute $50 and more to the national organization. Dozens of corporations, such as Jack Daniel Distillery, The Chase Manhattan Bank, and Eli Lilly Company, also contribute $10,000 or more. Foundations, including the MacArthur Foundation and the AT&T Foundation, donate sums ranging from $500 to $300,000. Hundreds of individuals give gifts of over $1,000 each year and numerous law firms donate time by preparing litigation for NTHP. In addition, the U.S. Department of Interior's Historic Preservation Division makes matching grants to the Trust.

NTHP has revenues of about $25 million, derived 26 percent from donations, 15 percent from membership dues, 21 percent from matching government grants, 7 percent from investments, and the remainder from sales, services, special events it runs, and publications. It expends over $20 million a year, 24 percent on preservation services, 28 percent on administering historic properties it owns, 12 percent on publications, and 12 percent on education. On support services, the Trust uses 8 percent of its 1986 budget on developing new members, 8 percent on general administration, and another 8 percent on fund-raising.

In the late 1980s NTHP had a board of trustees consisting of 32 members known for their fund-raising prowess and interest in historic preservation, including corporate executives from such companies as Atlantic Richfield and the Rockefeller Brothers, as well as representatives from local historic preservation foundations such as Colonial Williamsburg. Seven regional offices are maintained in Philadelphia, Chicago, Boston, Charleston, Denver, Fort Worth, and San Francisco. The national headquarters in Washington houses a staff of 150 headed by J. Jackson Walter, president of the Trust.

### POLICY CONCERNS

In 1966 Congress passed the National Historic Preservation Act, which NTHP had lobbied for since its beginning. Through this law it is possible to have particular sites designated as national historic sites, which affords them some degree of protection from destruction. The local affiliates of the Trust are primarily concerned with preventing developers from tearing down historic landmarks in communities and replacing them with modern buildings. In order to achieve this it is sometimes necessary to purchase and preserve the site themselves. However, they also try to influence property owners to rehabilitate historic properties, restoring them to their former elegance and to find some economic use for them. Ad hoc groups organized to protect particular properties have initiated many lawsuits to prevent a highway, shopping mall, or high-rise development from being constructed on historic sites. In other cases they have been successful in convincing developers that more profit could be derived by using the historic sites in their original form. The Trust attempts to negotiate and cooperate with business and developers as often as possible.

The Economic Recovery Tax Act of 1981 provided for tax benefits to be given to developers and other property owners for rehabilitating historic sites and buildings. In 1987 some members of Congress attempted to eliminate this tax credit, but the NTHP successfully defended this tax advantage. The new law provides for a 20 percent investment tax credit for rehabilitation of historic structures certified by the National Park Service through state historic preservation offices. Nonhistoric structures built before 1936 are eligible for a 10 percent tax credit.

The Trust has also taken on such causes as the condition of historic buildings in the national parks. It advocates the restoration and maintenance of such historic buildings as Fort Yellowstone in Yellowstone Park. It has for years testified for a larger budget for the National Park Service to be able to afford to keep up the archeological and architectural treasures within the national park system. It argues that lack of resources have caused irreparable damage in many parks and leads to ever more costly rehabilitation needs because of lack of planning. In 1988 NHTP succeeded in convincing Congress to appropriate money to acquire a tract of land next to the Manassas National Battlefield Park that had been slated for the development of a 1.2 million square foot shopping mall.

In 1987 the Trust editorialized to support the findings of a commission appointed by President Reagan in 1985 to examine the need for outdoor recreation in the United States. The report, *Americans Outdoors: The Legacy, The Challenge,* a $1 billion trust fund to finance preservation of recreational areas with particular emphasis on metropolitan areas; it was ignored by the Reagan administration.

*TACTICS*

NTHP owns and maintains sixteen historic sites around the United States, from Montpelier in Virginia, James Madison's estate, to the Woodrow Wilson House in Washington, D.C., and the Frank Lloyd Wright home and studio in Oak Park, Illinois. These estates have generally been donated to the Trust by various philanthropists, and some are maintained by local associations. Members of the Trust are dedicated to finding and preserving sites important to the American heritage whether for historic, architectural, cultural, or other reasons. The national and regional offices serve as clearinghouses for local heritage societies dedicated to preserving a part of the past in their local communities. It provides expertise and information about organizing such groups and provides grants to them for obtaining, rehabilitating, and maintaining such properties.

NTHP awards grants to cities and organizations to preserve buildings and rehabilitate historic buildings and sites. In 1986 it gave financial assistance to 143 preservation projects in 35 states and the District of Columbia. Such grants are mostly seed money designed to encourage local fund-raising to more than match the outside assistance. Two specific programs are of particular moment. The Inner City Ventures Fund makes low-interest loans to neighborhood organizations in cities to create housing units for low- and moderate-income residents in historic neighborhoods. The Main Street Network focuses on revitalizing the downtown areas of moderate-sized towns.

NTHP organizes an annual conference on preservation, the 44th one being held in Philadelphia in October 1990. It also organizes tours and excursions for its members to historic sites in the United States and abroad. The National Trust publishes *Historic Preservation* every other month featuring articles about successful rehabilitation and preservation projects. It also informs its membership about techniques and developments in the rehabilitation field. The Preservation Press, owned by the Trust, publishes books on such subjects as *America's Country Schools* or *Fabrics for Historic Buildings*. In addition it publishes a monthly newspaper, *Preservation News*, that features stories about regional developments.

### FURTHER INFORMATION

*Annual Report 1988* (1989). Washington, D.C.: NTHP.
*Historic Preservation* (1989). Washington, D.C.: NTHP, March-April.
*Preservation News* (1989). Washington, D.C.: NTHP, May.

## NATIONAL WATER RESOURCES ASSOCIATION (NWRA)
955 L'Enfant Plaza, North Building, S.W.
Washington, D.C. 20024

### HISTORY AND DEVELOPMENT

In 1891 a National Irrigation Congress was held in Salt Lake City, Utah, to promote the interests of western farmers who sought funds from government to help them turn arid land into arable land. In 1902 Theodore Roosevelt signed into law the Reclamation Act, and the Department of Interior's Bureau of Reclamation (BuRec) began building dams to store water for irrigating croplands in the seventeen western states. Over the years water supply projects, including canals as well as other distribution systems, in addition to the storage facilities, have expanded their goals to include hydroelectric production, municipal and industrial water supply, flood control, and recreation purposes.

In 1932 the National Reclamation Association was founded, consisting of representatives of the states that constitute the primary beneficiaries of BuRec projects. The program was greatly expanded during the depression in conjunction with the Public Works Administration to provide jobs for the unemployed in the west. Almost since its inception the reclamation program of the U.S. government has been opposed by some conservation groups such as the Sierra Club* because of the flooding of spectacular natural views such as Dinosaur National Monument, the reduction of wildlife habitat, and the general alteration of the western landscape from free-flowing streams to channelized lakes. For the most part, these protests were unsuccessful, and BuRec's program expanded.

In the 1960s and 1970s, however, conservation opposition grew and focused more on the expenditure of federal funds to benefit a small part of the country, especially large landholders in the western states. In 1972 the association changed its name to the National Water Resources Association (NWRA) in order to change its image and increase its support around the country for continued funding of reclamation projects. During the Carter administration, efforts were made to reduce the number of water projects mostly without success because of tremendous support within Congress for individual projects for specific states. With the advent of the Reagan administration additional pressure was put on all government projects to demonstrate their cost-effectiveness.

## ORGANIZATION AND RESOURCES

The NWRA has about 5,000 individual members: cities, counties, irrigation districts, conservancy districts in the west, as well as industrial and commercial firms benefiting from public water supplies. It is divided into 17 individual state chapters and has an annual budget of about $250,000 contributed primarily by its state affiliates. Corporate members pay between $250 and $500 in dues. Its president is Jeffry L. Nelson, and Thomas F. Donnelly, who heads a staff of 4, is both executive vice-president and editor of the monthly *National Water Line*.

## POLICY CONCERNS

NWRA's sole goal is to continue and increase federal funding for water projects in its seventeen member-states. Unlike most other federal subsides, it argues, water project costs are partially recovered by the national treasury through the sale of irrigation water to farmers and the sale of electricity to users. It argues also that the program returns dividends to the entire nation through increased agricultural productivity and reduced food prices to the consumer.

In 1982 a Reclamation Reform Act was passed that required farmers to pay full costs for water going to lands leased in excess of 160-acre landholdings (or 320 acres for husband/wife combinations). However, in writing the regulations to implement this law, Secretary of Interior Donald Hodel's BuRec interpreted it in such a way that according to the author of the law, "the rules allow farmers to engage in the very same practices we found prior to the 1982 Act" *(National Water Line*, April, 1987). Opposition members of Congress have also introduced legislation to force states that irrigate much of their cropland with federally funded water to protect their ground water by controlling the fertilizers and pesticides that farmers spray on their fields.

In recent years eastern legislators have introduced bills in Congress to increase the cost of irrigation water and power to westerners on the grounds that the entire nation should not have to subsidize one sector that is doing very well economically. In 1987 an irrigation subsidy reform bill was introduced that would have forced farmers to pay the full cost of irrigating crops that were declared to be surplus and bought to be stored by the Department of Agriculture, but it was easily defeated by the water and agriculture lobbies. Generally, NWRA has been highly successful in defending its members against any conservation or environmental legislation directed against them. NWRA opposes all wilderness, scenic rivers, and endangered species legislation for fear that these laws would impinge on the areas that could be flooded for new water projects.

## TACTICS

The NWRA traditionally formed one leg of a stereotypical "iron triangle," or subgovernment in U.S. policy-making. Its members had close ties both to the BuRec in the Interior Department and to the western congressional representatives who sat on the House and Senate subcommittees on water and power resources. There was no need for large expenditures of dollars to lobby for its program because there was no effective opposition. No one complained about the expenditure of general revenue funds to benefit a limited number of western farmers, stockgrowers, and industrialists because there were no other participants in this subgovernment. All careerists in the BuRec and politicians on the appropriate congressional committees were committed to the goals of the private interest they represented.

Only in the 1970s has the NWRA felt sufficiently challenged to offer an extensive public education program to the media to explain the utility of its goals. Even today it depends on the representations of its grass-roots members and such dedicated loyalists as Senator Alan K. Simpson to speak for them before Congress. Few western members of Congress, including liberal Democrats such as Morris Udall of Arizona, can afford to oppose massive public works projects designed to benefit their immediate constituents. NWRA publishes a monthly newsletter, *National Water Line*, to keep members alert to developments in Washington. It holds an annual conference and urges members to make their interests known to the local representatives.

## FURTHER INFORMATION

Culhane, Paul J. (1984). "Sagebrush Rebels in Office: Jim Watt's Land and Water Policies." In *Environmental Policy in the 1980s*, edited by Norman Vig and Michael Kraft. Washington, D.C.: Congressional Quarterly Press.
Foss, Phillip (1960). *Politics and Grass*. Seattle: University of Washington Press.
*A National Investment* (1985). Washington, D.C.: NWRA.
*National Water Line* (1987). Washington, D.C.: NWRA, April, May

## NATIONAL WILDLIFE FEDERATION (NWF)
1400 16th Street, N.W.
Washington, D.C. 20036

### HISTORY AND DEVELOPMENT

In 1911 various gun manufacturers led by the Winchester Repeating Arms Company, which had been rebuffed by the National Audubon Society,* formed the American Game Protective Association (AGPA). Its goal was to protect and increase the availability of game for hunters, and it worked throughout the 1920s to obtain legislation that would have created a series of federal refuges that could be used as public shooting grounds. However, this was stalemated in Congress by such conservation organizations as the National Audubon Society and the Izaak Walton League of America.* In 1935 the American Wildlife Institute replaced AGPA and represented all industries with a stake in hunting and advocated restoration of wildlife habitat that had been vastly depleted by the dust-bowl conditions of the Great Depression. In 1936 under the auspices of President Franklin Roosevelt it sponsored a North American Wildlife conference attended by some 1,500 sportsmen.

Out of this meeting came the General Wildlife Federation, which changed its name to the National Wildlife Federation (NWF) in 1938, dedicated to "conserving and restoring the vanishing wildlife resources of a continent," which gradually replaced the Izaak Walton League as the largest mass-membership conservation association in the United States. During its early days NWF was beset by financial difficulties and was largely dependent on the American Wildlife Institute and the gun industry. It opposed gun control legislation, insisting, as did the National Rifle Association, on the constitutional right of all Americans to bear arms. Occasionally it also opposed creation of new national parks because it would take some of the national forest lands out of the hunters' domain.

## ORGANIZATION AND RESOURCES

In 1988, NWF celebrated its fiftieth anniversary with 4.8 million members in 51 state and 650 local associations. Fifty state affiliates are serviced by 7 regional offices of NWF in Atlanta, Georgia; Portland, Oregon; Missoula, Montana; Ann Arbor, Michigan; Boulder, Colorado; Bismarck, North Dakota; and Anchorage, Alaska. Its national headquarters are in Washington, where a new building constructed in 1986 houses the NWF's Washington staff as well as the Conservation Hall of Fame and other public exhibits depicting North American wildlife.

It has a 29-member board of directors whose members reside from New York City to Tacoma, Washington. NWF's president is Jay D. Hair. Organized like a pyramid, local rod and gun clubs elect state representatives who select the national leadership. Staff in Washington number over 400, and 28 additional staff are employed in regional offices.

In the late 1980s the NWF's revenues were about $67 million, divided among member dues, 22 percent; junior memberships, including *Ranger Rick* subscriptions, 15 percent; donations and bequests, 17 percent; sales of educational materials, 32 percent; sales of *Your Big Backyard*, 7 percent; and investments and grants, 7 percent. In addition, its 50 state affiliates had budgets totaling $13.5 million. Expenditures went to pay for administration and fund-raising, 11 percent; development of new members and publications, 22 percent; provision for future activities, 5 percent; and conservation education and programs, 62 percent. This last category includes production of *Ranger Rick* and other educational materials as well as advocacy of policy positions in state and local governments.

## POLICY CONCERNS

Policies are set for local matters by state affiliates, and national headquarters develops positions for the NWF on national issues. NWF is one of the best established of the conservation organizations in the United States and continues to draw significant support from local rod and gun clubs around the country. In recent decades, concerned by the growing degradation of the environment and rapid depletion of wildlife, the NWF has become a major supporter for a wide variety of environmental policies from endangered species to strip-mining controls and wetlands protection.

Generally the national organization opposes subsidized construction of dams and other water projects. In the 99th Congress it supported an Omnibus Water Resources bill to force users of water projects to pay a percentage of the cost of those projects rather than having them funded by general revenues. It also testified for years against the North Dakota Garrison Division Unit project. This was finally resolved in a congressional compromise whereby the Department of Interior's Bureau of Reclamation agreed to mitigate some damage to wildlife habitat created by the project. In 1987 NWF succeeded in obtaining an agreement with the Arizona congressional delegation to scuttle plans for Cliff Dam on the Verde River, which would have flooded the habitat of desert bald eagles. The Maine Wildlife Association opposed construction of a hydroelectric project on the Penobscot River to prevent destruction of white-water boating there.

NWF also opposes sales of natural resources owned by the U.S. government at prices that it considers to be below fair market value. In the 1980s, national leadership was particularly concerned about the Forest Service and Department of Interior's sales of grazing rights, timber rights, and mineral rights to industry for less than market value. It believes that if these subsidies to industry were reduced, the federal budget could achieve a better balance and it would be unnecessary to cut back on essential conservation activities such as wilderness preservation. Its state affiliates regularly argue for inclusion of tracts of land in the national wilderness system and for the Forest Service to protect old-growth timber and not sell it to timber companies. Its national representatives frequently request Congress to cut the Forest Service's road-building budget into national forests to accommodate timber cutting there.

In recent years, NWF has focused on the destruction of wildlife habitat caused by strip mining. In 1987 it successfully advocated that Congress close a loophole in the Surface Mining Control and Reclamation Act (SMCRA) that allowed mineral companies to mine small areas without reclaiming the land. National representatives of NWF have often urged the Office of Surface Mining in the Department of Interior to enforce more forcefully the strip mining law. When negotiations with federal administrators failed, it attempted to force the Kentucky Department of Natural Resources and other state governments to enforce the SMCRA more effectively. NWF has also negotiated directly with industry, as for example when the Wyoming Wildlife Federation signed a pact with Rocky

Mountain Energy to hold off on mining in the most sensitive area of Red Rim Canyon until it could demonstrate that the area can be restored.

Although the NWF began as a support system for hunters, its members now include some opponents of hunting. Its national leadership now supports predator restoration projects in national parks, and its March 1989 meeting theme was "Predators: They're Part of the Picture." John Denver and Muppet Kermit the Frog were cochairs of Wildlife Week that year. Through the 1980s it joined other environmental groups in urging reauthorization of the Endangered Species Act, which Congress did in 1988.

In recent years NWF has become involved in lobbying for traditional pollution control laws, as well as natural resources policies. Representatives of NWF lobby Congress on such varied issues as renewal of the hazardous waste cleanup under Superfund, reauthorization of the Clean Air and Clean Water acts, and stricter controls on industry under the Federal Insecticide, Fungicide and Rodenticide Act. It counted as two of its major victories in the 100th Congress the passage over President Reagan's veto amendments to the Clean Water Act and the Senate's ratification of a treaty banning dumping of plastics in the oceans. NWF urged both the Corps of Engineers and the U.S. Environmental Protection Agency (EPA) to protect and restore wetlands under the Clean Water Act. Representatives testified on the Resource Conservation and Recovery Act in 1983 that Congress should ban landfilling and ocean dumping of hazardous wastes and broaden the definition of hazardous waste. During the 101st Congress, it broadcast radio advertisements urging its constituents to support a much strengthened clean air bill that would include drastic reductions in sulphur oxide emissions to control the problem of acid rain, over the Bush administration's more conservative approach to the problem.

NWF, like other conservation groups, is concerned about the buildup of carbon dioxide, the depletion of ozone in the atmosphere, and global warming. It argues for preservation of tropical rain forests and in 1988 editorialized against the killing of Francisco "Chico" Mendes Filho, organizer of Brazilian rubber tappers, who object to the clear-cutting of jungles to make way for agriculture. It urges the banking community and the U.S. Agency for International Development to allow debt-for-nature swaps, forgiving part of third world countries' debt in exchange for their designating areas as protected natural resources.

*TACTICS*

In 1988 NWF joined with seventeen other environmental groups, including the National Audubon Society and the Sierra Club,* in drafting a *Blueprint for the Environment* to present to the Bush administration that urged it to give attention to the global environmental crisis that conservationists view as crucial in the 1990s. That report included a recommendation that EPA be elevated to cabinet status. In frustration over recent administrative intransigence over environmental issues, in the 1990s NWF considered supporting a call for a constitutional amendment to guarantee all Americans a clean environment.

Nevertheless, NWF remains a relatively conservative mainstream organization that relies on government intervention to achieve its goals. The causes it selects have usually been pioneered by other conservation groups. Its president, Jay D. Hair, has called Earth Firsters "outlaws" and "terrorists." He is accepted as a representative of the environmental establishment and was appointed to the EPA's Biotechnology Science Coordinating Committee to investigate the need to regulate genetic engineering.

If it is unsuccessful in winning over administrative agencies or Congress to its point of view, NWF will turn its attention to state government in the hope of influencing them to take up the slack in some of the federal programs that are being turned over to them. In addition, it sometimes goes to court, as when it sued the National Park Service to close a campground in Yellowstone National Park to protect the endangered grizzly bear whose habitat was being disrupted by visitors. It also sued to force both the Departments of Interior and Agriculture to increase their grazing fees on public lands in order to prevent elimination of wildlife food sources. It also has been involved in suits against the Fish and Wildlife Service for permitting waterfowl hunting with lead shot, which poisons species such as the bald eagle, and against the Bureau of Land Management for allowing ranchers to fence off areas to wildlife and cut off their food supply.

National representatives of NWF are convinced that conciliation and negotiation are better tools that confrontation, and frequently they will seek to reach agreement with industry amicably. In 1982 NWF founded a Corporate Conservation Council (CCC) by which NWF officials hoped to be able to persuade corporate managers to adopt more conservation-oriented policies toward natural resources. Members of the CCC include Atlantic Richfield, Du Pont, Dow Chemical, Duke Power, Exxon, Miller Brewing, 3M, Monsanto, Tennoco, TVA, USX, and Weyerhaeuser corporations. In 1986 the CCC focused on the problem of groundwater and attempted to work out a compromise between industry and conservation organizations on the disposal of hazardous wastes. NWF's goal was to reduce the landfilling of these wastes and to find alternative methods of disposal.

From its inception, the NWF has focused on educating the public to the need to conserve the life-sustaining resources of earth, and to promote appreciation of these values. It gives financial assistance to conservation causes and fellowships for graduate study in ecology. In 1985 it initiated a nature newsbreak that airs on National Public Radio. In 1988 it began "Conserving America," a public television series about wildlife. It mails educational guides to public schools for use in conjunction with the TV series. It also produces video news releases on issues such as acid rain and toxic wastes.

*National Wildlife*, NWF's flagship bimonthly magazine, was started in 1962 and now has a circulation of over 900,000 to whom it gives information about endangered species. *International Wildlife* was started in 1971 to bring public attention to the problems of wildlife around the world and is also published bimonthly. *Ranger Rick*, first published in 1967, teaches children about the wonders of wildlife; it also offers contests, games, and puzzles that involve various nature themes. *Naturescope* was begun in 1984 as an environmental science series for elementary school teachers. *Conservation* is a biweekly newsletter for members interested in congressional and administrative actions on conservation issues. *Your Big Backyard*, with a circulation of 500,000, is devoted to preschoolers. *The Leader* gives 17,000 NWF-affiliated volunteers monthly news about natural resource issues.

## FURTHER INFORMATION

*Annual Report* (1986, 1987, 1988). Washington, D.C.: NWF.

Caldwell, Lynton Keith (1989). "A Constitutional Law for the Environment." *Environmental Action* 31 (December): 6–28.

Fox, Steven (1981). *John Muir and His Legacy: The American Conservation Movement.* Boston: Little, Brown.

*International Wildlife* (1988, 1989). Washington, D.C.: NWF, March-April.

Mitchell, John G. (1987). "A Man Called Bird." *Audubon*, November, pp. 81–104.

*National Wildlife* (February-March, April-May, June-July, August-September, October-November, 1988; February-March, April-May, 1989). Washington, D.C.: NWF.

Watkins, T. H. (1989). "Untrammeled by Man." *Audubon*, November, pp. 74–91.

## NATURAL GAS SUPPLY ASSOCIATION (NGSA)

1129 20th Street, N.W., Suite 300
Washington, D.C. 20036

### HISTORY AND DEVELOPMENT

The Natural Gas Supply Association (NGSA) was founded in 1965 as a trade association for companies that produce natural gas. In 1938 Congress mandated that the Federal Power Commission (succeeded by the Federal Energy Regulatory Commission, FERC) begin regulating the price of natural gas distributed by interstate pipelines. In 1954 the Supreme Court ruled that this law should apply to the wellhead price of gas that would be distributed in interstate commerce. Hence, prices charged for gas supplied to intrastate users rose as interstate prices remained more stable, and a larger share of the supply became concentrated in the intrastate market. Industry began to organize to oppose the control of prices at the wellhead. In 1978 the Natural Gas Policy Act (NGPA) was passed which lessened the distinction between inter- and intrastate markets, but increased that between old gas (pre–1977 discoveries that would be price controlled) and new gas whose price would be allowed to fluctuate with the demand.

### ORGANIZATION AND RESOURCES

In the late 1980s NGSA had sixty-five member corporations that together produced 80 percent of all U.S. natural gas. It represents major international corporations, many of which also belong to the American Petroleum Institute (API)* because much natural gas is found in association with petroleum. It also represents small and medium-sized independent suppliers whose interests sometimes diverge from those of the major energy corporations, especially regarding quotas for foreign oil. NGSA has a thirteen-person staff in its Washington office headed by Nicholas J. Bush, president. Dues for its corporate members vary according to volume of business. It has an annual budget of over $2 million.

## POLICY CONCERNS

NGSA, like the API, favors tax breaks for industry on the grounds that mineral exploration is a risky business and needs protection in the form of tax write-offs for most of its exploration activities. It also advocates a gas and oil depreciation allowance for natural resources removed from the ground in a given year. It advocates opening up all federal lands to exploration for gas sources, especially the outer continental shelf and the Alaskan wilderness lands.

The NGSA was founded to oppose federal intervention in the market for natural gas. It opposes any price control on natural gas on the grounds that it is not a natural monopoly, that competition in the industry will keep prices down, and that depressing the price of gas will discourage exploration and thus decrease the proven reserves available for development. Its representatives argue that the energy crisis in the middle 1970s was brought on by federal regulation of the price of natural gas which kept the supply low.

In 1978 the NGPA extended price controls to all natural gas at the wellhead to halt the discrimination between gas sold by interstate and by intrastate pipelines. The NGPA, however, differentiated between new and old gas. Old gas remained price controlled, but gas discovered after 1977 was not. In the 1980s NGSA testified to Congress that any reregulation of gas would be unfair, because the NGPA had induced industry to develop expensive deep wells, and to put controls on the prices they could charge would mean changing the rules of the game in midstream. At the same time it argued to amend the NGPA so that all gas, even old gas, would be decontrolled. It argues that allowing the price of all natural gas to float free will not drive the price up, as the industry will compete to discover new supplies and industry will stop using old gas.

NGSA favors take-or-pay contracts for pipelines. These prevent distributors from getting out of their old contracts if they find a less expensive supplier. It also favors FERC rules that require some distribution system be available for all sources of natural gas. It argues that this mandate improves the chances of all customers obtaining a guaranteed supply. In these particular issues, the production part of the industry is at odds with the distribution and sales part represented by such trade associations as the American Gas Association* and the Interstate Natural Gas Association of America.*

The gas industry is united in its desire to expand use of natural gas in order to increase its own market. On issues such as controls for coal emissions, it favors a strict air pollution control law in order to make natural gas more competitive with coal as a fuel for powerplants. It also worked hard to eliminate the prohibition against use of natural gas for industrial purposes during the energy crisis of the mid–1970s. In 1987 a compromise was worked out whereby natural gas could be used in industrial boilers and electricity-generating plants as long as they could be converted to burn coal.

## TACTICS

NGSA relies on officers of some of its major member corporations to do much of its testifying before Congress, FERC, and the Department of Energy. It issues a newsletter, *FYI*, ten times a year to its members about relevant court actions as well as congressional and administrative agency events.

## FURTHER INFORMATION

Chubb, John E. (1983). *Interest Groups and the Bureaucracy*. Stanford, Calif.: Stanford University Press.
McFarland, Andrew (1984). "Energy Lobbies." *Annual Review of Energy* 9: 501–527.
Rosenbaum, Walter A. (1987). *Energy, Politics, and Public Policy*, 2d ed. Washington, D.C.: Congressional Quarterly Press.
Stobaugh, Robert, and Daniel Yergin, eds. (1983). *Energy Future*, 3d ed. New York: Vintage Press.

## NATURAL RESOURCES DEFENSE COUNCIL (NRDC)
40 West 20th Street
New York, New York 10011

### ORGANIZATION AND RESOURCES

The Natural Resources Defense Council (NRDC) was founded with a Ford Foundation grant in 1970 by six lawyers concerned with environmental issues. After twenty years of operation, it had a forty-two person board of trustees, including nine original board members, several partners in major law firms, law professors such as David Sive, and well-known celebrity-environmentalists such as Robert Redford, John B. Oakes, and Laurance Rockefeller. Adrian W. DeWind is the board's chair, and its executive director is John H. Adams. The trustees meet each year to set policy for the organization and recruit additional trustees.

NRDC maintains 5 offices: in New York, Washington, San Francisco, Los Angeles, and Honolulu. Its national headquarters is in New York, where it purchased its own building in 1988 and refurbished it for energy efficiency in 1989. Its primary lobbying activities take place in Washington. In 1989 it had 150 attorneys, scientists, resource specialists, consultants, administrators, support staff, interns, and fellows on its staff in the 5 offices. In January 1990 its membership passed the 125,000 mark.

NRDC received revenues of over $13 million in 1989. Dues range from $10 to $100 a year, and additional contributions are regularly solicited from members. Over 900 individuals were listed as contributing $1,000 or more in 1989. In addition, NRDC received funds from such foundations as Beinecke, Bulitt, Carnegie, Clark, Field, Ford, Greve, Hughes, Joyce, Merck, McIntosh, Skaggs, Streisand, Strong, and Weeden. Forty-nine percent of its revenues were obtained from member contributions, 42 percent came from foundation grants, and 9 percent from attorneys' fees, contracts, and miscellaneous revenue. NRDC spent in the same year slightly over $12 million: 8 percent on membership services, 10 percent on general administration and management, 8 percent on fund-raising, and 74 percent on program services. The latter were divided further into environmental programs, 39 percent; public education, 18 percent; and scientific support, 8 percent. Only 1 percent of NRDC's expenses were used for legislative activities and a like amount for its intern program in 1989.

## POLICY CONCERNS

One of NRDC's main priorities is pollution control. It advocates strengthening the Clean Air and Water acts (CAA, CWA). In its early years, it challenged numerous state implementation plans to enforce the CAA, successfully arguing that building taller stacks was not a pollution control strategy. It continues to oppose the use of tall stacks to disperse sulfur dioxide emissions and advocates strict controls on all industrial boilers emitting sulfur oxides. NRDC representatives worked throughout the 1980s, in association with the National Clean Air Coalition, to reauthorize the CAA, but all compromises fell through at the end of the 100th Congress. Its staff hoped that after the drought and heat wave of 1988 the 101st Congress would be more receptive to arguments about the need for greater controls on sulfur oxides, chlorofluorocarbons, and toxic emissions. In 1989 NRDC severely criticized President Bush's proposal for changing the CAA, arguing that its specific suggestions for extending smog control deadlines for two more decades and allowing increased emissions for powerplants near national parks fell far short of the rhetoric with which he introduced the plan. In addition to lobbying Congress, NRDC representatives argue regularly in EPA hearings against the loosening of standards for all emissions and against the extended use of the "bubble concept" that allows industry to trade emission reductions at one source for increased emissions in the same area. NRDC staff argue that these trades often are simply paper exercises whose outcome is increased total emissions.

In the field of water pollution control, NRDC representatives testified for ten years preceding the 1986 amendments to the Safe Drinking Water Act (SDWA) and the 1987 amendments to the Clean Water Act, which were passed over President Reagan's veto. The new laws mandate that industry pretreat toxic wastes that it sends to municipal treatment facilities on which the latter have little impact. These laws also regulate urban storm water and agricultural runoff, significant sources of toxic pollutants, such as pesticides. NRDC's goal now is to see these requirements carried out.

In 1986, NRDC attorney Albert Meyerhoff participated in the Campaign for Pesticide Reform through which forty-one organizations negotiated with the agricultural chemicals industry to reach an agreement in principle. Out of this evolved several proposed amendments to the Federal Insecticide, Fungicide and Rodenticide Act (FIFRA), some of which the 100th Congress passed in 1988. NRDC considered this merely the first step on a long road to pesticide reform and continues to argue for stricter limits to pesticide residues on agricultural products. In 1988 it published *Pesticide Alert: A Guide to Pesticides in Fruits and Vegetables* to alert the public to the dangers of consuming such residues. This received considerable media attention when NRDC spokespersons focused on the risk to children from eating Alar, a pesticide commonly used on apples.

NRDC is also much concerned about the disposal of solid wastes, especially hazardous wastes. Its representatives argued before Congress concerning amendments to both the Resource Conservation and Recovery Act (RCRA) and Superfund. They argued for more government research on alternative technologies to landfilling solid wastes, including recycling and reduction of waste generation. They opposed lifetime landfill permits and the continued use of deep-well injection and landfills to dispose of hazardous wastes. They also advocated stricter controls on the incineration of hazardous wastes and a ban on various carcinogens such as asbestos in the United States.

Another major priority of NRDC is to influence government agencies to manage public lands with greater sensitivity to ecological concerns. In the 1980s NRDC developed economic cost/benefit arguments, showing that it costs the Forest Service more to administer many of its timber harvesting programs than the lumber generates in revenues. NRDC often joins local conservation groups in arguing that the Forest Service should reconsider wasteful and environmentally damaging logging programs in old-growth national forests. In 1988 NRDC opened an office in Hawaii in order to try to preserve what is left of tropical forests there.

NRDC works through the Public Lands Institute to protect wildlife and publicly owned wilderness areas managed by the Bureau of Land Management. It argues for increasing grazing fees to reflect the true costs of the program and reducing the number of livestock permitted on public lands to halt the degradation and erosion of such public lands. It also opposes the federal coal leasing program, arguing that it constitutes a giveaway program, selling to industry below market value resources that belong to the U.S. taxpayer. Like other conservation groups, NRDC believes many water projects in the west subsidize industrial farming at the expense of the taxpayer. They have argued before Congress that such recipients of government largesse should pay a larger percentage of the costs of such projects. NRDC also lobbied with other groups for reauthorization of the Endangered Species Act in 1988.

NRDC opposes all contamination of the ocean. It used the crisis on the beaches of the Northeast in summer 1988 to argue for phasing out all dumping in the oceans. It considers the Department of Interior's offshore oil and gas leasing program one of the greatest threats to the ocean environment. In January 1988 it issued a report documenting environmental abuses in the oil industry's development of North Slope oil in Alaska over a year before the *Exxon Valdez* ran aground and spilled 11 million gallons of crude oil into Prince William Sound. NRDC uses this report to argue against the opening to similar development of the Arctic National Wildlife Refuge.

NRDC has also been active in the nuclear debate. It made a 1986 agreement with the Soviet Academy of Sciences to establish six monitoring stations near nuclear weapons test sites in the United States and the USSR. Seismic equipment was installed in the Soviet Union in July 1987 and in the United States in March 1988 in order to demonstrate the ease of monitoring each other's tests and the futility of trying to maintain secrecy. NRDC urged the U.S. Department of Energy (DOE) to produce environmental impact statements for many of its nuclear experiments and has urged more congressional oversight of DOE reactors. NRDC representatives regularly argue for greater energy conservation through more energy-efficient appliances and more efficient use of power in buildings. In 1989 it refurbished its New York headquarters as a model of energy conservation technology.

### TACTICS

Originally designed to litigate cases, the NRDC in its early years initiated many landmark law cases designed to force the U.S. Environmental Protection Agency (EPA) to enforce crucial environmental statutes, such as the Clean Air and Water acts. It challenged many nuclear reactors, arguing that the environmental impact statements written for them were inadequate and did not take into consideration many of the real threats to human health from radiation. It also challenged numerous Department of Interior drilling projects in wilderness lands in the western United States.

While it maintains an active litigation schedule, members of the staff in the Washington office have in recent years testified on numerous legislative issues and argued before agency hearing officers. NRDC has become involved in several projects whereby it negotiates directly with industry when government seems unable to solve problems, as in the FIFRA discussion project. It also points out violations of environmental statutes to administrative agencies in order to influence enforcement actions. In 1982 it started a citizens' legal action program in which its attorneys sue industrial polluters directly when they feel that the government is unwilling to take such actions.

NRDC conducts educational workshops in many law schools for lawyers interested in becoming involved in environmental law; it also provides scientific and legal internships to graduate students each year. Since 1979 it has published *The Amicus Journal* on a quarterly basis, which it distributes to its membership. This journal contains feature articles of several pages on timely issues such as industry's proposal to open Alaskan wilderness areas to oil exploration, book reviews on environmental publications, and shorter articles on events in the courts, agencies, and Congress, as well as editorials. It also publishes a monthly NRDC *Newsline* for membership giving details on court case outcomes, agency hearings, and congressional actions on proposed bills. In addition, NRDC scientists research and publish monographs on specific topics, such as the risk to humans from pesticide residues, when it believes government agencies are not doing a sufficient job of informing the public.

## FURTHER INFORMATION

*The Amicus Journal* (Winter 1986, 1987, 1988, 1989).

*Deeper Problems: Limits to Underground Injection as a Hazardous Waste Disposal Method* (1987). New York: NRDC.

*Intolerable Risk: Pesticides in our Children's Food* (1989). New York: NRDC.

Mott, Lawrie, and Martha Broad (1984). *Pesticides in Food: What the Public Needs to Know*. New York: NRDC, March.

*NRDC Annual Report 1985–86, 1986–87, 1987–88* (1987, 1988, 1989). New York: NRDC.

*NRDC Fifteen-Year Report 1970–1985* (1986). New York: NRDC.

*NRDC Newsline* (September-October, 1987; May-June, July-August, September-October, November-December, 1988; March-April 1989). New York: NRDC.

*Our Ailing Public Rangelands: Condition Report—1985* (1986). New York: NRDC.

*Tall Stacks: A Decade of Illegal Use, A Decade of Damage Downwind* (1985). New York: NRDC.

Taylor, Robert E. (1986). "Group's Influence on U.S. Environmental Laws, Policies Earns It a Reputation as a Shadow EPA." *The Wall Street Journal*, January 13, p. 4.

*Turning off the Tap on Federal Water Subsidies* (1985). New York: NRDC.

*Twenty Years Defending the Environment: NRDC 1970–(1990)*. New York: NRDC.

Washington office: 11350 New York Avenue, N.W., Washington, D.C. 20005

## THE NATURE CONSERVANCY
1815 North Lynn Street
Arlington, Virginia 22209

### ORGANIZATION AND RESOURCES

The Nature Conservancy was incorporated in 1951 originally as the Ecological Society of America, "to find, study, protect, and maintain the best examples of ecosystems, lands and waters supporting the best examples of all elements of the natural world." It is a private, nonprofit, tax-exempt corporation under Section 501(c)(3) of the IRS code. It has a board of governors numbering 35 people, who select the president. The Conservancy has a staff of over 900 professionals distributed among some 52 field offices and in the national office, which has 170 staff members.

The Nature Conservancy has 436,407 individual members who pay $15 yearly dues and 437 corporate associates, such as Booth Newspapers, W. Atlee Burpee Company, Humana, Ford, McArthur, Weeden, and Yawkey foundations, and real estate and power companies. These corporations contribute between $1,000 and $10,000 a year to the operations of the Conservancy. Individuals may become life members by contributing $1,000 at one time.

In 1989, the Nature Conservancy raised $168.5 million through dues and contributions: 66 percent from individuals, 28 percent from foundations, and 6 percent from corporations. It expended $156 million: 11 percent on fund-raising, 4 percent on general administration, and 2.4 percent on miscellaneous; the remainder was spent on purchasing and managing lands as well as donating lands to government agencies. It reported a total of over $400 million worth of lands held for conservation at the end of 1989, which amounted to nearly 4 million acres in the United States, Canada, Latin America, and the Caribbean.

### POLICY CONCERNS

The Nature Conservancy advocates government preservation of natural areas in the form of parks and wildlife preserves and refuges. It supplies Congress with information about the need for ecological preservation. It supported the creation of the Land and Water Conservation Fund and argues in favor of the American Heritage Trust Fund, to be used exclusively for the national government to acquire more parklands. It also urges state governments to devote resources to preserving part of their natural heritage and donates lands to states to manage. It helps states develop management plans for natural areas and lobbies state houses to provide stable funding for such lands. However, its primary focus is to supplement publicly held lands with privately donated lands that are also preserved for future generations through individual and corporate philanthropy. It works with private organizations in Latin America to protect tropical rain forests and savannas there.

### TACTICS

The Conservancy owns and manages over 1,000 tracts of land itself, but has turned over many others to public and private organizations to manage. It encourages members and contributors to turn over ecologically important lands to the Conservancy for protection and solicits trade lands of no particular ecological value, which it trades or sells to raise money for purchasing ecologically sensitive areas. In the 1980s, it launched a major endeavor to protect and preserve wetlands around the United States and internationally. With the cooperation of state governments it inventories ecologically rare areas and habitats of endangered species and attempts to purchase them for conservation or to convince their private owners to protect them. In 1989 Alaska and Alabama joined this effort, bringing all fifty state governments into the heritage program. The Conservancy has extended this identification program to ten countries in Latin America and the Caribbean.

It issues a bimonthly, *The Nature Conservancy News*, to its members in which it describes the kinds of lands that it has added to its holdings. Individual state chapters also periodically issue newsletters entitled *The Conservator* about events in specific regions of the country. Members in state chapters engage in volunteer activities such as harvesting seeds of natural plant life and using these to restore other areas to their native species.

## FURTHER INFORMATION

*Annual Report* (1986, 1988, 1989). Washington, D.C.: The Nature Conservancy.
*The Conservator Illinois Chapter* (1987, 1988, 1989). Summer, all years.
*The Nature Conservancy Magazine* (1987, 1988, 1989). Washington, D.C.: The Nature
        Conservancy, all issues.

## NORTH AMERICAN ELECTRIC RELIABILITY COUNCIL (NERC)
101 College Road East
Princeton, New Jersey 08540

### ORGANIZATION AND RESOURCES

In 1965 there was a major blackout in the electricity supplied to the northeastern section of the United States, and the industry responded by forming the National Electric Reliability Council in 1968. It changed its name to the North American Electric Reliability Council (NERC) in 1981. This is a federation of nine regional reliability councils throughout the United States and parts of Canada. Members of each council represent investor-owned, state- and municipal-owned, rural cooperative, and federal utilities. Their primary purpose is to ensure that a steady supply of electricity is available to all customers by networking and sharing supplies in times of emergency when some sources may be interrupted.

Activities of NERC are directed by a twenty-five member board of trustees with two representatives from each regional council and additional members elected to assure representation from each type of utility. The U.S. Department of Energy (DOE), the Federal Energy Regulatory Commission (FERC), and the Canadian government attend meetings, as well as the Edison Electric Institute,* the American Public Power Association,* and the National Rural Electric Cooperative Association. The main headquarters are located in Princeton, New Jersey, but there are small staffs in each one of the nine regional councils.

### POLICY CONCERNS

NERC's primary concern is to improve and maintain the image of the entire electric utility industry as a reliable supplier of power to its customers. Its members are concerned about the costs of generating electricity and hope to minimize the impact of economic and environmental regulations on those costs. NERC is especially concerned about forecasting demand for electric energy in order to maintain a sufficient supply and avoid outages. Consumer groups both at the national and state levels have argued that utilities tend to overestimate demand in order to convince state commissions that regulate prices of utilities to allow more construction into the rate base of the various companies. Hence, the regional councils continually try to reassure regulators that the utility estimates of need for more power plants are not overstated. To achieve this goal NERC has instituted a movement to replace the term *reserve margin* with *capacity margin* or *operating margin*.

The 1978 Public Utility Regulatory Policies Act (PURPA) mandates that utilities purchase from cogenerators any excess electricity they produce that is not consumed on site. The electric utility industry at first resisted this type of competition as unfair as it is unregulated by state commissions, but it has accepted the reality of PURPA and now integrates such supplies into their reliability network and plans for future needs. It continues to maintain that such supplies are less predictable than utility sources and complicates the councils' task. It argues that competition within the industry is now so great that there is less need for any type of regulation whether from the state or federal level.

## TACTICS

NERC does not consider itself a trade association and has no official lobbying operation in Washington. Yet its studies of projected demands by the various councils and its plans for wheeling power from one system to another in time of need form a major part of the public policy regarding the energy supply. Government representatives attend all NERC meetings, and NERC officials have regular inputs into the discussions of electric supply in DOE. Officials of NERC are also utility executives who are represented before government in such organizations as the Edison Electric Institute. Hence, NERC forms an important part of the policy network for energy in the United States. It issues many technical reports to its members for planning purposes, and it has a substantial public-relations program designed to convince the public of the concern of the industry for the public interest.

## FURTHER INFORMATION

*Annual Report 1988* (1989). Princeton, N.J.: NERC.

# O

---- / ----

## OCEAN COMMERCIAL USERS ASSOCIATION
*See* National Ocean Industries Association.

## OCEANIC SOCIETY
*See* Environmental Policy Institute and Friends of the Earth.

## OXYGENATED FUELS ASSOCIATION (OFA)
1330 Connecticut Avenue, N.W.
Washington, D.C. 20036–1702

### ORGANIZATION AND RESOURCES

In 1983 some corporations involved in the production of oxygenated fuels, especially methanol alcohol, formed the Oxygenated Fuels Association (OFA). By the end of the 1980s it had fifteen members, including some major energy corporations: Arco Chemical, Standard Oil, Sun Refining, Tenneco Oil; chemical companies: Celanese, Union Carbide, Borden, EBASCO-Humphreys & Glasgow, and Ocelot Chemical; and more-specialized companies: Methanor V.O.F.; and even foreign and U.S. government entities: National Energy Corporation of Trinidad and the Tennessee Valley Authority. Membership is limited to businesses engaged in manufacturing methanol or other alcohol fuels, blending these fuels with hydrocarbon fuels, or producing internal combustion engines. Dues range from $1,000 for small businesses to $30,000. It is affiliated with the Organic Chemical Manufacturers.

### POLICY CONCERNS

OFA is primarily interested in promoting the use of methanol and ethanol fuels by mixing them with gasoline and diesel fuel. It seeks to reduce the cost of such fuels and to develop technologies that can use such fuels without damaging engines. It also seeks to reduce consumer resistance to using such blends that are now available on the market and to convince the government and consumers that these products can reduce the environmental impact of hydrocarbon fuels.

OFA does not disapprove of the labeling law in some states which requires sellers of oxygenated fuels to indicate what percentage of methanol or ethanol the fuel contains. It also wants to have the American Society for Testing and Materials (ASTM) certify that each blend meets its motor fuel standards and periodically sample and test to make sure blenders are adhering to standards. This new policy, it feels, would reassure consumers about the noncorrosive nature of alcohol blends.

The oil industry is divided on the issue of promoting oxygenated fuels, as some companies have devoted more research to developing oxygenated blends than have others that prefer to refine only gasoline and diesel oil. In 1989 Congress began consideration of a plan to force automotive manufacturers to produce cars that can run on alternate fuels, following the lead of California and some eastern states that took air pollution control into their own hands during the 1980s while the national government was doing little to improve air quality. In response, the American Petroleum Institute (API)* and Motor Vehicle Manufacturers of the U.S.* began a crash program to reblend gasoline without such polluting additives as lead and benzene to produce a nonpolluting gasoline to compete with the alcohol blends. For thirty years petroleum companies have argued that such a development was impossible, but when an economic alternative became possible through the actions of regulatory agencies the oil industry began seriously considering cleaning up their product. Hence OFA cannot depend on the API to represents its interests on this issue. In fact two major petroleum manufacturers, Arco and Mobil, that were originally interested in oxygenated fuels have joined the move to reformulated gasoline products and argue against use of methanol blends.

### TACTICS

OFA publishes a monthly newsletter to its members. It provides liaison with the Departments of Energy, Commerce, and Transportation, as well as the Environmental Protection Agency. It does research on the emissions from oxygenated fuels in order to provide information to the regulatory agencies. It also works with automotive manufacturers to try to improve engine technology that can use alcohol blends, and distributes information among consumer groups about the environmental benefits of oxygenates.

### FURTHER INFORMATION

ARCO (1989). "The Clean Air Agenda." *The New York Times*, October 11, p.5.

*Fuel for Thought* (1985). McLean, Va.: Written by Stackig/Swanston Public Relations
    for Arco Chemical Company.
Mobil Oil (1989). "More Problems with Methanol." *The New York Times*, September
    2.

# P
—————————— / ——————————

**PENNSYLVANIA WATERWORKS ASSOCIATION**
*See* National Association of Water Companies.

**THE PETROCHEMICAL ENERGY GROUP (PEG)**
1100 15th Street, N.W., Suite 1200
Washington, D.C. 20005

*ORGANIZATION AND RESOURCES*

The Petrochemical Energy Group (PEG) was founded in 1972 by seven companies that all use gas and oil as the feedstock for their products. PEG has nine members and a seven-person board of directors. Dena E. Wiggins is its administrator in Washington. It has a small budget and hires professional lobbyists to represent its interests.

*POLICY CONCERNS*

PEG's interests do not diverge substantially from those of the large trade associations representing the chemical, petroleum, and plastics industries. It opposes all controls on the price of natural gas because it believes if the price is allowed to float free it will come down. It believes that regulation can only favor the producers and distributors.

PEG also opposed the renewal of the Superfund Act in 1986. It believes that the tax on the petrochemical industry is unfair and keeps the costs of oil abnormally high. It did succeed in convincing Congress to add an industry-wide tax to Superfund. Like other trade associations, PEG opposes any victim compensation clause in the law on the grounds that it would be too expensive for industry to fund.

It opposes any import tax on foreign oil on the grounds this will increase costs of doing business for all its firms. If the petrochemical industry were to have to pay more for its imported feedstocks, it argues, this would mean it would be at a disadvantage to foreign competitors producing the same finished products. Since this industry is one of the few that actually has a favorable balance of trade abroad, PEG argues, this would increase the U.S. trade imbalance rather than improve it, as tax advocates argue.

## TACTICS

PEG holds an annual meeting for its corporate members in the fall and a monthly strategy meeting in Washington.

## PETROLEUM MARKETERS ASSOCIATION OF AMERICA (PMAA)
1120 Vermont Avenue, N.W.
Washington, D.C. 20005

## ORGANIZATION AND RESOURCES

In 1909 a group of entrepreneurs in the business of distributing petroleum products in the United States banded together to represent their interests to state, local, and federal government, but it eventually died out. In 1940 it was revived under the name of the Council of Petroleum Marketers Associations, which in 1948 changed its name to the National Oil Jobbers Council. In 1984 it changed its name again to the Petroleum Marketers Association of America (PMAA). Throughout this time, however, the organization has consistently represented the interests and concerns of businesses that retail petroleum products. In 1974 it absorbed the National Oil Fuel Institute, founded in 1961, which in turn replaced the Oil Burner Institute, founded in 1942, and the Oil Heating Institute, started in 1930.

PMAA now claims a membership of about 11,000 small businesses in the United States and some 54 major corporations such as Exxon. PMAA's members are in the business of selling motor fuels and heating fuels. About half its membership supply both heating and motor fuels, and 10 percent deal exclusively with residential, commercial, and industrial fuels, while 40 percent work only in the transportation sector. Of those involved exclusively with motor fuels, 35 percent own and operate their own businesses, 37 percent are lessees of major corporations, and 28 percent are bulk users of the fuel.

PMAA is organized along state and regional lines with forty-one state or regional affiliates, representing the petroleum markets in their areas. Each of the forty-one affiliates selects a member to send to the board of directors of the organization. The board has an executive committee of ten persons representing the major areas of the country. There are ten standing committees that handle issues such as finances and legislative liaison. The association meets twice yearly, in a spring convention and a fall convention and trade show where the latest marketing techniques and equipment are displayed. There is a professional staff of eight in Washington headed by Phillip R. Chisholm, executive vice-president, who is selected by the board.

In 1989 the budget was about $1.4 million, derived 55 percent from membership dues and 45 percent from fund-raising, usually done at the trade shows and conventions, although publications do produce some revenue. The dues are on a sliding scale, and depend on the gallons of petroleum products sold by the individual members. The state affiliates collect these dues and contribute to the national organization according to their volume of business.

## POLICY CONCERNS

As a trade association whose members earn their livelihood from sales of petroleum products, PMAA advocates increasing production of gasoline and fuel oils both at home and abroad. It favors the depletion allowance for oil producers, just as the American Petroleum Institute* and the Independent Petroleum Association of America* do. It opposes any tax on foreign oil imports as a way to increase the cost to themselves and thereby depress the market. It advocates opening all natural resources on public lands to exploration and development.

PMAA is especially concerned about environmental regulations that affect individual business people who operate gas stations and fuel oil delivery services. It opposes any tightening of the Clean Air Act (CAA) which would make its members' business more problematic. It opposed especially any crackdown on cities and regions not meeting the 1987 deadline for ozone levels. Its representatives argued before congressional hearings and U.S. Environmental Protection Agency (EPA) hearings that since so few areas of the country exceed the standards and these violations only occur a few days a year, they should be ignored for the time being. If any action is taken, PMAA favors individual vehicle canisters for vapor recovery from volatile gas rather than stage II controls on gas stations for vapor recovery while gasoline is being pumped into cars. It argued that the initial outlay of $12,000 a service station would be excessive if this equipment eventually became obsolete and canisters for individual vehicles had to be supplied eventually by the auto industry.

PMAA opposed drafting underground storage tank regulations under the Comprehensive Environmental Response, Compensation, and Liability Act (CERCLA, or Superfund) and helped form an ad hoc committee of underground storage tank operators for over thirty trade associations. It succeeded in preventing the 99th Congress from including underground storage tanks in its definition of toxic waste dumps in its rewriting of Superfund in 1986. Storage tanks are still controlled under the Resource Conservation and Recovery Act (RCRA). PMAA has testified frequently before EPA about setting standards for underground storage tanks. It seeks to reduce the stringency of the regulations and argues that EPA's survey of leaking tanks exaggerates the danger and does not follow industry practices in defining a leak. EPA regulations exclude farm and residential gasoline tanks and small tanks for noncommercial purposes. PMAA supports all such exclusions and argues that EPA's proposed regulations are excessive. However, it agreed to some regulations under RCRA in order to avoid having the underground tanks placed under CERCLA controls, which are more stringent and tend to favor recovery for victims under strict and joint liability laws.

PMAA also opposed the regulation of used oil as a hazardous waste. Its representatives argued that placing used oil in this category would constitute a tremendous setback for the recycling industry, and this would be environmentally damaging itself. It argued that a few incidents such as the mixing of PCBs into used oil sprayed on roadways in Times Beach, Missouri, give the public a false impression of the hazardous nature of used oil. It also advocates burning used oil as a fuel and has testified against EPA regulations to prevent the use of waste oil as a fuel in residential boilers.

## TACTICS

PMAA publishes *Petroleum Marketing Management* bimonthly for its members, giving them tips on the industry and keeping them abreast of developments in Washington. Its *Weekly Review* has more-timely pieces about legislation being debated in Congress and the need for members to write to their legislators as well as regulations being discussed in the agencies, such as the EPA.

## FURTHER INFORMATION

*Petroleum Marketing Management* (1989). Washington, D.C.: PMAA, January-February.
*Weekly Review* (1989). Washington, D.C.: Petroleum Marketers Association of America, May, September.

## PLANNED PARENTHOOD FEDERATION OF AMERICA (PPFA)
810 Seventh Avenue
New York, New York 10019

## ORGANIZATION AND RESOURCES

In 1915 Planned Parenthood was founded by physicians concerned about the need for birth control facilities in the United States. By 1989 it had expanded to include some 250,000 individual donors. Its president is Faye Wattleton, who heads a paid and volunteer staff of about 24,000 around the United States in 850 family planning clinics. PPFA has a 36-person board of directors.

PPFA has an annual income of about $300 million. Of this over $260 million is raised and spent in local affiliates; approximately $40 million is used in the national office in New York. Nearly $4 million goes to the Alan Guttmacher Institute, a special affiliate of PPFA, to conduct research and policy analysis on reproductive health issues. On the income side, about 35 percent comes from government sources, 24 percent from private contributions, 34 percent from clinic income, and the remainder comes from miscellaneous sources. PPFA spends some 53 percent of its income on patient services, 10 percent on international programs, 8 percent on community education, 14 percent on management support, 4 percent on fund-raising, and 11 percent on other services and payments.

## POLICY CONCERNS

PPFA is committed to providing quality health care and reproductive choices to American women and women in the Third World. Its single policy issue is closely connected to many environmental issues because the total number of people on earth have a tremendous impact on the natural resources and pollution stress created by industrialization. Therefore, PPFA is closely associated with many groups such as Population-Environment Balance,* the National Audubon Society,* and the Sierra Club.*

PPFA has been on the cutting edge of new birth control technology. In 1988 a new drug, RU 486, was developed in France that safely ends a pregnancy without surgery. Anti-abortion forces caused the manufacturer to withdraw the drug from the market. But PPFA and the international medical community urged the French government to order the drug company to proceed with distribution. PPFA maintains that all women should have the right to an abortion if they so desire and believes that RU 486 should cut down substantially on self-induced abortions that kill about 200,000 women in the developing world each year.

PPFA advocates comprehensive sexual education for all school children. In 1986 it published *How to Talk with Your Child About Sexuality* for parents and has sold 40,000 copies. Family Planning International Assistance (FPIA), PPFA's international affiliate, supports international assistance for family planning and opposed the 1985 Reagan administration's withdrawal of U.S. support for foreign birth control centers that counsel abortion. FPIA refused to stop aiding clinics that provide abortion services and the U.S. government withdrew its support. FPIA has sued on the grounds that such policy is unconstitutional and has tried to make up the deficit with additional private contributions.

## TACTICS

PPFA's clinics provide birth control counseling services to 2.2 million men, women, and teenagers each year; in addition, FPIA provides family planning services to 1.4 million needy individuals in the developing world each year. PPFA also trains nurse practitioners for birth control clinics and conducts seminars to keep health professionals informed of the latest developments in birth control methods. It provides information to its state affiliates about the latest contraceptive technology as well. It conducts an annual meeting and distributes a newsletter, *New Directions in Health Care Financing for PPFA Affiliates*. In the late 1980s PPFA added testing and counseling for the human immunodeficiency virus (HIV) that can cause AIDS to its services. It also regularly screens 1.4 million women for cervical cancer each year and provides abortions for over 100,000 and voluntary sterilization for men and women.

PPFA closely monitors federal, state, and local legislative action on reproductive health issues. It drafts legislation and presents testimony to congressional committees and maintains strong coalitions with environmental groups that advocate population control as one method of improving the quality of life for the world's 4 billion people. It works to bring RU 486 to the United States. PPFA seeks to broaden public understanding of family planning issues. It issues press releases on Medicaid's lack of funding for poor women's abortions and other problems. Its medical staff regularly briefs science and medical reporters about reproductive issues.

In 1988 PPFA established a special fund, the Katharine Houghton Hepburn Fund, to ensure future generations will have freedom of choice in reproduction. This fund was launched by a benefit tribute to Ms. Hepburn and her mother, who was a active feminist, and was co-hosted by Angela Lansbury and Walter Cronkite. Other celebrity participants included Barbara Walters and Martina Navratilova. After the U.S. Supreme Court announced its *Webster v. Reproductive Health Clinic* decision in 1989, PPFA joined with many environmental, civil liberties, and women's groups to advocate pro-choice positions in all state legislatures. It successfully supported many political campaigns of pro-choice candidates at the state level and lobbied every state legislature that was under pressure to pass more restrictive legislation on abortion.

## FURTHER INFORMATION

*Annual Report 1988* (1989). New York: PPFA.
*Choice* (1989). Chicago: Illinois Campaign for Choice, November-December.
Washington Office: 2010 Massachusetts Avenue, N.W., Washington, D. C. 20036.

## POPULATION-ENVIRONMENT BALANCE, INCORPORATED
1325 G Street, N. W.
Washington, D. C.20005

## ORGANIZATION AND RESOURCES

In 1972 a group of scientists and private citizens who believe that population growth is the root cause of most environmental problems formed The Environmental Fund. This occurred immediately after the issuance of a report by a Special Commission on Population Growth and the American Future, headed by John D. Rockefeller 3rd. In 1986 the name was changed to Population-Environment Balance, Inc. Balance is a nonprofit membership organization dedicated to maintaining and improving the quality of life in the United States through stabilizing the population. Its seven-person board of directors has as its honorary chair the biologist Garrett Hardin, author of "The Tragedy of the Commons." Policy is formulated for Balance by this board and a national advisory board of eighteen additional individuals, including Linus Pauling, Norman Cousins, and former secretary of the interior Stewart Udall.

In 1989 Balance had 5,500 members who paid $25 or more each year to produce a budget of about $750,000. Almost all of this came from individual contributions, plus a small amount from interest income. In its early years, it was funded in large part from foundation grants, for example, from the David and Lucille Packard, George Gund, Mellon, and Starrett foundations, and the budget was large. There were also some contracts for research projects from such groups as the Open Space Institute. Thirteen percent of its budget is spent on fund-raising and membership promotion, 29 percent on office management and administration, and 58 percent on public education, publications, and other program services. In 1986 its status was changed from a private foundation to a public charity under Section 501 (c)(3) of the Internal Revenue Code. Its executive director is Rose Hanes, who heads a four-person staff in Washington.

*POLICY CONCERNS*

In 1986 Balance worked for the passage of the Immigration Reform Act, signed into law in November of that year. It supported the concept of restricting entry into the United States for illegal aliens and of imposing sanctions on employers who attract and use undocumented workers. It also supports government funding for birth control clinics and aid to foreign countries to assist them in population control programs. It, together with other population control groups, such as Zero Population Growth,* have advocated the passage of a U.S. population policy bill for years. In 1987 such suggested legislation was introduced into Congress by a Democrat from Florida, Rep. Buddy MacKay, and by Senator Mark Hatfield, a Republican from Oregon. Balance continues to advocate restricting legal immigration to 200,000 people each year rather than the over 600,000 who are presently admitted, not including asylees and refugees. It opposed all Reagan administration cutbacks on funding for abortions and birth control agencies in the United States and abroad. It opposes the U.S. Supreme Court's dilution of abortion rights on both population and civil liberties grounds.

In 1985 Balance conducted a Connecticut River Basin study in which it illustrated the relationship between population growth and increased stress on the environment, natural resources, and quality of life. It used this in 1986 to undertake an analysis of increased expenditures by local governments on schools, roads, sewer, water, and other public services to support urban sprawl at the request of the Chesapeake Bay Foundation.

*TACTICS*

Balance issues *Balance Data* monthly describing population growth and economic development in the United States, such as water projects and transportation networks that replace agricultural lands and other natural resources, and urban sprawl and demand for more mineral development. It also publishes and distributes to its membership on a bimonthly basis *Balance Report*, which goes into issues such as the need for birth control clinics and advertisement of condoms. It also publishes monographs such as Garrett Hardin's classic essay on the public good, "The Tragedy of the Commons." It has produced a ten-minute video cassette education program to explain the problems of population in classrooms.

## FURTHER INFORMATION

*Annual Report* (1988). Washington, D.C.: Population-Environment Balance, March.
*Balance Data* (1987). Washington, D.C.: Population-Environment Balance, April.
*Balance Report* (1987). Washington, D.C.: Population-Environment Balance, May-June.
Caldwell, Lynton K. (1985). *Population and Environment: Inseparable Policy Issues.*
 Washington, D.C.: Population-Environment Balance, March.
Hardin, Garrett (1968). "Tragedy of the Commons." *Science* 162, pp. 1234–1245.

## PROCESS GAS CONSUMERS GROUP (PGCG)
1275 Pennsylvania Avenue, N.W.
Washington, D.C. 20004

### ORGANIZATION AND RESOURCES

The Process Gas Consumers Group (PGCG), founded in 1978, is a trade association of eighteen major corporations, including the Aluminum Company of America, Armco, Bethlehem Steel, Chrysler, Corning Glass Works, Eaton, PPG Industries, and LTV Steel, which consume a large amount of natural gas for which there is no alternative fuel. PGCG is dedicated to keeping the price of natural gas for its members down as low as possible and to guarantee them a constant supply. Its dues depend on the profitability of the member companies as well as the volume of process gas used. All members have representation on the board of directors. Jan Vlcek is general counsel and chief lobbyist.

### POLICY CONCERNS

PGCG says it favors competition in all phases of the natural gas industry, and it supported partial deregulation of the wellhead price of gas. However, it also believes that pipelines and local distribution companies sometimes occupy monopoly positions in the market for natural gas and unfairly restrict access to gas supplies or charge exorbitant rates for supplying consumers who have no alternative supply. Representatives of PGCG testified before the Senate Energy and Natural Resources Committee in 1985 that gas producers were overcharging consumers for new uncontrolled gas and the Federal Energy Regulatory Commission (FERC) should regulate it. It also opposed having suppliers sell the cheapest gas to customers with the longest term contracts.

It agreed with the American Gas Association* in 1987 that the Powerplant and Industrial Fuel Use Act (PIFUA) should be repealed to allow gas to be used in industrial plants. But it disagreed that this would solve all industry supply problems. It argued for competitive access to all supplies and against take-or-pay contracts which raise the price consumers must pay for gas contracted for before cheaper supplies were found. It wants bloc prices to reflect actual costs of delivery to customers, as this will lower the price for large volume users and raise it for residential and smaller commercial users. It agrees with the gas suppliers that all resources should be developed, but it opposes guaranteeing pipelines a return on their investment, as this only gives incentives to distributors to invest in inefficient equipment and techniques of distribution.

In 1985 PGCG argued successfully for FERC Order 436 to pipeline companies to provide nondiscriminatory transportation to all purchasers of gas and was subsequently disappointed by later court action that modified this order. It then sought congressional action to force greater access to transportation services for its members. It argues that pipeline companies prefer to discriminate against end users of natural gas as compared to local community distributors, whose purchases are larger.

### TACTICS

The PGCG is a small trade association as compared to the American Gas Association. Consequently it relies largely on the testimony of executive officers of its member corporations, such as Bethlehem Steel and General Motors, that maintain much larger lobbying offices in Washington than PGCG does. They all coordinate their activities and testimony before FERC and Congress concerning price controls on transportation services for natural gas as well as equal access to supplies. PGCG issues a quarterly journal and sponsors a meeting every three years.

### FURTHER INFORMATION

A Call to Compete (1985). Washington, D.C.: PGCG.
Chubb, John E. (1983). Interest Groups and the Bureaucracy. Stanford, Calif.: Stanford University Press.

## PUBLIC CITIZEN
P.O. Box 19404
Washington, D.C. 20036

### ORGANIZATION AND RESOURCES

In 1971, Ralph Nader, the consumer activist, founded Public Citizen from which several subsidiaries have evolved. The parent organization, whose president is Joan Claybrook, reported an operating budget for 1988 of about $3 million: 26 percent for administrative services, 41 percent for fund-raising, and 33 percent for other programs, and support from over 100,000 people. Most of Public Citizen's funds come from individual contributions solicited through direct mail advertising, but it also raises money from foundations and hired a consultant in 1988 to increase its success in this regard.

The Health Research Group was started in the same year, 1971, that Public Citizen began. Its director, Dr. Sidney Wolfe, has an operating budget of about $450,000 with a staff of nine. Congress Watch was created in 1973 to lobby Congress on all issues considered important to Public Citizen's various affiliates. It is now headed by Craig McDonald who has an operating budget of about $300,000 with a staff of eight; his legislative director is Michael Waldman.

The Field Organizing Project was formed to create Student Public Interest Research Groups and other grass-roots groups throughout the United States in 1972. It now claims over 4,000 activists in various parts of the country who can be called upon to work on any of the organization's concerns from nuclear power to insurance reform. This project has a budget of around $375,000 and is headed by Tom Tobin.

Two affiliates of Public Citizen are of particular importance in the energy field. The Critical Mass Energy Project,* directed by Ken Bossong, has a staff of four and an operating budget of around $1 million. Buyers Up, founded in 1983, is a cooperative fuel oil purchasing group that resells fuel oil to its members in Washington, Baltimore, Philadelphia, Richmond, and Wilmington. It operates with a staff of seventeen and a budget of $200,000, headed by Jason Adkins. The Citizens Utility Board Campaign (CUB) is also headquartered in Public Citizen. It is a two-person clearinghouse, headed by Tom Tobin, for CUB organizations in Wisconsin, Illinois, Oregon, and California.

## POLICY CONCERNS

Public Citizen's interests are wideranging and include interest rates charged by banks and credit card companies, the safety of consumer products, including the contents and side effects of drugs and food additives as well as a healthful environment and safe energy supply. Congress Watch has lobbied for such diverse policies as consumers' right to know bank and credit card rates of interest, Superfund to clean up toxic wastes, the 1977 Toxic Substances Act, and the Freedom of Information Act. In the 1980s it worked to convince Congress to reauthorize Superfund and not to reduce the impact of the Freedom of Information Act. It supports full product liability and resists attempts by the insurance industry to change the liability laws in various states to reduce victim compensation under tort litigation. In 1988 it testified against the nomination of Judge Robert Bork for Supreme Court justice because of the judge's preference for business litigants and against antitrust legislation.

The Health Group focuses on the Food and Drug Administration and the Occupational Health and Safety Administration, attempting to get drugs and food additives it considers unsafe off the market, and to improve the safety of working conditions and workers' right to know about the risks present in the materials and devices with which they work.

In 1986 Public Citizen sponsored a tax reform research group that claimed credit for several of the changes in the 1986 tax reform law. It argued for closing loopholes and for shifting a larger tax burden onto business and away from the individual citizen.

Energy groups like Buyers Up and Critical Mass advocate conservation of energy and less dependence both on imported oil and nuclear power. State groups supported by CUB are voluntary citizen organizations that attempt to counter industry's arguments for price increases for electricity, telephone, and other public utilities regulated by public utility boards in the various states. It also provides free energy audits and recommendations to improve energy efficiency of residences and nonprofit community organizations' headquarters.

## TACTICS

Public Citizen publishes the magazine *Public Citizen* bimonthly and distributes it to all members who contribute $20 a year or more to the organization. This journal informs the membership about group projects and contains articles of general interest about health, safety, economic, and social issues from a consumer perspective. The Health Research Group publishes the monthly *Health Letter*; Buyers Up produces the quarterly *Buyers Up News*. Public Citizen also publishes books for sale to members and the public about such varied issues as how to act as your own attorney, *Representing Yourself*; the history of regulatory agencies in the United States, *Freedom from Harm: The Civilizing Influence of Health, Safety and Environmental Regulations*; the voting records of all members of Congress on consumer and environmental issues, *Congressional Voting Index, 1985–86*; and tax shelters' inequitable effect for most taxpayers, *Running for Shelter*. Public Citizen also litigates whenever it believes actions taken by Congress or administrative agencies are against the public interest, as when it argued to require the Food and Drug Administration to prevent foodstuffs from being sprayed with carcinogenic pesticides.

## FURTHER INFORMATION

*Annual Report* (1987, 1988). Washington, D.C.: Public Citizen.
*Buyers Up News* (1986, 1987, 1988). Washington, D.C.: Public Citizen, Spring.
*Health Letter* (1987, 1988). Washington, D.C.: Public Citizen, June.
*Public Citizen* (1989). Washington, D.C.: Public Citizen.

## PUBLIC LANDS COUNCIL (PLC)
1301 Pennsylvania Avenue, N.W., Suite 300
Washington, D.C. 20004

## ORGANIZATION AND RESOURCES

In 1968 ranchers who use public lands in the west for grazing their livestock banded together to form the Public Lands Council (PLC) to represent their interests in Washington. In 1989 the Council had approximately 27,000 federal permittees as members located in 13 western states: Arizona, California, Colorado, Idaho, Montana, Oregon, Nevada, New Mexico, North Dakota, South Dakota, Utah, Washington, and Wyoming. Its budget in 1989 was $180,000, derived entirely from contributions made either by individual members or state affiliates.

PLC is governed by an eighteen-member board of directors made up of one voting delegate from each member state and one representative each from the National Cattlemen's Association, National Wool Growers Association, and the Association of National Grasslands. The executive director is Patty McDonald, who maintains an office of five staffers in Washington to represent the council before Congress and the executive branch. Four voting members from each state meet annually to determine policy, and the general membership is kept up with news reports from the national office as the need arises.

## POLICY CONCERNS

The purpose of PLC is to keep as much federally owned land, managed by the U.S. Department of Interior's Bureau of Land Management (BLM) or the Agriculture Department's Forest Service (FS) open to grazing by privately owned livestock at the lowest possible fee. The national office holds workshops on issues such as wilderness set-asides and endangered species protection that are of interest to the membership from time to time. It was highly successful during the Reagan years in obtaining low grazing fees for ranchers using public lands. President Reagan signed an executive order extending the existing grazing fee formula despite efforts on the part of environmental groups to raise those fees.

Individual ranchers are usually highly influential in the communities where they live and have close relationships with the BLM's representatives in western states. The BLM and FS both have advisory boards elected by grazing licensees who effectively represent the interests of the ranchers. Although ranchers tend to regard the federal government as an intruder into "their" lands and have argued for public lands to be turned over to private ownership, they usually have a close working relationship with the local FS and BLM representatives. Under secretaries of the interior James Watt and Donald Hodel, they have also been well represented in Washington within the federal government's executive branch. The organization issues a *PLC Newsletter* quarterly and holds an annual meeting in September.

In 1987 the PLC established the Foundation for Renewable Natural Resources as a non-profit, tax exempt, charitable foundation under Section 501(c)(3) of the Internal Revenue Code. It was created to educate the public, the media, and politicians about the benefits of multiple use, including livestock grazing, on the nation's public lands. This was done to counter the information given the press by conservation and wildlife protective associations that were perceived by PLC as being too influential in public opinion. In 1989 PLC scored a major victory when President Bush appointed James E. Cason, a protege of James Watt who held office in the Department of the Interior during the Reagan administration, to be assistant secretary of agriculture for natural resources and the environment.

## TACTICS

Members of PLC have testified in all hearings concerning the FS's and BLM's review of their wilderness areas in order to urge maximum use of these lands for stock raising. It enters litigation initiated by such conservation organizations as the Natural Resources Defense Council* as intervenors or friends of the court on the side of government to argue against NRDC's complaints against over-grazing or grazing fees that are below fair market prices. PLC argues that it is more expensive to graze their animals on public lands than the $1.86 animal unit per month fee indicates. Livestock permittees (who hold their permits for ten year periods) sometimes must pay a part of the price of water supplies through public works projects. They also argue that the number of stock now grazing on public lands has been reduced in recent years and that the lands could support more animals.

PLC testified in hearings to amend the Endangered Species Act to reduce the amount of habitat reserved for wildlife and the Public Rangeland Improvement Act to increase the number of livestock permitted to use the ranges. It has also worked against bills to protect natural diversity and nongame species proposed by conservationists in the 1980s and against the coal slurry pipeline proposed by the coal industry, which ranchers do not want crossing public rangelands. PLC representatives regularly testify against any further wilderness "lockups" of public lands and against the reintroduction of wolves into various national parks such as Yellowstone. However, stockmen also argue that they are the "original conservationists" and that their control of weeds, provision of salt licks, and maintenance of trails in the public lands also benefit wildlife that share the range with livestock.

## FURTHER INFORMATION

Culhane, Paul J. (1981) *Public Lands Politics*. Baltimore, Md.: Johns Hopkins Press, Resources for the Future.

McDonald, Patty (1988). "Public Lands Livestock Grazing: The Success Story." *California Cattleman*, October, p. 11.

Oakes, John B. (1989). "Bush Nominates Watt II." *The New York Times*, November 15, p. 8.

# R

## /

**RACHEL CARSON COUNCIL**
8940 Jones Mill Road
Chevy Chase, Maryland 20815

### ORGANIZATION AND RESOURCES

In December 1965, a little over a year after the death of Rachel Carson, friends and colleagues of the well-known publicist and author of *Silent Spring* formed the Rachel Carson Trust for the Living Environment, which later changed its name to the Rachel Carson Council. It was dedicated to advancing Ms. Carson's philosophy of conserving the natural environment and reducing dependence on chemical pesticides. Its president is Dr. Samuel S. Epstein, a toxicologist on the staff of the University of Illinois at Chicago School of Public Health. Its executive director is Shirley A. Briggs, who has served in this capacity since the creation of the council, and heads a staff of four. There is an eighteen-person board of directors and a six-person advisory committee to make policy for the Council. The Council charges $15 a year for individuals to become associates.

### POLICY CONCERNS

The Council responds to individual requests for information about the impact of toxic chemicals on the environment and human health and seeks to inform the public through publications about the hazards of pesticides. Representatives have testified before Congress about the Federal Insecticide, Fungicide and Rodenticide Act (FIFRA). It argued for years against the practice of paying manufacturers for disposal of stocks of chemicals declared unsafe for use by the U.S. Environmental Protection Agency (EPA), which was accomplished by the 1989 amendments to FIFRA.

*TACTICS*

In 1987 the twenty-fifth anniversary of the publication of *Silent Spring*, which warned the public of the dangerous impact of indiscriminate use of pesticides, there were many remembrances of Rachel Carson. The Council assisted local activists in Maryland in obtaining a statewide right-to-know law governing commercial application of landscape pesticides. This law requires that signs be posted on sprayed areas to prevent public exposure to the chemicals. The Council publishes monographs about the dangers of pesticides and methods for controlling pests without chemicals.

*FURTHER INFORMATION*

Bean, Dr. George A. (1971). *Healthy Lawns without Toxic Chemicals.* Chevy Chase, Md.: Rachel Carson Council.
Rainer, Ellen M., and Cynthia T. French (1985). *Pesticides in Contract Lawn Maintenance.* Chevy Chase, Md.: Rachel Carson Council.

## RACHEL CARSON TRUST FOR THE LIVING ENVIRONMENT
*See* Rachel Carson Council.

## RENEW AMERICA (RA)
1001 Connecticut Avenue, N.W., Suite 719
Washington, D.C. 20036

*ORGANIZATION AND RESOURCES*

The Fund for Renewable Energy and the Environment (FREE) was formed in 1986 from the Center for Renewable Resources and the Solar Lobby, both of which were founded in 1978 in response to the energy crisis. However, a number of letters to the editor complained about the connotations of the new acronym, FREE, and argued for a return to a more conservative title for the organization. It changed its name to Renew America (RA) in 1988. It has a twelve-person board of directors, including Denis Hayes, former head of the Solar Lobby; Eddie Albert, actor; Amory and Hunter Lovins of the Rocky Mountain Institute; and Robert Rodale of the Rodale Press. Tina Hobson is the executive director of a thirteen-person staff in Washington. Policy is set by discussion among the staff and board and by polling the membership. In 1989 RA had 15,000 members who contributed $25 a year. The total budget was $650,000, the balance of which was made up by foundation grants from such organizations as the George Gund, William and Flora Hewlett, and New Land foundations.

*POLICY CONCERNS*

RA's primary goal is to convince government agencies, especially the U.S. Department of Energy (DOE), to plan for a post-petroleum future. It criticized the Reagan administration's single-minded commitment to encourage more oil exploration and development and its refusal to consider other options, such as energy conservation. In 1987 RA published *The Oil Rollercoaster*, a report in which its authors argued against restoring the oil depletion allowance as a tax incentive to the oil industry in order to produce more oil. They advocated instead a $1 a gallon tax on gasoline to increase government revenues, bring U.S. prices closer to world levels, and induce conservation of energy. They argued that the United States is becoming increasingly dependent on oil imports, reaching the same level of imports that we experienced in the mid–1970s when the energy crisis occurred. RA opposes opening the California coast and the Alaskan wildlife refuge to exploration and drilling on the grounds that such programs will only provide a stopgap measure, supplying the nation with oil for a limited number of weeks at a tremendous cost to the environment.

RA advocates developing renewable energy technology, especially solar, wind, geothermal, and hydropower. It advocated efficiency standards for household appliances passed into law in 1987. It also hopes to re-establish incentives for insulating new buildings and installing renewable energy technologies. RA supports stricter gas mileage standards for automobiles than have been set. It argues that only through such conservation and renewable energy programs can the transition to an oil-less economy be achieved. It argues against dependence on coal and nuclear energy as equally damaging to the environment and at best only temporary solutions.

In 1987 RA published its first annual *State of the States* report, in which it ranked the fifty state governments according to the efforts they put into six major programs to improve the environment: air pollution reduction, soil conservation, groundwater protection, hazardous waste management, solid waste disposal and recycling, and renewable energy and conservation. The three top states, Wisconsin, California and New Jersey, had aggressive programs in several of these categories, including strong laws as well as extensive funding and enforcement actions. States ranked low, such as Mississippi, West Virginia, Wyoming, and Utah, tended to be non-affluent states with minimum government programs in many areas, not necessarily those with the largest environmental problems. RA now focuses its attention on state programs to preserve the environment and to influence state decision makers in becoming more aware of the need for such programs in the era of new federalism in which much of the responsibility for controlling pollution falls on the states.

## TACTICS

RA issues *Renew America* quarterly to its membership. It also issues periodic research reports and sees as its first priority educating the public and its membership through research and convincing them to influence their elected representatives to adopt more energy conserving policies.

## FURTHER INFORMATION

*The Free Report* (1987). Washington, D.C.: R.A., vol 1, no. 2, April-June.

*The Oil Rollercoaster* (1988). Washington, D.C.: RA.
*State of the States* (1987). Washington, D.C.: RA.

## RESOURCE POLICY INSTITUTE (RPI)
P.O. Box 39185
Washington, D.C. 20016

### ORGANIZATION AND RESOURCES

The Resource Policy Institute (RPI) was founded in 1975 by Albert J. Fritsch, a chemist who had earlier formed the Center for Science in the Public Interest (CSPI), and Arthur H. Purcell, an engineer who had worked for the American Association for the Advancement of Science. In February 1975, they incorporated as the Technical Information Project, renamed in 1982 the Resource Policy Institute (RPI). Over a four-year period they conducted a series of regional workshops bringing together consumer and public interest representatives, industry managers, educators, and government officials to discuss waste management. A participant in one of those conferences set up the Colorado Project, a RPI division in Boulder. Albert Fritsch returned to Kentucky in 1977, and CSPI gradually evolved into a center concerned exclusively with food and nutrition issues. Fritsch later set up Appalachia Science in the Public Interest, still affiliated with RPI. RPI remains a small operation in Washington, with two affiliates in Colorado and Kentucky. It obtains small private grants on occasion and also solicits contributions from the public. It has about 2,000 members.

### POLICY CONCERNS

RPI is primarily interested in environmental and energy conservation issues, especially the reduction of waste production in the United States. Purcell testified before Congress for CSPI on the Resource Conservation and Recovery Act, and CSPI was invited to submit a proposal to EPA to develop and conduct workshops on national and regional waste issues. During the 1980s RPI experienced a reduction in government funding for its projects. It did receive some grant assistance from the Department of Energy and the National Science Foundation to conduct work on municipal energy conservation. During that time it has emphasized the need to reduce the generation of waste materials, particularly toxic wastes.

### TACTICS

In 1977 the directors of RPI held a conference on controlling toxic substances and testified for the passage of the Toxic Substances Control Act. It continues to advocate the creation of alternative methods of disposing all waste materials, especially the conservation of energy and waste reduction at the source. Its director serves as consultant to municipalities and states interested in reducing costs of waste management. It has published papers and reports on waste reduction and resource conservation.

*FURTHER INFORMATION*

Purcell, Arthur H. (1980). *The Waste Watchers*. New York: Doubleday/Anchor Press.

## RESOURCES FOR THE FUTURE (RFF)
1616 P Street, N.W.
Washington, D.C. 20036

*ORGANIZATION AND RESOURCES*

Resources for the Future (RFF) was founded in 1952 through a Ford Foundation grant by economists and other social scientists interested in doing research on natural resource management and environmental questions. Its president is Robert W. Fri, and its vice-president is John F. Ahearne. RFF has a twenty-person board of directors, consisting primarily of academics, such as Charles Bishop formerly of the University of Houston; industrialists, such as Macauley Whiting, retired president of Dow Chemical International; government officials, such as John H. Gibbons from the Office of Technology Assessment; and environmentalists, such as Frederic D. Krupp of the Environmental Defense Fund.*

RFF has approximately sixty professional fellows conducting research in its Washington office. It also has a resident fellowship program that brings in visiting scholars from academic institutions for work on particular research projects.

At the end of the 1980s it had an annual budget of between $6 and $7 million. It also has a reserve fund of about $30 million. It derives about 30 percent of its revenues from investments and 10 percent from rental income; the remainder comes from foundation grants, contracts to undertake particular kinds of research, and sales of its publications. It obtains funding from a wide variety of sources, from the Exxon Corporation and the World Bank to the National Science Foundation and the Andrew Mellon Foundation. It expends approximately 28 percent of its budget on general administration, 13 percent on building operations, 8 percent on education and communication, and 3 percent on grants that it awards to academics to do their own research. The remaining 48 percent is expended on its own research program which is divided among energy and materials, quality of the environment, renewable resources, and risk assessment.

*POLICY CONCERNS*

RFF is divided into five units: energy and materials, quality of the environment, renewable resources divisions, the national center for food and agricultural policy, and the center for risk assessment. In the energy field, RFF researchers have studied the linkage between energy supply, price, and general economic prosperity and employment levels. They have compared how the economies of several industrial countries have adjusted to energy price shocks in the 1970s and 1980s both in the private sector and through government intervention. The energy and materials division also examines the demand for mineral resources in international trade and the potential commercial uses for space transportation, satellite communications, and earth observation. It has investigated the future role of coal in the U.S. energy mix, studying the leasing of federal lands containing coal, regulation of railroad rates as they affect coal transportation, and how new regulations to control acid rain may affect coal use. The energy and materials division has also taken up the issue of disposal of nuclear waste from power plants. It analyzes such problems as how to identify the best geologic site for nuclear wastes, how to isolate them through engineered barriers, and how to convince jurisdictions to agree to host such sites. Researchers there have also examined the impact of the 1986 oil price reduction on future levels of exploration for petroleum and on the impact on the U.S. market from a projected oil import fee. The division has also projected costs of producing electricity by varied new technologies, such as coal gasification and fluidized bed combustion, in order to estimate the future market for electricity. Sponsors of this research include the Edison Electric Institute,* the U.S. Bureau of Mines, and the World Bank.

The quality of the environment division has explored such questions as what the outcomes would be if various states were allowed to set their own individualized ambient air quality standards rather than conforming to national ones. Economists and scientists in the division have examined the relationship between air pollution and human health and made other efforts to quantify the social costs of pollution in order to compare these with the costs of pollution control. The division has investigated such questions as the utility of using economic incentives to control air and water pollution rather than a regulatory approach and how to value publicly owned natural resources. It also has pioneered in the contingent valuation method of asking consumers how much they would be willing to pay for environmental improvement rather than estimating changes in values of goods and services such as real estate prices. The division has also outlined the steps needed for obtaining information about future locations of cost-effective solid waste management facilities. It has also developed models for estimating the costs of mitigating environmental damage from hydroelectric developments.

In 1987 RFF created a new Center for Risk Management in order to develop methods for estimating the risks to health and the environment involved in such threats as acid rain, toxic substances, pesticides, hazardous wastes, and ozone depletion. Scientists in this area compare the methods that different government agencies, such as EPA and OSHA, use to estimate risks and to determine what levels of exposure are safe. They have considered questions about what concentrations of dioxin can be permitted in soil and how much benzene can be allowed to leak into the atmosphere. Endemic in all such studies are questions about the uncertainty involved in any such estimates. The center has also investigated such questions as the costs of sheltering people during a toxic chemical emergency as opposed to evacuating them from the area. It has also focused on the costs to human health from incinerating hazardous wastes and landfilling the ashes, which may leach into groundwater supplies. These projects are funded by a variety of corporate sponsors, including Union Carbide, Waste Management, and the Motor Vehicle Manufacturers Association* as well as government agencies such as the Environmental Protection Agency (EPA) and the National Science Foundation.

The Renewable Resources Division focuses on economic theories applicable to problems of multiple-use management of public forestlands, cropland erosion, and pesticide use. Economists in the division have examined the Forest Service's planning models for national forest management and the way in which timber harvests affect watershed programs and water available for use in hydroelectric and irrigation projects. They have also examined the problem of below-cost timber sales and implications for long-range forest management. The division has launched a program to investigate the effect on agriculture and silviculture that global warming may have. The Soil Conservation Service of the U.S. Department of Agriculture has sponsored RFF research on the impact of soil erosion on water quality and the payback to farmers from investments in erosion control. The Georgia Pacific Corporation and the U.S. Geological Survey are among the sponsors of these projects.

The National Center for Food and Agriculture Policy with the Renewable Resources Division has been funded by a grant from the W. K. Kellogg Foundation to study policies affecting food and nutrition, international trade, and environmental impacts of such technology as pesticides and fertilizers. Economists in RFF have studied the relationship between U.S. agricultural policies and U.S. exports of food affected both by international demand and the General Agreement on Tariffs and Trade. They have explored methods of making American farmers less dependent on federal price supports through increasing markets in such commodities as ethanol as a fuel alternative. They placed special emphasis on the impact of liberalizing trade between the United States and Canada prior to the free trade agreement in 1989. Under the auspices of the National Climate Program of the National Oceanic and Atmospheric Administration, scientists in the division are also concerned about the possible impact of new technologies on the global climate and the latter's effect on agriculture. They estimated the impact of the 1988 drought on foreign markets for American exports and on world nutrition levels.

*TACTICS*

RFF's primary purpose is to conduct research into important timely environmental and natural resource problems. Its primary output is research reports and books, normally published by the Johns Hopkins Press. It also publishes a quarterly, *Resources*, which describes recent research and is distributed free to anyone interested in developments in natural resources and the environment. RFF sponsors public affairs radio programs that are broadcast over the National Public Radio Network, and issues regular press releases about its ongoing research. It also sponsors a resident fellowship program for academics from various universities and has an annual competition for small grants among university researchers.

RFF also sponsors several conferences each year on timely issues such as global warming and risk assessment. Although RFF takes no official stance and does not lobby Congress, its economists and scientists often testify before Congress concerning their findings and are available as resource people for agency and congressional staff. They frequently do research sponsored by such agencies as the Departments of Agriculture and Interior and the EPA, as well as business corporations. However, they are under no obligation to suppress their findings if they do not correspond to the policy preferences of the sponsors. Its staff view themselves as objective scientists, not as advocates for any policy position.

*FURTHER INFORMATION*

*Annual Report* (1988). Washington, D.C.: RFF.

## RUBBER AND PLASTIC ADHESIVE AND SEALANT COUNCIL

*See* Adhesive and Sealant Council.

# S

## / 

**SAFE ENERGY COMMUNICATION COUNCIL (SECC)**
1717 Massachusetts Avenue, N.W., Suite LL215
Washington, D.C. 20036

### ORGANIZATION AND RESOURCES

The Safe Energy Communication Council (SECC) was founded in 1980 to counter advertisements by the nuclear power industry, specifically the U.S. Council for Energy Awareness (USCEA).* The SECC has a budget of about $100,000 a year obtained from about fifteen environmental groups such as the Sierra Club,* who are also represented on SECC's board of directors. It has no members and does not solicit contributions by mail.

### POLICY CONCERNS

SECC advocates that state regulatory commissions deny rate increases to public utilities whose increased costs are due to excess capacity, especially from nuclear reactors. It argues that conservation measures and alternative fuels enabled the United States to weather the energy crises of the 1970s and that conservation techniques, cogeneration, and development of renewable energy can fill U.S. energy needs well into the twenty-first century.

In 1987, SECC argued against the reauthorization of the Price-Anderson Act, which relieves industry of much of the liability in the event of a nuclear accident. It argued that taxpayers will be asked to pay the cost instead, and relieving industry of liability reduces their incentive to operate safely. SECC also countered industry's assurances after the Chernobyl accident, stating that the containment system in use there was similar in principle to some American reactors, and there was no reason to believe that Soviet technology was comparatively inferior to that of the United States.

### TACTICS

SECC does little direct lobbying with Congress, but seeks to influence the print and electronic media through its periodic publication, *Viewpoint*. In this publication SECC writers argue that the electric utilities have overbuilt and charge customers, both residential and business, for their own mismanagement. SECC's news releases have focused since its inception on the advertisements put out by USCEA, which advocates greater capacity for American utilities. SECC argues that USCEA's ads are deceptive because they imply that nuclear energy can replace petroleum while the United States uses almost no oil for generating electricity, but rather for transportation where nuclear power cannot be substituted.

SECC has relied in the past on the fairness doctrine of the Federal Communications Commission to force television and radio to give equal time to antinuclear groups to counter these ads. Under SECC's guidance local organizations have obtained free air time in various parts of the country. However, in 1987 the fairness doctrine was eliminated, and it seems likely that SECC will have to adopt new tactics in future.

### FURTHER INFORMATION

*Viewpoint* (1989). Washington, D.C.: SECC, August.

## SCIENTISTS INSTITUTE FOR PUBLIC INFORMATION (SIPI)
355 Lexington Avenue, 16th Floor
New York, New York 10017

### ORGANIZATION AND RESOURCES

The Scientists Institute for Public Information (SIPI) was founded in 1963 to bridge the gap between the scientific community and the mass media and public. There is a thirty-one-member board of trustees, headed by Dr. Lewis Thomas, chair, and Alan McGowan, president. Trustees include journalists and scientists, as well as William D. Ruckelshaus, former head of the U.S. Environmental Protection Agency (EPA), and Russell E. Train, former head of the Council on Environmental Quality. There is in addition a twenty-two-person media resource service advisory committee, with Walter Cronkite as its honorary chair.

Individual members pay from $25 to $100 a year, depending on their preference. Institutions may become associates for $1,000 a year, and major sponsors pay as much as $10,000. There is a media sponsor council which helps fund SIPI, including the Hearst Corporation, New York Times Foundation, and the Washington Post Company. In addition, corporate foundations, such as AT&T, Bristol-Myers, Ford, Exxon, and Xerox also contributed. SIPI has a budget of over $1.3 million a year, most of which comes from contributions and grants.

Over 80 percent is spent on program services, with the remainder going to support services, fund-raising, and general administration.

## POLICY CONCERNS

SIPI takes no official stands on any public policies and does not officially seek to influence policy makers. Its members are primarily concerned with disseminating information to the media on such subjects as health and medicine, environment, life sciences, and high technology, including energy issues.

## TACTICS

In 1980, after the 1979 Three Mile Island accident deluged the offices of SIPI with inquiries about nuclear power, SIPI began its media resource service (MRS). This project links individual journalists writing stories about health, technology, environment, energy, and other physical science issues to appropriate experts in the field. SIPI maintains a toll-free number (800/223–1730) for members of the working press to call and describe the information or type of specialist needed. Then MRS staff search their computer data base to find appropriate experts. It broke down its calls in 1986 into topics: health and medicine 33 percent; environment 21 percent; social science and psychology 10 percent; life sciences (gene manipulation, in vitro fertilization) 7 percent; high technology (robotics, fiber optics) 6 percent; energy, 4 percent; agriculture (famine, food additives) 4 percent; military technology (star wars, chemical warfare), 3 percent; natural disasters, 2.2 percent; and other, 10 percent.

During its first year of operation MRS grew to include 5,000 scientists in its files. By 1988, MRS included more than 20,000 participating experts in science, technology, and medicine. The MRS staff fields about 50 calls a week from print and broadcast journalists and refers these calls to relevant experts in the region. Experts are all volunteers and are obtained from research institutions and scientific societies. Questionnaires are mailed to participants asking for their educational background, positions held, and areas of expertise. MRS attempts to keep on file representatives of all points of view on controversial scientific issues. When queried about lead in gasoline, MRS referred journalists both to spokespersons for oil companies as well as to researchers in children's hospitals on the impact of lead on human health. Sponsors of MRS include major networks such as ABC, CBS, and NBC news organizations, major newspaper chains, such as Knight-Ridder, as well as individual papers, such as the *Christian Science Monitor* and the *San Francisco Chronicle*, and magazines, both general (*The Reader's Digest Association*) and specialized journals (*Medical World News*).

SIPI publishes *SIPISCOPE* quarterly which covers controversial scientific issues such as recombinant DNA research. It also conducts seminars on such issues as reporting on toxic chemical spills, inviting such participants as representatives of chemical manufacturers as well as representatives of the U.S. Environmental Protection Agency and journalists. It conducts surveys of science editors for major newspapers to determine how much science coverage there is and in what forms.

It also publishes *Environment Magazine* for its membership, which presents stories about major science issues. These stories represent a variety of points of view on scientific controversies for the public and media.

### FURTHER INFORMATION

*Media Resource Service 1987* (1988). New York: SIPI.
*SIPISCOPE* (Autumn, 1986, 1987, 1988). New York: SIPI.

## SERVICE STATION DEALERS OF AMERICA (SSDA)
304 Pennsylvania Avenue, S.E.
Washington, D.C. 20003

### ORGANIZATION AND RESOURCES

In 1947 a group of service station dealers formed a trade association, the National Congress of Petroleum Retailers. In 1980 the name was changed to Service Station Dealers of America (SSDA). In the 1930s several state associations of gasoline retailers had sprung up to try to prevent below-cost selling that was devastating many industries. In 1937 Michigan passed a fair trade law to stop the price wars there that had eliminated many dealers. Rankin Peck was the leader of dealers in Michigan and was instrumental in founding the organization. After nearly going bankrupt in the 1960s, SSDA was reconstituted, and has been especially active in representing its membership in their negotiations with their suppliers, the major oil corporations. During the oil crisis in 1973 NCPR held a rally on Capitol Hill which succeeded in getting Congress to order the Cost of Living Council to allow dealers to pass through wholesaler price increases to customers. In 1974 NCPR moved its headquarters to Washington to be closer to national policy makers. It continues to lobby state legislatures also for laws protecting the individual dealer against monopolistic practices by the oil companies.

SSDA is the major representative for independent businesses who retail gasoline from the major oil companies. It has forty-four state affiliates, retail gasoline sales and auto repair organizations, each of which pays dues according to the volume of sales done by its members. These produce a budget of about $600,000 a year to support a staff of four in Washington.

### POLICY CONCERNS

The most important policy victory that service station dealers achieved came in 1978 when Congress passed the Petroleum Marketing Practices Act (PMPA), which protects individual dealers from monopolistic practices by the franchisors from whom they obtain their supplies. PMPA prevents the oil companies from terminating a franchise without cause and regulates the relationship between supplier and retailer. Several states, such as New Jersey, Maryland, and Connecticut, had passed laws designed to help the retailers earlier, and the federal law preempted these safeguards, but today the same rights hold for all dealers across the United States. In the 1980s SSDA obtained a settlement of $58 million for dealers from oil companies for overcharging their retailers during the period 1973–1989 when oil prices were controlled.

In the 1970s and early 1980s SSDA fought to have service stations exempted from the hazardous wastes requirements of Resource Conservation and Recovery Act (RCRA), and originally any generator of hazardous wastes under 1,000 kilograms a month was considered too small to come under the requirements of the law. However, in 1987 this was changed to 100 kilograms which includes many more small generators. For several years the U.S. Environmental Protection Agency (EPA) debated whether used motor oil should be declared a hazardous waste. However, SSDA was successful in convincing EPA that do-it-yourselfers would simply dump their used oil in sewers if service station dealers could not collect it. Therefore EPA ruled that dealers who turn over used oil to recyclers are exempt from responsibility under Superfund if the oil is disposed of improperly.

Under RCRA, EPA also imposed regulations on underground storage tanks for gasoline in service stations. It now requires that these tanks be monitored for leaks and replaced, but SSDA was able to obtain a lengthy phase-in period and to prevent a requirement that all tanks be replaced regularly regardless of whether they leak. It also managed to limit the liability for leaking tanks for dealers, whereas the oil companies have a larger liability.

Under the Clean Air Act (CAA) EPA has sought to control volatile organic compounds (VOCs) that escape when cars and trucks are refueled. Stage I nozzle guards have been in use for several years, but Stage II nozzles would cost $5,000 a ton VOC reduction for gas stations to implement according to SSDA, which argues for an amendment to the CAA to withdraw the Stage II requirements. SSDA argues that another requirement in the CAA, which mandates canisters on new 1991 cars to recover VOCs, is more practical. The automobile industry counters that the canister option is too expensive for the limited improvement it would make, and that Stage II vapor recovery should only be required in areas not meeting CAA ozone standards.

Another method of reducing emissions from cars, inspection and maintenance of old vehicles, is written into the CAA, and SSDA advocates use of this method. In so doing it joins its sister organizations, such as the Automotive Service Association (ASA)* in supporting an option that will bring more business to its members, many of whom also run auto repair and maintenance shops.

*TACTICS*

SSDA has forty-four affiliate organizations from various states, and representatives from these groups lobby on Capitol Hill and before EPA. It often coordinates its defenses against environmental legislation with such giants as the American Petroleum Institute* and with smaller groups like ASA. In other instances it attempts to shift the costs of compliance to its oil company suppliers or to another part of the transportation industry, the automotive manufacturers.

SSDA issues an annual report to its members each year and sponsors a convention at which dealers learn about each other's troubles with suppliers and new technology in the business. It also issues weekly *Washington Actiongrams* to its members to keep them informed of developments in Washington and to ask their support for particular programs in writing and phoning their congressional representatives.

### FURTHER INFORMATION

*The American Dealer Yearbook—1988* (1989). Washington, D.C.: SSDA.
*SSDA Washington Actiongram* (1981). Washington, D.C.:SSDA, June 17, July 2

## SIERRA CLUB
330 Pennsylvania Avenue, N.W.
Washington, D.C. 20003

### HISTORY AND DEVELOPMENT

In the latter part of the nineteenth century, John Muir, born in Scotland but raised and educated in Wisconsin, migrated to the California Sierra Nevada mountain range and spent the remainder of his life attempting to preserve some of it for succeeding generations. A naturalist who preferred solitary mountain climbing to city life, Muir turned to writing and lecturing about his wilderness experiences in order to enlist others in his cause. He was befriended by Robert U. Johnson, editor of the prestigious eastern *Century* magazine, who provided an outlet for Muir's essays and suggested to him the possibility of forming an association to help preserve California's natural wonders. In 1892, with the help of some professors from the University of California, Muir conducted the first meeting in San Francisco of the Sierra Club, modeled on the Appalachian Mountain Club. Its charter proclaimed the purpose of the fledgling organization:

to explore, enjoy and preserve the Sierra Nevada and other scenic resources of the United States and its forests, waters, wildlife, and wilderness; to undertake and to publish scientific, literary, and education studies concerning them; to educate the people with regard to the national and state forests, parks, monuments, and other natural resources of scenic beauty and to enlist public cooperation in protecting them.

Its first major victory was the expansion and protection of Yosemite National Park which Muir had helped found in 1890. The Club also succeeded in getting California to return Yosemite Valley to federal management, thereby reducing the commercialization of the park. It failed in its attempt to preserve the Hetch Hetchy Valley, which was turned into a water reservoir for San Francisco in the early twentieth century. Muir and the Sierra Club attempted to influence the U.S. government to adopt a preservationist attitude toward its natural resource heritage, but generally lost out to Gifford Pinchot, the first director of the Forest Service, and his arguments for the most utilitarian use of all natural resources.

John Muir remained as president of the Sierra Club from 1892 until his death in 1914 and generally urged that the Club depend on volunteers to run it and keep its amateur status. It engaged in some of the earliest struggles for preserving part of the American wilderness, but it remained essentially a California-based club while other groups were becoming nationally oriented during the early twentieth century. It was not until after World War II and an influx of new members that the Sierra Club began to change and assume a leadership position again. In the early days, Club members used mules to make trips into the wilderness, but in the 1940s, they decided that the animals were too destructive of mountain meadows and adopted a backpacking philosophy that encouraged members to make as little impact on the ecology they visited as possible.

David Brower, whom some have called the reincarnation of John Muir, joined the Club in 1935 and became editor of the *Bulletin* in 1946 on his return from the war. He was appointed the first professional executive director of the Club in 1952 by then president Richard Leonard. Under Brower's editorship, the *Bulletin* came to emphasize more political action instead of focusing exclusively on camaraderie in the outings sponsored by the Club's local chapters. Membership grew at a phenomenal pace, and chapters sprang up outside California as many political activists were attracted to the cause. In the 1950s Sierra joined forces with the Wilderness Society* to prevent the flooding of part of Dinosaur National Monument in Colorado. In 1964 Congress passed the Wilderness Act to preserve more unspoiled areas in the United States, albeit with a caveat that permitted new mining claims in them until 1984.

## ORGANIZATION AND RESOURCES

The Sierra Club is the oldest voluntary membership conservation organization in the United States. It has a membership of nearly 500,000 who pay dues of $33 a year which includes a subscription to *Sierra*, formerly the *Sierra Club Bulletin*. There are 56 local chapters throughout the United States and Canada, ranging in size from about 600 to 40,000 members. These chapters are in turn divided into about 350 groups which hold regular meetings.

Sierra Club national policy is set by its 5 elected officers and a 15-person board of directors, elected for 3-year terms by mailed ballot from the membership. The nominating committee solicits candidates for the board from the entire membership before each election, searching for individuals who have been active in local chapters and have exhibited commitment to the principles of the Club. The board has authority to remove officers and board members for cause based on acts inimical to the Club's purposes. Since 1892, the board has included some of the nation's eminent naturalists, including Ansel Adams, the nature photographer; John Oakes, retired *New York Times* editorial director; and David Brower. Mr. Brower also served as executive director until 1969 when he was forced out over fiscal issues and left to found the more militant Friends of the Earth* and, later, Earth Island Institute.* He remains as an honorary vice-president, however. The Sierra Club has had only four executive directors in its long history: Mr. Brower until 1969, Mike McCloskey from 1969 to 1985, and Douglas Wheeler, who resigned in 1986 over policy differences with the board and fiscal problems, and the present director, Michael L. Fischer. President of the 15-person board is Richard Cellarius. In addition the Club has 21 vice-presidents, of whom 13 are regional vice-presidents, and a professional staff of almost 300.

The national headquarters for the Sierra Club is in San Francisco, where its bimonthly magazine *Sierra* is published. In 1985 the National Headquarters Association, a partnership of Sierra Club supporters, purchased a building and leased space to the Sierra Club. In 1985 the board of directors decided not to move its national headquarters to Washington in order to maintain the Club's identity with the California area. It does, however, maintain an office in Washington from which the Club conducts campaigns to influence national policy regarding natural resources. San Francisco remains the editorial office for *Sierra*. It added regional offices throughout the years and now maintains offices for Alaska in Anchorage; Appalachia in Annapolis, Maryland; Canada in Victoria and Ontario; the Midwest in Madison, Wisconsin; the Northeast in Philadelphia, Pennsylvania; Northern California/Nevada in Oakland, California; the Northern Plains in Sheridan, Wyoming; the Northwest in Seattle, Washington; the Southeast in Knoxville, Tennessee; Southern California in Los Angeles; the Southern Plains in Dallas, Texas; and the Southwest in Boulder, Colorado.

At the end of the 1980s the Sierra Club's revenues totalled about $35 million: 37 percent from member dues, 29 percent from the Sierra Club Foundation and Legal Defense Fund, 12 percent from sales of catalog merchandise and publications, 7 percent from outings and lodge fees, 11 percent from advertising and royalties, and 4 percent from reimbursement for services. After expenditures for administration, 13 percent; membership activities, 13 percent; and fund-raising, 8 percent, the Club spent 22 percent on its information and education program, 26 percent on public policy influencing programs, 7 percent on its outdoor activities, and 6 percent on chapter allocations, which left 5 percent for investment and contribution to net worth.

*POLICY CONCERNS*

Originally organized to promote conservation policies in the western part of the United States, the Sierra Club has expanded its mission in the twentieth century as new issues have arisen. Individual officers and members have continuously advocated establishment and conservation of national forests and parks. After its successful drive to preserve Dinosaur National Monument from being flooded by government reclamation projects, the Club became active in urging Congress to adopt wilderness legislation such as the Wilderness Preservation Act of 1964 and the Wild and Scenic Rivers Act of 1968. Individual chapters frequently suggest tracts to be included in the wilderness holdings of the United States and have been active participants in the Forest Service and Department of Interior's roadless area review and evaluation process mandated by the Federal

Land Policy and Management Act. In these local disputes Sierrans usually face timber, mining, and ranching interests who urge the development of all publicly held lands for multiple uses. Club members also frequently identify rivers and streams they believe are good candidates for designation as wild and scenic rivers and try to prevent the government from damming, channeling, or otherwise developing them.

The Sierra Club's staff in national headquarters frequently argues against the expenditure of public funds for reclamation projects that it views as reducing the quality of natural resources through changing the natural flow of streams and rivers. It argues against excessive leasing of public lands for grazing and mineral exploration, believing these actions decrease the potential for other uses such as wildlife refuges and human recreation. It also opposes most National Park Service attempts to develop the national parks by adding more access roads, hotels, and other accommodations inside the parks. It advocates splitting off the National Park Service from the Department of the Interior because it regards the latter as devoted to exploiting rather than conserving natural resources.

The Sierra Club views as two of the most serious threats to the climate and ecology of the planet recent deforestation and proposals to open the Arctic to mineral exploration. It opposes clear-cutting timber in the national forests, which escalated in the 1980s in the northwestern part of the country despite Sierra Club law suits. It supported reenactment of the Endangered Species Act in 1988 and argues that the numbers of endangered species can only be increased by protecting their habitats and maintaining wildlife refuges. It has opposed opening all wilderness and off-shore lands to exploration for mineral resources and views as one of its top priorities the defense of the Arctic National Wildlife Refuge against oil development.

In addition to its primary concern for preserving wilderness, the Club has taken on many pollution control causes in the 1970s and 1980s. The Washington staff has testified in favor of strengthening the Clean Air and Clean Water Acts, arguing for more-stringent regulations and enforcement. It believes that acid rain is a major threat to the health of streams and forests and has advocated reducing sulfur oxide emissions by 15 million tons in the 1990s. In 1983 and again in 1987 Sierra Club representatives testified to the Senate over amendments to the Resource Conservation and Recovery Act, arguing that the Environmental Protection Agency should stop all land disposal of hazardous wastes, especially in liquid form.

In 1986–87 the Club was active in the campaign to reauthorize the Superfund to clean up toxic waste dumps around the United States, which resulted in the Superfund Amendments and Reauthorization Act. It supported the passage of the Federal Insecticide, Fungicide and Rodenticide Act of 1988, sponsored by an environmental/industrial coalition, but would have preferred that it be stronger.

## TACTICS

The Internal Revenue Service removed the Sierra Club's tax-exempt status in 1969 because it ran newspaper advertisements protesting the possibility of flooding the Grand Canyon. At that time the Sierra Club Foundation and Legal Defense Fund (LDF) were created as legally distinct tax exempt entities, in order to fund research and litigation to preserve natural resources.

The Sierra Club also has a Committee on Political Education (SCOPE), a political action committee, that contributes to individual political candidates for public office on all levels. There is an eight-person committee appointed by the executive committee who select candidates to endorse at the national level. Local chapters may also select their own candidates to support. The Club not only helps to finance, but fields volunteer workers for political campaigns. It urges its own members to run political campaigns based on conservation issues and to become delegates to political parties' annual conventions. It also conducts workshops for volunteers, and issues a *Handbook on Electoral Politics*.

When the Club's lobbying efforts before Congress or the agencies fail, LDF uses the courts by suing the Department of Interior or the Forest Service over many tracts of land the government seeks to develop for private enterprise. It has also used the National Environmental Policy Act to force other agencies, such as the Corps of Engineers, to write environment impact statements about public works projects they propose. It has used the California Environmental Quality Act to force the state government to go through the same kind of exercise for state projects. When the Reagan administration was unwilling to take polluters to court, the LDF stepped up its efforts to sue industry directly for violating the clean air and water acts, under private attorneys general provisions written into those laws.

In addition to its professional lobbyists who are employed in the Washington office, the Sierra Club sends out regular bulletins alerting its membership to legislative and administrative developments of importance to Club policies. Members are urged to write or call their congressional representatives expressing their interest and opinion about the proposals before them. In 1986, the Club felt its grass-roots campaign was crucial in obtaining a favorable outcome to the Superfund fight. In addition to news bulletins and a Washington hotline maintained for members to learn about issues, the *Sierra* magazine, issued bimonthly to all members, discusses major environmental issues in depth.

It publishes books designed to inform the public about a broad range of environmental issues, and *In Brief*, a quarterly newsletter about environmental cases in court. It also sponsors outdoor activities, such as hiking, backpacking, bicycling, and float trips for its members and other outdoor enthusiasts. Some of these outings are service oriented, with Club members performing maintenance services along the trails; some are entirely for pleasure. All minimize human impact on the natural environment.

*FURTHER INFORMATION*

Culhane, Paul J. (1981). *Public Lands Politics*. Baltimore, Md.: Johns Hopkins Press, Resources for the Future.

Fox, Steven (1981). *John Muir and His Legacy: The American Conservation Movement.*
    Boston: Little,Brown.
*Sierra* (various issues, 1987–90). San Francisco: Sierra Club.
Udall, James R. (1989). "Climate Shock." *Sierra*, July-August, pp. 26–33.

## SOCIETY OF AMERICAN FORESTERS (SAF)
5400 Grosvenor Lane
Bethesda, Maryland 20814

### ORGANIZATION AND RESOURCES

The Society of American Foresters (SAF) was founded by Gifford Pinchot in 1900 to represent the interests of the new profession of foresters in the United States. At the end of the 1980s its membership stabilized at approximately 20,000 members who pay $45 a year to belong. SAF is the official accreditation agency for schools of forestry around the nation. Its members include public-sector employees of the Department of Agriculture's Forest Service, as well as employees of state forestry departments and the Department of the Interior; employees from the private sector who work for pulp and paper manufacturers, timber companies, and consultants for small woodlot owners; as well as academics who teach or study in the 47 accredited programs in the United States.

Dues account for about 46 percent of the SAF's revenues; publications and merchandise, 29 percent; conventions, 11 percent; investments, 8 percent; with voluntary contributions making up the difference. SAF spends about 32 percent of its revenues on publishing its journal, 21 percent on administrative expenses; 9 percent on executive expenses, 11 percent on conventions, 5 percent for member services, 10 percent on educating the public, 4 percent on resource policy, and the remainder on public affairs and miscellaneous expenses. At the end of the 1980s, SAF's annual budget was approximately $2.3 million. Usually its revenues exceed its expenses, and it has built up a financial reserve of nearly $3 million.

SAF has an eleven-person elected council, which represents each of several regional associations, and a president elected each year at its annual convention. The executive vice-president is William H. Banzhaf who heads a nine-person staff in the national headquarters in Maryland.

### POLICY CONCERNS

SAF is primarily concerned with the profession of forestry. It has a code of ethics that was first promulgated by the society in 1948 and has since been amended. It generally pledges its members to behave in a professional manner regarding their employers and the public. It is devoted to managing natural resources in a balanced manner in order to derive maximum human use from them. Most of its members derive their income from consumptive use of forests and are primarily concerned with a sustained yield of lumber products from the publicly and privately held forests in the United States. Yet its members obviously enjoy nature and many of them advocate other uses for the national forests, including wildlife habitat and watershed protection.

One major issue in managing the public forests of the United States is that raised by the practice of the Forest Service of selling timber below cost to industry. SAF takes the position that the sale price to timber companies may sometimes be less than the total costs of reforestation, building roads into the area to be timbered, and administrative costs of the sale. These may sometimes be offset by such public benefits as employment, however. SAF seeks to increase efficiency by minimizing timber management costs and controlling road building. It hopes that the Forest Service's Timber Sale Program Information Reporting System (TSPIRS), developed in the 1980s, will increase cost effectiveness.

SAF deplores the precipitous reduction in budgetary resources made available for natural resource management purposes in the federal government during the 1980s. It supports the practice of clear-cutting large areas of forests as a tree regeneration method, but it argues this should only be used under appropriate ecological conditions. SAF argues that forest fires should be controlled or allowed to burn according to the landowners' objectives. It recognizes that some forest fires can regenerate areas and may be appropriate for wilderness as long as provisions are made to protect adjacent property. It advocates harvesting timber killed by fire in opposition to some conservation organizations that prefer to allow the area to regenerate naturally. SAF supports the use of chemicals and biological materials registered with the U.S. Environmental Protection Agency (EPA) to control vegetation and forest pests, depending on the resource management objectives of the owners.

SAF supports discretion for the Forest Service and the Bureau of Land Management to develop plans for forest tracts. It opposes congressional interference with this discretion. It argues some old-growth forests should be preserved for biological diversity, but others should be managed by harvesting old growth for economic purposes. It argues policy positions in the agencies should be filled by nonpartisan career professionals and not political appointees. It argues for tax treatment that will encourage private owners to manage their woodlots in an ecologically responsible manner.

Professional foresters and environmental groups agree on certain issues, such as the threat from global warming and the need to keep healthy stands of trees throughout the earth. SAF is engaged in many international activities whereby they encourage professional management of forests and jungles abroad. It advocates financial support to developing nations to assist them in stopping massive deforestation.

## TACTICS

SAF publishes the *Journal of Forestry* monthly which contains refereed professional articles of interest to foresters. Within its pages debates are conducted regarding major issues in the profession, such as the conservation ethic as espoused by Aldo Leopold in a letter to the editor in the April 1936 volume of the *Journal*.

Once a year a convention is held where panels are organized around such issues as silviculture, estimating board-feet harvests from remote sensing, windbreak technology, and soil management. SAF representatives can and do share their opinions with members of congressional committees on issues such as the implementation of the Federal Land Policy and Management Act. However, their leadership is primarily concerned with improving its communications with the public and its image as an objective, professional group representing a middle ground between the timber producers and the conservation community.

### FURTHER INFORMATION

*Briefings on Federal Forest Policy* (1988). Bethesda, Md.: SAF.
*Journal of Forestry* (February, June, August 1988; January, April, June, July, September, October 1989). Bethesda, Md.: SAF.

## SOCIETY OF THE PLASTICS INDUSTRY (SPI)
1275 K Street, N.W.
Washington, D.C. 20005

### ORGANIZATION AND RESOURCES

In 1937 the new plastics industry formed its own trade association, the Society of the Plastics Industry (SPI). By the end of the 1980s it had grown to an organization of over 2,000 member companies, representing all segments of the plastics industry. It has committees designed to address the problems of resin manufacturers, distributors, machinery manufacturers, plastics processors, and mold makers. Its president is elected by the 55-person board of directors. It has an annual budget of around $15 million, derived half from corporate dues and half from annual meetings and other fund-raising efforts among its members. Dues range from $400 a year for firms doing less than $1.5 million worth of business in plastics to $100,000 for those doing over $800 million worth. This budget supports a national office with 95 staffers in Washington and 4 regional offices for the New England, east, midwest and western regions.

### POLICY CONCERNS

Much of SPI's membership overlaps with that of the American Petroleum Institute* and the Chemical Manufacturers Association,* and SPI shares their concerns about corporate taxes and labor issues. It also seeks to protect its membership from all manner of governmental regulation, and therefore has an interest in most environmental policies. During the debate over the Superfund Amendments and Reauthorization Act of 1986 (SARA) SPI opposed the institution of any kind of community right-to-know law on the grounds it would be excessively expensive for the plastics industry. It also opposed numerous right-to-know laws at the state level on the grounds that these should be preempted by a uniform federal regulation. SPI approved the idea of extending the tax to include industries, especially the waste management industry, other than the petrochemical feedstock industry, because the latter includes the plastics industry. But it opposed setting the total amount of the fund any higher than it had been in the original Superfund because SPI believed the U.S. Environmental Protection Agency (EPA) could not use the funds efficiently.

Under the Clean Air Act (CAA), SPI opposed most definitions proposed by EPA of hazardous air pollutants. Many of the substances that could be regulated under this part of the CAA would affect the plastics industry drastically, and the plastics industry does not believe the costs of regulation would be worth the benefits to society of avoiding toxic releases. SPI generally urges EPA to take its time in setting standards for such substances and to be certain that each one is a threat to public health before doing so. SPI also supports the extension of deadlines for cities to comply with the ozone standards of the CAA because of the costs of controlling hydrocarbons emitted by the plastics industry.

For many years EPA has had under consideration proposals to regulate storm-water runoff from industrial plants in order to protect groundwater and drinking water supplies dependent on groundwater. SPI opposes any such regulation on the grounds that the information it would have to provide the government about potential contaminants from chemicals stored on plant sites would be enormously expensive and would not improve groundwater quality substantially. It was successful, along with other industrial representatives, in preventing EPA from taking action through the Reagan administration and now focuses its attention on stopping Congress from amending the Clean Water Act to force EPA to take action.

SPI opposes any regulation of chlorofluorocarbons (CFCs), which scientists say are eliminating the protective ozone layer in the upper atmosphere. It argues that if such regulations prove necessary, it will take the industry ten years to find suitable replacements for spray foam insulation material, and this time should be allowed before the United States takes unilateral action against CFCs. SPI has supported legislation against ocean dumping by ships of plastic debris that contributes to marine life loss, but it opposes any mandatory degradability requirement for plastic materials.

The plastics industry's raw materials are derived from petroleum and natural gas, and SPI therefore opposes any tax on such fossil fuels, such as a tax on oil imports proposed by some members of Congress to help solve the budget deficit problem and to prevent the United States from becoming too dependent on foreign oil. This was successfully avoided by the oil and plastics industries through the Reagan administrations. SPI also opposes any regulation of the price of natural gas, believing that if the price is allowed to float free in the market this will give industry the greatest incentive to find more supplies. By the end of the 1980s, however, some old gas was still regulated at the wellhead under the Natural Gas Policy Act of 1978. SPI also supports the energy industry in seeking to open all publicly owned lands to oil and gas exploration.

Structural polymers, used by resin manufacturers, are regulated under the Toxic Substances Control Act (TSCA), and SPI has regularly tried to get EPA to differentiate between structural polymers and other new polymers without success. Hence it now focuses on amending TSCA through Congress to achieve the same objective.

SPI opposes any legislation at the state level to force the plastics industry to recycle its containers. It opposes laws that favor glass and metal containers over plastic ones because of their greater recyclability. It also seeks to allay fears about the creation of dioxins from burning plastics and argues to state legislatures that incineration of solid wastes is the logical solution to limited land space for landfills in metropolitan areas. It argues that federal laws that control solid waste disposal should preempt any state initiatives along these lines.

Similarly SPI opposes any state initiatives regulating the transportation of hazardous materials. It argues the national Hazardous Materials Transportation Act is sufficient control for all substances and does not need strengthening. SPI also supports the transportation industry in arguing that maximum loads on trucks should be permitted in all states to minimize transit costs for its products.

## TACTICS

SPI coordinates most of its activities in Washington with the American Petroleum Institute and various chemical manufacturers trade associations. Its membership list overlaps with those groups, and many CEOs in such corporations as Union Carbide testify for all three organizations at the same time. It issues a biweekly *Washington Memo* for its membership which keeps them apprised of legislative and regulatory developments, and regular news releases to the media to keep them informed about SPI's stands on policy issues.

## FURTHER INFORMATION

*Member Services Guide* (1989). Washington, D.C.: SPI.
*Washington Memo* (1989). Washington, D.C.: SPI, April 24, May 8, June 5, June 19.

# SOLAR ENERGY INDUSTRIES ASSOCIATION (SEIA)
1730 North Lynn, Suite 610
Arlington, Virginia 22209

## ORGANIZATION AND RESOURCES

The Solar Energy Industries Association (SEIA) was created in 1974 as a national trade association for the solar industry. It represented at the end of the 1980s more than 300 solar manufacturers, distributors, dealers, installers, and component suppliers. Major energy corporations, such as Mobil Solar Energy and Arco Solar, are involved, as well as General Electric and Du Pont Chemicals. However, small local developers and companies specializing in heat pumps or solar collectors also belong. They pay for membership according to their capital investment and profits. There are 18 state and regional chapters which involve about 900 companies. Its total annual budget is about $300,000.

SEIA is divided into three major technical divisions: photovoltaics, (the technology of producing electricity by solar power), solar thermal power (producing heat for industrial processes), and solar heating and cooling (both active and passive systems for space heating in residential and commercial properties, with emphasis on hot water production). There is a chair and vice-chair for each of the three divisions, as well as some at-large directors, who together constitute a fifteen-person board of directors. The executive director who directs the Arlington, Virginia, office and makes representation to Congress is Scott Sklar. SEIA has a Solar Energy Research and Education Foundation.

### POLICY CONCERNS

During the period from 1981 to 1989, SEIA saw a 70 percent decline in federal budget support for solar research and development, a situation that its members considered to be a disaster for the United States and unfair given continued government support for fossil fuel and nuclear power. SEIA representatives argued consistently before Congress for additional funds beyond those sought by the Reagan administration for the U.S. Department of Energy's (DOE) solar building, thermal power, and photovoltaics programs. They believe that the energy glut of the 1980s is not likely to continue, and the government should begin planning for another energy crisis similar to that in the mid–1970s. They call for the federal government to procure more solar equipment and monitor federal buildings to ensure use of solar technology there.

During the 1970s a solar residential tax credit was initiated to encourage use of solar technology in residential buildings. This program was eliminated by the Reagan administration, and SEIA has consistently urged its reinstatement by Congress. Its representatives argue that nuclear, coal, oil, and natural gas are partially subsidized, and solar power needs equivalent market incentives in order to be able to compete. Federal loan programs such as Fannie Mae and the Federal Housing Administration do allow higher debt-to-loan levels if energy-conserving (including solar) equipment is installed because operating costs should be lower. But SEIA argues these congressional mandates have never been completely implemented by federal agencies. It urges such agencies as the Small Business Administration to encourage use of solar technology through this method.

A third priority for SEIA is to increase the international market for U.S.-manufactured solar equipment. It argues that the trade imbalance could be improved for the United States if the federal government were willing to grant incentives to export U.S. solar technology. It also calls regularly for all federal agencies, especially the U.S. Department of Defense (DOD), to purchase solar energy equipment whenever cost-effective. Since the DOD operates buildings and consumes electricity in some of the most remote parts of the globe, SEIA feels it should be a prime user of solar energy.

It argued before the 100th Congress against taxing solar energy production to help pay for acid rain cleanup if the nuclear industry were to be granted a waiver. SEIA believes that taxes derived from acid rain cleanup should be used partly to pay for solar peak power plants to substitute for fossil fuel–fired ones. It was eager to publicize a presidentially authorized study on the security of the domestic energy industry, as it believes solar energy can make the United States more energy independent in the future. It also supported continuation of the Public Utilities Regulatory Policy Act (PURPA) which forces utilities to buy power that their customers may generate from their own resources, such as wind and solar devices.

## TACTICS

There is a U.S. Export Council for Renewable Energy* to which SEIA belongs. This umbrella group of renewable energy trade associations tries to identify foreign markets where U.S. solar products will do best and provide information to domestic producers. In 1984 Congress passed a law creating the Committee for Renewable Energy Commerce and Trade (CORECT), which SEIA hopes will become more active in the future in helping U.S. firms to enter international markets. It urges Congress to impose protective tariffs against countries that have imposed barriers to importation of U.S. solar products. In the late 1980s, however, several of the major energy corporations, including Exxon, Shell Oil, and Motorola left the solar field. ARCO threatened to sell its solar division in 1989, and analysts in the field speculated that U.S. firms might be cut out if German and Japanese corporations continue to develop the field.

SEIA publishes *SEIA News* eight times a year in order to keep its members informed of developments in government that affect them. It also runs an annual meeting and trade show where members can display their products to others, and developments in the field are discussed.

## FURTHER INFORMATION

*SEIA News* (1989). Arlington, Va.: SEIA, March, April, May.
Wald, Matthew L. (1989). "U.S. Companies Losing Interest in Solar Energy." *The New York Times*, March 7, p.1.

## SOLAR LOBBY
*See* Renew America.

## STATE AND TERRITORIAL AIR POLLUTION PROGRAM ADMINISTRATORS (STAPPA)/ASSOCIATION OF LOCAL AIR POLLUTION CONTROL OFFICIALS (ALAPCO)
444 North Capitol Street, N.W., Suite 306
Washington, D.C. 20001

## ORGANIZATION AND RESOURCES

Each state and many metropolitan areas have an air pollution control agency that manages the local air quality program. The State and Territorial Air Pollution Program Administrators (STAPPA) is the national association of state air quality officials in 53 states and territories of the United States. The Association of

Local Air Pollution Control Officials (ALAPCO) is the national association representing such officials in 150 major metropolitan areas. Formed in 1968 to coordinate activities with each other and with the U.S. Environmental Protection Agency (EPA), STAPPA and ALAPCO are very similar in organization to the Association of State and Interstate Water Pollution Control Administrators.*

To some degree the existence of STAPPA and ALAPCO depend on the Clean Air Act (CAA), passed by Congress in the 1960s and amended drastically in the 1970s. However, some cities had air pollution control officials long before it became a national issue. The CAA nationalized the problem and provided an incentive for the various city administrators to band together to face their mutual problems. There is a common board of governors with nine representatives from STAPPA and seven from ALAPCO. They are elected annually at the annual meeting, as is the president. The executive director is S. William Becker who heads a staff of three in Washington. Together STAPPA and ALAPCO have a modest budget of about $200,000 a year assessed from all its members.

### POLICY CONCERNS

Both STAPPA and ALAPCO advocate greater federal spending on air pollution control. Like their water pollution control counterparts, they opposed the Reagan administration's cuts in spending on air pollution throughout the 1980s, especially the reduction in federal aid to states and cities. They argued before Congress against changes to the CAA that would have reduced the standards for national ambient air quality around the United States. They supported both the prevention of significant deterioration of air quality in clean areas and the improvement of air quality in areas not meeting standards. The EPA under President Reagan greatly extended the use of "bubbles" to allow new sources of pollution to offset their emissions by reducing some old sources in the same area. STAPPA and ALAPCO both opposed this offset policy when it had the effect of allowing new sources to be built without the best available control technology, on the grounds that this policy sets back the national goal of cleaner air.

Both STAPPA and ALAPCO support federal deadlines for achieving ambient air quality standards in nonattainment areas, but they believe EPA should provide extensions for areas such as Los Angeles that experience severe problems in meeting those standards. They also argue that the lowest achievable emission rate is unrealistic and should be dropped even in nonattainment areas. They also believe that EPA's method of assigning increments of pollution admissible in clean areas is too complex and should be simplified. For ozone control specifically, STAPPA/ALAPCO's preferred strategy is to abandon the complex method of modeling and predicting emissions and assigning reduction percentages to specific sources. Instead, they would substitute a mandated technology approach, similar to that under the Clean Water Act, under which all new sources would have to install the best available control technology rather than having each source treated individually and through offsets sometimes avoid any regulation.

The primary method for controlling air pollution is the state implementation plan for which states have primary responsibility. STAPPA would like to increase all states autonomy over their plans and their ability to change plans without having to prove to EPA that the plans will work. STAPPA recognizes that the interstate nature of long-range transported air pollution which causes acid deposition will require federal attention. It advocates amending the CAA to increase control of sulfur oxides by from 8 to 10 million tons, and it hopes federal funds will be made available for this purpose.

STAPPA and ALAPCO both are concerned about hazardous air pollutants and the length of time it has taken EPA to identify them and begin to create standards for their emissions. Under EPA's system of risk assessment in the 1980s, EPA could determine that the national risk is insufficient to warrant control of certain substances that in some local areas pose major risks to individuals. State and local officials, therefore, argue that Congress should simplify and accelerate the process for listing hazardous air compounds by grouping classes of toxics and creating generic standards.

## TACTICS

Like their counterparts in water pollution control, STAPPA and ALAPCO both seek an expanded federal role in funding pollution control efforts by the states and at the same time greater discretion for state agencies. They combine forces with pollution control interest groups when EPA's budget is being attacked or other efforts made to reduce the pollution control program. As government officials, they are often called upon by EPA and congressional committees to give expert opinions about how the program can be effectively carried out. STAPPA/ALAPCO publishes *Washington Update* monthly for its members as well as specific position papers on the CAA.

## FURTHER INFORMATION

*STAPPA's Recommendation for Revising the Clean Air Act* (1987). Washington, D.C.: STAPPA.

U.S. Congress. House Committee on Energy and Commerce (1987). *Hearings on Oversight of Clean Air Act.* Washington, D.C: Government Printing Office.

U.S. Congress. Senate Committee on Environment and Public Works (1987). *Hearing on S. 1384, Amendments to Clean Air Act.* Washington, D.C.: Government Printing Office.

*Washington Update* (1989). Washington, D.C.: STAPPA and ALAPCO.

# T

------------------------ / ------------------------

**TECHNICAL INFORMATION PROJECT**
*See* Resource Policy Institute.

**TRIAL LAWYERS FOR PUBLIC JUSTICE (TLPJ)**
2000 P Street, N.W., Suite 611
Washington, D.C. 20036

*ORGANIZATION AND RESOURCES*

In 1982, a group of trial lawyers, those who litigate for plaintiffs involved in personal injury law suits, banded together to form the Trial Lawyers for Public Justice (TLPJ). They included such consumer advocates as Ralph Nader and Joan Claybrook of Public Citizen, as well as famous personal injury lawyers such as Phil Corboy of Chicago. TLPJ merged the legal talents of some prominent trial lawyers with the goals of some public interest organizations, such as the Environmental Defense Fund* and the Natural Resources Defense Council.* It is dedicated to recovering monetary damages from both business and government for individual victims of misconduct.

In the late 1980s TLPJ had about 500 members, both firms and individual trial lawyers. Individual sponsoring attorneys pay $1,000 a year to belong, although law students and attorneys in practice fewer than five years can pay only $100 a year. Patrons pay $10,000 or more and include foundations such as McIntosh, Rockefeller, and Playboy, as well as individual attorneys. Lifetime members pay $5,000. One goal of the organization is to become self-supporting with lawyers' fees recovered in litigation covering all its costs, as well as being able to make donations to other public-interest law firms.

Revenues are nearly $200,000 yearly, 80 percent of which comes from membership dues, and 8 percent from grants and contributions and from attorneys' fees. The remainder comes from miscellaneous sources. Expenses amount to nearly $300,000, 56 percent of which are salaries; other categories of expenses included, rent, telephones, travel, printing, copying, and depositions. Most of these expenses go toward litigation, although a small amount is used for representation before Congress. The shortfall is made up by loans from foundations which are repayable usually only in the event that the case is won and expenses are recovered from the opponents through attorneys' fees.

There is a forty-six person board of directors. Supporters contribute to the Citizens Legal Clinic, a tax-exempt charitable membership foundation which operates the TLPJ. The board holds quarterly meetings to discuss which cases to take and what the policies of the association should be. There is a staff of eleven in Washington headed by Anthony Roisman, executive director, which administers the litigation strategy of the firm. Individual members, however, also donate their time and expertise to particular cases around the country.

## POLICY CONCERNS

In order to be accepted by TLPJ, a case must be approved by the litigation approval committee. The criteria for acceptance are three: it should have a far-reaching effect on public policy and set precedents for similar cases, it should have potential for large monetary damage awards, and it should involve unique legal issues that demonstrate creative use of law for the public good.

There are four major types of cases that TLPJ has been involved in to date: toxic torts, whistleblower, civil rights, and consumer rights. Toxic torts include cases in which groups of people argue they have suffered health impacts from exposure to hazardous chemicals in drinking water or from being sprayed or otherwise exposed to chemicals. The usual defendants in such cases are chemical corporations, although the U.S. Environmental Protection Agency (EPA) has also been sued for not controlling the environment properly. Consumer rights are also emphasized through tort suits against manufacturers of defective products, auto manufacturers for refusing to put airbags in cars, and insurance companies for raising rates and refusing to insure certain types of clients, such as day-care centers. TLPJ also attempts to protect the rights of whistleblowers, workers who are harassed by their employer (either government or industry) for speaking out about safety problems that affect the public. Beyond public health and safety issues, TLPJ also seeks to force the government to implement civil rights laws, such as the regulation that women athletes should not be discriminated against by having fewer resources spent by educational institutions on their sports.

## TACTICS

Although the primary strategy of TLPJ is to litigate and force wrong-doers to pay for their actions and thus prevent similar actions in the future, its staff also lobbies for laws that will reduce personal injuries. Representatives testified for keeping the common law of tort to compensate victims of chemical contamination during CERCLA hearings in 1983. They also argued for citizen intervention in nuclear licensing procedures in 1986. TLPJ advocates clauses in environmental laws that provide for private attorney general (citizen action) suits, for class action suits, and for strict liability rules. It also seeks to keep open the possibility of seeking common-law remedies for personal injuries caused by nuclear power plants, toxic chemical plants and dumps, and any other business or government actions that threaten the public or private health. One of its major priorities is to prevent the insurance industry from convincing state legislatures to pass laws restricting the awards that juries may give to personal injury victims.

Trial Lawyers publishes the *TLPJ Newsletter* quarterly. It also published a five-year report including its activities from 1982 through 1986.

### FURTHER INFORMATION

*Five Year Report: 1982–1986* (1987). Washington, D.C.: TLPJ.
*TLPJ Newsletter* (1986). Washington, D.C.: TLPJ, September.

## TROUT UNLIMITED (TU)
501 Church Street, N.E.
Vienna, Virginia 22180

### ORGANIZATION AND RESOURCES

In 1959, 15 anglers with a common interest in sportfishing for cold water fish, such as trout and salmon met in Michigan to form a club. Since that time Trout Unlimited (TU) has grown to over 50,000 individual members in 400 chapters and 25 state councils around the United States. In addition there are affiliated organizations in New Zealand, Canada, and Japan that claim 30,000 members.

Dues are $20 a year, and most of TU's budget of $1.7 million comes from these dues as well as from fund-raising on the part of local chapters. In addition, a few corporate entities such as the Atlantic Richfield, Coors Brewery, and Marshall Field corporations belong, and some funds come from foundation grants. It is a nonprofit conservation organization with tax-exempt status from the IRS. The board of 100 directors is elected at the annual meeting and has representatives from five regions as well as active individual members elected at large. Policy is developed by the board in cooperation with 20 professional staff members in the Washington headquarters, headed by Robert Herbst, executive director.

### POLICY CONCERNS

Officers and members of TU are primarily concerned about maintaining fish habitat in the United States for sport fishermen. In so doing, they undertake projects in their local chapters to clean up streams and rivers that have become polluted and choked with debris. At both state and federal levels, their representatives advocate keeping public lands, such as national parks and forests, open to sport fishing and stocking waterways with salmon and trout, working closely with the Department of Interior's Fish and Wildlife Service and state departments of natural resources.

TU also attempts to influence individual water project managers, including the Corps of Engineers in the east and the Department of Interior's Bureau of Reclamation to minimize their projects' impact on fishlife, and ameliorate negative impacts by building fish ladders around dams in order to facilitate fish migration. They also argue for strict enforcement of clean water laws designed to reduce pollution of waterways. One major concern is the lack of control on nonpoint sources of chemical contamination from pesticides and fertilizers, produced by the agriculture and silviculture industries, which contribute to the poisoning of streams. Trout Unlimited also works with the Department of Agriculture's Soil Conservation Service to minimize loss of topsoil through runoff and siltation.

In July 1986, a delegation of TU officers and members traveled to the Soviet Union to negotiate a bilateral agreement whereby the Russian Society of Hunters and Fishermen agreed to facilitate opportunities for Americans to hunt and fish there. It was not sponsored by the U.S. government, although negotiators also addressed increasing export of U.S. sporting goods to the Soviet Union.

## TACTICS

TU's Washington staff keeps abreast of developments in the Clean Water Act and many natural resources laws, such as the Federal Land Policy and Management Act, Endangered Species, Wild and Scenic Rivers, and Wilderness Preservation acts. Trout Unlimited publishes a quarterly magazine for its membership describing fishing techniques, areas for outdoor recreation, and policy developments that affect fishlife. Through a conservation network of active members who receive public policy alerts, it attempts to influence individual congressional votes. It coordinates its activities with other hunting, fishing, and conservation groups, such as the Sport Fisherman Institute. Some state councils also issue newsletters to their membership alerting them to state policy affecting fisheries in their areas. Local chapters hold monthly meetings at which matters of local concern to fishermen are discussed.

## FURTHER INFORMATION

*Trout* (1988). Bend, Oregon: TU, Winter.

# U

## UNION OF CONCERNED SCIENTISTS (UCS)
26 Church Street
Cambridge, Massachusetts 02238

### ORGANIZATION AND RESOURCES

In 1969 a group of Massachusetts Institute of Technology (MIT) faculty and students formed the Union of Concerned Scientists (UCS), which now has a contributing membership of about 100,000 scientists and a 32-person staff in Cambridge and Washington. In the late 1980s it had both revenues and expenditures of approximately $3.5 million, over twice its funding level of $1.5 million in 1980. About 70 percent of its revenues came from individual donations, and the remainder from sales of publications and grants. It is a nonprofit corporation with 501(c)(3) tax exempt status from IRS.

Professor Henry W. Kendall, a high-energy physicist at MIT, was one of the founding members and has served as chair of the board since 1973. There are six other members, chosen by Dr. Kendall and past board members. Howard C. Ris, Jr., has served as executive director since 1984.

### POLICY CONCERNS

Originally the Union was dedicated entirely to the principle of nuclear arms reduction and stabilization of national security policy. It devotes approximately 75 percent of its resources to promoting nuclear arms control. Since 1983, the Union has been critical of the Strategic Defense Initiative (SDI or Star Wars) advocated by the Reagan administration, publishing *The Fallacy of Star Wars* in 1984, and *The Empty Promise: The Growing Case Against Star Wars* in 1986. It achieved few successes in the early 1980s, but argued before Congress in

1986 to extend a moratorium on antisatellite weapons and reduce Star Wars funding, both of which passed.

The other 25 percent of its resources are devoted to criticism of the nuclear power industry. UCS argues that the United States should phase out its current generation of nuclear plants which it does not consider safe. Safe use of nuclear power will require new reactor and safety system designs and vastly improved management and regulatory supervision. Scientists from UCS have become the chief alternative source of information on nuclear power issues to the government. They have appeared on numerous news and discussion shows such as ABC's Nightline to argue that the Nuclear Regulatory Commission (NRC) is not an effective regulatory force over the nuclear industry.

UCS's legislative counsel testified to the Senate Committee on Energy in 1986 against the idea of standardizing nuclear plants in the United States because it would lead to speedier licensing. It is the Union's policy position that all plants should be considered separately for safety. It argued unsuccessfully before the NRC that it should shut down eight reactors similar in design to the reactor involved in the accident at Three Mile Island in 1979. It also initiated a lawsuit against NRC's ruling that safety benefits must be balanced against costs of any safety improvements. It advocates changing the Price-Anderson Act to increase industry liability for accidents and to overhaul the NRC, creating an independent safety board more receptive to intervenors' demands for greater safety measures.

## TACTICS

UCS has many members around the United States in various universities, and it has recruited a Scientists' Action Network of about 8,000 to educate the public and media in their areas about the hazardous nature of the nuclear arms race.

UCS publishes a quarterly report to its members, entitled *Nucleus*, informing them about the major public policy debates in Washington about nuclear arms control and nuclear power safety. It also provides briefing papers for its members' use in their public education activities.

## FURTHER INFORMATION

*Annual Report* (1988). Washington, D.C.: Union of Concerned Scientists.
Ford, Daniel. (1981). *Three Mile Island: Three Minutes to Meltdown.* New York: Penguin Books.
Kendall, Henry, and Steven Nadis, eds. (1980). *Energy Strategies: Toward a Solar Future.* New York: Ballinger.
*Nucleus* (vol. 8 no. 4, 1987; vol. 9, no. 4, 1988; vol. 10 no. 4, 1989). Washington, D.C.: UCS.


## UNITED AUTO WORKERS (UAW)
8000 East Jefferson
Detroit, Michigan 48214

## ORGANIZATION AND RESOURCES

The United Auto Workers (UAW) was founded in 1935 by Walter Reuther in order to represent workers in the burgeoning automobile industry. Unlike the AFL-CIO,* it was organized on an industry, not a craft, basis and has tended to be a militant organization. In the late 1980s it had about 2 million members, although membership has dropped off in all unions in recent years. During its early years it was successful in obtaining closed shops in most of the auto manufacturing industry. However, with the advent of Japanese manufacturing plants in the United States, there are some nonunion shops in this formerly highly unionized industry.

## POLICY CONCERNS

The UAW takes radical stances regarding universal health insurance for all workers, wage maintenance, and protection of U.S. industry from foreign competition. Its leadership also argues for a safe work environment for its own members and was instrumental in passing the Occupational Safety and Health Act. It also advocates worker and community right-to-know laws about dangerous chemicals used and stored in industrial plants.

However, the auto workers' union has stood with the auto industry consistently in resisting increased strictness concerning auto emissions in the hope of keeping new car prices down and sales up in order to save jobs in the industry. At the same time the UAW Conservation Department has developed an ''Adopt-A-Dump'' program to assist communities where leaking hazardous waste sites are located. Working-class residential areas have typically been located near manufacturing plants where industrial wastes were for many years disposed of without regard for their impact on nearby water tables and homes.

## TACTICS

The UAW frequently allies itself with the automotive manufacturers when the issue is one of amending the CAA to make emission controls stricter. It also on occasion allies itself with the environmental movement when it perceives the issue as affecting worker health. It publishes *Solidarity* monthly for its membership, making them aware of legislative proposals that affect labor/management relations and labor negotiations in the auto industry around the United States.

## U.S. ASSOCIATION FOR THE CLUB OF ROME
1325 G Street, N.W. Suite 1003
Washington, D.C. 20005

## ORGANIZATION AND RESOURCES

In 1968 Dr. Aurelio Peccei founded the Club of Rome dedicated to stimulating debate on global problems such as population growth, consumption of natural resources, and pollution control. This Club is small and informal, consisting of only from 80 to 100 members from 20 to 30 different countries. This informal network of people includes industrialists, educators, humanists, scientists, and civil servants. It sponsors future-oriented research and conferences devoted to understanding the interdependence of global systems.

The U.S. Association for the Club of Rome was founded in 1976 by a group of concerned Americans committed to "building a humane and sustainable future for all residents of spaceship earth." About 215 people belong and nominate and elect new members who pay $100 a year dues. It has a budget of $30,000 derived half from membership dues and half from other fund-raising. One professional part-time employee, Linda Kovan, is the executive administrator in Washington. There is a elected executive board of 7 members, including Donald R. Lesh, executive director of Global Tomorrow Coalition,* and the chair, John E. Fobes, former Deputy Director General of UNESCO.

*POLICY CONCERNS*

The Club of Rome sponsored a series of research reports on future problems from 1968 to 1982. It emphasizes that its members believe in varied ideologies and do not necessarily subscribe to the conclusions of all of its reports. The first and most famous was commissioned from the Massachusetts Institute of Technology under the direction of Dr. Dennis L. Meadows, *Limits to Growth*, which argued that those limits would be reached on earth in the next 100 years. The authors argued for changes in public policy and individual behavior in order to create a sustainable economy not dependent on continual growth.

Since then it has sponsored a number of other studies focusing on some of the hazards involved in uncontrolled global growth, including problems of inequality in the distribution of the world's resources, the need to educate the world's population with values and skills required in the future, problems of world capital formation, energy consumption, conversion and conservation, and finally microelectronics and other technical innovations that are changing lifestyles around the globe.

USACOR issues a newsletter to its membership about five times a year, informing them about developments in global issues: renewable energy, rapid urban growth, food resources, and population growth.

*FURTHER INFORMATION*

Meadows, Dennis, et al. (1974). *Dynamics of Growth in a Finite World*. Cambridge, Mass.: Wright-Allen Press.
Meadows, Donella, and Dennis Meadows (1972). *The Limits to Growth*. New York: Universe Books.

**U.S. CHAMBER OF COMMERCE**
1615 H Street, N.W.
Washington, D.C. 20062

## HISTORY AND DEVELOPMENT

Like the National Association of Manufacturers (NAM),* the U.S. Chamber of Commerce has had a lengthy history of primarily conservative politics. Founded in 1912 at the suggestion of President Taft, it originally opposed labor unions, welfare measures, and most environmental legislation, but its primary focus was on defending the business community from taxation at the state, local, or federal level.

Through the 1950s, it was successful in obtaining most of the policies it wanted from the U.S. government, not because of any expertise in lobbying but because the general political climate tended to favor business, and there was little opposition to its point of view. Not all businesses agreed about policies affecting them, as shown in the classic study about business lobbying over the protective tariff (Bauer, Pool, and Dexter, 1972). Peak associations such as the Chamber did not always form a united front because of internal divisions. In the late 1960s, however, the business community began to take a more militant stand, believing that it needed to counter the actions of newly emerging public interest groups, such as consumers and environmentalists (Wilson, 1981).

## ORGANIZATION AND RESOURCES

The Chamber of Commerce now has 180,000 member companies, ranging in size from small local companies with fewer than 100 employees to all the Fortune 500. There are more than 2,500 local, state, and regional chambers; more than 1,000 trade and professional associations also belong. Its budget of over $60 million comes from dues ranging from $100 to.01 percent of invested capital for the largest members. Thus it has 10 times the number of members and nearly 5 times as much money as the NAM.

It has a board of directors of 65 people primarily representing the smaller members, but much of its budget is dependent on the large national and international corporations that belong. It employs 300 staffers in Washington and an additional 200 throughout the rest of the United States in various regional offices. Its policies are formulated by 30 standing committees, composed of officials from its membership. Because of its tremendous size, the Chamber has a more difficult job even than the NAM of coordinating policy goals for its diverse membership.

## POLICY CONCERNS

The Chamber considers itself to be the official voice of business, free enterprise, and a general proponent for relaxing excessive government regulation of business. Its primary focus is on fiscal matters: reducing the corporate income tax and not increasing the minimum wage. However, it also takes stands on particular environmental issues.

Representatives from the Chamber have testified on amendments to the Resource Conservation and Recovery Act (RCRA) frequently, arguing that regulation of small generators of hazardous wastes is unfair. Nevertheless the law was changed in 1987, defining small generators as those producing less than 100 kilograms of hazardous waste a month rather than 1,000 kilograms. The Chamber has also argued that the limits and deadlines set by the U.S. Environmental Protection Agency (EPA) for RCRA are unrealistic and not worth the costs to business.

The Chamber also opposed the 1986 amendments to refund the Comprehensive Environmental Response, Compensation, and Liability Act (CERCLA, or Superfund) on the grounds they were extreme, excessive, and arbitrary. It argued that the issue of leaking toxic dumps needed more study and analysis before any action should be taken. It also argued strenuously against strict, joint, and several liability for users and operators of abandoned dumps.

The Chamber also opposes any action that would raise the cost of energy to its members. It joined the oil industry initiative to eliminate the windfall profits tax on crude oil in the 100th Congress. It also testifies against an oil import duty along with the petrochemical industry and some consumer groups on the grounds that it would increase the price and hurt the economy generally. It also advocates opening up all federally owned lands to exploration for oil and other minerals in order to free the United States from dependence on foreign supplies.

Through the 1980s, Chamber representatives testified to the House and Senate against legislating about acid rain. They argued that all the evidence is not yet in and there is no need to regulate sulfur oxides any more strictly than they are at present and that additional reductions would increase the costs of energy beyond what business could afford. They also tried to delay the EPA's definition of hazardous air pollutants, and argued for the need to prove that the benefits outweigh the costs of each regulation.

The Chamber advocates the development of all sources of energy, including nuclear power. Representatives argue that the United States needs to standardize nuclear plant design in order to facilitate licensing and get more plants on-line quickly in order to bring down the price of electricity.

## TACTICS

Like the NAM, the Chamber does not endorse parties, but it contributes heavily to the campaign chests of individual politicians. It originally concentrated on Republican politicians in the early twentieth century, but tended in the 1980s to contribute heavily to most incumbents' campaigns, regardless of party. The Chamber, like other business groups, is constantly solicited for funds and has easy access to most influential members of Congress. The Federal Election Campaign Law limited the amounts that can be contributed by any one group, which simply led to the proliferation of political action committees (PACs).

Individual corporations increased their presence in Washington tremendously in the 1980s, and the Chamber as well as smaller trade associations cannot compete with them on individual issues. It does play a role in coordinating business pressure on Congress on many issues as does the NAM. While the

NAM focuses on major corporate problems, the Chamber emphasizes the needs of smaller businesses. Because of the numbers of its members it can launch a major grass-roots lobbying effort from around the country on such issues as opposition to an import tax on oil. It produces a yearly *Congressional Handbook* and directory of members of Congress for use by its members in their lobbying activities. On most economic issues the business community is united against workers, consumers, or environmental groups. However, the diversity of membership of the Chamber does create coordination problems for the leadership in some policy areas.

In addition to lobbying Congress, the Chamber also focuses on improving its media image, seeking a positive image in the press and in the public. The American people's skepticism about the intentions of business and the morality of major corporate executives has grown in the era of corporate buyouts. The Chamber has stepped up its efforts to communicate at the local level to convince the residents there that the business community represents the best interest of every town and city in America. It publishes the monthly *Nation's Business*, which has a circulation of 860,000. It produces the "Nation's Business Today," a radio news program for business, "Ask Washington," a daily national television program, and "It's Your Business," a weekly TV debate program.

### FURTHER INFORMATION

*Annual Report* (1989). Washington, D.C.: U.S. Chamber of Commerce.

Bauer, Raymond, Ithiel de Sola Poole, and Raymond Dexter (1972). *American Business and Public Policy.* 2d ed. New York: Aldine-Atherton.

Vogel, David (1989). *Fluctuating Fortunes.* New York: Basic Books.

Wilson, Graham K. (1981). *Interest Groups in the United States.* Oxford, Eng.: Clarendon Press.

## U.S. CONFERENCE OF MAYORS (USCM)
1620 I Street, N.W.
Washington, D.C. 20006

### ORGANIZATION AND RESOURCES

The U.S. Conference of Mayors (USCM) was founded in 1932 in the midst of the most important depression to occur in the United States by mayors who felt the need to band together to obtain federal assistance for their fiscally stressed jurisdictions. In the beginning its leadership focused on obtaining welfare programs passed by the New Deal and in obtaining federal assistance for low-cost housing for the poor in cities. In the late 1980s it included 800 mayors of cities with populations of over 30,000 in the United States. Dues are assessed in proportion to the population of each city and produce $4 million annually. A president is elected at each annual conference along with an advisory board of between 15 and 23 members. It has an executive director, J. Thomas Cochran, who heads a staff of 36 in Washington.

## POLICY CONCERNS

In the 1980s the USCM was concerned with a number of issues having to do with the environment. Chief among these was concern over the disposal of solid wastes, especially hazardous wastes. Many metropolitan areas are running out of space for landfills, and in all American cities it is becoming more expensive to dispose of the daily collection of garbage generated by their residents. The mayors supported passage of the Resource Conservation and Recovery Act (RCRA) in 1976, and in the 1980s they testified in favor of increasing controls over hazardous wastes. USCM also argues that cities should not be held responsible for the landfills they inherit, but that the federal government needs to play a role in helping to clean up these dumps. It also argues that cities and other local governments should play a role in determining where new hazardous waste treatment facilities are to be placed and what kinds of solutions should be adopted for the lack of space for solid waste disposal. Some cities have begun to turn to resource recovery plants to solve their garbage problems, and USCM has called on Congress to consult municipal governments in regulating such facilities.

USCM also supported the Superfund Amendments and Reauthorization Act (SARA) of 1986, arguing that the federal government needed to refund Superfund at higher levels than originally set in 1980. It argued for oil spill coverage in SARA, but this was deleted by Congress. The Conference was successful in having written into SARA protection for municipal aquifers and community right-to-know about chemical substances stored in their jurisdictions. It also succeeded in having municipal owners of abandoned dumps excused from liability in all but negligence cases. The Conference of Mayors also argues for local authority to regulate transportation of hazardous substances through their jurisdictions and for localities to play a role in designating which sites should be put on the national priority list to be cleaned up.

Since passage of the Water Pollution Control Act of 1956, USCM has supported the effort to clean up United States waterways. It regularly testified to increase the federal component of funding for publicly owned sewage treatment plants through the 1970s and supported Congress's override of President Reagan's veto of the Clean Water Act amendments in 1987. The mayors argued that the impact of their efforts to improve the quality of surface water by increasing sewage treatment has been reduced because of nonpoint sources such as agricultural and urban runoff, and the new law mandates attention to nonpoint sources. The Conference, however, opposes forcing cities to apply for a discharge permit for every stormwater drainage facility.

The Clean Air Act (CAA) set a December 1987 deadline for all cities that failed to meet national ambient air quality standards. The Conference of Mayors argued for extension of this deadline throughout the 1980s on the grounds that the proposed sanction, withdrawal of federal funds for sewage treatment plants and highways, would only set back cities in desperate need of federal money.

The deadline was extended by administrative decision as arguments over amending the CAA continued in Congress. The mayors also argued that federal decisions about developing gas and oil in federal waters in the outer continental shelf also affect air quality in coastal cities. Yet the states and localities are not permitted any discretion over such decisions, and USCM believes this should be changed. The mayors advocate finding a remedy for the acid rain problem without penalizing regions that have already controlled their sulfur emissions or hurting the economies of any cities. They advocate eliminating lead from gasoline in order to reduce the impact on city residents' health and encouraging EPA to speed up the process for establishing limits for toxic emissions.

## TACTICS

The Conference of Mayors by definition includes among its members some of the more powerful politicians in the United States. These mayors frequently testify before Congress and use their influence with their fellow party members to influence legislative decisions affecting cities. They visit Washington many times each year in addition to their annual conference and are always available to advise appropriate committees in formulating policies. *The Mayor*, a semimonthly publication, is sent to all members to keep them informed of developments at the federal level.

## FURTHER INFORMATION

*Solving Urban Environmental Problems* (1988). Washington, D.C.: USCM.

## U.S. COUNCIL FOR ENERGY AWARENESS (USCEA)
1735 I Street, N.W. Suite 500
Washington, D.C. 20006

## ORGANIZATION AND RESOURCES

The U.S. Committee for Energy Awareness was formed in 1979 by representatives of the nuclear industry in order to counter the bad publicity it received from the Three Mile Island nuclear plant accident. During the 1970s nuclear power, which had been predicted to produce 20 percent of the electricity in the United States by 1990, went into decline partially as a result of criticisms made about it by such groups as Public Citizen* and the Union of Concerned Scientists.* The nuclear industry felt it needed to consolidate its opposition to such groups. The USCA changed its name to the U.S. Council for Energy Awareness (USCEA) in 1987 when it absorbed the Atomic Industrial Forum, an independent pronuclear lobby.

The USCEA consists of approximately 380 corporations that either produce electricity with nuclear power or are involved in the production of reactors or other supplies for the nuclear industry, such as Bechtel, Westinghouse, and General Electric. It has an annual budget of about $21 million, all of which is derived from contributions of its corporate members. All donations are tax deductible as USCEA is a nonprofit educational organization. Harold B. Finger is president and director of a 70-person staff in Washington; he responds to a governing board of representatives of the member organizations.

## POLICY CONCERNS

USCEA has a single purpose: to promote the revitalization of the nuclear power industry in the United States which dropped off sharply in the 1970s as utilities reduced their orders for new plants. Its representatives argue that the United States is becoming dangerously dependent on imported oil as it was in the mid–1970s when the energy crisis occurred. It argues that America has an abundant supply of both coal and uranium and these two sources of energy need to be utilized more to produce electricity which can replace other sources of residential and commercial heat, as well as fuels for industrial processes.

USCEA argues that the decline in the nuclear industry has been due to hysterical arguments of a few individuals, such as Ralph Nader and Jane Fonda. It estimates the electricity demands of the American population to be much greater than those made by conservation organizations and argues that U.S. utilities need to begin a construction program now if the needs of the twenty-first century are to be met. It deplores the cancellation of many nuclear plants in the 1980s and argues that these have come about because of over-regulation and public fears that have prevented new sites from being selected. It points out that many other industrial nations are more dependent on nuclear power than the United States.

USCEA argues that the problems of nuclear waste disposal are merely political, not technical, and that we could be glassifying and storing our high level and low level wastes in deep deposits in the earth now rather than keeping them in temporary water-cooled storage facilities. It denigrates the idea that it will be costly to deactivate nuclear plants as they go out of use and argues that the economic and environmental costs of producing electricity by other means are greater. During the late 1980s discussion of global warming caused by increased levels of carbon dioxide in the atmosphere, USCEA emphasized the need to substitute nuclear plants for coal- and oil-fired burners, which add to the acid rain problem as well as carbon dioxide buildup.

## TACTICS

USCEA does little direct lobbying with Congress. Rather, its focus is on educating the public to its point of view regarding nuclear power and U.S. vulnerability to foreign oil supplies. It spends most of its budget running major advertising campaigns in the press, on TV, and on radio. It also trains speakers to talk at school and civic group meetings and produces video programs explaining how safe, practical, and necessary nuclear power is for a healthy industrial economy.

## FURTHER INFORMATION

*Energy and the Greenhouse Effect* (1989). Washington, D.C.: USCEA.

*Energy Independence* (1985). Washington, D.C.: USCEA.
Griffin, Melanie (1986). "Setting the Record Straight." *Sierra*, March-April, p. 26–28.
Meadows, Donella (1987). "The Nuclear Goliath Will Eventually Trip over Its Own
    Lies." *Valley News*, White River Junction, Vt., June 20, p. 1

## U.S. EXPORT COUNCIL FOR RENEWABLE ENERGY (US ECRE)
P.O. Box 10095
Arlington, Virginia 22210–9998

### ORGANIZATION AND RESOURCES

Eight U.S. renewable energy associations banded together in 1983 to form
the U. S. Export Council for Renewable Energy (US ECRE) in order to lobby
more effectively for government support for exporting their products. The eight
associations are American Wind Energy, National Hydropower, National Wood
Energy, Renewable Fuels, Renewable Energy Institute, Solar Energy Industries
Association,* Volunteers in Technical Assistance, and Wood Heating Alliance;
all contribute modest amounts to US ECRE's support. It maintains a small office
in Arlington, Virginia, under the direction of Scott Sklar, executive director.

### POLICY CONCERNS

US ECRE argues that the renewable energy industry is a high-technology
industry that the government ought to be interested in promoting abroad. It was
successful in getting a law passed by the 98th Congress which created the
Committee on Renewable Energy Commerce and Trade (CORECT), an interagency group chaired by the Department of Energy and including the Department
of Commerce. It has worked to promote exports of alcohol fuels, biomass,
cogeneration, hydropower, passive solar, photovoltaics, solar thermal, wind,
and wood energy technologies. These sources of energy, its representatives
argue, should be especially useful to developing nations and helpful to the United
States in improving its balance of trade.

In the 1980s, however, the renewable energy industry experienced reductions
in tax incentives for its technology, while nonrenewable energy industries, such
as oil, have not been equally burdened. The federal government has also cut
back on research and development moneys spent to promote renewable resources,
partly because of the increased availability of conventional fuels and their subsequent lowered prices.

US ECRE has conducted surveys of market opportunities in areas such as
Greece, India, the Philippines, Guatemala, Jamaica, and Barbados where the
need for energy is great and the potential for utilizing solar sources is high. It
argues that the developing world affords an immense potential market, since 75
percent of the world's population does not have access to electricity for in-home
use. However, the U.S. renewable energy industry will not be able to take
advantage of this market unless it is able to expand in the United States through

increased government funding for research. Despite such arguments, however, federal funding for renewable energy continued to decline in the 1980s.

## TACTICS

US ECRE is tiny in comparison to any one of the fossil fuel organizations. It uses officers in its constituent organizations whenever possible just as the larger trade associations do, but they do not have a large presence in Washington. US ECRE also allies itself with environmental groups whenever possible to promote renewable resources, although it does not join them in criticizing fossil fuels and nuclear technologies.

## FURTHER INFORMATION

McFarland, Andrew (1984). "Energy Lobbies." *Annual Review of Energy* 9: 501–527.
Rosenbaum, Walter A. (1987). *Energy, Politics, and Public Policy.* 2d ed. Washington, D.C.: Congressional Quarterly Press.
Sklar, Scott (1987). "Testimony before the House Science Space and Technology Committee." US ECRE. Washington, D.C., July.
Stobaugh, Robert, and Daniel Yergin, eds. (1983). *Energy Future.* 3d ed. New York: Vintage Press.

# W

————————————— / —————————————

## WATER AND WASTEWATER EQUIPMENT MANUFACTURERS ASSOCIATION (WWEMA)
P.O. Box 17402, Dulles International Airport
Washington, D.C.20014

*ORGANIZATION AND RESOURCES*

Corporations that manufacture equipment and chemicals for treating water and wastewater founded their own trade association in 1908 under the name Water Works Manufacturers Association. Since changing its name to the Water and Wastewater Equipment Manufacturers Association (WWEMA), it has grown to include eighty-five firms. There is a board of directors of eighteen people selected by member ballot who direct policy for the association. WWEMA has an annual budget of about $250,000, derived primarily from corporate dues that depend upon the volume of business each company does in a given year.

*POLICY CONCERNS*

WWEMA, as do other trade associations whose members are in the pollution control business, depends partially for its continued existence and prosperity on government policy, especially the Clean Water Act (CWA) and the Safe Drinking Water Act (SDWA). It has supported both pieces of legislation since their inception and regularly testifies about amendments to both laws. It has two interests: to increase its business, much of which is linked to government programs, and to decrease government regulation of its business. These two goals place WWEMA in an ambiguous position vis-à-vis federal and state governments.

WWEMA consistently argues in favor of increased federal spending for construction grants under the CWA. Under this program Congress has provided some assistance to local governments to construct sewage treatment plants since the 1950s. Through the 1970s, the federal contribution increased, but in the Reagan administration this trend was reversed, and state and local governments had to assume more responsibility for providing this essential public service. In 1987 Congress passed substantial amendments to the CWA, phasing out all federal grants by 1990 and replacing them with a federal loan program for the states until 1994, at which time the states are to assume full responsibility for funding publicly owned sewage treatment plants in the United States. President Reagan vetoed the legislation because he considered it too costly, and Congress passed it over his veto. WWEMA would have preferred continued federal grants, but since passage of the law its representatives have argued before Congress's appropriations committees to ensure full funding of the law's authorization for spending $18 billion over an eight-year period. It regularly favors more spending for sewage treatment plants than the amount requested by the U.S. Environmental Protection Agency (EPA) each year.

In the 1990s WWEMA will have to turn to local and state governments for more investment in sewage treatment plants if it is to sustain its normal level of business. In addition to its concern about having less public money available for purchasing their equipment, the wastewater equipment manufacturers are worried that fifty different state procurement systems will multiply the government regulations with which they will have to contend. Hence WWEMA is taking an active role in trying to influence EPA in drafting guidelines to administer state loan programs and in advising state governments about how to spend the money.

WWEMA supported changes in the CWA in 1987 which increased the requirements for safe disposal of sewage sludge because it foresaw increased business for its members. Under the new law EPA must develop criteria for toxic contaminants in sludge, which WWEMA argues should be as strict as possible because of the potential contamination of groundwater. Under the Resource Conservation and Recovery Act (RCRA), which WWEMA also supported, contaminated sludge can no longer be buried in landfills, and this may mean municipal treatment plants will have to use additional treatment techniques or require industry to pretreat its sewage before sending it through municipal sewers. WWEMA argues that since it has the expertise needed to determine what level of treatment is possible, it should play a major role in EPA's rule-making on sludge disposal. WWEMA also supported increased administrative civil penalties for noncompliance with the CWA in the hope that this too would lead to an upswing in demand for its members' products.

WWEMA also supported the passage of the Superfund Amendments and Reauthorization Act (SARA) in 1986, which extended the cleanup of leaking hazardous dumps around the country. It believes that the only effective method of cleaning up a toxic dump is to treat the contaminated soil and water at the site and not simply remove the soil to another location to be reburied. The latter technique was most commonly used during the Reagan administration and benefited the solid waste disposal industry more than pollution control equipment manufacturers. WWEMA also argues that hazardous waste sites owned by the U.S. government, especially on military installations, should be thoroughly cleaned up.

WWEMA also testified concerning amendments to the Safe Drinking Water Act (SDWA) in 1986 in order to force EPA to set maximum contaminant standards for eighty-three different substances found in public water supplies in the United States. It argued on public health grounds, but also that it would increase business for U.S.-made filtration and disinfection equipment. WWEMA also argues it should play a major role in setting such standards on the grounds that its members have the necessary expertise to inform the government about what treatment is possible.

One of the major issues that WWEMA sees as important in the 1990s is the creation of comprehensive federal legislation to protect groundwater in a manner similar to the way the CWA protects surface water. The beginnings of such a program have been made under RCRA and CERCLA, but WWEMA representatives argue that there must be systematic control of surface impoundments, lagoons, landfills, oil and gas operations, mining wastes, injection wells, and pesticide and fertilizer applications to protect the integrity of America's aquifers. Legislation has been introduced into Congress to begin evaluating the quality of U.S. groundwater and developing plans to protect this valuable resource. WWEMA supports this effort, but argues further that the Congress should develop a goal of nondegradation of all aquifers and a requirement for treatment of all discharges over or near aquifers.

As do all other trade associations, however, WWEMA takes a defensive posture concerning taxes, labor/management relations, and product liability laws. It argues against any EPA regulations concerning the reliability of the equipment manufactured by its members. It believes that industry expertise in pollution control is greater than that of government, and the industry should be allowed to set its own standards for equipment and police the behavior of its members itself.

## TACTICS

WWEMA works with the Water Pollution Control Federation,* the American Consulting Engineers Council,* and government agencies such as the National League of Cities* to coordinate testimony about the need for additional treatment of water and wastewater in the United States. Congressional committees and EPA call upon it to assist them in formulating new policies and to inform them about the technical capacity of the industry. It publishes *Washington Analysis* for its members on a monthly basis and research reports about various aspects of the industry. It provides an analysis of the process by which Congress passes laws and agencies set regulations in order to encourage members to become involved and participate in the lobbying effort.

*FURTHER INFORMATION*

*Washington Analysis* (1989). Washington, D.C.: WWEMA.

## WATER POLLUTION CONTROL FEDERATION (WPCF)
601 Wythe Street
Alexandria, Virginia 22314–1994

*ORGANIZATION AND RESOURCES*

The Water Pollution Control Federation (WPCF), founded in 1928, is an umbrella organization for associations of professionals who work in waste water treatment plants. There are 44 affiliates in the United States, mostly individual state associations, with some regional groups, such as the Kentucky-Tennessee and the Rocky Mountain regions. In addition there are some 23 affiliates from other countries from New Zealand to Venezuela and South Africa. Within these affiliates there are some 30,500 individual members, and 1,000 corporate members such as wastewater equipment companies and engineering firms that earn all or part of their income in the wastewater business.

WPCF has an annual budget of about $6.5 million. Annual dues are $45 for each individual member, and corporate dues depend on the volume of business transacted by each company. Its president is elected by its board of directors of ninety members. Its executive director is Dr. Quincalee Brown, who heads a staff of sixty-two.

*POLICY CONCERNS*

The primary public policy concern of WPCF is the Clean Water Act (CWA) since all its members are professionally involved either in manufacturing wastewater treatment products or in operating municipally or privately owned waste treatment plants. Clearly the requirements of the CWA concern them intimately in their careers. WPCF has testified in favor of most amendments to the CWA over many years, arguing in favor of more-complete treatment of effluents and expansion of government funding for treatment plants, especially for training personnel to operate those plants. It has long advocated upgrading the training requirements for wastewater engineers in order to improve the image of the profession.

At the same time WPCF members are affected by the requirements of the CWA and seek to reduce the amount of reporting that they have to do to comply with the act. Many members work for municipal sewer districts and seek to increase state and local autonomy over how to conduct their affairs and resist federal standards. Some members advocate complete pretreatment of wastes by industry before release into publicly owned treatment plants in order to minimize the burden on such plants, as called for in the CWA. Yet a technical committee of WPCF argued in December 1986 that industry should receive pretreatment credit for reduction of effluents by the publicly owned sewage plants to which it sends its wastewater because this is a pragmatic solution to the problem. WPCF membership is ambivalent about the need for federal coercion to force industry to comply with the law and the desirability of state control of water pollution programs.

WPCF advocates other environmental policies that will reduce the problems of treating wastewater. It has generally supported such legislation as the Resource Conservation and Recovery Act (RCRA) and the Superfund Amendments and Reauthorization Act (SARA) which should help to prevent the contamination of groundwater. However, it opposed EPA's proposed rule to declare recycled oil a hazardous waste in 1987 because this may have led to more illegal dumping of such oil into municipal sewers that could foul sewage treatment plants. Thus the interest of a professional group in cleaning up one natural resource, water, may lead to less support for controlling contamination of another resource, land.

## TACTICS

WPCF's membership overlaps somewhat with that of the Water and Wastewater Equipment Manufacturers Association,* but WPCF is a much larger and better financed organization with thousands of individual members, which enables it to mount grass-roots lobbying efforts more effectively. It coordinates its operations with WWEMA and to some degree with environmental organizations when they testify for strengthening the CWA.

WPCF publishes two monthly journals for its membership: *WPCF Journal*, which includes much technical information about wastewater treatment and news about policy developments, and the *Operations Forum*, which is primarily a technical publication.

## FURTHER INFORMATION

*WPCF Journal* (1988). Washington, D.C.: WPCF, February.

## WATER RESOURCES CONGRESS (WRC)
3800 North Fairfax Drive, Suite 7
Arlington, Virginia 22203

## HISTORY AND DEVELOPMENT

The Army Corps of Engineers, since its inception, has been responsible for keeping clear the nation's navigable waterways and facilitating traffic along them. During the heyday of navigation as a major system of transportation in the United States, the Corps built numerous canals and channelized many streams and rivers for the purpose of moving the nation's goods. It also constructed innumerable dams and locks along the major rivers and minor tributaries in the United States, usually at the behest of local communities and politicians who perceived the construction projects as boons to the local economies. At first the dams were built primarily for flood control purposes. Later, power generation and storage of irrigation waters were added. An entire industry grew up around this public works program: the civilian contractors and engineering firms that contracted with the Corps to carry out this work.

During most of its history the Corps of Engineers had no opposition to its program and was considered the fair-haired agency in Congress that could do no wrong. It practically could determine its own budget because nearly all members of Congress were eager to have a major construction project in their own districts. Similarly, the industry that lived off these contracts was unchallenged because most communities viewed them as useful to their economies. Nevertheless, trade associations were formed by this industry.

## ORGANIZATION AND RESOURCES

The Water Resources Congress (WRC) was founded in 1971 when the Mississippi Valley Association and the National Rivers and Harbors Congress, founded in 1901, merged to form one trade association to promote building water projects, such as dams, locks, and channelization projects. It now represents the interests of about 300 engineering and construction firms interested in obtaining government contracts to build dams primarily in the eastern half of the United States. Its dues are $300 for firms and $150 for individuals, which provides it with a budget of about $55,000 annually. Its president is Raymond G. Leonard, its only permanent representative in Washington. Its thirty-member board of directors represents the major firms in its membership.

## POLICY CONCERNS

The only policy that concerns the WRC is the continued funding of the Corps of Engineers' programs to dredge and clear the nation's waterways for navigation and to build new water projects to provide water for irrigation, water supply, and power, as well as flood prevention. It seeks to convince the public of the need for these kinds of projects in the face of growing opposition from conservation organizations and wildlife preservation groups that contend that the projects are not worth the taxpayer's investment in them and that they are actually destructive of the environment and water resources they seek to protect.

Like the National Water Resources Association,* representatives of the WRC argue that the projects built by its members benefit not only the construction industry and the communities in which the jobs are generated but also the entire nation's economy. They argue that the transportation of goods down the Ohio, Mississippi, and other rivers kept open by the Corps benefits all consumers. They also believe that the flood control projects benefit not only the landowners whose holdings are saved but also consumers of the crops grown on such lands and irrigated by the waters stored behind these dams.

Like the irrigation farmers in the west, the business interests that formed the WRC, the Corps of Engineers, and congressional public works committees formed an unassailable policy network for many years. None of the projects they proposed, funded, and built were challenged by any other interest for the first half of the twentieth century. In the 1960s, however, conservation groups began having an impact on the policy, and since then the WRC has emphasized the need to conserve water by storing it for future use and the recreation uses that can be made of reservoirs and lakes for motor boat traffic.

### FURTHER INFORMATION

Maass, Arthur (1962). *Muddy Waters: The Army Engineers and the Nation's Rivers.* Cambridge, Mass.: Harvard University Press.

## WATER WORKS MANUFACTURERS ASSOCIATION
*See* Water and Wastewater Equipment Manufacturers Association.

## WESTERN PETROLEUM REFINERS ASSOCIATION
*See* National Petroleum Refiners Association.

## WHALE PROTECTION FUND
*See* Center for Marine Conservation.

## THE WILDERNESS SOCIETY
1400 I Street, N.W.
Washington, D.C. 20005

### HISTORY AND DEVELOPMENT

The Wilderness Society was founded in 1935 by five men, including Aldo Leopold, author of *The Preservation Ethic* and *A Sand County Almanac*. Leopold over his lifetime shifted from a Gifford Pinchot–like attitude of managing natural resources for utilitarian purposes to a more John Muir-like philosophy of nature worship. All the founders were conservationists concerned about dust-bowl conditions in the United State and dedicated to preserving wilderness areas and to promoting a land ethic among the American people. Their leader was Robert Marshall, a fervent New Dealer who worked in both Franklin Roosevelt's Department of Interior under Harold Ickes and later in the Forest Service in the Department of Agriculture. The first president was Robert Sterling Yard, a seventy-four-year-old conservationist, because it was viewed as a conflict of interest for a government employee to head the Society. However, Bob Marshall dominated policy-making in its early years and was the single most important financial contributor to it.

In 1939 the Society was instrumental in getting the Kings Canyon National Park established under terms that precluded much of the commercialization of Yosemite and Yellowstone. By the 1950s the Society had a membership of around 5,000 and was considered an exclusive group that opposed making wilderness accessible to everyone and preferred ardent mountaineers and hikers. Its membership base shifted from the east coast to the western region of the United States although it maintained its headquarters in Washington. It became somewhat more democratic and less oligarchic under the strong leadership of Howard Zahniser, the executive director in Washington, who joined with the Sierra Club in defending Dinosaur National Monument from development. His greatest feat, however, was the drafting of a wilderness bill which he successfully pushed through Congress in 1964. During that period the Society increased its membership to 27,000.

In 1980 Dave Foreman, a staffer who had worked for the Wilderness Society since 1973, resigned to form the militant Earth First!* He argued that the staff was coming to be dominated by former federal bureaucrats and that the council was controlled by people overly concerned with raising money and attracting millionaires with a "vague environmental interest" onto the council. This was exemplified by the replacement of the grass-roots-oriented executive director Celia Hunter with the more management-oriented Bill Turnage.

## ORGANIZATION AND RESOURCES

The society has a staff of eighty-five headquartered in Washington, with ten regional offices: Northeast, Southeast, Northwest, Southwest, Northern Rockies, Central Rockies, Intermountain, California, Alaska, and Florida. It has a governing council of twenty-three and an executive committee of fourteen drawn from the council and its executive officers. Its president is George T. Frampton, Jr.; the chair of its governing council is Alice Rivlin, former head of the Congressional Budget Office; its legal counsel is Gaylord Nelson, former senator from Wisconsin. Its council includes politicians such as John Seiberling, former member of congress from Ohio, academics, and conservationists.

The Society has a membership of 160,000 from whom it obtains $30 a year dues that include a subscription to its quarterly, *Wilderness*. Individual donations range from $100 to $10,000 and each of its major donors is listed in an issue of its quarterly *Wilderness*. At the end of the 1980s its annual budget was about $15 million, up from about $4 million in 1983. Its largest single source of revenues is membership dues, 55 percent; special contributions solicited from its members garner another 15 percent; and bequests, 4 percent. Grants from foundations such as the Beefeater, Bitterroot, Cudahy, Frick, Harriman, and Joyce foundations, and businesses, such as the CIGNA, Federal Express, Little, Brown, and Co., and New York Times corporations produce 10 percent, and the balance is made up from investments, advertising income, and telemarketing. The Wilderness Society expended 12 percent of its budget in the late 1980s on member services and recruitment, 9 percent on general management, and 4 percent on fund-raising. The remaining 75 percent was spent on programs: 20 percent on member services, 28 percent on public education about wilderness issues, and 27 percent on conservation.

## POLICY CONCERNS

The Society focuses on public lands issues, arguing to preserve wilderness areas in their natural state, to create more national parks, protect wetlands, and purchase more forest lands for inclusion in national forests. During the 1980s it was mostly on the defensive, working against building roads into national forests to facilitate timber sales and against leasing mineral rights to energy corporations, both of which have been expanded by the Department of Interior's (DOI) Bureau of Land Management (BLM). Society spokespersons argued that BLM spends more money to develop areas than it obtains from selling the timber to companies, thus producing a net loss for taxpayers. The Society's primary mission is to protect western wilderness areas managed by BLM and to slow the U.S. Forest Service's long-range plan to accelerate logging and road building in the national forests, including the Tongass National Forest in southeastern Alaska.

One of the Society's highest priorities in the 1980s was its opposition to opening 1.5 million acres in the Arctic National Wildlife Refuge to oil and gas drilling that was recommended to Congress by Secretary of the Interior Donald Hodel. It criticized DOI's report issued in January 1987 on the ground that the report itself showed that there would be irreparable damage to wildlife and wilderness values there. It argued that if the Reagan administration had been genuinely concerned about an expected energy crisis, it would not have rolled back new-car mileage standards, increased the speed limit on rural roads, and reduced federal spending on conservation and renewable energy sources. After the 1989 oil spill in Prince William Sound, the Society redoubled its efforts to prevent further exploration in Alaskan wilderness areas.

In 1986 Society representatives testified against a Senate bill to pave a road in Utah through national parklands. They also testified in favor of a desert protection bill introduced by Senator Alan Cranston of California, which failed passage in the 99th Congress. This bill would have upgraded Death Valley and Joshua Tree national monuments into national parks by creating Mojave National Park and designating 4.5 million acres of BLM land as wilderness.

A continuing interest of The Wilderness Society for many years has been the roadless area review and evaluation process taking place in both the BLM and the Forest Service to determine which lands should be set aside for wilderness and which may be economically developed. The Society seeks to maximize the amount of land set aside for wilderness. In the 99th Congress, it tried but failed to reduce the appropriation of $165 million for road construction in the national forests. In 1988 the Society filed an administrative appeal against the Forest Service's fifty-year plan for opening most of the Clearwater National Forest in Idaho and the Gallatin National Forest in Montana to logging, road building, and other development. The Society failed to get a reform bill passed in the 100th Congress to prevent sales in the Tongass National Forest to timber companies that lost money for the Forest Service, but it reintroduced the bill into the 101st Congress in 1989.

In the first years of the Reagan administration, Congress reduced funding for the Land and Water Conservation Fund, but in 1986 the Society scored a victory when the 99th Congress increased appropriations for acquisition of sixty-five projects including parks, wildlife refuges and forests. New wilderness set-asides were created in Georgia, Tennessee, and Nebraska, but bills to create wilderness areas in Alabama, Colorado, Michigan, and Montana died for various reasons.

Nevada's first national park was established in 1986, and the Columbia River Gorge National Scenic Area was created. In 1988 the Big Cypress National Preserve in Florida was increased in size through the efforts of the governor and the congressional delegation. A wilderness tract set-aside failed in Alabama, however, because the Society was unwilling to agree to the chemical control of pine beetle infestation in wilderness areas.

After the West Coast fires of 1987 and the Yellowstone fire of 1988, the Society opposed salvage sales of damaged trees to timber companies on the grounds that many could regenerate themselves or produce seeds for the next generation if they were allowed to stand. The Forest Service proposed to build logging roads into the burned areas to facilitate the salvage operation, and this would lead to eliminating them for consideration as wilderness areas later. It also opposes selling off the remaining old-growth forests in the northwestern part of the United States to timber companies to be exported to the lucrative Japanese market.

The Society also opposes conversion of tropical rain forests in Asia, Africa, and Latin America to cattle ranching and other agricultural uses to produce commodities for U.S. and European markets. It argues for a sustained agriforestry economy for those nations that should be supported by such agencies as the World Bank and the U.S. Agency for International Development.

## TACTICS

The Society divides its resources among three main activities: research and analysis of issues, education and constituency building among the public, and policy advocacy within Congress and the agencies with which it is most intimately involved. Society staff and council members testify before Congress on crucial issues, maintain an activist mailing list of those to be notified of the need to write Congress as conservation issues arise there, sponsor conferences to consider conservation issues, and join with other groups such as the Sierra Club* Legal Defense Fund to litigate such issues as BLM's review of mines on public lands in the West.

Although the Society is more dedicated to adding lands to the wilderness preservation program than any other group than Earth First!, it works within the system. It gives a yearly Ansel Adams Award to public figures its board believes have contributed to conservation causes. In 1986 it gave this award to Representative Sidney R. Yates of Illinois and in 1982 to John Sieberling, congressman from Ohio at that time. In 1989, President George T. Frampton presented the second annual Olaus and Margaret Murie Award to Jeff DeBonis, a timber sale planner for the Willamette National Forest, because he helped found the Association of Forest Service Employees for Environmental Ethics, a new professional organization that places increased emphasis on resource stewardship and less on extraction.

The Society publishes a professionally edited quarterly, *Wilderness*, which includes feature articles with photographic essays on major ecological areas such as the Everglades, as well as news of events in Washington including its staff's efforts to influence policy. *Field Notes* keep members up on events around the United States and the world, and members are offered the option of being placed on activist mailing lists to be informed about specific issues to write their representatives and government agencies about.

### FOR FURTHER INFORMATION

*Earth First!* (1982). Tucson, Ariz.: Earth First!, February 2, Bridgid edition.
Fox, Steven (1981). *John Muir and His Legacy: The American Conservation Movement.* Boston: Little, Brown.
*Wilderness* (Winter, 1986; Spring, 1987; Winter, 1987; Spring, Winter, Fall, 1988; Spring, 1989). Washington, D.C.: Wilderness Society.

## WORLD WILDLIFE FUND (WWF)
1250 24th Street, N.W.
Washington, D.C. 10037

### ORGANIZATION AND RESOURCES

The World Wildlife Fund (WWF) was founded in 1961 by conservationists dedicated to the proposition that the remaining variety of flora and fauna in the world needs to be conserved through public and private action. World Wildlife Fund–U.S.A. is now affiliated with a network of national wildlife organizations in twenty-three countries with an international secretariat in Switzerland. In October 1985, World Wildlife Fund–U.S.A. affiliated with The Conservation Foundation* with which it shares a new headquarters in Washington. It was intended to combine the Fund's knowledge of ecological and biological systems with the Foundation's expertise in social science, policy analysis, and experience with U.S. environmental policy. Their common executive officer, William K. Reilly, was appointed by President Bush as administrator of the Environmental Protection Agency in 1989.

At the end of the 1980s, the World Wildlife Fund had grown to over 220,000 members with a $23 million budget. About 67 percent of the budget comes from individual contributions, 8 percent from foundations, 3 percent from corporate sponsors and government contracts, 10 percent from investment earnings, and the balance from miscellaneous sources. Its expenditures include 13 percent for membership development, 10 percent for fund-raising, and 4 percent for general administration. Dues for individuals are $15 a year.

The board of directors has sixty-five members, whose chair is Russell E. Train, former head of the U.S. Environment Protection Agency (EPA). Another former administrator of EPA, William Ruckelshaus, also sits on the board, along with other U.S. politicians, ex-governors Bruce Babbitt and Richard Lamm, and socially prominent individuals, such as Robin Chandler Duke and Helen B.

Spaulding. H.R.H. The Prince Philip, Duke of Edinburgh, is international president of World Wildlife and a major patron of its activities.

## POLICY CONCERNS

The World Wildlife Fund expends most of its budget on educating the public to the threat to endangered species and the need for conservation, protecting parks, wildlife habitat, and individual species, and educating and training conservation officers. It has special projects to preserve tropical forests and tries to convince various governments to stop the illegal traffic in endangered species. WWF scientists also study primates and marine ecosystems. Its programs are distributed around the world but are concentrated currently in Latin America and the Caribbean. African and Asian projects also receive considerable attention, as do global projects designed to have a general impact.

Individual projects include helping to establish and manage wildlife parks with the cooperation of local governments, such as the Central Kalahari Game Reserve in Botswana; supporting scholars who study the habits and numbers of endangered species, such as gorillas in Zaire and humpback whales in the Caribbean; training programs in U.S. universities and conferences for graduate students from Asia, Africa, and Latin America interested in wildlife management; studying the minimal critical size for ecosystems in the Amazon Basin of Brazil; and establishing an office to prevent trafficking in endangered species in South America.

Originally WWF focused on identifying endangered species around the world and assessing ways of preserving them. As a result, its early projects were to help set aside land for parks and nature preserves to protect the habitat of endangered species. In recent years emphasis has been placed on slowing the rapid elimination of tropical rain forests, wetlands, and other valuable ecological systems on which life may ultimately depend. In so doing, WWF has attempted to work cooperatively with local governments in finding ways to provide sustainable sources of fuel and food for the local human population. It seeks to influence such international financial institutions as the World Bank to fund projects that will conserve natural resources and build a sustainable economy in developing nations rather than deplete nonrenewable resources. The Fund seeks to work cooperatively with all governments whose jurisdictions include critical habitats.

WWF counts among its victories the establishment of a system of national parks in Costa Rica; the signing of the Convention on International Trade in Endangered Species by ninety-four nations who have agreed to control such traffic in their jurisdictions; and Mexico's establishing a ecological reserve for monarch butterflies' wintering site. In the United States, the Endangered Species Act and legislation preserving wilderness areas and their implementation are of great importance to WWF. It also attempts to influence foreign aid programs in developing areas to assume a benign attitude toward endangered species around the globe.

## TACTICS

World Wildlife Fund's staff testifies regularly before Congress on issues involving endangered species, and it seeks to educate the public concerning these issues as well. It publishes *Focus*, a bimonthly newsletter, to keep its membership informed of developments in various projects around the world, and *Traffic*, a quarterly newsletter covering trends in wildlife trade. It sponsors scientific research on biological diversity and preservation and publishes research reports and occasional books, as well as video programs on particular species.

## FURTHER INFORMATION

*Focus* (January-February, November-December, 1986; January-February, 1987). Washington, D.C.: WWF.

Oates, J. C. (1986). *Action Plan for African Primate Conservation: 1986–90*. Washington. D.C.: WWF.

Train, Russell (1984). *Corporate Use of Information Regarding Natural Resources and Environmental Quality*. Washington, D.C.: WWF.

## WORLDWATCH INSTITUTE
1776 Massachusetts Avenue, N.W.
Washington, D.C. 20036

### ORGANIZATION AND RESOURCES

The Worldwatch Institute was founded in 1974 by William M. Dietel of the Rockefeller Brothers Fund and Lester R. Brown, who continue in the 1990s as the president and senior researcher. It is a nonprofit research organization designed to alert policy makers and the public about emerging global trends in the availability and management of human and natural resources. Its policy is directed by an international board of directors, including Lester Brown, five other U.S. citizens, and one representative each from Italy, Pakistan, Switzerland, and Algeria. Chair of the board is Orville Freeman, a former secretary of agriculture.

Worldwatch has a staff of 19 who collect information from some 200 periodicals and government agencies from around the world in the fields of science, economics, demography, energy, agriculture, environment, and development. Financial support comes from major foundations, including the Rockefeller, Hewlett, Mellon, Noble, Noyes, Clark, and Dodge foundations. It also earns substantial income from sale of its publications throughout the world.

### POLICY CONCERNS

Worldwatch is a research and education institution attempting to influence public policy indirectly through informing the public and educators in particular about global environmental problems. Its representatives do, however, testify before congressional hearings on such matters as ways of disposing of solid and nuclear wastes. It is highly critical of such Reagan administration policies as withdrawing support for international family planning programs and its lack of interest in conserving energy resources, including the president's veto of national energy standards for household appliances.

## TACTICS

Worldwatch publishes a biweekly feature service on current events in resource management to more than 100 newspapers around the world. It sells subscriptions to all its papers and books for an annual fee of $25. It also provides single or multiple copies of individual papers on specific issues to educational institutions and government agencies. It has also produced several books and about 80 papers on issues from energy and food supply to environmental problems and economics of the third world. In 1984 it published the first *State of the World*, which describes the progress that has been made toward a sustainable international economic system, and has updated it annually since then.

## FURTHER INFORMATION

Brown, Lester R., et al. (1989, 1990). *State of the World*. New York: W. W. Norton.
Eckholm, Eik (1978). *The Dispossessed of the Earth: Land Reform and Sustainable Development*. New York: W. W. Norton.
Postel, Sandra (1986). *Altering the Earth's Chemistry: Assessing the Risks*. New York: W. W. Norton.

# Z

———————————— / ————————————

## ZERO POPULATION GROWTH (ZPG)
4080 Fabian Way
Palo Alto, Calif. 94303

### ORGANIZATION AND RESOURCES

Zero Population Growth (ZPG) was begun in 1968 by demographers, biologists, and others concerned about the density of the human species on the planet Earth. At the end of the 1980s it had 30,000 members who paid dues of $20 a year. Many members, however, choose to donate between $100 to $500 a year. ZPG's honorary president is Paul R. Ehrlich, the eminent demographer; its president is Timothy Lovain. Its executive director is Susan Weber. ZPG has many scientists, such as Linus Pauling, Garrett Hardin, and B. F. Skinner, as well as many environmentalists such as Lester Brown, David Brower, and Roger Tory Peterson, and politicians, such as Stewart Udall on its board of sponsors. It has 3 lobbyists working in Washington D.C., but its national office is in Palo Alto, California. It has 300 active local chapters concentrating on educating the public at the grass-roots level.

### POLICY CONCERNS

ZPG has only one purpose: to stabilize the population of the United States, which it views as the key to controlling other serious social, environmental, and resource problems. It uses political, educational, and legal means to achieve its objective and has never sought tax deductible status because it needs freedom to actively lobby for legislation designed to control the population. Originally it set as its goal a stabilized population of around 230 million for 1990 but saw this goal eroded over the years.

ZPG argues for a massive education campaign to inform all citizens of the need to restrict their numbers to zero, one, or two children per couple. It urges that all forms of birth control be made available to all members of society and that government fund birth control research to improve the technology available. It opposes pronatalist public policies such as taxes that favor families and urges career opportunities for women that will direct them away from the traditional child-bearing role. It also advocates recycling, reducing consumption in the United States, and making industry processes more ecologically sound. It opposes compulsory birth control and emphasizes that parenthood should be voluntary and decided upon by the individual in society. It argues for abortion facilities to be available to all women, regardless of income.

During the 1980s, the Reagan administration withdrew support from the United Nations Population Fund and prevented U.S. foreign aid money from being used by groups in foreign countries that counsel about abortion. ZPG and other population groups such as Population-Environment Balance* opposed this move and urged the 101st Congress to repeal these actions.

ZPG argues that, contrary to popular belief, tax rates do not decline as cities grow. Rather, city services decline and problems multiply with population density, including crime, poverty, and pollution. ZPG members feel that stabilization is not a substitute for programs to preserve ecosystems that support life on earth but that no effort to combat environmental problems will succeed unless population is also controlled. ZPG argued in 1989 that there were approximately 5.2 billion humans on earth, many of whom subsist on an inadequate diet because there is only food for 4 billion on healthful diets. Demographers now project that the world population will level off at about 14 billion in the middle of the twenty-first century at present growth rates. This is not a sustainable population, according to ZPG, and "Human beings must not be so vain as to believe that only their species has the right to inhabit this planet" (ZPG, 1988).

## TACTICS

ZPG publishes a monthly *ZPG National Reporter* and seeks media coverage of the population problems by distributing TV and radio public service announcements, literature, buttons, bumper stickers, and posters. In 1989 ZPG joined with the National Organization of Women, Planned Parenthood Federation of America,* and other pro-choice groups to march on Washington and "mobilize for women's lives."

## FURTHER INFORMATION

Ehrlich, Paul R. (1968). *The Population Bomb*. New York: Ballentine Books.
*The ZPG Reporter* (1989). Vol. 21, no. 5, October; vol. 6, December.
*Zero Population Growth* (1988). Organizing Brochure. Palo Alto, Calif.: ZPA.

Washington office: 1400 Sixteenth St., N.W., Washington, D.C. 20036

# APPENDIX A: Directory of Additional Environmental Interest Groups

————————— / —————————

American Academy of Environmental Engineers
132 Holiday Court
Annapolis, Maryland 21401
State-licensed environmental engineers who have passed examinations given by the academy in air pollution control, solid waste management, water supply, or wastewater management

American Bituminous Contractors
2020 K Street, N.W.
Washington, D.C. 20006
Independent and general contractors who build coal mines

American Clean Water Association
7308 Birch Avenue
Tacoma Park, Maryland 20912
Engineers, equipment manufacturers, and municipal officials involved in water and waste management field

American Coal Ash Association
1000 16th Street, N.W., Suite 507
Washington, D.C. 20036
Electric utilities that use coal to produce electricity; ash marketing companies

American Coke and Coal Chemicals Institute
1255 23rd Street, N.W.
Washington, D.C. 20037
Producers of oven coke, metallurgical coal, and chemicals; coke sales agents and builders of coke ovens and byproduct plants

American Independent Refiners Association
649 Olive Street
Los Angeles, California 90014
Fosters the interests of independent petroleum refiners

American Pulpwood Association
1025 Vermont Avenue, N.W.
Washington, D.C. 20005
Consumers and suppliers of pulpwood

American Sheep Producers Council
200 Clayton Street
Denver, Colorado 80206
Promotes lamb and wool consumption; seeks use of public land for grazing sheep. Belongs to Public Lands Council

American Waterways Operators
1600 Wilson Blvd., Suite 1000
Arlington, Virginia 22209
Trade association for tugboat and barge operators, shipyards, terminal operators, and suppliers; seeks to keep waterways open at taxpayer expense

American Wood Preservers Institute
1945 Old Gallows Road
Vienna, Virginia 22180
Wood preservers, including manufacturers, formulators of wood preserving chemicals, and wood treating companies

Americans for the Environment
1400 16th Street, N.W.
Washington, D.C. 20036
Educational organization concerned with protecting natural resources by influencing public policy

Animal Legal Defense Fund
333 Market Street, Suite 2300
San Francisco, California 94105
Promotes humane treatment of animals

Animal Welfare Institute
P.O. Box 3650
Washington, D.C. 20007
Promotes humane treatment of animals

Association of National Grasslands, Inc.
Box 1028
Hettinger, North Dakota 58639
Trade association of livestock growers who use public lands

Association of State and Territorial Solid Waste Management Officials
444 North Capitol Street, N.W., Suite 388
Washington, D.C. 20001
State solid and hazardous wastes professionals who work in public sector

Better World Society
1100 17th Street, N.W., Suite 502
Washington, D.C. 20036
Individuals, corporations, foundations, and government agencies dedicated to fostering
international awareness about sustainability of life on earth

Bituminous Coal Operators Association
303 World Center Building
918 16th Street, N.W.
Washington, D.C. 20006
Firms that mine bituminous coal

Citizens for Sensible Control of Acid Rain (CSCAR)
1301 Connecticut Avenue N.W., Suite 700
Washington, D.C. 20036
Founded 1983; 135,000 members from electricity, coal, and manufacturing companies
formed to educate public about acid rain and clean coal technology

Citizens/Labor/Energy Coalition
1300 Connecticut Avenue, N.W., Room 401
Washington, D.C. 20036

Coastal Society
5410 Grosvenor Lane
Bethesda, MD 20814
Scientists, engineers, lawyers, government officials, public interest groups, and managers
concerned with problems confronting coastal environments

Coastal States Organization
444 North Capitol Street, N.W.
Washington, D.C. 20001
Representative organization of governors of thirty-five coastal states and territories in-
terested in managing the country's coastal and marine resources. Affiliated with the
National Governors Association

Conference of State Health and Environmental Managers
3909 Cresthill Drive
Austin, Texas 78731
Chiefs, sanitary engineers, and environmental officials in state agencies of public health
and environment

Council on Economic Priorities
30 Irving Place
New York, N.Y. 10003
Researches social responsibility of corporations in the areas of environmental control, energy planning, and employee health

Environmental Industry Council
1825 K Street, N.W.
Washington, D.C. 20006
Manufacturers of pollution control equipment and systems

Federal Water Quality Association
10167 Woodbury Drive
Manassas, Virginia 22110
Professional society of federal government employees, and engineers, interested in sewage control. Formerly called Federal Sewage Resources Association

Ferrous Scrap Consumers Coalition
1055 Thomas Jefferson Street, N.W.
Washington, D.C. 20007
Cold metal scrap steel firms, ferrous metal foundries, and unions representing employees of such companies

Fund for Animals
200 West 57th Street
New York, New York 10019
Works to protect wildlife and fight cruelty to domestic and wild animals

Independent Liquid Terminals Association
1133 15th Street, N.W.
Washington, D.C. 20005
Commercial operators of bulk liquid terminals and tank storage facilities, including those for crude oil and petroleum

Institute for Local Self Reliance
2425 18th Street, N.W.
Washington, D.C. 20009
Research and technical assistance organization that sponsors local projects for energy conservation and production of renewable energies

Institute for Policy Studies
1601 Connecticut Avenue, N.W.
Washington, D.C. 20009
Research organization that focuses on human rights and problems of rich nations dominating poor ones

Institute of Scrap Recycling Industries
1627 K Street, N.W., Suite 700
Washington, D.C. 20006
Processors and consumers of ferrous, nonferrous, and non-metallic scrap. Merged with
Institute of Scrap Iron and Steel and Rubber Reclaimers

International Association for Energy Economics
1133 15th Street, N.W.
Washington, D.C. 20005
Individuals from energy industries, universities, government, and research organizations
interested in energy economics. Formerly International Association of Energy Economists

National Association of Conservation Districts
509 Capitol Court
Washington, D.C. 20002
Soil and water conservation districts organized by local landowners; a subdivision of state
government

National Association of Regulatory Utility Commissioners
12th Street and Constitution Avenue, N.W.
Washington, D.C. 20044
Members of state and federal regulatory commissions with jurisdiction over utilities and
their rates

National Association of State Utility Consumer Advocates
1101 14th Street, N.W.
Washington, D.C. 20005
Public advocates offices authorized by each state to represent rate-payer interests before
state and federal utility regulatory commissions

National Cattlemen's Association
P.O. Box 3469
5420 South Quebec Street
Englewood, Colorado 80155
Corporation of 48 state and 23 beef breed registry associations, representing 230,000
farmers, ranchers, breeds, and feeders of beef cattle

National Constructors Association
1101 15th Street, N.W.
Washington, D.C. 20005
Designers and builders of oil refineries, chemical plants, steel mills, power plants, and
other industrial facilities

National Energy Resources Organization
11529 Montgomery Road
Beltsville, Maryland 20705

Representatives of government, industry, educational institutions, and others interested
in all forms of energy

National Fisheries Institute
2000 M Street, N.W.
Washington, D.C. 20036
Producers, processors, wholesalers, importers, and brokers of fish and shellfish

National Food Processors
1401 New York Avenue, N.W.
Washington, D.C. 20005
Food processing companies and suppliers

National Hydropower Association
1516 King Street
Alexandria, Virginia 22314
Owners of dam sites and promoters of electricity generated by water

National Inholders Association
P.O. Box 588
Sonoma, California 95476
Individuals who own homes, property, or other equity interests within federal or state-
managed areas

National Pest Control Association
8100 Oak Street
Dunn Loring, Virginia 22027
Pest control operators who seek less regulation by the Environmental Protection Agency
for chemicals used to control weeds, insects, and rodents

National Recycling Coalition
P.O. Box 80729
Lincoln, Nebraska 68501
Public officials, community recycling groups, environmentalists, waste disposal com-
panies, and consultants

National Rural Electric Cooperative Association
1800 Massachuetts Avenue, N.W.
Washington, D.C. 20036
Rural electric cooperative systems, public power districts, and public utility districts

National Woolgrowers Association
1301 Pennsylvania Avenue, N.W., Room 300
Washington, D.C. 20004
Established in 1865 to represent sheep growers, it has seven staffers and twenty-eight
state affiliates. It has a political action committee entitled RAMPAC

Oil, Chemical, and Atomic Workers Union
P.O. Box 2812
Denver, Colorado 80201

1126 16th St., N.W.
Washington, D.C. 20005
Concerned with worker safety

Population Council
One Dag Hammarskjold Plaza
New York, New York 10017
Dedicated to developing improved birth control methods and to increase public under-
standing of population trends

Quail Unlimited
P.O. Box 10041
Augusta, Georgia 30903
Hunters who work for quail habitat conservation and management

Rainforest Action Network
301 Broadway
San Francisco, Calif. 94133
Dedicated to preserving rainforests

Rainforest Alliance
295 Madison Ave.
New York, New York 10017
Dedicated to preserving rainforests

Renewable Fuels Association
201 Massachusetts Avenue, N.E., Suite C4
Washington, D.C. 20002
Companies, state governments, and people working in ethanol and methanol fuels

Renewable Natural Resources Foundation
5430 Grosvenor Lane
Bethesda, Maryland 20814
Consortium of professional, scientific, and educational organizations, including the Amer-
ican Fisheries Society, American Society of Landscape Architects, American Water
Research Association, Coastal Society, Wildlife Society, Resources for the Future, and
Nature Conservancy

Sea Shepherd Conservation Society
P.O. Box 7000 S.
Redondo Beach, California 90277
Activist conservation society concerned with protecting marine mammals. Affiliated with
Earth First!

United Mine Workers of America
15th Street, N.W.
Washington, D.C. 20005
Supports protection for workers in the mine workplace, but opposes strict strip mining legislation to restrict places where coal can be strip mined on the basis that it would reduce jobs in the mining industry

U.S. Public Interest Research Group
215 Pennsylvania Avenue, S.E.
Washington, D.C. 20003
Research groups that coordinate grass-roots efforts to advance environmental protection laws

Wildlife Management Institute
1101 14th Street, N.W., 7th Floor
Washington, D.C. 20005
Research and consulting organization that provides technical services and information about renewable resources

World Resources Institute
1709 New York Avenue, N.W.
Washington, D.C. 20006
Does research on human needs and environmental integrity

# APPENDIX B: *Survey of Energy and Environmental Groups*

——————————— / ———————————

Please complete the form as fully as possible, using the reverse side, if necessary.

Name of organization_____

Name and title of head of organization_____
Selected by Member Ballot____ Annual Meeting ____ Governing Board ____ Other (specify)_____

Is there a board of directors/governors? _____yes _____no Number of members _____
Selected by Member Ballot____ Annual Meeting ____ Governing Board ____ Other (specify)_____

Year organization was founded_____ By whom?_____

Goals of organization:   Represent interests of members_____
                         Conserve natural resources_____
                         Other (specify)_____

How many individual members does organization have?_____

Members are defined by:   Type of business_____
                          Profession_____
                          Shared philosophy_____
                          Other (specify)_____

How many local/state affiliates does organization have?_____

What are the annual dues of your group:   for individual_____
                                          for corporation_____
                                          for affiliates_____
                                          others (specify)_____

What was the total annual budget last year? _____

Approximately what percentage of your annual budget do you obtain from:
Individual membership dues_____
Corporate membership dues_____
Additional fundraising from members_____
Foundation grants_____
Government funding_____
Other (specify)_____

What services does the organization provide for its membership:
Represents their interests in national government_____
Informs them of public policy developments of interest_____
Obtains group rates for insurance, travel, lodging, etc?_____
Sponsors educational trips, excursions, etc._____
Other (specify)_____

How many professional staff do you employ?  in Washington_____ Nationwide_____

In policy formulation for the organization, of what importance are:

| | Very | Moderate | Minor | None |
|---|---|---|---|---|
| Professional staff recommendations_____ | | | | |
| Board of directors/governors discussion___ | | | | |
| Executive officer's decisions_____ | | | | |
| Annual Meeting discussion_____ | | | | |
| Poll of membership_____ | | | | |
| Other (please specify)_____ | | | | |

Among the following strategies for influencing public policy, how important is each for your organization?  What percentage of its resources do you estimate are devoted to that strategy?

| | IMPORTANCE | | | | |
|---|---|---|---|---|---|
| | Very | Some | Minor | None | % Resources |
| Hire professional representatives_____ | | | | | |
| Testify in congressional hearings_____ | | | | | |
| Supply congressmen, senators, and staff with information_____ | | | | | |
| Contribute to political parties_____ | | | | | |
| Endorse/fund candidates_____ | | | | | |
| Monitor voting record of Congress_____ | | | | | |
| Testify at agency/departmental hearings___ | | | | | |
| Make written comments on proposed regs___ | | | | | |
| Seek administrative review of agency or departmental decisions_____ | | | | | |
| Educate membership with publications____ | | | | | |
| Encourage members to write Congress____ | | | | | |
| Educate public through press releases___ | | | | | |
| Direct action/political demonstrations___ | | | | | |
| Conduct and publish research on issues___ | | | | | |
| File court cases_____ | | | | | |
| Litigate cases_____ | | | | | |
| Coordinate with similar organizations____ | | | | | |

If the last option is important to you, please specify some groups with whom you would be most likely to coordinate your actions.

How important is each of the following federal acts to your organization's public policy concerns? What degree of change does each need?

| | IMPORTANCE | | | | Drastic Change | Minor Change | Maintain Status quo | Reauthor Extend |
|---|---|---|---|---|---|---|---|---|
| | Very | Some | Minor | None | | | | |
| National Environmental Policy (NEPA)_____ | | | | | | | | |
| Clean Air_____ | | | | | | | | |
| Clean Water_____ | | | | | | | | |
| Safe Drinking Water_____ | | | | | | | | |
| Ports and Waterways_____ | | | | | | | | |
| Marine Protection, Research, and Sanctuaries_____ | | | | | | | | |
| Coastal Zone Management_____ | | | | | | | | |
| Outer Continental Shelf Lands_____ | | | | | | | | |
| Resource Conservation and Recovery Act (RCRA)_____ | | | | | | | | |
| Comprehensive Emergency Response, Compensation, and Liability_____ | | | | | | | | |
| Toxic Substances Control_____ | | | | | | | | |
| Hazardous Materials Transportation_ | | | | | | | | |
| Insecticide, Fungicide and Rodenticide (FIFRA)_____ | | | | | | | | |
| Surface Mining Control and Reclamation (SMCRA)_____ | | | | | | | | |
| Minerals Leasing (1920)_____ | | | | | | | | |
| Federal Power_____ | | | | | | | | |
| Energy Supply and Environmental Coordination_____ | | | | | | | | |
| Energy Policy Conservation_____ | | | | | | | | |
| Public Utilities Regulatory Policy_ | | | | | | | | |
| Petroleum Marketing Practice__ ___ | | | | | | | | |
| Natural Gas Pricing_____ | | | | | | | | |
| Solar Energy Conservation_____ | | | | | | | | |
| Atomic Energy_____ | | | | | | | | |
| Price Anderson_____ | | | | | | | | |
| Nuclear Waste Policy_____ | | | | | | | | |
| Taylor Grazing Act_____ | | | | | | | | |
| Forest and Rangeland Renewable Resources_____ | | | | | | | | |
| Land Policy and Management_____ | | | | | | | | |
| Multiple Use/Sustained Yield_____ | | | | | | | | |
| Park System Act_____ | | | | | | | | |
| Land and Water Conservation Fund__ | | | | | | | | |
| Public Rangeland Improvement_____ | | | | | | | | |
| Wilderness Preservation System_____ | | | | | | | | |
| Wild and Scenic Rivers_____ | | | | | | | | |
| Alaska National Lands_____ | | | | | | | | |
| Barrier Islands_____ | | | | | | | | |
| National Historic Preservation_____ | | | | | | | | |
| Endangered Species_____ | | | | | | | | |
| Marine Mammal Protection_____ | | | | | | | | |
| Fish/Wildlife Coordination_____ | | | | | | | | |
| Wild/Free Roaming Horse/Burro_____ | | | | | | | | |
| Wildlife Refuge_____ | | | | | | | | |

For those laws in which your organization would like to see major changes, how should those changes be couched?

Increase the strictness of the law for greater environmental control. _____Yes _____No
Allow more consideration for economic costs and benefits of the law. _____Yes _____No
Make deadlines more precise; force timely action by administrative department. _____Yes _____No
Extend deadlines and allow for flexibility for individual situations. _____Yes _____No
Centralize authority and make more uniform the standards being developed. _____Yes _____No
Give states and localities more autonomy in the implementation of the law. _____Yes _____No

In addition to the laws listed on the previous page, what other policies, if any, is your organization concerned about, and why?

In the past six years, what were the most important new pieces of legislation or amendments to earlier laws needed and passed by the U.S. Congress?

What level of influence, if any, do you believe your organization had in the passage of these acts/amendments?

In the past six years, what were the worst initiatives or changes made to energy or environmental laws, in the view of your organization?

To what do you attribute their passage?

Comparatively speaking, were the laws and amendments passed in the 1980s better or worse than legislation passed in the 1970s?

Among the various types of issues with which your organization concerns itself, where do environmental and energy issues rank in importance and urgency? _____

What, if any, kinds of publications does your organization produce, and how often?
   Annual Report _____yes _____no  Research reports _____yes _____no  Frequency_____
   Newsletter for membership _____yes _____no  Frequency_____
   Journal for public sale/consumption _____yes _____no  Frequency_____
   Other (please specify) _____

# REFERENCES
————————— / —————————

Abbey, Edward (1968). *Desert Solitaire*. New York: Ballantine Books.
————— (1975). *The Monkey Wrench Gang*. Philadelphia: Lippincott.
American Forest Resource Alliance (1989). "The Balance between Man and Nature."
   *The New York Times* op-ed advertisement, September 15, p. 23.
Audette, Rose Marie (1989). "The Greenhouse Effect." *Environmental Action*, January-
   December, pp. 17–19.
Bartlett, Robert (1980). *The Reserve Mining Controversy*. Bloomington: Indiana Uni-
   versity Press.
Bastow, Thomas F. (1986). *"This Vast Pollution . . ."* Washington, D.C.: Green Fields
   Books.
*Battle for Natural Resources, The* (1983). Washington, D.C.: Congressional Quarterly
   Incorporated.
Bauer, Raymond, Ithiel de Sola Pool, and Raymond Dexter (1972). *American Business
   and Public Policy*. 2d ed. New York: Aldine-Atherton.
Bernstein, Marver (1955). *Regulating Business by Independent Commission*. Princeton,
   N.J.: Princeton University Press.
Berry, Jeffrey (1977). *Lobbying for the People*. Princeton, N.J.: Princeton University
   Press.
————— (1984). *Interest Group Society*. Boston: Little, Brown.
Bingham, Gail (1986). *Resolving Environmental Disputes: A Decade of Experience*.
   Washington, D.C.: Conservation Foundation.
Birrell, George A. et al. (1986). *The American Law Institute and Corporate Governance*.
   Washington, D.C.: National Legal Center for the Public Interest.
Blair, John M. (1976). *The Control of Oil*. New York: Pantheon.
Brower, David. (1984). "In Wilderness Wanders David Brower, Still Seeking to Preserve
   the World." *California Magazine*, September, pp. 115–167.
————— (1990). *For Earth's Sake: The Life and Times of David Brower*. New York:
   Peregrine Smith.

Brower, Kenneth (1988). "Mr. Monkeywrench." *Harrowsmith* 40 (September-October): 40–51.

Brown, Lester R., et al. (1989, 1990). *State of the World*. New York: W. W. Norton.

Caldwell, Lynton Keith (1989). "A Constitutional Law for the Environment." *Environmental Action* 31 (December): 6–28.

Christrup, Judy and Robert Schaeffer (1990). "Not in Anyone's Backyard." *Greenpeace* 15, (January-February):14–19.

Chubb, John E.(1983). *Interest Groups and the Bureaucracy*. Stanford, Calif.: Stanford University Press.

Cook, Constance Ewing (1980). *Nuclear Power and Legal Advocacy*. Lexington, Mass.: D.C. Heath.

Culhane, Paul J. (1981). *Public Lands Politics*. Baltimore, Md.: Johns Hopkins Press, Resources for the Future.

———— (1984). "Sagebrush Rebels in Office: Jim Watt's Land and Water Policies." In *Environmental Policy in the 1980s*, edited by Norman Vig and Michael Kraft. Washington, D.C.: Congressional Quarterly Press, pp. 293–317.

Davies, J. Clarence III, and Barbara S. Davies (1975). *The Politics of Pollution*. 2d ed. Indianapolis, Ind.: Bobbs-Merrill.

Davis, David Howard (1982). *Energy Politics*. 3d ed. New York: St. Martin's Press.

Domhoff, G. William (1967). *Who Rules America?* Englewood Cliffs, N.J.: Prentice-Hall.

Downs, Matthew (1988). "Producing Oil on Public Lands." *The Lamp* 70: 6–11.

Eckholm, Erik (1978). *The Dispossessed of the Earth: Land Reform and Sustainable Development*. New York: W. W. Norton.

Edwards, Rob (1985). "Friends of the Earth Cook Their Own Goose." *New Statesman* 23 (August): 11–12.

*Encyclopedia of Associations* (1990). 24th ed. 3 vols. Detroit, Michigan: Gale Research.

Epstein, Samuel, Lester O. Brown, and Carl Pope (1982). *Hazardous Wastes in America*. San Francisco: Sierra Club Books.

Federal Election Commission (1988). *Receipts and Disbursements*. Washington, D.C., 1987–88.

Fergus, Jim (1988). "The Anarchist's Progress." *Outside*, November, pp. 51–129.

Flavin, Christopher (1981). *Wind Power: A Turning Point*. Washington, D.C.: Worldwatch Institute.

Ford, Daniel (1981). *Three Mile Island: Three Minutes to Meltdown*. New York: Penguin Books.

Foreman, Dave (1981). "Earth First!" *The Progressive* (October): 39–42.

———— (1985). *Ecodefense: A Field Guide to Monkeywrenching*. Tucson, Ariz.: Ned Ludd Books.

Foss, Phillip (1960). *Politics and Grass*. Seattle: University of Washington Press.

Fox, Steven (1981). *John Muir and His Legacy: The American Conservation Movement*. Boston: Little, Brown.

Fowler, Linda L., and Ronald G. Shaiko (1987). "The Grass Roots Connection: Environmental Activists and Senate Roll Calls." *American Journal of Political Science* 31 (August): 484–510.

Fritschler, A. Lee (1989). Smoking and Politics. 4th ed. Englewood Cliffs, N. J.: Prentice-Hall.

*Fuel for Thought* (1988). McLean, Virginia: Written by Stackig/Swanston Public Relations for Arco Chemical Company.

Gibbs, Lois Marie (as told to Murray Levine) (1982). *Love Canal: My Story*. Albany: State University of New York Press.

Godwin, R. Kenneth (1988a). "Lobbying within a Social Movement: The Case of Environmental Groups." Unpublished paper. University of Arizona.

——— (1988b). *One Billion Dollars of Influence*. Chatham, N.J.: Chatham House.

Godwin, R. Kenneth, and Robert C. Mitchell (1984). "The Impact of Direct Mail on American Political Institutions." *Social Science Quarterly*.

Gold, Allan R. (1989). "Bush Proposal for Clean Air Is Dealt a Blow." *The New York Times*, October 12, p. 1.

——— (1989). "Shift on Clean Air." *The New York Times*, October 5, p.11.

Gordon, Joshua (1986). *Nuclear Power Safety Report 1979–1985*. Washington, D.C.: Public Citizen Critical Mass Energy Project, May 3.

Gottlieb, Robert, and Helen Ingram (1988). "The New Environmentalists." *The Progressive* (August): 14–15.

Grant, Wyn (1989). "Business Interest Organization and the Politics of Collective Consumption: An Analysis of the Forest and Forest Products Industry in the U.S., Canada, and the U.K." Paper presented at the annual meeting of the American Political Science Association, Atlanta, Ga.

Hardin, Garrett (1968). "Tragedy of the Commons." *Science* 162, pp. 1243–1245.

Hays, Samuel P. (1987). *Beauty, Health and Permanence: Environment Policies in the U.S., 1965–1985*. Cambridge, Eng.: Cambridge University Press.

Heclo, Hugh (1978). "Issue Networks and the Executive Establishment." In *The New American Political System*, edited by A. King. Washington, D.C.: American Enterprise Institute, pp. 87–124.

Holcomb, John M (1986). "Citizen Group Strategies and Regulatory Politics: Adapting to the Reagan Agenda." Paper presented at the annual meeting of the American Political Science Association, Washington, D.C., September.

Inglehart, Ronald (1988). "The Renaissance of Political Culture." *American Political Science Review* 82 (December): 1203–1230.

Ingram, Helen, and Dean Mann (1989). "Interest Groups and Environmental Policy." In *Environmental Politics and Policy: Theories and Evidence*, edited by James Lester. Durham, N.C.: Duke University Press. pp 135–137.

Kalter, Robert J., and William A. Vogely, eds. (1976). *Energy Supply and Government Policy*. Ithaca, N.Y.: Cornell University Press.

Kendall, Henry, and Steven Nadis, eds. (1980). *Energy Srategies: Toward a Solar Future*. New York: Ballinger.

Knoke, David, and Edward O. Laumann (1983). "Issue Publics in National Policy Domains." Paper presented at the American Sociology Association, Detroit, September.

Kosowatz, John J. (1988). "Mediating Toxic Responsibility." *Environment and Natural Resources*, May 26.

Langton, Stuart, ed. (1984). *Environmental Leadership*. Lexington, Mass.: Lexington Books.

*Least-Cost Electrical Strategies* (1987). Washington, D.C.: Energy Conservation Coalition.

Ledbetter, Sandra (1988). "Environmental Action's Dirty Dozen of 1988." *Environmental Action*, September-October, pp. 10–15.

Levin, Doron P. (1989). "Auto Makers' Plea on Pollution." *The New York Times*, July 21, p. 20.

Lindblom, Charles E. (1977). *Politics and Markets*. New York: Basic Books.

Liroff, Richard A. (1986). *Reforming Air Pollution Regulation: The Toil and Trouble of EPA's Bubble*. Washington, D.C.: The Conservation Foundation.

*Love Canal: A Chronology of Events that Shaped a Movement* (1985). Washington, D.C.: Citizens Clearing House for Hazardous Wastes.

Lowi, Theodore J. (1969). *The End of Liberalism*. New York: Norton Press.

Luoma, Jon R. (1989). "Logging of Old Trees in Alaska Is Found to Threaten Eagles." *The New York Times*, November 7, p. 19.

Maass, Arthur (1962). *Muddy Waters: The Army Engineers and the Nation's Rivers*. Cambridge, Mass.: Harvard University Press.

Malanowski, Jamie (1987). "Money-Wrenching Around." *The Nation*, May 2, pp. 568–570.

McAvoy, Gregory E. (1989). "The Context for Entrepreneurship: Reconsidering Truman's Disturbance Theory." Paper presented at the annual meeting of the American Political Science Association, Atlanta, Ga., September.

McConnell, Grant (1966). *Private Power and American Democracy*. New York: Alfred Knopf.

McFarland, Andrew (1976). *Public Interest Lobbies*. Washington, D.C.: American Enterprise Institute.

———— (1984). "Energy Lobbies." *Annual Review of Energy* 9: 501–527.

———— (1987). "Interest Group Theory and Policy Implementation Studies." Midwest Political Science Association Meeting.

McPhee, John (1971). *Encounters with the Archdruid*. New York: Farrar, Straus and Giroux.

Meadows, Dennis, et al. (1974). *Dynamics of Growth in a Finite World*. Cambridge, Mass.: Wright-Allen Press.

Meadows, Donella, and Dennis Meadows (1972). *The Limits to Growth*. New York: Universe Books.

Meredith, Pamela Louise, et al. (1986). *American Enterprise, the Law, and the Commercial Use of Space*. Washington, D.C.: American Enterprise Institute.

Milbrath, Lester (1963). *Washington Lobbyists*. Evanston, Ill.: Northwestern University Press.

Millar, Fred (1988). "Every Towns Needs a Hazard Analysis. " *Environmental Action* 20, no.2 (September-October): 22–23.

Miller, Taylor O., et al. (1986). *The Salty Colorado*. Washington, D.C.: The Conservation Foundation.

Mitchell, John G. (1987). "A Man Called Bird." *Audubon*, November, pp. 81–104.

———— (1988). "The Mountains, The Miners, and Mister Caudill." *Audubon*, November, pp. 80–102.

Mobil Oil (1989). "More Problems with Methanol." *The New York Times*, September 23, p. 22.

Moe, Terry (1984). "The New Economics of Organization." *American Journal of Political Science* 28 (November): 739–777.

Moore, A (1986). *Making Polluters Pay: A Citizens' Guide to Legal Action and Organizing*. Washington, D.C.: Environmental Action.

Morrison, Denton E. (1983). "The Environmental Movement in the U.S. : A Development and Conceptual Examination." In *Handbook of Environmental Sociology*.

Mosher, Lawrence (1989). "Washington's Green Giants." *The Amicus Journal* (Fall):34–39.

Mott, Lawrie, and Martha Broad (1984). *Pesticides in Food: What the Public Needs to Know*. New York: Natural Resources Defense Council, March.

*National Trade and Professional Associations of the United States* (1989). 24th ed. Washington, D.C.: Columbia Books.

Noogee, Alan (1987). *Gambling for Gigawatts: Excess Capacity in the Electric Utility Industry*. Washington, D.C.: Environmental Action.

Nosburgh, Paul V. (1983). *Commercial Applications of Wind Power*. Alexandria, Va.: American Wind Energy Association.

Olson, Mancur (1965). *The Logic of Collective Action*. Cambridge, Mass.: Harvard University Press.

Oppenheimer, Bruce (1974). *Oil and the Congressional Process: The Limits of Symbolic Politics*. Lexington, Mass.: Lexington Books.

Osborn, Fairfield (1948). *Our Plundered Planet*. New York: Pyramid Brooks.

Postel, Sandra (1986). *Altering the Earth's Chemistry: Assessing the Risks*. New York: W. W. Norton.

*Public Interest Profiles 1988–1989* (1988). Washington, D.C.: Congressional Quarterly, Inc., Foundation for Public Affairs.

Purcell, Arthur H. (1980). *The Waste Watchers*. New York: Doubleday/Anchor Press.

Rabe, Barry G. (1986). *Fragmentation and Integration in State Environmental Management*. Washington, D.C.: The Conservation Foundation.

Rauber, Paul (1986). "With Friends Like These . . . " *Mother Jones*, November, pp. 35–49.

Reilly, William K. (1987). "Shaping an Environmental Policy for the 1990s." *The Woodlands Forum*. Houston, Tex.: Center for Growth Studies, Fall, pp. 6–7.

Reinhold, Robert (1989). "California Alliance Proposes Vote on Broad Environmental Measure." *The New York Times*, October 11, p. 1.

Renner, Michael (1988). *Rethinking the Role of the Automobile*. Washington, D.C.: Worldwatch.

Rifkin, Jeremy (1980). *Entropy*. New York: Viking Press.

Rikleen, Lauren Stiller (1985). "Superfund Settlements: Key to Accelerated Waste Cleanups." *The Environmental Forum*. Washington, D.C.: Environmental Law Institute, August, pp. 51–54.

*Role of Energy Conservation in Acid Rain Control in the Midwest, The* (1987). Washington, D.C.: Environmental Action.

Rosenbaum, Walter A. (1987). *Energy, Politics, and Public Policy*. 2d ed. Washington, D.C.: Congressional Quarterly Press.

Rudolph, Richard, and Scott Ridley (1986). *Power Struggle: The Hundred-Year War Over Electricity.*. New York: Harper and Row.

Russell, Dick (1987). "The Monkeywrenchers." *The Amicus Journal* 9, no. 4 (Fall): 28–42.

——— (1989). "Nicaraguan Journey." *The Amicus Journal* (Summer): 32–37.

Sabatier, Paul (1975). "Social Movements and Regulatory Agencies: Toward a More

Adequate—and Less Pessimistic—Theory of 'Clientele Capture'." *Policy Sciences* 6: 301–342.

Sale, Kirkpatrick (1986). "The Forest for the Trees." *Mother Jones*, November, pp. 25–58.

Salisbury, Robert (1969). "An Exchange Theory of Interest Groups." *Midwest Journal of Political Science* 13 (February).

Schattschneider, E. E. (1960). *The Semisovereign People*. Hinsdale, Ill.: Dryden Press.

Schaumburg, Frank D. (1976). *Judgment Reserved; A Landmark Environmental Case*. Reston, Va.: Reston Publishing.

——— (1984). "Interest Representation: The Dominance of Institutions." *American Political Science Review* 78 (March) 137–147.

Schlozman, Kay, and John Tierney (1985). *Organized Interests and American Democracy*. New York: Harper and Row.

Soloman, Burt (1987). "Measuring Clout." *National Journal*, July 4, pp. 1706–1711.

Sperling, Daniel (1988). *New Transportation Fuels*. Berkeley: University of California Press.

Stanfield, Rochelle L. (1986). "Alaska Face-Off: Crude Oil v. Habitat." *National Journal*, December 13, pp. 3028–3029.

——— (1986). "Reaching a Compromise." *National Journal*, July 26, pp. 1829–1831.

——— (1986). "Wildlife Chief Avoids 'Kamikaze' Shrillness." *National Journal*, August 9, p. 1964.

——— (1987). "Another Oil Crisis?" *National Journal*, January 17, pp. 131–133.

——— (1987). "A Standout Lobbyist for the Out-of-Doors." *National Journal*, February 28, p. 509.

——— (1987). "Legalized Poisons." *National Journal*, May 2, pp. 1062–1066.

——— (1987). "Paying for Nothing." *National Journal*, April 4, pp. 812–814.

Steger, Mary Ann E., and John C. Pierce. (1988). "The Role of Environmental Interest Groups in Educating Members on Acid Rain Issues: A Canadian–U.S. Comparison." Paper presented at the annual meeting of the American Political Science Association, Washington, D.C.

Steinhart, Peter (1987). "Respecting the Law." *Audubon*, November, pp. 10–13.

Stobaugh, Robert, and Daniel Yergin, ed. (1983). *Energy Future*. 3d ed. New York: Vintage Press.

Taylor, Robert E. (1986). "Group's Influence on U.S. Environmental Laws, Policies Earns It a Reputation as a Shadow EPA." *The Wall Street Journal*, January 13, p. 4.

Tivnan, Edward (1988). "Jeremy Rifkin Just Says No." *The New York Times Magazine*, October 16, 38–46.

Truman, David (1951). *The Governmental Process*. New York: Alfred A. Knopf.

Udall, James R. (1989). "Climate Shock." *Sierra*, July-August, pp. 26–33.

Udall, Stewart (1988). *The Quiet Crisis and the Next Generation*. Layton, Utah: Gibbs Smith.

U.S. Congress. House Committee on Energy (1986). *Hearing on National Appliance Energy Conservation Act*. Washington, D.C.: Government Printing Office.

——— House Committee on Energy and Commerce (1983). *Hearings on RCRA*. Washington, D.C.: Government Printing Office.

——— House Committee on Science and Technology (1983). *Hearings on Hazardous Waste Disposal*. Washington, D.C.: Government Printing Office.

———— House Committee on Small Business (1983). *Hearings on Hazardous Waste and Enforcement Act*. Washington, D.C.: Government Printing Office.

———— Senate Committee on Energy and Natural Resources (1984),. *Hearings on Off-shore Drilling Moratorium*. Washington, D.C: Government Printing Office.

———— Senate Committee on Energy and Natural Resources (1986). *Hearings on PURPA*. Washington, D.C.: Government Printing Office.

———— Senate Committee on Energy and Natural Resources (1986). *Hearings on the Clean Air Act*. Washington, D.C.: Government Printing Office.

———— Senate Committee on Energy and Natural Resources (1987). *Hearing on Ground-water Protection*. Washington, D.C.: Government Printing Office.

———— Senate Committee on Environment and Public Works (1984). *Hearings on CER-CLA*. Washington, D.C.: Government Printing Office.

———— Senate Committee on Environment and Public Works (1987). *Hearings on Acid Rain Legislation*. Washington, D.C.: Government Printing Office.

———— Senate Committee on Environment and Public Works (1987). *Hearings on the Clean Air Act Enforcement*. Washington, D.C.: Government Printing Office.

Vogel, David. (1989). *Fluctuating Fortunes*. New York: Basic Books.

Walker, Jack (1983). "The Origins and Maintenance of Interest Groups in America." *American Political Science Review* 77: 390–406.

Walton, Izaak (1948). *The Compleat Angler*. New York: Limited Edition Club.

Watkins, T. H. (1989). "Untrammeled by Man." *Audubon*, November, pp. 74–91.

Wenner, Lettie M. (1982). *The Environmental Decade in Court*. Bloomington: Indiana University Press.

Wilson, Graham K. (1981). *Interest Groups in the United States*. New York: Oxford University Press.

Wishart, Ronald S. (1988). "The Lessons of Bhopal." *The Woodlands Forum* 5: 1–3.

Wootton, Graham (1985). *Interest Groups: Policy and Politics in America*. Englewood Cliffs, N.J.: Prentice Hall.

# INDEX

/

Page numbers in **bold** refer to main entries.

**About the Author**

LETTIE McSPADDEN WENNER is Professor and Chair of the Political Science Department at Northern Illinois University. She is the author of *The Environmental Decade in Court* (1982) and *One Environment Under Law* (1976). She has published numerous articles and book chapters on judicial behavior and environmental policies.